INTERPRETING THE MOVING IMAGE

Interpreting the Moving Image is a collection of essays by one of the most astute critics of cinema at work today. This volume provides a close analysis of major films of both the narrative and the avant-garde traditions. Written in accessible and engaging language, it also serves as a guide to such classics as *The Cabinet of Dr. Caligari* and *Citizen Kane*, as well as the art of cinema in the postmodern era.

D1288227

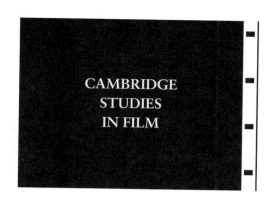

CAMBRIDGE
STUDIES
IN FILM

GENERAL EDITORS

William Rothman, University of Miami
Dudley Andrew, University of Iowa

OTHER BOOKS IN THE SERIES

Another Frank Capra, by Leland Poague
Documentary Film Classics, by William Rothman
Projecting Illusion: Film Spectatorship and the Impression of Reality,
by Richard Allen
Theorizing the Moving Image, by Noël Carroll

INTERPRETING
THE MOVING IMAGE

NOËL CARROLL

University of Wisconsin, Madison

CAMBRIDGE
UNIVERSITY PRESS

PUBLISHED BY THE PRESS SYNDICATE OF THE UNIVERSITY OF CAMBRIDGE
The Pitt Building, Trumpington Street, Cambridge CB2 1RP, United Kingdom

CAMBRIDGE UNIVERSITY PRESS
The Edinburgh Building, Cambridge CB2 2RU, United Kingdom
40 West 20th Street, New York, NY-10011-4211, USA
10 Stamford Road, Oakleigh Melbourne 3166, Australia

First published 1998

Printed in the United States of America

Typeset in Sabon by Thomson Press (India) Ltd., New Delhi

Library of Congress Cataloging-in-Publication Data
Carroll, Noël (Noël E.)
     Interpreting the moving image / Noël Carroll.
          p.   cm. – (Cambridge studies in film)
     Includes bibliographical references.
     ISBN 0-521-58039-0 (hc). – ISBN 0-521-58970-3 (pbk.)
     1. Motion pictures.   I. Title.   II. Series.
PN 1995.C3547   1998   97-22892
791.43 – dc21   CIP

A catalog record for this book is available from
the British Library

ISBN 0 521 58039 0 hardback
ISBN 0 521 58970 3 paperback

To
David Bordwell

Contents

Foreword
Through Carroll's
Looking Glass of
Criticism
by Tom Gunning

"I meant by 'impenetrability' that we've had enough of that subject, and it would be just as well if you'd mention what you mean to do next, as I suppose you don't mean to stop here all the rest of your life."

"That's a great deal to make one word mean," Alice said in a thoughtful tone.

"When I make a word do a lot of work like that," said Humpty Dumpty, "I always pay it extra."

– Lewis Carroll, *Through the Looking Glass*

In a critique of the film theory of André Bazin that is both penetrating in its logic and devastating to Bazin's theoretical argument and yet seems somehow nearly irrelevant to what most of us would agree is the importance of Bazin to film studies, Noël Carroll proposes a distinction between film theory and film criticism. Redefining Bazin's theory of cinematic realism, Carroll claims it is best approached as an argument in favor of a particular film style rather than definition of the essence of cinema. Instead of a coherent argument about the nature of the film image, Bazin offers, as Carroll puts it, "an astute appreciation of an important stylistic shift." Acknowledging that the weakness of Bazin's theoretical metalogic does not gainsay his deep insight into a stylistic change in film history, Carroll admits, with the sort of disarming candor that so often strikes one in his work, "What fails as theory may excel as criticism."

Most of the film studies community (as well as students of aesthetics) know Noël Carroll as a theorist, specifically as a philosopher of art who with undeviating logic skewers the pretensions of film theory for a lack of argument and logical consistency, as well as puncturing its ambition of constructing a theory that could reveal the deep structures not only of all narrative film but of the spectators who watch films as well. In a project that has endured for more than a decade, Carroll has subjected the dominant film theory to the sort of critique it would seem to invite, given its claims to have dispelled the illusions upon which rest the basic assumptions of Western subjectivity. In this almost military campaign, employing both sniping and all-out strategic assaults, Carroll has burst open the agenda of film theory to a variety of concerns that formerly seemed tangential to the master plotting of subject formation. In the course of whipping up this new omelet he has scrambled a large number of eggs, and, for some of us, come perilously close to tossing the baby out with the bath water (water which, unqestionably, had been long due for a change). But there is no question that Carroll's persistent interrogation of film theory has helped rescue a still youthful discipline from a premature hardening of the dogmatic arteries.

Whether Carroll has swept film theory clean of persistent bugaboos or merely demanded that a developing discourse fit into a procrustean bed recalling the protocols of a college forensic society will continue to be debated over the next decade, I am sure. But there is no question that he has helped change the agenda in film studies, emerging as a major theorist whose demands for clarity and argument should strengthen any serious theoretical position, including those opposed to his. Perhaps most important, he has deflated the idea of Film Theory as a Capital Letter, singular noun, fracturing it into a series of theories each suited to focused and tangible questions, rather than supplying the single answer to the Ultimate Question about the nature of cinema. Carroll advises us to chew and digest only as much as we can bite off, rather than nearly choking and reeling in a bout of perpetual indigestion and possibly beneficial nausea that the bulimia of Seventies Theory seemed to invite. Further, the menu *chez* Noël is varied. He allows us to rediscover cinema in all its variety and range of practices. I believe that in Carroll's approach (perhaps paradoxically) the range of differences within film history and practice can be fully acknowledged, while the avowedly radical project of apparatus theory envisioned a cinema machine that cranked out an amazingly homogenous imaginary sausage.

Despite the fact that I find Carroll a formidable figure in film theory however, I have to confess that for me his greatest contribution to film studies is his lesser known role as a film critic and analyst. If at some points I can find Carroll's theoretical arguments as sophistic as they are sophisticated, his criticism consistently deals with the intricacies of stylistic structure with both clarity and originality. This should come as no surprise to someone who has read his theory carefully, because what Carroll calls "piecemeal theory" is actually theory tailored to the needs of specific issues, including the structures of specific genres (such as the horror film); specific narrative techniques (such as suspense); or specific devices within films (such as point of view editing). In other words, Carroll envisions a theory that accounts for the way films work within a variety of perspectives and contexts, a theory that, while it maintains a purely speculative value as well, can be trained upon individual films and movements in film style in a way that highlights and reveals their differing organizing principles. If I sometimes feel that Carroll's ongoing forays against what he calls "The Theory" begin to take on something of the obsessive and possibly necrophilic pleasure of beating a dead horse, it is the sort of detailed analysis offered in this volume that supplies the proof of the pudding, the insight that a piecemeal conception of film theory makes possible.

Further, these insights, while enabled by the theoretical positions Carroll is known for, rarely rely upon them as premises. As Carroll has stressed, interpretations that simply turn texts into mirrors of the basic tenets of a particular theory hardly stand as interpretations in a true sense. Rather than allegories of his pet projects, Carroll's essays function as gateways to the films themselves, that is, to a probing of their structures, their assumptions and their social and political backgrounds. What succeeds as criticism here need not entail or demonstrate any single theoretical viewpoint. This anthology, then, performs the extremely valuable task of corralling Carroll's often vagrant critical pieces, rounded up from an enormous range of publications, and making them available to a field that, I hope, is ready to appreciate this neglected side of his work on film.

A great deal of Carroll's writing in film theory belongs to the realm of analytical philosophy, submitting, as in his first published book, *Philosophical Problems of Classical Film Theory*, film theories to the scrutiny required of philosophical argument. His possession of a doctorate in philosophy and his tenure in a number of departments of philosophy in his teaching career, as well as his many publications in philosophical journals, have often led people to describe him as a philosopher who often works on film in the distinguished tradition of such diverse writers as Stanley Cavell, George Wilson, Arthur Danto and others. However, I always hasten to point out to my students and colleagues that Carroll also holds a doctorate in film studies and that his first university position was in the Department of Cinema Studies at New York University (where for two semesters I served as his teaching assistant, cribbing from him numerous insights and interpretations and some of the best jokes now lodged within my repertoire as a lecturer). Carroll does not come to cinema as a dilettante, or as an outside professional, or hired gun, but as the product of the first doctoral program in cinema studies in this country, and, as this anthology records, as a participant in the vital film culture of New York City in the seventies and early eighties.

His intense and even obsessive immersion in cinema should be obvious to anyone one who has followed the range of references contained in his theoretical work, but the complete dimensions of Carroll's cinematic consumption becomes fully displayed only in this anthology. What is remarkable is not simply his range of references (it is almost *de rigeur* for academics writing on film to juxtapose discussions of pop masterpieces like *King Kong* with more elitist works such as the films of Werner Herzog), but for the depth of his erudition within this gamut of material. He doesn't merely refer in passing to *Tarzan*, but can discourse at length on the difference between Caspak and Mars in Edgar Rice Burroughs's pulp writings, as thoroughly as he can trace the relation between post-modernist strategies in Yvonne Rainer's dance pieces and her films. One does not find in this volume simply a series of intelligent remarks and penetrating insights on the expansive canon of film culture, but rather readings of the films of Chaplin, Keaton, Harry Smith, Herzog, Rainer, Kenneth Anger, Orson Welles that I feel rank as essential and, at points, even definitive statements on these works. I think that Carroll's writings on the silent comedy of Chaplin and Keaton actually supply the most thoroughly thought out and clearly demonstrated basis for a discussion of this body of film once felt to be at the center of film study (and now often lost sight of in the drive to uncover gender complications in yet another Hollywood sound film). Also, Carroll's firsthand understanding of the variety of practices among the primarily New York – based avant-garde filmmakers of the seventies and early eighties (another area rarely discussed in the unacknowledged canon of the purportedly anti-canonical field of film study) matches the insight of his masterful treatment of the echo chamber of recent Hollywood filmmaking in "The Future of an Allusion,"possibly the best single essay on what is often described as "Post-Classical" Hollywood.

This volume is filled with surprises, especially for those readers primarily aware of Carroll's more recent theoretical work. As the title indicates, this is a book dedicated to interpretation, a term often viewed with some suspicion in the domains of "Post-Theory" cinema studies, but a task that Carroll clearly feels is essential to the full encounter with films and their forms and meanings. Indeed, the meanings most frequently discussed in these films involve cinema's relation to social issues and politics, issues that Carroll hardly approaches from a neo-conservative viewpoint. As Carroll has argued elsewhere, and demonstrates in these essays, the investigation of films and politics (and, in fact, progressive politics), need not (according to Carroll, *must* not) be restricted to pronouncements on the ideological entailments of particular techniques of classical cinema. In this volume Carroll engages with politics as an essential aspect of the formal organization and rhetorical argument of specific films, whether discussing "social problem" films (as in his essay on the relation between sixties racial issues in *The Cool World* and *Nothing But a Man*, showing both the insights and limitations of the liberal integrationist horizon of these films), analyzing the attempt to create a visual form of political analysis and argument in Eisenstein's intellectual montage sequences of *October*, or uncovering the implicit social background of Social Darwinism in *King Kong*. However, although I feel that Carroll's engagement with politics in his criticism is essential to his value as a critic, I should immediately differentiate his criticism from some other forms of political criticism. Carroll is not primarily interested in using film to establish his own political credentials (although his progressivist, reformist attitudes are evident). Rather, he deals with politics as motivation for the formal organization and rhetorical stance of individual works. Carroll's interest in interpretation and uncovering meaning lies not so much in coming up with a new reading or pronouncing a moral to a film as in showing the way certain meanings structure the films as organic (or at least organizationally complex) wholes.

Another surprise may come from the fact that one of the thinkers who frequently supplies Carroll with a means for describing the relation between meaning and the choice of formal devices in a film is Sigmund Freud. While I think it would be quite misleading to describe Carroll the critic as a Freudian (and not only because Carroll the theorist has taken an aggressively anti-psychoanalytical stance), nonetheless in a number of essays included here (admittedly early ones) he cites Freud's concept of "dramatization" within the dream work as a model for understanding how films express ideas in visual forms. Although I think that Carroll's adoption of Freud's term does not entail key aspects of Freud's theory of dream interpretation (especially the ideas of repression and the unconscious that constitute the uniquely Freudian contribution to interpretation), I also think that his use of this Freudian term reveals how, for Carroll, meanings can motivate devices and structures within films, and how much speculation on meaning is needed to make film analysis more than simple formalism (and, I might add, how much formal analysis is needed to make film analyses more than simple allegories of intellectual concepts). A great deal of Carroll's interpretations revolve around the process that "dramatization" refers to: the visualizing of contents that are usually carried by verbal means. Therefore for Carroll these filmic "translations" might be thought to *begin* with meanings, rather than to *end* with them. Meaning functions in Carroll's criticism both as motivation for visual style and as an integrating force. It is the process of making meaning through film images, sound and editing that occupies him in these essays, rather than the critic's imagination in deriving unique meanings and interpretations. Freud's concept appeared in Carroll's early writings (later he uses the term "literalization" apparently to mean the same thing) because it supplied not so much a master key to interpretation as a glimpse into the process by which films arrive at some aspects of their style from attempting to communicate ideas.

Carroll's work as a critic is unabashedly formalist, if one means by that term a scrutiny of the formal devices within a film and a mapping of their integration into larger structures. But Carroll's commitment to a formalism that involves interpretation makes any view of this work as isolated (or insulated) from larger issues of politics and history absurd. As Roland Barthes indicated, a little formalism may take the text out of history, but a thorough commitment to formal analysis brings it right back. Carroll's in-depth consideration of the way films work includes consideration of the way they process their relation to surrounding ideologies and also the means by which they can try to revise dominant conceptions. In addition, history filters through Carroll's criticism not only because he relates texts to larger social contexts through their individual forms, but also because, like Bazin, he records a series of stylistic shifts that were occurring before his eyes.

Reading this anthology, encountering essays that in some cases I had not reread for more than a decade, I experienced a sort of flashback to American film culture (and more specifically New York film culture) over the past two decades in which the essays were originally written.

These essays capture a period crucial in the development of film studies, and show something of its excitement about (and, indeed, appetite for) cinema as a newly opened domain of study: a vast, unclaimed territory that ranged from popular Hollywood genres recently given cultural respectability to avant-garde films filled with nearly millennial ambitions. Part of Carroll's later disillusionment with the field of film study may derive from the lack of fulfilment of this promise, so strongly sensed in several of the earlier essays in this volume.

This direct engagement with defining a new field as it was emerging partly explains the vitality of Carroll's essays on both the Hollywood cinema and the avant-garde cinema of the seventies and early eighties, charting changes and transformations as they occurred. Also during these decades, certain historic luminaries and films were rediscovered or reevaluated (not only Buster Keaton, most obviously, on whom Carroll wrote his doctoral dissertation at New York University, but also, in some sense, classics such as *The Cabinet of Dr. Caligari* and *Vampyr*). Further, although Carroll was certainly not an auteurist, his serious treatment and obvious enjoyment of aspects of American genre film displays the legacy of sixties debate over the value of American cinema.

Carroll has the gift of making films he dissects seem like discoveries, the result of a completely contemporary experience, regardless of their period in film history. This is most evident when Carroll deals with long established classics such as *Caligari* or *Citizen Kane* or *The Gold Rush*. In these essays Carroll not only returns our attention to films thoroughly familiar from the repertoire of film history courses and film society screenings, but also makes us rediscover traditional readings of these films. Rather than producing radical deconstructions of these classic texts, Carroll reveals approaches that at first appear to be little more than readings of manifest content, but that as they unfold reveal a structural complexity not previously acknowledged. Carroll can defend or redescribe such chestnuts as the Rosebud theme in *Kane*, the framing flashback of *Caligari* or the role of pathos in Chaplin and make us experience them as elements with a new vitality. Rather than seeking out distant horizons of exotic interpretation, Carroll shows us how seemingly surface meanings can motivate elegant and complex structures within a work, provided we are willing to use meanings to help us trace the intricacies of the film's from and narrative structure, rather than approach the interpretation of a film as a chance to demonstrate the critic's clever originality and ingenuity in discovering unexpected readings. Although I frequently disagree with Carroll's criticism and interpretation, and would not want to think of his readings as the final word, the clarity and specificity of his vision and argument always demands that the reader reexperience the film. Agreeing or disagreeing with the reading, one experiences a renewal of the film as an aesthetic work. What more could one ask for from a critic?

A final surprise triggered by the juxtaposition of these essays lies in following the range of Carroll's critical voice. This anthology not only records his growing confidence as a writer and therefore a sort of stylistic maturation, but also shows Carroll employing several styles of rhetoric and modes of argument. Carroll can write as if he were delivering a lecture to a foundation course in logic, but he can also strut a deviously mordant sense of humor and sarcasm, worthy of the urbane wit of New York literary and theater criticism from a bygone era. It may reveal a perverse angle to my pleasure in reading Carroll's prose that I delight in the fact that the dry logician comes forward to analyze the gags of Buster Keaton, while the witty wag is likely to discuss modernist genres within American avant-garde film. While one tone or the other may dominate specific essays, Carroll also can move between registers within an argument in an often surprising and invigorating manner. Carroll's criticism is typified by a clarity of exposition and a desire to make sure the reader is following every turn of the discussion (offering in abundance definitions of terms, summaries of the argument and even full rehearsals of possible objections, clarifications to which obscurantist film theorists of the seventies would never have stooped), yet it is never possible to predict completely what he will come up with next. Like his namesake, the Reverend Charles Dodgson, creator of logical puzzles and chess problems, as well as the story of the little girl who fell down rabbit holes and passed through mirrors, Noël Carroll finds the constraints of logic to be the mother of invention, and the turns of argument frequent occasions for surprise.

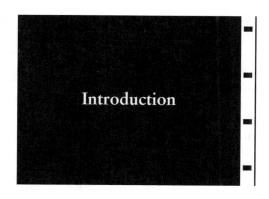

Introduction

This volume is a collection of some of my critical analyses of selected films and videoworks – what I call moving images.[1] Written between 1971 and 1990, most of these essays (though not all) are of the nature of what is often called "close readings." This is not a label that I endorse, since I do not think that film is a language, and hence I do not believe that films are read (closely or otherwise).[2] Thus, I prefer to say that these articles are close *analyses* of individual films (where "close" is meant to signal an attention to detail).

My inclination to approach films in this way undoubtedly reflects the concerns that attended my entry into the field of film studies. And though I no longer believe all of the things that predisposed me toward close analysis back then, perhaps the best way to begin to introduce these essays is to remind readers of some of the prejudices that influenced me, and people like me, when I started studying film professionally.

That began in 1970 when I enrolled in the Cinema Studies Department at New York University. The NYU department was, at that time, in the process of having its Ph.D. program accredited. The NYU program was one of the first of its kind in the United States – an academic department of film history and theory, without a practical filmmaking wing. Thus it was a time when anxieties about the legitimacy of film studies loomed large. One felt the pressure to demonstrate that film studies was a full-fledged academic discipline.

Close analysis of film seemed like an obvious way to go in that context. Why? Perhaps – first and foremost – because it accorded with a popular model of literary analysis, especially as practiced by those tutored in the New Criticism. Consequently, if one were in the business of inventing a new discipline, one straightforward strategy was to imitate a going concern like literary studies.

Morever, I suspect that some of us also thought that close analysis might provide an oblique vindication of film studies. For, if films (or, at

1

least *some* films) were such that they could sustain close analysis, then it appeared fair to suppose that they possessed aesthetic value. That is, close analysis would show that films were capable of rewarding the type of interpretive activity that was one of the acknowledged sources of value in the accepted sorority of the arts (that is to say: the arts with their own academic departments).

Close analysis also struck many of us at the time as more rigorous than other alternatives. Compared to the global style of sociologizing, as exemplified, for instance, by McLuhanism, close analysis was grounded in the data. It was neither impressionistic nor vague. It paid attention to detail, and, in that sense, it had the virtue of appearing empirical. And that, too, appealed to our academic super-ego.

Close analysis was also reinforced by the standard practice of film pedagogy – the one class/one film format. If one spent so much of one's class time watching a film, it seemed natural to devote at least as much time analyzing that experience. Rather than using the film to talk about something else, it appeared clear that we should address in depth our experience of the films themselves. This was something that rarely occurred in film criticism as we knew it. But, at the same time, it also presented itself as one of the leading reasons that we needed a field of film studies – to look closely at what was at the heart of film-going (the experience of the individual work) but which, at the same time, was usually passed over in other, nonspecialized discourses about film.

Undeniably, there was also an aesthetic prejudice behind the disposition toward close analysis. Its basic unit was the individual work, conceived of as the discrete object of film experience. The other arts all possessed masterpieces, and, with respect to those other practices, their title to the status of arthood appeared to reside in the fact that these masterworks served as the loci of experiences of great value. This was confirmed by the fact that these works could support close analyses that revealed the presence of sophisticated structures and themes (and inter-relations thereof) which, in turn, provided the basis for complex and rich aesthetic experiences on the part of discerning spectators. Importing these biases into film studies, close analysis appeared to justify the film experience itself, thereby legitimatizing the academic field of film studies by way of legitimatizing its subject matter.

Of course, close analysis was not the only critical strategy for legitimatizing film studies in the late sixties and early seventies. Auteurism was another option, and perhaps a better known one.[3] Auteurism claimed value for film – especially American film – by trumpeting a certain romantic myth of the film director. The film director was an artist possessed of a unique, personal vision.

Against studio odds, the auteurs were able to express that vision, despite the putatively impersonalizing forces of the film industry. Auteurs were able to seize individuality from the jaws of anonymity. They defeated the system by projecting their own concerns, often evident in the recurring motifs in their oeuvres. Value in the auteurist scenario was located in the triumph of the human spirit.

Film studies, on this view, was the documentation of the victories of the auteurs over industrial adversity. And this implied that the legitimacy of film studies rested upon the mission of recording and acknowledging the trials and breakthroughs of embattled cinematic geniuses.

Though I learnt a great deal from auteurist critics, I was always skeptical of their underlying assumptions. Never convinced that the auteurs were typically at war with their corporate employers, I did not buy, for example, the idea that Hawks's achievement rested upon his expression of a vision that was antithetical to Hollywood. Weren't Hawks's preoccupations quite congenial, or, at least, compatible with Hollywood's?

That is, I suspected the very myth upon which auteurism seemed founded. And, as well, I also wondered whether the auteurist's automatic attribution of authorship to the director wasn't often dubiously axiomatic rather than empirically motivated.

Furthermore, I was influenced enough by New Criticism that I worried that auteurism was a form of biographism, if not misplaced hero worship. What difference did it make that a filmmaker expressed a personal vision? Surely it was the sophistication of that vision as it was complexly articulated that mattered. Mere possession of a personal vision (or tick) did not seem valuable to me *a priori*. That was to mistake the dancer for the dance. And surely it was the dance that we cared about. Or so I thought.

Moreover, at the level of practical criticism, auteurism seemed routinely to evince certain shortcomings. On the one hand, auteurist critics appeared prone to confuse mannerisms for expressions of personal vision, so that unimaginative repetitions of certain devices – as in some of the later films of Lang – came to be prized as hypostatizations of the filmmaker's vision. This, in turn, frequently had the untoward consequence that the more schematic ("phoned-in") works of master filmmakers came to be valued over their more canonical accomplishments.

Furthermore, in a related vein, auteurist critics seemed remiss when it came to distinguishing between features of films attributable to the influence of genre versus directorial choice, and they often misconstrued genre données as personal statements.

On the other hand, auteurism, as it was generally practiced, tended also to favor thematic criticism. Of course, there was no reason why, in principle, auteurism had to be thematic criticism, but that is how it generally worked out. Hawks, for instance, was tagged with the ethos of professionalism through a summary of his recurring narrative motifs, and scant attention was paid to his visual style. And this seemed to me, at least, a failure to come to terms with much of our experience of his films.

Needless to say, close analysis and auteurism were not mutually exclusive options. Some critics, like Fred Camper, promised to marry auteurism and close analysis. However, even in the most felicitous of cases, I remained suspicious of auteurism because of my own fundamental commitments to the value of the artwork over the value of the artist. Auteurism struck me as too invested in the cult of the genius personality. For some, auteurism might have provided an avenue for legitimatizing film studies, but not one that was readily open to someone like me and many of my fellow students at NYU.

However, even among those of us who were attracted to close analysis, there were differences of opinion. Some, claiming the authority of phenomenology, opted for what was briefly called descriptive criticism.[4] This, as I remember it, was an exercise in describing films as closely as possible – especially in terms of their visual and aural articulations – in an effort to remain as true to the moment-to-moment experience of film (bracketed phenomenologically) as one could be in the medium of script. Moreover, this approach appeared to correspond to critical techniques in the fore in adjacent artforms – like dance, painting, sculpture, and theater – and thus participated in the general modernist animus against interpretation that flourished in the sixties and early seventies in New York.[5]

But, though I benefitted by being exposed to the demanding precision of descriptive criticism, I found it difficult to subscribe to its rationale. Whereas descriptive criticism made a certain amount of sense with respect to writing about dance and theater – before the advent of inexpensive video recording – since those arts are transitory and required documentation for posterity, I saw little point to it with respect to film, where the object was publicly available over generations. I could also agree that some works of art – particularly avant-garde films of the period (e.g., structural films) – were designed to be seen and heard, rather than to be (thematically, semantically, or allegorically) interpreted, but I did not see how this supported a methodology appropriate to *all* films. Indeed, I even thought that identifying the point of a film as being reductively concerned with the experience (itself!) of seeing and hearing was a form of interpretation. This is not to say that I see no distinction between describing a film and interpreting it. Rather, I was never convinced that the primary goal of close analysis was always description.

Maybe descriptive criticism performed a certain pedagogical role in inspiring students to pay attention to cinematic phenomena. It forced students to look carefully at what they often heretofore had ignored or neglected. Descriptive criticism was a formalist adventure in seeing afresh. And in that regard, descriptive criticism was salutary.

But for me, it seemed that was only part of the job. One not only had to get students to see what was there. One had to encourage them to ask why what we got them to see was there. Otherwise, what point was there to improving their perceptual skills?

This bias, of course, predisposed me toward interpretation, which I understand to be, at root, a matter of explanation – a matter of answering the question of why a work has the parts it has and/or of saying why the parts it has are related in the ways they are. Thus, close analysis was and continues to be for me primarily an affair of interpretation.

By means of this brief narrative, I have tried to indicate how I came to place such emphasis on the task of film interpretation. Given various existing choices on offer – such as McLuhanism, auteurism, and descriptive criticism[6] – it seemed to me when I began my career in cinema studies that the close interpretation of films was the royal road of film inquiry. This is not an argument in favor of film interpretation. It is merely an attempt to give a causal account of how I got into the interpretation business. Perhaps I once thought that an argument for the primacy of film interpretation could be cobbled together out of considerations like those just cited. But I no longer do.

I now think that there are many roads for film inquiry and that there is no reason to argue for the primacy of any of them – just as there is probably no longer any reason to debate the legitimacy of film studies. But that is not to deny that there is still a point to film interpretation. Film interpretation, as represented in this book, may not be the overriding concern of film studies – that for which all other forms of film inquiry (theory, historical poetics, industrial history, and so on) exist. But it continues to have a justifiable function. And perhaps the best way to substantiate that claim is to talk a bit about what film interpretation is – or, at least, about what I think it to be.

As I noted earlier, interpretation for me is a form of explanation. Interpreting a feature of a film is to offer an account of why that feature is present in the film. To interpret a film is a matter of explaining the presence of its features and the interrelationships thereof (or, at least, of explaining a substantial number of the pertinent features and interrelationships in the film in question). These features may be formal, expressive, and/or representational, and their interrelationships may be explained thematically in terms of what might be broadly called "meaning," or in terms of their putative effects.[7]

On some views of interpretation, it must address what is nonobvious. And, though this may typically be the case, I see no reason to require it as a necessary condition of interpretation. A putative interpretation is still interpretation if it explains why a feature is present in a work, even if the presence of that feature is obvious. To note the function of the way in which African-Americans are depicted in Griffith's *Birth of a Nation* is interpretive, even if the racist message is baldly apparent.

My view of film interpretation is close to what David Bordwell calls "explicatory criticism"; however, it is not quite the same thing, since he describes explicatory criticism as an activity that regards the ascription of implicit meanings to film as the principal goal of criticism.[8] I, on the other hand, do not regard the derivation of implicit meanings as either the whole or even the principal aim of interpretation.[9] My view of explication – or, rather, of explanatory close analysis – is wider. Though it includes the explication of meaning (in the broadest sense of the term), it is a more commodious concept, countenancing all sorts of explanations, including also functional and causal ones, under the rubric of *interpretation*.

This is not to say that Bordwell is mistaken in alleging that interpretation as explication, as currently practiced, is primarily concerned with implicit meanings. But if one thinks that what I practice is interpretation as explication, then it should be understood that I, at least, do not regard this as a commitment that restricts my attention to the discovery of implicit meanings. Again, for me, interpretation is the explanation of the presence of a feature or a set of features in a film, whether such explanation is (broadly semantic or) thematic, or functional or even causal (in terms, for example, of emotional effects).

This view of interpretation is on display throughout this volume. By way of a brief preview: "The Cabinet of Dr. Kracauer" tries to account for the actual significance of the framing story in *The Cabinet of Dr. Caligari*. In "*Entr'acte*, Paris and Dada," I try to explain the imagery of the race that concludes Clair's film. "*The Gold Rush*" addresses the interrelation of Chaplin's ensemble of techniques, just as the two essays on *The General* address Keaton's ensemble of techniques. "For God and Country" hypothesizes the way in which I think that sequence in Eisenstein's *October* is designed to work. "Land, Pabst and Sound" plumbs the alternative motivations behind the contrasting styles of *M* and *Kameradschaft*, while "Notes on Dreyer's *Vampyr*" speculates on the function of difficulty in that film.

In "*King Kong*: Ape and Essence," I try to answer the question of why the imagery on Skull Island rhymes with the imagery of Kong's rampage in Manhatten. "Becky Sharp Takes Over" deals with the rationale for the use of emphatic artifice in Mamoulian's *Becky Sharp*. "Interpreting *Citizen Kane*" advances an explanation of that film's explicitly contradictory thematics. "The Moral Ecology of Melodrama" considers the function of what I call the family plot in Sirk's *Magnificent Obsession*. "Welles and Kafka" attempts to disclose the point of Welles's disjunctive editing in *The Trial*, while "*Nothing but a Man* and *The Cool World*" contrasts the stylistic alternatives present in those two films with an eye to explaining the political goals they aspire to implement.

Many of the essays in this volume are devoted to close analyses of specific avant-garde works. These articles include: "Mind, Medium and Metaphor in Harry Smith's *Heaven and Earth Magic*," "Identity and Difference: From Ritual Symbolism to Condensation in Anger's *Inauguration of the Pleasure Dome*," "*Text of Light*," "Joan Jonas: Making the Image Visible," "Introduction to *Journeys from Berlin/1971*," and "Amy Taubin's Bag." Inasmuch as these works are avant-garde, they are designedly nonobvious and, therefore, they call out for interpretation on the part of virtually every viewer. My essays with regard to these films attempt to pick out some of their most salient features and to explain how they work in concert. These explications represent an effort of appreciation on my part, in the first instance, and they are meant to guide or to enable the appreciation of these films by others, in the second instance.

So far I have wavered somewhat amorphously in the direction of my view of interpretation, and I have tried to indicate how it is in evidence in many of the essays in this volume. But earlier, I promised something more – to establish that interpreting films has a point, even if it is not the *summum bonum* of film inquiry. What is that point?

In fact, I have already alluded to it in my remarks on avant-garde film. Film interpretation is a form of film appreciation, in the first instance, and then a guide to others about the ways in which they too can come to appreciate the value (and, in some cases, the disvalue) of the films in question. If appreciation is a matter of contemplating the organization (or disorganization) of features of works, or of works as a whole, then interpretation is a primary medium of film appreciation. That is one of the points of interpretation and, in fact, the predominating point of interpretation in this volume.

This is not to say that aesthetic appreciation is the only point of interpretation. Ideology critique may be another. It is only to say that appreciation is a leading point of interpretation – one that grounds the activity – and that it is perhaps the major purpose that motivates me in the essays in this volume.[10]

By speaking of aesthetic appreciation, I open the door to being charged with formalism. However, I think that charge would be misguided for at least two reasons. First, I have claimed that appreciation is only *one* aim of interpretation. I question whether anyone could deny that, and, furthermore, whether anyone would deny that it is even among the major goals of interpretation. However, I have not precluded that there are other purposes, including political ones. And even though appreciation is generally my aim in the close analyses in this volume, a number of these essays do engage political interpretation.

Second, I am not a formalist, if by that one has in mind an interpreter who restricts her attention either (1) to only formal devices, or (2) to features that are said to be exclusively internal to the work. Clearly, throughout these essays I am concerned with representational and expressive as well as formal features, and, in addition, in endeavoring to explain why these features are present in the works in question, I frequently advert to contextual factors, including not only film and art historical ones, but ones pertaining to politics and broader cultural factors as well. I do conceive of interpretation as explanation. But I am not a narrow aesthetic autonomist about where I am willing to look for the ingredients of those interpretations.[11]

In *Interpreting Films*, Janet Staiger criticizes people like Jonathan Culler for portraying interpretive competence as an idealization that is at variance with what historically situated audiences do.[12] *If* this is meant to suggest that our interpretations of films should model the actual interpretive activities of film viewers, then Staiger's conception of interpretation is radically different from my own. I should not be taken in this volume to be presenting accounts of what I conjecture actual, historically situated viewers thought about while watching the films in question. If these essays document anything, it is my own considered assessment – upon reflection and reviewing – of how these films work.

At points, I may speculate about how a device moves viewers. But my account of why the device is designed that way and about how it achieves its postulated purpose should rarely be taken as a claim about the way in which the audience actually conceptualized the relevant feature or features of the film in question. The interpretations are my own hypotheses. They are not meant to stand in as reports of the surmises of the average audience member (whoever that might be).

Moreover, this, I would argue, is the way in which we standardly understand interpretations – in film and the other arts. Interpreters do not write interpretations in order to tell other people – the historical viewers – what they already think. If that were what interpreters did, the rest of us would not have any interest in reading them. We already know what we think. Why would we look to someone else to find that out? Primarily, we read interpretations in order to gain *new* insights concerning the way films work.

We applaud certain interpreters (our academic stars) for their brilliance, because they point out and explain features of films that we had failed to notice or to understand. This would make no sense if interpreters were typically persons who reported on what we already have in mind. Interpreters with respect to the standards of achievement that typically govern our existing critical practices attempt to cast work in a new light, rather than merely to recycle received wisdom.

Interpretation is not reducible to reception studies, even if reception studies, suitably deployed, can enhance interpretation. This is not to disparage reception studies, but only to plead that they not be conflated with interpretation. Conceptually, interpretation and reception studies are logically distinct activities.

Of course, in drawing this distinction, I do not mean to imply that interpreters have no relation whatsoever with audiences. I do not think that my interpretations reconstruct anyone's actual experience while viewing a film. But they may inform other people's experience subsequent to their consideration of my interpretations. That is, I hope that readers will test my interpretations in their encounters with the films I discuss, where this testing involves not only ascertaining whether my conjectures are objectively plausible attributions – given the work and its historical context – but also seeing whether it enhances their appreciative activity (their contemplation, comprehension, and understanding of the film and its features).[13]

For me, an interpreter is not an archivist of audience responses but a co-creator of appreciation (along with the filmmakers and their intended viewers). And that is the sentiment that underwrites my close analyses of individual films throughout this volume.

I have noted that my view is more like what David Bordwell has called interpretation as explication than other options. Like interpretation as explication, my approach (let us call it "interpretation as explanation") contrasts with another current view of interpretation – what Bordwell labels symptomatic interpretation.[14] I make this correlation because I think that my practice of interpretation, like interpretation as explication, tends to be holistic or organic or functional. I interpret features of films, for the most part, in light of their relation to hypotheses about the *unity* of the works in question. In this, I do not imagine that my interpretations account for every detail of the films I discuss (I am talking about *relative* unity, not totalized unity), nor do I claim that there may not be other (compatible) interpretations of the works I examine. But I do operate with a presumption that the films I examine are relatively unified, whereas symptomatic criticism, I think, presupposes that works are necessarily, essentially disunified – rent with contradictions, often ideological contradictions, that are submerged in the work, but that can be detected "against the grain."

I have no doubt that some films are contradictory in this way. I have no principled argument against symptomatic interpretation. However, given the popularity of symptomatic interpretation nowadays, some readers may be tempted to think that symptomatic interpretation renders obsolete the holistic approach that people like me embrace. How can exegetes continue to operate with the presumption of unity after a brush with the metaphysics of disunity? Shouldn't we all be symptomatic interpreters all of the time?

Symptomatic interpretation, it seems to me, has its origin in Claude Levi-Strauss's discussion of myth.[15] For Levi-Strauss, the function of myth was to display the contradictions of a culture. This view of myth, then, was appropriated for art by theoreticians like Pierre Macheray[16] and Louis Althusser.[17] They proposed that the function of artworks was to exhibit the contradictions within a society.

In a way, the initial move to symptomatic interpretation was aesthetically conservative. Artworks were still conceptualized as objects of contemplation, though what was contemplated was not the unity of the work, but its disunity – the way in which the work symptomatically revealed the often repressed contradictions of the culture. Art, on this view, still maintained a privileged cultural position. Like an oracle, it spoke the truth, even if the artist him- or herself did not understand what was being said. The artwork displayed cultural contradictions for audiences – or at least critics – to track.

In this respect, art is still conceptualized as performing a positive service to the commonweal. This approach still regards art as a source of beneficial social value. Art discloses important social contradictions – often more by way of what the work unsuccessfully attempts strenuously to exclude than by what it underlines. These exclusions are thought of as *structuring absences*. They are symptoms. Interpreting artworks involves isolating these structuring absences – these symptoms of unsuccessfully coordinated purposes – and explaining their social significance.

Symptomatic criticism found its way into film studies through the influence of such seminal articles as "John Ford's *Young Mr. Lincoln*" by the editors of *Cahiers du Cinema*.[18] However, whereas symptomatic criticism originally seems to have cast art in a favorable light, in film studies, symptomatic criticism primarily empowered a hermeneutics of suspicion. Whereas Althusser placed art outside ideology, symptomatic critics in cinema studies regarded film as an instrument of ideology, including not only capitalist ideology, but sexism as well. Neither art nor film was privileged any longer. The function of each was presumed to be inherently ideological, dedicated to occluding pernicious contradictions from view. Symptomatic criticism, in turn, was a tool for unmasking these machinations.

Given the stridently political posture of film studies over the past two decades, symptomatic interpretation as a species of ideological criticism became the leading tendency. In this context, the presupposition that films were disunified assumed the status of a dominant heuristic. To demur from that assumption was taken to be either ontologically misguided or politically reactionary or, more likely, both. Symptomatic criticism, in other words, came to command priority over other forms of interpretation, both in terms of the construction of films as cultural objects, and in terms of critical/political practice.

In this regard, holistic interpretation can appear to be a throwback, both metaphysically and morally. Thus, for me to present a volume of essays explicitly committed to holistic interpretation at this late date will probably strike many film scholars as irretrievably retrograde. What, it might be asked, can possibly justify an endorsement of holistic interpretation in the wake of symptomatic criticism?

Perhaps I can begin to answer that question by pointing out that holistic interpretation and symptomatic interpretation are not necessarily incompatible rivals. The reason for this, quite simply, is that even symptomatic criticism requires some measure of holistic interpretation. The symptomatic critic is not concerned simply with what is absent from a film or an artwork. For any given work, so much is absent. Simply to catalogue what is absent from a work would be virtually interminable as well as pointless and boring to boot. Reference to New Zealand is absent from *Spartacus*, but so what? The symptomatic critic is not interested in any old absence, but in *structuring absences*.

Yet how does one go about identifying structuring absences? Obviously by determining the overall direction or tendency (generally thematic) of a film in order to detect the countervailing tendencies that the work aspires to mask. But that, of course, involves holistic interpretation, and the assumption of some relative unity in the work. In order to interpret against the grain, one needs to find the grain in the first place. And holistic interpretation is indispensable to this end. Thus, symptomatic interpretation cannot be thought to undermine the prospects of holistic interpretation entirely, since holistic interpretation – to an important degree – is material to the practice of symptomatic interpretation. A taste for symptomatic interpretation does not banish the need for holistic interpretation. Actually, it requires a measure of holistic interpretation.

Moreover, this is a result that should have been expected. As H. G. Gadamer has argued persuasively, all interpretation is holistic in the sense that it strives to establish reflective equilibrium in the movement from part to whole and back again.[19] To interpret a feature or a fragment of a work invokes hypotheses about the whole (or, at least, larger segments of the work) at the same time that a conception of larger complexes in built up from the interpretations of fragments. As George Wilson puts it, we must develop a "reiterated sense of the holistic character of all interpretive work."[20] In this respect, holistic interpretation is conceptually prior to other sorts of interpretation. A proclivity for symptomatic interpretation does not preclude holistic interpretation, for the simple reason that symptomatic interpretation itself cannot do altogether without holistic interpretation.

Though I claim that holistic interpretation is, in a certain sense, logically prior to symptomatic interpretation, it is also the case that I do not think it precludes symptomatic interpretation across the board.

Some films do mask social contradictions, and it is important to point this out. But in these cases, holistic interpretation and the presumption of the relative unity of the film in question will work hand-in-hand with symptomatic criticism. Finding that a film is relatively unified as a result of holistic interpretation is compatible with finding that it is also disunified in certain important respects. In point of logic, to find that a film is disunified in certain respects already requires the presumption that it is somehow unified in others.

There is, in short, logical space enough for holistic interpretation and symptomatic interpretation to co-exist. To think otherwise is sheer polemics. Whether or not predominantly holistic interpretation or predominantly symptomatic interpretation is apposite is something that can be determined only on a case-by-case basis.

In this book, the interpretations that I offer are predominantly holistic. But I do not take that to show that this is always the case, nor should readers take me to be implying this. In my practice, I favor holistic criticism, but this is not a brief against symptomatic criticism *tout court*.

Until now, I have been speaking as though this volume contains only close interpretive analyses of individual films and videos. Most of the essays do fall into this catergory, but not all. "Herzog, Presence and Paradox" attempts to provide an overview of a single filmmaker's oeuvre, and "Lang, Pabst and Sound" tries to situate *M* and *Kameradschaft* in a broader, film-historical context, while "The Future of Allusion: Hollywood in the Seventies (and Beyond)," "Back to Basics," and "Film in the Age of Postmodernism" are efforts in the "state of the art" genre of critical writing – they try to chart striking filmworld tendencies as they seemed to emerge in the seventies and early eighties. These essays, along with my faltering attempts at film theory, reflect my growing awareness that the interpretation of films is not enough – that there is more to film inquiry than close analysis. This is not to renege on my belief in the value of close interpretation, but only to acknowledge that it needs to be supplemented by other sorts of investigations.

There is at least one apparently glaring anomaly in this book that many readers are bound to notice and that deserves comment. As a film theorist, I have turned railing against psychoanalytic film theory into a veritable cottage industry. And yet, in a number of these essays, especially those written early in my career, I make use of psychoanalytic concepts. What is going on here? Curious readers want to know.

Well, I will now confess in print that in the early seventies I did flirt with psychoanalysis (though not the Lacanian version, I hasten to add). But, as has often happened to me, adopting a position led me to begin to see its shortcomings from the inside (so to speak). So, though initially disposed sympathetically toward psychoanalysis, I began to become its critic in a way that parallels my evolution from a cinematic essentialist to the position of a hectoring anti-essentialist. I suppose it was all presaged by my teenage transition from being a fervent Catholic to becoming what for all intents and purposes is a knee-jerk anti-clerical atheist.

It has been my blessing or my curse to bounce from belief to skepticism many times in my life. Maybe this is one reason that you should hope that I am never on your side, since it immediately raises the question, "For how long?" In any event, the explanation for what psychoanalysis there is in this volume is that I was once a fellow traveler, and, through having to talk the talk, I had to listen to myself long enough to know when I had to be faking it.

Of course, that might invite someone to respond by saying, "That may be interesting biographically, but why, if you no longer subscribe to psychoanalysis, do you include work of that sort in this volume?" Shouldn't I exclude these pieces as juvenalia and retire them to the dustbin of bad ideas? I have not, because I think that they are still instructive, even though I now question the authority of psychoanalytic theory.

How is that possible? I have several answers. First, much of the psychoanalytic vocabulary that I employ belongs to what I would call the descriptive part of psychoanalysis, rather than to psychoanalytic theory proper. I advert often to symbol-making structures like the dream processes of condensation and dramatization. I think that Freud was often an acute and sensitive observer of phenomena, even if I have grave reservations about his more theoretical speculations. And I think that his identification of these structures is insightful and well grounded, so that even a born-again non–psychoanalytically inclined critic like me can use these descriptive categories with a clear conscience.

Furthermore, in other writings, I have proposed non-psychoanalytic characterizations of these symbol-making structures, in essays such as "A Note on Film Metaphor" and "Language and Cinema."[21] Thus, I think that it is possible to "translate" my early discussions of processes such as condensation and dramatization in these essays into the idiom of what I call strict cinematic metaphor and verbal images. Consequently, with the appropriate adjustments in vocabulary, these essays can be recuperated, to an astonishing extent, for cognitivists.

This, however, does not account for all the invocations of psychoanalysis in this book. How can I justify the remainder? By pointing out that psychoanalytic ideas permeated the cultural environs in which many of the films I discuss emerged. Therefore, in mobilizing psychoanalytic concepts in interpreting various films, I am not committing myself to the truth of psychoanalysis, but commenting on intellectual influences abroad in the context of the films under consideration.

One does not have to be a Roman Catholic to cite medieval theological ideas in order to explain works by Dante, nor does one have to believe in pataphysics to explicate *Ubu Roi*. Similarly, interpretations of the films of German Expressionism, Dadaism, and the mythopoetic company of the American avant-garde can be grounded in intellectual history.

In analyzing the writings of Stephen King, one would be well advised to invoke psychoanalytic concepts, because King himself believes some (culturally diluted) version of them, and, in point of fact, he uses them in his works, as does Clive Barker. Psychoanalytic concepts, however diffuse, influence their imagery, and reference to them enhances our historical understanding of what King and Barker are about. I claim no more than this for the articles in this volume that deploy psychoanalytic concepts.

Indeed, this historicist viewpoint was even presupposed, and explicitly voiced, when I wrote these articles in the first place, despite the fact that, at the time, I was more charitably disposed toward psychoanalysis than I am now. Unlike many psychoanalytic critics, I never assumed that the use of psychoanalysis in criticism was grounded in its putative scientific authority as a general explanation of all things human, including films.

I have always used psychoanalysis in a historically constrained manner, restricting its application to cases where I thought it was plausible to do so, supposing that psychoanalytic thinking was part of the intellectual milieu in which the relevant films were imagined and created. Thus, even though I no longer have any sympathy for psychoanalytic theory whatsoever, I still think that the articles that employ psychoanalytic concepts in this volume provide reasonable interpretations of the pertinent works on the grounds of cultural history.

I have chosen to organize the essays in this book in a way that roughly corresponds to the progression of film history, rather than to the chronological order in which the articles were written. Indeed, the fact that many of the articles concern canonical classics of film history, or (less politely) "old war horses," probably makes it evident that for a substantial period of my life I taught film history courses (and attended screenings at MOMA and the Thalia and rented films from Janus, New Yorker Films, the Filmmakers Co-Op, and Audio Brandon). As a result, it is one of my fondest fantasies that some people may find this book to be a useful supplementary text in introductory film history courses.

I realize that many of these articles may not be as historiographically up to speed as the current state of film studies requires. However, insofar as undergraduate film history courses are also typically introductions to film appreciation, I think that this text can be profitably combined with a reliable film history text. Where such historical overviews provide sweep, this book can add interpretive detail with reference to many of the films that students still routinely spend most of their time watching in introductory courses.

I am very grateful to Cambridge University Press – to Beatrice Rehl and Bill Rothman – for providing me with the opportunity to assemble these articles in one place. Many of them were written for journals that have ceased to exist and that, in any case, never circulated widely. I suspect that many of these essays will find a larger audience in this incarnation than they ever did in their previous lives.

For me, gathering these articles together is to some degree an exercise in nostalgia. As I have indicated, the close interpretation of film was my first love. In recent years, I have not had the occasion to indulge it as often as I would like. Intellectual commitments to other issues have drawn me elsewhere. Some day I hope to return to it, though at this juncture in my career, it seems more likely that I would be led to developing a theory of film interpretation.

Reading Tom Gunning's gracious and altogether overly generous preface to this anthology, I too recalled a time gone by. Tom, in fact, was the first person I spoke to (I learned he was from Ohio, as I remember) when we both queued up for our first graduate course in cinema studies at NYU. [22] I can only wish that these essays do something to rekindle the excitement, commitment, and intensity of our mutual generation's "discovery" (rediscovery?) of film.

1

The Cabinet of Dr. Kracauer

Though it would be foolhardy to attempt to trace the development of the early avant-garde the way one sketches the rise of the silent narrative tradition, I think it is at least plausible to assess the importance of *The Cabinet of Dr. Caligari* for the avant-garde, as comparable to the importance of *The Birth of a Nation* for the popular film. That is, *Caligari* is the best remembered early venture in avant-garde film experimentation just as *The Birth of a Nation* is the most memorable forebear of the commercial narrative. Of course, *Caligari* was both narrative and commercial, and its influence has never totally disappeared in the popular tradition. Yet it also has special significance for the avant-garde in that it is the most distinguished early attempt to articulate the concerns of a contemporary art movement, Expressionism, in film.

The place of *Caligari* in film history is secure. It appears wherever the classics are convoked. But its reputation is another matter. Though much seen, it is also much maligned. Two kinds of charges plague it. The first relies on one or another myth of the cinematic. Either *Caligari* is too theatrical or it violates film's supposed commitment to realism.[1]

The other charge is partly political, but it is also aesthetic since it amounts to the claim that the film is castrated. This argument, enshrined by Siegfried Kracauer,[2] holds that *Caligari*, though initially a radical denunciation of authoritarianism, was reduced to hollow conformism by the addition of the psychiatric framing story. The problem here is not only that the film is right-wing (and, for Kracauer, proto-Nazi), but also that it is an imperfect masterpiece whose authentic message has been garbled.

Of these two kinds of arguments, the first sort seems the least serious because they lean so heavily on discredited theories of film. Also, the theatricality of *Caligari* can be justified internally in the film as a

"The Cabinet of Dr. Kracauer," *Millennium Film Journal*, no. 2 (Spring/Summer 1978), pp. 77–85.

quotation of theatrical staginess that emphatically fosters the sense of society as both artificial and externally directed, two major assertions of the film.

The Kracauer position, however, seems to require a more detailed response. His approach does not presuppose a dated film theory. Consequently, it can be embraced by critics of almost every aesthetic allegiance. Indeed, some commentators on Weimar film merely repeat the Kracauer story whole.[3] Kracauer's explanation has spread like a pernicious rumor, making the forerunner of the avant-garde film seem like a botched job.

What did Kracauer say? Basing his speculations on a manuscript about the origin of *Caligari*, by one of the film's co-authors (Hans Janowitz), Kracauer explains that originally the story had a specific pacifist intention. Carl Mayer and Janowitz meant their tale as an allegory, "animated by hatred of an authority which had sent millions of men to death."

Cesare stands for the common man, virtually hypnotized by the malevolent Caligari, who manipulates the somnabulist like a puppet to do his murderous bidding. Absolute authority, Caligari, is characterized as an impostor and as insane. The central metaphor of the original script is that unchecked authority is mad; the implication warns that authority leads to homicidal mania, the poets' analogue for war. Power inevitably spirals into frenzy and bloodbath.

But the original script was not filmed as Mayer and Janowitz planned. A framing story, purportedly suggested by Fritz Lang, was added which established the saga of the mad psychiatrist and his factotum as the fantasy of the protagonist, Francis. This deviation, directed by Robert Wiene, reportedly infuriated Mayer and Janowitz. In Kracauer's words

. . . it perverted, if not reversed their intrinsic intentions. While the original exposed the madness inherent in authority, Wiene's *Caligari* glorified authority and convicted its antagonist of madness. A revolutionary film was thus turned into a conformist one – following the much used pattern of declaring some normal but troublesome individual insane and sending him to a lunatic asylum.[4]

For Kracauer, the framing story vitiates the project. The denunciation of authority metamorphoses into the hostility of a patient for his doctor. The madman reverses the order of things, relocating his own insanity in his psychiatrist and projecting his own aggression into other characters and the threatening environment. Perhaps, following Kracauer, we could go so far as to interpret Alan's murder as a displacement of Francis' morbid wish to do away with his one rival for the affections of Jane.

Cesare's abduction of Jane might be a manifestation of Francis' un-acknowledged desire to rape her. Francis, Caligari and Cesare could be read respectively as the super-ego, ego and id of the paranoid fabulator, the ever-present triangles of the set, an emblem of this psychic hierarchy.

Kracauer is undoubtedly correct in holding that the framing story makes a difference. But is it the difference Kracauer asserts? Kracauer has the film changing from day to night, from revolutionary to con-formist, in one easy step. Could a work that is intrinsically radical be subverted so effortlessly? In Kracauer's account, the original story seems to function like a shot in montage – by juxtaposing it to the framing story, its significance shifts completely.

There is something disconcertingly facile in this analysis. It virtually denies that the core of the film has any internal integrity. It is one-sided, giving the framing story too determinant a position in terms of establish-ing the meaning of the film.

Against Kracauer, I would urge a more dialectical reading, one that would consider how the original, radical conception of the film makes the framing story work in its favor. Far from a cripple, *Caligari* is stylis-tically and thematically an organic whole. Kracauer's approach is too mechanical, insensitive to the interplay of the various elements of the film. He supposes that a complex aesthetic system has no powers of recuperation; for him, it can be disabled as simply as putting sand in the gasoline tank of a car.

My strategy for defending the unity of *Caligari* is simple. The framing story does transform Holstenwall from an allegory to a fantasy. The vio-lence is relocated in Francis. But this does not make the film conformist because, dialectically, it raises a new question, viz., what is the source of Francis' madness? The film assures us that Francis can be cured; but why was he afflicted? I think that *Caligari* has an answer to this question, one that resides in the core of the film, the part Kracauer thought had been defanged. In terms of the whole film, the framing story doesn't subvert social criticism so much as resituate it in a psychoanalytic context where the core of the film, the fantasy, dialectically supplies enough evidence for us to charge that Francis has been maddened by his environment.

In order to say how the film supplies this evidence, I must put my psychoanalytic cards on the table. Throughout this article, I will hold that the symptoms of the psychotic often contain a symbolic account of the source of his madness. Consequently, I intend to examine Francis' tale and its imagery from two perspectives: both as indications of his madness and as a symbolic expression of the factors that maddened him.

I am very sympathetic to Morton Schatzman's recent rereading of Daniel Paul Schreber's paranoid fantasies as a symbolic transformation of the unbearable regimes to which his father subjected him in the name of hygiene. That is, Schreber's "feelings of persecution can be adequately explained as transformations of his real persecution."[5] Similarly, I will argue that Francis' fantasies are not only symptoms, as Kracauer holds, but also, dialectically, indices of the source of that madness. From this perspective, I interpret what is given as Francis' representation of Holstenwall as an accusation to the effect that the inhumanity and hostility of the environment are the causes of his madness.

Unlike Kracauer, I don't regard the framing story as a debilitating appendage, an excrescence, but rather as a healthy organ neatly segued with the central story. The difference its addition makes vis-à-vis the Mayer/Janowitz version is unequivocally to ground their visionary symbolism in the language of the unconscious. Some may bridle, charging that this effect is quite philistine, insofar as it involves naturalizing or psychologizing poetry. Yet, within the framework of Expressionist literature, the complaint is hardly compelling because the Expressionists often seem to mime explicitly the language of madness. For example, their experiments in telegraphic writing sometimes recall the structure of psychotic word salads. In this context, the psychologism of *Caligari* merely makes the already apparent source of the imagery more apparent.

Madness, of course, was a favorite Expressionist theme. Expressionism might even be called the art of the traumatized. Though often couching their diatribes in the rhetoric of cosmic estrangement, the Expressionists were responding to concrete social conditions. The personal anxiety, the alienation and the sense of crisis of artists, first in reaction to the rapid industrialization of Germany after 1870 and then against the world war, led them to madness as a likely subject. Madness could embody the experience of shock, derangement standing for the feeling of acute disorientation that accompanies convulsive social change.

The Expressionists were rebellious rather than revolutionary. Apart from vague utopian promises, they rarely espoused political programs. Instead, one might argue that the political function of their art was to serve as an index of anguish, despair, uncertainty and hysteria. In the face of social upheaval and dislocation, they were lightning rods galvanizing the prevailing sense of *angst* into powerful currents of expression. Intense psychological states and characters literally driven mad were natural analogues for their own subjective experience of social chaos and collapse.

Madness supplied Expressionism not only with content, but also with technique. The language of madness, based on the structures of the primary process, could be intuitively mobilized by artists in their quest to project a symbol system that would appropriately and expressively communicate their extreme sense of crisis. Discussing *Job*, Walter Sokel remarks, "Intimately related to the dream and the workings of the human subconscious, as expounded by Freud in his *Interpretation of Dreams* and *Wit and Its Relation to the Unconscious*, Kokoschka's method constitutes the dramatic parallel to Kafka's art of projecting the repressed content of the mind into mysterious events."[6]

The use of the structures of the primary process as a means of communication is apparent as the very basis of Mayer's and Janowitz's original idea for *Caligari*. Their central theme, that authority is mad, is articulated metaphorically by identifying the authority figure as a madman. This form of symbolism is one that is quite common in dreams. Freud called it condensation. It operates by uniting two disparate elements, in this case authority and madness, for the sake of identifying them.

Condensation is an apt symbolic device for dreams because dreams are primarily visual, not linguistic. The yoking together of disparate elements supplies a means for overcoming the lack of the term "is" in the vocabulary of the dreamwork. Silent film is also primarily visual. Therefore, it is not surprising to find the makers of *Caligari* resorting to condensation as a means of articulating their themes, especially since the basic story is founded on a condensation.

The search for further condensations in the plastic elements of *Caligari* is rewarding. In many of the sets, the shape of a knife seems incongruously joined with – indeed, superimposed over – other disparate entities. When Jane and Francis discuss Alan's murder, there are painted, knifelike shadows on the garden wall behind them. One of them is especially pronounced in the shooting – it seems to be a black version of Cesare's white, steel dagger.

Pointed angular shapes echo throughout the film. The two bannisters at the entrance to the fairground seem modeled on cutlery. The window at the discovery of the first mysterious murder looks like a stiletto ominously pointed at the bed. Indeed, windows throughout are often triangular, not only suggesting authority, but pretending to the shape of a knife. Extremely narrow buildings jut out against the horizon, their sharp tips and edges hyperbolized. Sometimes these distorted buildings are described as shards. This is close, but I think not quite right. The architecture and the attendant network of shadows are rather based on the knife as their basic form, condensing its shape with the man-made environment. This condensationg is based not only on pointed figures, but on a persistent theme of long edges throughout the film.

The natural world continues this condensatory motif. Note the fields Caligari races across as he returns to the asylum after Cesare's death. Here we find what are quite literally *blades* of grass; the knolls are depicted as a series of teeth of some fantastic chain saw. This grass also recalls the earlier backdrop of the hillside town of Holstenwall. Both the natural and architectural environment seem hostile because they are weapon-like. Leafless trees, such as those underneath the bridge Cesare crosses, are shaped and sharpened like spears. The physical environment, in short, is an oneiric arsenal, surrounding and enclosing the drama like veritable knives pointed at the frail human characters. The set designers, Hermann Warm, Walter Reiman and Walter Rohrig, have created a milieu that is nothing less than a colossal Iron Maiden.

The distortion of the sets should not simply be explained as having a single message – "this is the vision of a distorted mind." The sets are more specific in their significations. One part of the meaning of this distortion is the condensation which identifies the environment as a forest of sabers and lances. But even where the environment is not overtly hostile, it is inhospitable. Rooms are not designed for human habitation. Their raked floors would be troublesome to navigate, while their slanted ceilings make much of the space useless for a person of average height. Likewise, the public streets that adjoin the square are precipitous, as well as so narrow that they crowd with the mildest traffic. Human life must be profoundly uncomfortable in the homes and on the boulevards of Holstenwall. And consider the thinness of many of the buildings – they signal symbolically an implosive sense of the environment closing in, contracting like a vise.

So far, it may appear that I haven't said anything that Kracauer couldn't absorb. He might account for the hostile portrayal of the environment as a projection of the paranoid Francis. The inhospitable nature of Holstenwall similarly is a reification of the phenomenology of psychosis, the implosive character of the physical world a correlate to the madman's experience of overwhelming pressure.

But I want to stress that these remarks are not where an analysis of *Caligari* should end, but where it should begin. Within the context of Expressionism, the distortion of the physical environment stands for the disruption and degradation of the social world. In the poetry of Trakl, the air is befouled with loathesome odors. Blood runs from slaughter houses into fetid canals, and the landscape is swarming with rats, worms, ravens and flies. Here, the emphasis on physical decay articulates the experience of social and cultural decay, just as Gottfried Benn's early collection of verse, *The Morgue* presents a microcosm of society in terms of an inventory of corpses whose rotting flesh compose the body politic. In "Weltende" by Jakob van Hoddis (the pseudonym of Hans Davidsohn), the premonition of the tumultuous decline and fall of bourgeois society is charted in images of roofs breaking apart and cascading, trains tumbling off bridges, an outbreak of influenza and floods breaking through embankments. Sickness, breakdown and deluge, attributes of the physical environment, represent the condition of society. Similarly, Francis' imagination plastically reconstructs society in the image of a physical world that is not only inhospitable but hostile, not only inhuman but closing in.

Another key symbolic process in *Caligari* is what Freud called dramatization. This is rather like a game of charades that the dream plays with the dreamer. Images literalize words, ideas and metaphors. A simple example is the famous chair scene in *Caligari*. When Caligari comes for a permit for his sideshow, he must importune the lofty town clerk perched appropriately on a seat that stands higher than Caligari's stooped shoulders. This is a picture of hierarchy. The linguistic expression that the official is "above" Caligari in the chain of civic authority is literalized, the metaphor made concrete in the imagery. This technique is also repeated in the police station where the constabulary, atop their swivel chairs, tower over the townspeople.

Much of the distortion in *Caligari* is of this sort. I have already mentioned the idea that the environment is implosive. There is also a suggestion in many of the rooms that the environment is in a state of imminent collapse. The slanted ceilings lower awesomely, as in Francis' private quarters. The bending buildings, crooked street lamps and cracked walls recall the buckling cityscapes of Ludwig Meidner (e.g. *Burning City*). Though the sets are sometimes compared to Feininger's paintings, the analogy seems wrong to me because the locked architectonic of Feininger's Cubist designs promotes a feeling of solidity. Holstenwall is unsteady. Throughout, top-heavy facades heave forward, literalizing the idea that society is on the brink of toppling.

This is a visual theme Wiene exploits even further in a subsequent film, *Raskolnikov*, where the motifs of broken windows and bannisters, sagging buildings, rooms that look like exploded mine shafts and apartments supported by jerry-built beams are pervasive. In *Raskolnikov*, the physical environment is literally coming apart; windows, for instance, are too big for their frames. The milieu is one that has cracked under its own weight, been patched up carelessly and is about to fall apart again. This sense of imminent collapse, though perhaps not as strident in *Caligari*, undeniably shapes Holstenwall. It constitutes the elements of Francis' fantasy, but also causes it. As such, it is an indictment as well as a symptom.

Francis' imbalance literally structures the ever-sloping sets. The night before Caligari is unmasked, there are interesting shots of him asleep where it is hard to tell whether the oblique image is a result of camera angulation or the sets. This ambiguity nicely encapsulates the question of whether the distortion is in the telling or in the world described.

Dramatization determines not only set design, but also acting. That the moral values Caligari represents are warped and diseased is inscribed in his gait. His corruption is virtually painted onto his decrepit complexion with splotchy greasepaint. The tendency of the authoritarian mentality to juxtapose obsequiousness with megalomania is represented, on the one hand, by his body bent into a hunched over bow and, on the other, with moments when he draws himself erect, shaking with exclamation. That Caligari is morally twisted is literalized in his movements – watch his hand as he is first tempted to become Caligari. In short, an entire vocabulary of scorn shapes his gestures.

Though it would be possible casually to compare Cesare with the vampire in *Nosferatu*, to me his movement seems different. The idea in *Nosferatu* is that the vampire is death. Stiffness is emphasized; Dracula, though moving, palpably evokes the idea of rigor mortis. Cesare is somewhat more flexible. Though an automaton, he sensuously presses his body against the wall in Jane's garden as he slinks toward her chamber. Here, the metaphor of pressure emerges again; he seems almost glued to the wall as if by some invisible centrifugal force.

More than any other character, Cesare seems the one best adapted to inhabit Francis' fantasy. His thinness, his angular posture and his black costume at times make him appear to blend into the two-dimensional elements of the set. As he dies, his gestures tend to refer the viewer to the painted trees in the background since his arms are an inverted pantomime of the lower branches of the tree behind him. The fact that Cesare can become a graphic element has symbolic overtones. It is part of a major visual theme in the film, a tension between two-dimensionality and three-dimensionality which may be read in terms of a sense of psychotic claustrophobia, the flatness suggesting life caught in an ontological crunch.

Of course, I don't pretend to have elucidated every kind of image in *Caligari*. There are also complexly developed visual motifs that involve confounding the organic with the inorganic and the internal with the external. These confusions articulate Francis' oceanic state. But, at times, they also contribute to the major theme of the film as I have described it. For instance, the wall outside Caligari's office has a crawling vine painted over it despite the fact that we presuppose the chamber is inside the large, well-kept asylum. The vine seems on the verge of taking over the hallway. This is an example of a recurrent vegetative motif which confounds the distinction between inside and outside. But it also participates in Francis' denunciation of society via the physical environment because it pejoratively suggests ruins; that stage in a civilization's life when it is overrun by nature since culture is long dead.

Caligari presents its core story as an hallucination, as a dream. The idea that it is a sort of rebus is evident, not only in terms of the psychiatric framework, but also in the way it uses outright symbols – letters and numbers – as design elements in the sets. The scene where the psychiatrist proclaims he must become Caligari puts the written word on a par with the physical environment. This should beckon us to attempt to read the iconography.

My major problem with Kracauer is that, in an important way, he did not try to decipher the imagery of the film. For the most part, he surmised that the distortion had one dominant message – Francis is mad. Given this monolithic reading, he postulated that the film subverted its animating conception and became reactionary. But a closer look at the imagery reveals that the original critical impulse is still intact.

It is true that I have not shown that the revised *Caligari* is the pacifist work Janowitz intended it to be. On the one hand, I wonder if without the framing story the film could be read so precisely. But even if a pacifist theme were lost that would not make the film reactionary, which is Kracauer's central claim, Francis is mad, but that madness is attributed to a hostile physical environment which, in the context of Expressionism, represents an attitude toward society that condemns the accelerated transformation of Germany into a capitalist state, the disruption and sense of rootlessness of rapid industrialization and the crisis of the war as anti-human. *Caligari* may be likened to a cry of pain. But it is also a consistent and coherent utterance which uses the language of the unconscious to express the maddening oppression of the social environment on the individual.

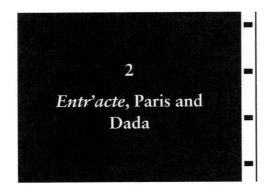

2

Entr'acte, Paris and Dada

Dada is a form of nihilism. But it would be a mistake to characterize it as a movement without a moral posture. Instead, it is of a piece with the kind of moral immoralism which emerges in the wake of Rousseau and de Sade, and which encompasses, among others, Baudelaire, Rimbaud and Gide. A basic gesture of the moral immoralist is to parade and to celebrate his infamies, outrages, excesses and sins, not in order to titillate, but rather to reveal hypocrisy. Certainly there were immoralists before Rousseau; but the great historical bounders, like Cellini, reveled in their antics to entertain. The moral nihilist presents his crimes in protest against existing morality and culture. He plays the boundary between morality conceived of as customary practice and the notion that there are deeper values that customary practice inhibits. The positive morality of the moral immoralist is often not systematically articulated; his role is generally negative. His gesture, though ostensibly lacking morality (customary morality), still constitutes an essentially moral act, namely that of condemnation.

Dada, significantly, began in reaction to the First World War. It was a protest against the bourgeois culture that caused such destruction. The Dadaist viewed bourgeois culture as an integral whole – art, morality and etiquette each being different faces of the same thing and going by the calling card of rationality. The protest of the Dadaist, consequently, was multi-dimensional, promoting anti-bourgeois art, anti-bourgeois morality and defiant rudeness. The moral stance was negation; for every bourgeois norm, its contrary was espoused. Tzara wrote:

The intelligent man has become the complete and normal type. What we need, what offers some interest, what is rare because it has the anomalies of a precious being and the freshness and freedom of great antimen, is the Idiot. Dada is working with all its forces toward the establishment of the idiot everywhere.

"*Entr'acte*, Paris and Dada," *Millennium Film Journal*, no.1 (Winter 1977–78), pp. 5–11.

Dada protest was provocative, not measured. Its most brilliant gestures could be interpreted in the way that followers of R. D. Laing decipher the symptomology of a psychotic, that is as a critique of the forces and customs that oppress. Tzara proposes that poems be made by cutting out words from books and magazines, shuffling them in a hat and drawing them out randomly. Such a method could be experienced only as brutal renunciation by a culture steeped in beliefs about the centrality of both craftsmanship and self-expression in poetry. Man Ray's *The Gift* defies the bourgeois commitment to functionalism. By welding nails to the bottom of an iron, his device no longer glides smoothly over well-tailored pants, but embeds itself, inert, in the ironing board. The very concept of this tool is subverted at just that point in its design which makes it useful. Contrariety is celebrated – the smooth bottom made jagged. And in the process, a core value of bourgeois culture is effaced.

As an integral whole of social practices and beliefs, bourgeois culture presents itself as rationality. The Dadaist, profoundly impressed by the oppression and destruction intrinsic to bourgeois culture, responds that if this be rational, let us be irrational. Rationality is regarded as a veil, disguising monumental hypocrisy. Dadaism is an act of revulsion, of protest, and of criticism. The Dadaist pursues irrationalism by rejecting whatever seems to constitute the standard, "rational" practice of art, communication, morality and etiquette. This rejection touches the core values, beliefs and customs of bourgeois culture like a dentist's drill hitting a nerve. Toying with the fundamentals of bourgeois culture is predicated on infuriating that culture. The mode of the Dadaist is indubitably humor, but it is aggressive humor, which is based, as Hobbes remarked, in a sense of superiority.

Entr'acte, by Réné Clair and Francis Picabia, is a complex work, unified by its Dadaist stance, by its contempt and disdain for the bourgeois version of culture. Though the humor of the piece may somewhat camouflage the sharpness of this Dadaist assault on one level, at another remove the humor itself is yet another gesture of contempt, a means of laughing at the complacency of its targets.

Entr'acte is a film born in the spirit of negation. Picabia casually composed the script at Maxim's, scribbling an inventory of images that he wanted in the film. The traditional notion of studied craftsmanship went by the boards as Picabia listed whatever popped into his head. The film was planned as an attraction to be screened during the intermission (hence the title) of a Dada performance of *Relâche*, a ballet whose name, signifying "no show today," obfuscates traditional codes of advertising by presenting an event in the standard vocabulary for cancelling an event.

Clair took Picabia's slapdash conglomeration of scenes and worked them into a coherent, purposively directed assault on the prevailing high culture. His attack is multi-dimensional, incorporating elements of style and content in an overarching diatribe. The film violates bourgeois morality – people are burnt, kicked and killed without recrimination. The funeral, a special moment of high seriousness in bourgeois culture, is turned into a farce. Etiquette is burlesqued – the undertaker has installed a fairground air hose on his doorstep so that the dresses of the bereaved blow into their faces as they offer their condolences to other friends of the deceased; members of the funeral entourage nibble at the decorations on the hearse as the trip to the cemetery begins.

High art is also disdained by direct buffoonery. Ballet comes in for an outright beating. The repeated crotch shots of the ballerina suggest a well-known pornographic interest in the art. The effusiveness of talk about dance, specifically in terms of the description of dance movements as "flowing," is challenged by contrasting a ballerina's "flowing" hands with water in a cut that renders the resemblance between the two insubstantial. And, of course, Clair finally insults the ballerina by substituting that ideal of female beauty with the image of a bearded, rather greasy and wholly unattractive man, an act akin to drawing a mustache on the *Mona Lisa*.

Obliquely, Clair challenges high art by his use of cinematic motifs culled from the most primitive days of early film. His imagery recalls the trick film and the Sennett chase, forms of film-making that belong to the days when film was still a rough proletarian art. What from the high art perspective of the period might be considered the most vulgar forms of entertainment are proffered as an appropriate supplement to that loftiest of arts, the ballet.

The use of Sennett, here, is quite tendentious. For Sennett, if he had one consistent aim, was devoted to attacking pretension. His representation of the bourgeois was generally ridiculous. Their makeup and costume are grotesque; they constantly suffer narrative indignities; their mannerisms and movements are always exaggerated. In *Entr'acte*, that animus remains intact. Clair even retains Sennett's use of the chase and of fast motion photography to reduce the bourgeois to physical absurdity. Clair adds slow motion to the chase for the same purpose.

Clair affronts expectation not only in his choice of subjects but also in his choice of structures. The temporal unity of the work as a whole is indeterminate. There are spurts of narrative, but most abort. Where a narrative appears somewhat sustained (e.g. toward the end of the film), it nevertheless lurches in inexplicable directions (e.g. the hearse riding the rails of the rollercoaster). The subversion of expectations, here, is based on two related, but distinguishable, motives. The first, and more obvious, is a continuation of the attack on the practice of bourgeois art, which in the realm of cinema traditionally was allied with narrative. To eschew the narrative "codes" of that art parallels the brutalities in the film that renounce codes of morality.

At the same time, the rejection of a consistent narrative structure is also deeply connected with an assault on rationality as such (here, I am using "rationality" in its specifically cognitive sense in contrast to the broader, multi-dimensional meaning employed earlier). Traditionally, narrativity and rationality stand in close relation. Narration is a form of explanation. It is a means of selecting and ordering experience so that later events are accounted for in terms of earlier ones. To narrate is to reason, to offer one kind of explanation. Indeed, narrative explanations are probably the most commonly used forms of explanation. By subverting narration in *Entr'acte*, Clair involved himself not only in an attack on an artistic institution, but also in an attack on the most customary practice of rational thought in bourgeois culture. *Entr'acte* does affront the narrative film as an art form just as it does ballet. However, the thrust is also deeper insofar as narrative structures also represent customary ways of thinking.

The processes that associate imagery in *Entr'acte* often are not causal. Instead, Clair substitutes causality, generally thought to be the backbone of narrativity, with kinds of connectives that we typically correlate with irrational mental processes. Cuts, as in the final chase, are based on sensuous associations between shots, e.g. shots on movement. In an earlier section of the film, Clair cuts from a superimposition involving water to a shooting gallery where the target, an artificial egg, is suspended on a jet of water; the only basis for the cut is the correspondence of the appearance of water in both images. When the sharpshooter hits the egg, the target bursts and a bird flies away – the events connected in virtue of an associative logic that relates birds and eggs. Other images are also linked by conceptual association – burning matches are superimposed over a man scratching his head because one also "scratches" a match to light it. Shot linkage based on rational, narrative thinking is displaced in favor of what is customarily thought of as irrational, associative structures corresponding to the operation of the primary processes of the unconscious.

Clair renounces the cinematic processes of articulation that can be correlated with rationality for irrational structures. And he uses these irrational structures to develop his polemic against bourgeois culture. This can be seen specifically in the series of pejorative cinematic metaphors that he develops about Paris.

One of the first of these critical metaphors involves shots of Paris streetlights at night and shots of boxing gloves. Clair changes the focus in the street light shots. The glare from the lamps expands – big, white orbs on a black background. At points these orbs grow until they are momentarily tangent. This is intercut with shots of white boxing gloves sparring on a black background. The two images are quite similar especially since the rapid focus alterations in the lamp shots yield the impression that the white orbs are moving at each other quickly. Cut against the boxing gloves, one has the feeling that the lamps are exchanging blows—as if Paris itself is a fight or a struggle.

Paris is also represented as a game. Duchamp and Man Ray stoop over a chess board. By superimposition, the chess game is identified with the busy Place de la Concorde. There are also shots of a massive, classic, official-looking building. Special shots select the columns in this building for emphasis, strengthening the chess game analogy through editing in virtue of the tubular, classic shape of both the chess pieces and these columns. Clair even deceptively pans his camera over these columns to suggest that they "move"—thereby referring to the typical function of chess pieces. Thus, both the everyday and official life of Paris are interpreted in the light of the metaphoric framework of a game.

A cascade of water falls on the game and by metaphoric extension onto Paris itself. This yields shots where Clair moves his camera in a kind of swinging action thereby making the buildings and landscape of the city sway to and fro. A child's boat, made from a folded newspaper, is superimposed on the rocking cityscape. The image becomes metaphoric – Paris is the sea, but a turbulent, troubled and storm-tossed sea, with each movement of the camera seen as a tempestuous wave.

The most famous pejorative metaphor of Paris, of course, is evolved in the chase scene. Unlike more typical cinematic metaphors, this one is notable for its length; the metaphor is sustained for many shots and for many minutes. Because of its length it is somewhat complex. One key structure in its articulation is the special cross-cutting employed to imply that all of Paris is involved in the chase after the casket. Bicyclists and scenes of everyday auto traffic are interwoven in order to suggest that the whole of Paris is involved in the chase after the hearse. The structure here reminds one of the finale of *Duck Soup* when the Marx Brothers' call for help is answered by the police, the fire department, marathon walkers and elephants. The function of this structure is incorporative, joining all these disparate elements into the same activity. In *Entr'acte*, because the structure generalizes the chase to all of Paris, the whole city is represented as involved in a moribund pursuit.

Speed is an important element in this chase. Clair emphasizes velocity in a number of ways. In the Sennett tradition, he undercranks part of the sequence. He employs shots, not only of the hearse, but also point-of-view shots from the hearse of passing objects, including tree-tops and walls. Here, the audience is supplied with a strong measure of the high velocity of movement by being given stationary objects in order to gauge the speed of the hearse. Clair also metaphorically develops the notion of speed by including point-of-view shots from a rollercoaster, referring the movement of the hearse to a recognized symbol of accelerated movement. As well, the accelerated motion of the ordinary bicyclists makes them appear as racers; they are tightly grouped, and, due to the under-cranking, they appear to be madly pumping their machines. This reference to racers also accentuates the sense of speed, characterizing the chase as a race, both a test and a contest of speed.

Chases function differently in different films. Often in Chaplin, the chase is a metaphoric device for developing the theme of the Tramp's alienation from society, i.e. the Tramp most often runs *away* from society. In other contexts, a chase articulates an anarchic urge because what is emphasized about the chase is the way that it interferes with and disrupts ordinary social processes. Here, the chase in *The Disorderly Orderly* is a prime example. Garbage pails are overturned, traffic interrupted and a supermarket reduced to mayhem. Lewis' chase is virtually aimed at the destruction of society. *French Connection I* presents a less profound use of the chase – a kind of wish fulfillment fantasy for owners of big, powerful American cars condemned to the slow pace of city traffic. *French Connection I* portrays the dream of, for once, using all that horsepower, unrestrained by law, pedestrians and traffic jams.

In *Entr'acte*, the function of the chase is also quite particular. It is not an anarchic chase; it doesn't emphasize the chase as disruptive. It emphasizes speed and also a particular consequence of that speed, namely the way the speed breaks up and disperses the entourage. The speed causes the bulk of the procession to fall away; the rather large entourage is reduced to a handful by the end of the chase. The camera pulls past the racers, as if to suggest that the race has passed them by, indeed that they have dropped away. This iconography, of course, has precedents in Sennett. As the Keystone Kops run to the rescue, members of the force are continually lost, continually dropping out. The force is perpetually disintegrating. In Sennett's race films, like *Lizzies of the Field*, the speed of the contests literally cause the cars to break up, leaving a trail of auto parts behind. Automobiles hurl through the air sending tires and gears in every direction. Part of the significance of Sennett chases involves the literalization of fears about the pace of modern life. That is, Sennett literalizes the belief that the accelerated pace of life, especially in light of the slow-paced, rural background of most of the proletarian audience, is inherently destructive; society would, like the lizzies, buckle and break apart under the intensified velocity. Clair selects this aspect of Sennett's iconography for *Entr'acte*. Though Clair does not emphasize characters actually falling down, the cumulative effect of the race is the dispersal of the procession, the emblem of bourgeois society. In certain shots, the image vibrates, acknowledging the pressure that the speed of the chase exerts on the recording mechanism. The chase is also a reckless one, changing direction continuously. Most of the mourners have disap-peared by the end of the chase; the speed of the moribund race has broken up society. The race is a self-destructive one, hurtling headlong and recklessly at a pace that breaks society apart.

The use of speed as a means to convey a disquieting vision of the des-tiny of a society is well-precedented. Gogol analogizes Russia to a galloping troika at the end of *Dead Souls*. And for Zola, the driverless train at the end of *La Bête Humaine* is his image of late 19th century France. For Clair, speed functions within a metaphoric construct that depicts the chase as a moribund race that inherently breaks up society under the pressure of its own reckless propulsion. The film introduces Paris as upside down. By the end the metaphoric significance of that inversion is clarified. Parisian society, locked in a topsy-turvy confusion of values, is a death race, falling apart through its own excesses.

Among the opening shots of *Entr'acte*, we find Satie and Picabia bouncing onto the screen in slow motion and aiming a cannon at Paris. The imagery defines the Dadaist relation to this center of bourgeois culture. Their posture is hostile, destructive. They fire a volley, metaphor-ically a moral salvo, that is echoed throughout the film, articulated through pejorative metaphors of Parisian society and aggressive renunci-ations of bourgeois aesthetic, ethical and social values. The film is ridiculous, irrational and immoral from the perspective of prevailing standards precisely for the purpose of renouncing those standards. Its nihilism is not a metaphysical denial of values as such; rather it is a systematic contempt for the specific ensemble of bourgeois cultural practices that in the wake of the war could be seen only as hypocritical.

3

The Gold Rush

During the sixties when Keaton's silent masterpieces were widely distributed, it was commonplace, at least in the company I kept, for some cognoscente to wonder aloud why for years Chaplin's reputation loomed so much larger than Keaton's. As often happens in aesthetic polemics, Keaton was upgraded by demoting Chaplin. A major complaint about Chaplin was that his cinematic style was quite primitive, never maturing past the formal innovations developed by 1915, wheras Keaton's deep-focus panoramas, graceful match cutting and ingenious special effects suggested that, had it not been for his personal tragedies, Keaton could have evolved as a modern director of any type of film.

This charge of "primitivism" is an old one. In a passage in *Film As Art*, Rudolf Arnheim summarizes a favorable analysis of some of Chaplin's achievements with a caveat that had already attained currency. He writes:

The incredible visual concreteness of every one of his scenes makes for a great part of Chaplin's art, and this should not be forgotten when it is said–as is often done and not without foundation–that his films are not really "*filmic*" (because his camera serves mainly as a recording machine).[1] [Emphasis added]

In the aesthetic context of silent film, "recording" was the fly in the ointment of film art. It could stand for at least two things, not always clearly distinguished in the minds of early theoreticians. On the one hand, the documentary reproduction of ordinary events and everyday scenes was inimical to film art. But more importantly, the slavish filming of theater was the major heresy. Chaplin was too beloved to be excommunicated, yet his reliance on the medium shot as an almost proscenium-like frame for his pantomime smacked of theater and forced the theoretician into gyrations of special pleading. In the sixties, when

"The Gold Rush," Wide Angle, vol.3, no. 2 (1979), pp. 42–49.

"cinematic" analysis locked horns with "literary" analysis, the charge that Chaplin merely recorded theatrical turns again became serious.

In this paper, I would like to focus on *The Gold Rush* (1925) in order to demonstrate that what is thought of as Chaplin's retrograde style is actually a rather sophisticated use of cinematic forms neatly coordinated with the thematic preoccupations that emerge from Chaplin's narrative structures and his gags. I don't mean to argue for Chaplin by disparaging Keaton (or anyone else for that matter), but instead I want to persuade the reader that Chaplin's comic vision is as complex and as cinematically integrated as that of any other master of film comedy.

Chaplin's composition is a special bone of contention because it may be condemmed as overly theatrical. The composition in *The Gold Rush* is, without a doubt, exceptionally studied. Chaplin again and again returns to the use of medium shots and medium long shots. His range is somewhat closer than Keaton's; it seems modeled on the relationship between an ideal spectator and a stage. Often there are strikingly composed shots, carefully setting off foreground/background juxtapositions. However, unlike in many Keaton films, this deliberate structuring is designed to depict social situations rather than to portray relations between man and nature.

When the Tramp enters the Monte Carlo Saloon, he stands alone in the foreground. In the background of this medium shot, the clientele of the bar mill about, in sharp contrast with the lonely silhouette in the foreground. Significantly, the clientele are all in groups, chattering animatedly to each other. The famous shot of the Tramp, outside the saloon on New Year's Eve, repeats this structure. The Tramp is in the foreground of the shot, gazing through the barrier of a glass window at the revelers in the background. Here, the foreground/background zones of the shot become associated with two modes of social being, the exile versus the community.

Chaplin supports this compositional theme of loneliness in numerous ways. First, he casts actors who are generally larger than himself, using scale to set himself off visually from others. He dresses quite differently from others in the film, appearing more as a tarnished dandy, in contrast to the basic lumberjack attire of the other men. And, of course, the Tramp walks in an absolutely unique fashion. Each of these devices makes the Tramp visually distinctive and can accrue more thematic connotations. Also, other characters are generally grouped together; blocking thereby emphasizes the theme of loneliness versus society. Through much of the first part of the saloon scene, Chaplin composes the situation in such a way that the Tramp is outside of virtually everyone else's sight lines. He is effectively invisible, socially nonexistent. He seems to be the only person not involved in a conversation or a dance.

This theme of social invisibility is stressed in the first comic encounter with Georgia where the Tramp mistakenly believes that Georgia is waving to him. The Tramp has picked up a torn photo of Georgia, whom he obviously admires. He is standing in a medium shot, looking at the photo; a tall man walks into the shot behind the Tramp. There is a cut to a two-shot of Georgia and one of her girlfriends. The girlfriend looks off-screen and then nudges Georgia to do likewise. As Georgia moves her head, Chaplin cuts to her point of view. This is a shot with both the Tramp and the man behind him, both looking, one surmises, at Georgia. The man behind the Tramp smiles; one assumes that he is an old acquaintance of Georgia's. The Tramp also smiles, though hesitantly; he believes that Georgia's attentions are directed at him. There is a cut to Georgia; she waves and begins to walk off-camera. Then, Chaplin shifts to a deep-focus, diagonally composed medium shot from behind the Tramp and from behind the man behind the Tramp. This shot composition gives special emphasis to Georgia's actual sight line; her line of vision shoots way over the Tramp to the taller man. At the same time, it is clear how someone, unaware of someone else behind him and standing where the Tramp is, could mistakenly think that Georgia is looking at him. The Tramp walks toward Georgia; she passes him, completely oblivious to his existence; they almost exchange screen positions. Here, the strong diagonal composition portrays the Tramp's condition of exclusion by depicting him as socially invisible. Added to the earlier foreground/background juxtaposition when the Tramp enters the Monte Carlo Saloon, as well as to Chaplin's manner of casting, blocking and even walking, this manipulation of sight lines communicates a powerful image of alienation from the community.

Many of the shots of the mining town, including those outside the Monte Carlo Saloon, are such that the Tramp is isolated in the foreground versus groups moving in the background. Again and again, Chaplin, the director, strives to isolate the Tramp. In the shot where Big Jim and the Tramp leave the cabin, Chaplin purposely holds the image after Big Jim departs in order to present yet another sustained portrait of the Tramp alone.

Throughout *The Gold Rush*, Chaplin proposes imagery that, given its visual organization, evokes concepts, like separateness, which have emotional as well as formal senses. In short, Chaplin is employing his medium shot in a way analogous to the dream process that Freud called dramatization. The themes of being alone, alienated and outside are dramatized by compositions where the character is visually isolated and outside, thus literalizing social relationships through visual ones.

The visual theme of alienation is much enhanced by the juxtapositions one finds in the editing schemas of *The Gold Rush*, which often involve counterposing or contrasting shots of groups with shots where the Tramp is the only person in the frame. For instance, the film begins with seven establishing shots of lines upon lines of men struggling to reach the Yukon gold field. Then there is a shot of the Tramp, alone on a ledge, wending his solitary way through the North country. Here, in the very first images of the film, a contrast is struck between a mass of humanity, represented as a society organized in lines, versus one person who is outside and apart.

This type of contrastive editing is, of course, brought to a crescendo in the New Year's Eve sequence. Between the image of the clock at twelve o'clock and the final shot of the Tramp standing outside the bar there are almost thirty images and subtitles. The basic alternation of images is between the Tramp, alone in his cabin, and the revelers, including Georgia, at the saloon. In the saloon, group shots predominate. There are overhead shots of the crowd. At one point the camera pans around the saloon community, and then cuts to the Tramp as if to underscore that he is outside the "circle" of the community. The camera also cuts around the circle, formed on the dance floor, and then cuts back to the Tramp. Everyone is singing "Auld Lang Syne." Everyone but the Tramp, the man apart. Most of the shots of the Tramp are the same. They are not added to convey new information, but to repeat the theme of loneliness again and again and again. In all, there are eight cuts from the group to the Tramp, each echoing the theme of exclusion.

Chaplin uses his medium shot compositions and his contrastive editing patterns to articulate visually a theme of alienation. This somewhat symbolic employment of technique occurs often in his films. In *The Circus* (1928), for instance, the visual theme of loneliness reaches almost epic proportions, as the circus, with the Tramp's unrequited love aboard, pulls out, leaving the Tramp in the middle of a huge circle where only a day before a circus tent, full of laughing, cheering people, had stood. The shooting and editing emphasize the circus as a social concert, a community, moving as one to its next destination. The editing emphasizes everything as moving away from the Tramp. The long shots stress how alone the Tramp is. It seems that, for miles around, he is the only person present.

The kind of compositional strategies and editing contrasts so far discussed can be readily seen as techniques with an effect that has long been acknowledged as Chaplin's forte, namely pathos. Pathos is a feeling of pity engendered in the audience. But it is a special sort of pity. In the nineteenth century, pathos was commonly associated with situations where a worthy character such as Heathcliff in *Wuthering Heights*, is *excluded* from membership in the community.[2] The audience is called upon to empathize with a character whose talent and virtue are great but unrecognized. The pathetic figure can also provoke audience identification verging on self-pity – e.g., "despite all my abilities, they still snub me."

Chaplin discovered the theme of pathos as a comic narrative theme in film. Like many comedians, Chaplin employed the marriage convention as a basic story device. As a genre convention, the marriage plot suggests an image of social reconciliation and integration.[3] It is, perhaps, a lingering vestige of the stabilizing functions of kinship systems as analyzed by Lévi-Strauss. That is, through marriage various different social classes and social types are integrated peacefully. Consider the screwball comedy: antagonism is buffered by drawing it into the web of affection and obligation within the family. Shakespearean tragedies end with mass murders, whereas the comedies end with mass marriages. The former symbolize the extreme of social disorder while the latter celebrate the height of social harmony, where all classes and factions amalgamate into complex tribal unities. What Chaplin realized about the marriage convention in comedy (specifically film comedy) was that insofar as success in marrying symbolized integration into society, an unrequited suit would suggest irreconcilable otherness.

In April of 1915, in his sixth short at Essanay, Chaplin made a two-reeler called *The Tramp*. In it, the Tramp fails to win the hand of the female lead, played by Edna Purviance. The film ends with the lonesome Tramp proverbially setting off down the road of life, an outcast from everyday society. In this film, Chaplin inaugurated the possibility of pathos in film comedy. He realized that the eternally serviceable marriage convention, insofar as it afforded the image of a fully integrated society, also afforded the possibility of alienation because an unrequited quest implied the contrary of a requited one.

Chaplin heightened emphasis on the female characters to a point where empathy with the Tramp's romantic quest becomes a felt focus of audience attention. The longing of the Tramp is framed in idolatrous closeups and point-of-view shots of his loved ones. Also some of his close shots include an explicit theme of desire. Compare the end of *The General* with the end of *The Gold Rush*. Both concern a kiss. In Chaplin's film, it is an erotic close shot that fully emphasizes Georgia's desirability. The Tramp and Georgia are posing for a photograph. The two characters move closer and closer. Their lips part; slowly and quite erotically they ease into a lusty embrace. In Keaton, the eroticism of the kiss is subverted. The occasion becomes another opportunity for Johnny Gray to solve a problem, namely how to kiss and salute at the same time. Keaton ends the film with a long shot which illustrates Johnny's solution. The difference between the two sequences is desire. For Chaplin, desire and longing are the crucial motivating factors of a quest that Chaplin wants the audience to be involved in emotionally. The formal means that he employs make the topic of the Tramp's love central. For Keaton, the marriage convention and the romantic quest provide merely a convenient armature, an exploitable plot structure, upon which to hang the finer points of the action. But Chaplin takes the marriage convention seriously, emphasizing themes of longing and desire through repetitive close shots in order to initiate the audience into the Tramp's quest empathetically.

In some films, like *The Tramp* and *The Circus*, the Tramp's quest fails. In *The Gold Rush*, the likelihood of a romantic resolution favorable to the Tramp remains only an outside and unpredictable possibility. Indeed, until the last reel, we believe that Georgia still loves Jack. Thus, almost to the very end, the audience is prompted to indulge itself in the sentimentality of unrequited love and of the Tramp's utter lack of connection to society. Chaplin, here, underscores the possibility that the Tramp may be forever exiled. This is symbolized in the narrative through the pervasive theme of unrequited love, which is not reversed until the last moments of the film.

The theme of the social outcast supplies the raison d'être for much of Chaplin's directorial technique in *The Gold Rush*. His way of visually underlining the difference between the Tramp and others by means of foreground/background juxtapositions, scale oppositions, blocking, sight lines and costuming continually individuate and differentiate the Tramp. Within the narrative context, that visual differentiation takes on thematic connotations, functioning as an iconographic marker of isolation. Chaplin renders the Tramp as absolutely distinctive in manner, bearing and dress. This uniqueness again provides an intensification of the gap between the Tramp and the social world around him. That the Tramp also appears as a lumpen proletarian is yet another emblem of his distance from civil society. The narrative theme of alienation is constantly reinforced through editing and compositional formats that suggest the pervasive difference of the main character and the surrounding community.

The primary direction of Chaplin's imagination is toward a specific depiction of social relations. This is not to deny that *The Gold Rush* also involves themes of man in relation to nature. The film devotes a great deal of attention to the subject of privation, especially to themes of hunger and exposure. One feels that these are concerns that are close to Chaplin and that they vividly recall the types of misery that he experienced as an orphan on the streets of London. Yet, these themes of privation seem secondary to the romantic preoccupation of the film, a preoccupation which provokes a powerful image of the social condition of alienation. To understand Chaplin's appeal to his contemporaries, one must locate him in a historical context where the transition to an urban, industrial society entailed a heightened degree of social alienation, a sense of loss of community. The subjective experience of alienation in modern mass society found an appropriate and compelling visual and narrative embodiment in Chaplin's work.

As mentioned, Chaplin seems to have failed to mature formally as a filmmaker. Some may argue that he remained a cinematic primitive, wedded to a frontally organized proscenium-like medium shot, occasionally relieved by simple Griffith editing. From the above analysis, one would hazard, however, the view that the reason for Chaplin's highly restricted vocabulary of forms is that, even by the twenties, Chaplin had learned to employ these minimal techniques in a way that perfectly expressed the theme of pathos which is what be sought. What is disdained as retrograde is actually an organic artistic program that has fully developed its potential and which can confidently rework its basic premises with little if any innovation.

So far, the narrative and compositional themes of *The Gold Rush* have been explored and it has been argued that they constitute an organic system that proposes a compelling theme of social alienation. But what is the relation of the gags to this system? Sadistic routines and mime gags preponderate. The brutality serves constantly to underline the fact that Chaplin narratives operate on the margins of civil society. The human body is continually punched, pulled, kicked and leaned on. In the Sennett tradition, it becomes a mere object, shorn of dignity. The mime gags, however, perform a different function.

The Chaplin character has the capacity, through gesture, to transform any object into a range of other objects. The scene with the clock in *The Pawnshop* (1919) is a famous example of this. The Tramp has a supremely metaphoric imagination.[4] In *The Gold Rush*, he transforms the wick of a lamp into an egg by substituting the behavior appropriate to a boiled egg to a piece of candle wick, salting and swallowing the thick white candle in the manner that one eats a hard-boiled egg. Likewise, Chaplin condenses various eating habits on an old shoe, thereby suggesting a vision of the old shoe as highly specific types of food. When Big Jim bites into the boot, the boot is just a boot. But when the Tramp tastes the leather, his carefully mimed interaction with the parts of the shoe evoke highly distinct images of the boot as part turkey and part spaghetti.

Chaplin's miming ability even comes into play in the big chicken gag, although the identification between the Tramp and the rooster is primarily communicated through literal superimposition. The scene evolves as follows: Big Jim is famished; all of a sudden, Big Jim sees the Tramp as a huge rooster. Big Jim's hallucination is signaled to the audience through the literal superimposition of Chaplin in a rooster costume over the image of Chaplin in the more familiar Tramp outfit. The imagery intermittently shifts between the Tramp as chicken and the Tramp as Tramp. Miming becomes important during the portions of the sequence where the Tramp appears as the Tramp. For in these moments, Chaplin shapes the Tramp's gestures to recall the movement of roosters. He abruptly shrugs his shoulders, suggesting the jerk of a wing; he shakes his head as if craning it. As he walks, he pauses on each foot, alluding to the barnyard strut of a rooster. When Big Jim hands the Tramp his shotgun, the Tramp buries it. And, as the Tramp walks away from that fateful digging, he suddenly kicks some snow behind him onto the buried gun, immediately bringing to mind a comparison with the way chickens scratch dirt. Here, Chaplin, the mime, directly addresses the audience, carefully setting out the visual basis for Big Jim's fantasy through gestures of a character who at moments is a perfect pantomime of a rooster. Indeed, one almost feels that Chaplin, as director, might have forgone the use of superimposition in this sequence, relying wholly on mime to enunciate Big Jim's hallucination.

The consummate visual imagination of Chaplin, the director, extends to the Tramp. The Oceana Roll dance marks the Tramp as a man who sees things differently from others. He sees things from the vantage point of a highly metaphoric visual imagination that can divorce objects from their utilitarian functions and project them onto a plane of pure aesthetic playfulness. The Tramp is a sort of Romantic artist. He sees the world differently from society and through his mime, he can communicate his alternate vision. This identification of the Tramp with the capacity for highly individual conceptions operates decisively within the context of Chaplin's concern with pathos, because it seems that it is exactly because the Tramp sees and thinks differently that he can be an apt object of pathos. His imagination makes him worthy of pathos. Moreover, a connection seems likely between the unique, original and highly individual consciousness of the Tramp and his alienation. The Tramp seems an outcast partly because he thinks differently. Society closes itself off from the inventive consciousness.

Chaplin's treatment of objects can be understood in light of the opposition between the exile and the community. For instance, when the Tramp dances with Georgia, his pants begin to fall down. In response, he swings his cane around and uses it as a hook to hold his pants up. Shortly after this coup, the Tramp ties a rope around his drooping drawers, hoping this will save the day. But he fails to notice that on the other end of the cord, there is an enormous dog. When a cat strays across the floor, the huge dog lurches after it, dumping a dazed Tramp on the ground. The Tramp's use of the cane to hold up his pants is important insofar as the Tramp puts the cane to a use that society never imagined. The Tramp's disastrous use of the rope, on the other hand, illustrates the Tramp's inability to use objects in the way society ordains. Many Chaplin gags return to this theme. Bazin remarked that the Tramp excels when he uses objects differently, i.e., when he invents new uses for them; but when he attempts to use a device in a conventional way, the result is often catastrophic.[5] The Tramp's success and failure with objects is an index of his alienation from society. Objects resist his control unless he uses them in his own unique manner. But it is that unique manner that in many ways keeps him apart.

It has been pointed out that the Tramp's otherness extends to his movement. This is immediately apparent in his gait, but it is also true of his comic evasive tactics. One source of humor in all Chaplin's films occurs as a result of the fast turns and changes in direction that he is able to execute when being chased. The Tramp can always find a hole in the world, so to speak. The humor is based on the subversion of the audience's expectations as well as those of Chaplin's pursuers. The momentum of the Tramp's movement, and of his pursuers, suggests that the Chaplin character will move in one direction and then, suddenly, the Tramp pivots and shoots along another pathway, often passing under the very nose of his assailant. These chase interludes contrast the agility of the Tramp against the more rigid and determined movement of his pursuers. The Tramp does not run like other men. Where others are locked into a single line of forward motion, the Tramp has a full circle of movement possibilities. Again, he is a man distinct, but the ultimate price of this multi-dimensional uniqueness is alienation.

The themes of the alienated individual and the isolated imagination pervade every aspect of the cinematic, comic and narrative organization of *The Gold Rush*. Whereas the Keaton character meditates on means rather than ends, the Tramp emotes about ends (marrying Georgia). This concentration on marriage and on symbolic integration into society provides an overarching unity to the shooting, editing, acting and joking throughout the film. In *The Gold Rush*, the Tramp's quest is successful, though the imagery of alienation is quite extreme. The overall effect is nine reels of almost unrelenting pathos. Every level of cinematic organization enhances this effect. *The Gold Rush* presents an image of the unique individual and society. Chaplin's cinematic and comic technique are consistently manipulated to threaten the irreconcilability of society and its exile. Chaplin's major aesthetic choices for *The Gold Rush* evolve around finding the best methods for wringing pathos out of his materials. The result is an organic unity where narrative content and cinematic style (composition and editing) reinforce each other in articulating a compelling theme of alienation.

Chaplin's work appealed to his contemporaries because in it they found a powerful expression of the subjective feelings of alienation and loss of community engendered in the transition to modern mass society. Moreover, Chaplin had discovered the cinematic means for expressing this early. When cinematic fashions changed, he had no aesthetic motivation to alter his methods. He had already found a perfect equilibrium point between style and theme. Thus, for him, the notion of improvement was incomprehensible.

4
Keaton: Film Acting as Action

I. Introduction

Certain images unavoidably conjure up the idea of silent film: Chaplin in his derby; Lillian Gish swathed in mountains of curls; and of course, Buster Keaton with his deadpan intensity and his porkpie hat. In one sense, Keaton played a number of different roles; but, in another sense. these were merely surface variations of one underlying character, one underlying set of preoccupations which Keaton explored in different fictional guises. The purpose of this paper is to isolate the core structure of the Keaton character as found in his mature silent films.

When we think of "film acting" what comes first to mind, generally, are the pretenses, mannerisms, and implied motives that a performer employs to give substance to a certain fictional being. However, when applying the notion to Keaton, we must also bear in mind a much more basic sense of "acting," viz., the sense of acting as being involved in a process of doing. Keaton's character, it could be said, is a product of a series of doings; his film acting, in a manner of speaking, is rooted in action. That is, in important respects, Keaton's character emerges not through declaiming, posturing, or emoting, but in the process of action, or better, in interactions, specifically with things. If such a rough distinction may be drawn, Keaton emphasizes the behavioral – the engagement with objects – rather than the psychological, where that category signals interest in the affective and in motivation. Moreover, the terrain of Keaton's activity is less significantly the social or the interpersonal and, more importantly, the realm of objects and the physical world. But though Keaton's traffic is most arrestingly with mute objects – or with people treated as objects, like so many weights in precarious balance – Keaton nevertheless is able to create a structurally rich and compelling

"Keaton: Film Acting as Action," in *Making Visible the Invisible*, ed. C. Zucker (Metuchen, Scarecrow Press, 1990), pp. 198–223.

character, one that calls attention to a dimension of human existence – what I call concrete intelligence – that is rarely explored in art, and even more rarely with the finesse found in Keaton's works.

Keaton's film acting is concerned, first and foremost, with the manipulation of objects and, by extension, with the manipulation of people as physical objects. This is not to say that Keaton's films lack dramatic or social dimensions, but rather that what is distinctive about the films and the character they are designed to showcase is a concern with the interaction between human life and things. Specifically, I shall claim, Keaton's preoccupation is with exemplifying what intelligence, and the lack thereof, amounts to in our interaction with things. The dramatic conflicts in the films and their subtending social relations are, for Keaton, pretexts for a series of feats and failures in the realm of micro-engineering.

Of course, other silent comics, such as Chaplin, build their characters through interactions with things. However, there is something special about the way in which the Keaton character approaches physical objects. One way to get a sense of this is to recall that many of the most memorable moments in Chaplin films involve the metaphoric transformation of objects into other kinds of objects; the alarm clock becomes a sardine can; the shoe laces become spaghetti; the buttons on a lady's dress become bolts. In Chaplin this transformative vision is the mark of the Tramp's imagination, of his ability to see the world differently. But Keaton's commerce with objects is generally much more mundane, and yet gloriously so. In his films, the physical world is not treated poetically and metaphorically, but manifests itself, as it were, through the sensibility of an engineer. It is a matter of weights and volumes, angles and balances, causes and effects, and of the special kind of human intelligence the physical world calls forth. Keaton's character, as he grapples with objects, shows us how things work and how things fail to work, and in the process the Keaton character shows us what it is to have and to lack a concrete intelligence of things – an ability to accommodate our actions to physical objects and forces, and to assimilate those objects and forces into our activities. Keaton's great theme, embodied in his "acting" (his "doings") is the mechanics of work and of ordinary life, and of the bodily intelligence they require.

I have asserted that Keaton's film acting is profitably approached as a series of doings, as a series of interactions with things in their physical dimensions. A convenient way to explore this issue is to focus on Keaton's gags; they are the crux of his films and the crux of his doings,

and it is through his gags that we primarily derive a sense of his character. In what follows, I will examine the recurrent gag structures in
Keaton's 1926 film *The General*, suggesting, as well, the extent to which
similar structures can be found throughout Keaton's silent work. I shall
argue that two significantly interrelated structures – what I call automatism gags and insight gags – dominate Keaton's work, and that the
contrast between the characters presupposed by these gags sets forth the
terms of the Keaton character's meditation on concrete intelligence.

II. Outline of *The General*

The story told in *The General* is based, ever so loosely, on an event that
occurred during the American Civil War – the hijacking of a Southern
locomotive, The General, by Union spies. In Keaton's uproariously fictional retelling, the engineer of The General, played by Buster himself, is
Johnny Gray. Johnny's abiding preoccupations are his locomotive and
his beloved Annabelle Lee. The opening of the film involves comic observations upon Johnny's courtship of Annabelle.

In the midst of their romance, however, the Civil War breaks out.
Annabelle's father and brother rush off to enlist. Johnny follows suit and
deftly reaches the head of the enlistment line. But the South needs engi-
neers to win the war, and Johnny's application for military service is
rejected. Johnny tries several ruses to enlist, but each is unmasked by the
conscription board, and Johnny is unceremoniously ejected with a swift
kick to the rear.

Annabelle's family sees Johnny and offers him a place with them on
the enlistment line. Recalling his aching bottom, Johnny declines, an
action Annabelle's family interprets to Johnny's discredit. Annabelle
seeks Johnny out and demands to know why he didn't enlist. When he
explains that they wouldn't take him, she accuses him of lying and says,
"I don't want you to speak to me again until you are in uniform." This
sets up two dominant questions whose answers we await until the end of
the story: Will Johnny re-win Annabelle's affections, and how, in order
to do that, will he ever be in a position to enlist?

After a short interlude – in which we are privy to the Union plan to
seize The General as part of a larger offensive – the hijacking scene com-
mences. The General is about to depart from Marietta, and Annabelle,
who is still not speaking to Johnny, is a passenger. When the train stops
for a layover, the hijackers make their move while Johnny is washing up.
But Annabelle is on board, checking her luggage. As the train pulls away,
Johnny pursues it on foot. Two more key narrative questions arise: Will

Johnny recapture The General, and, in the process, will he rescue Annabelle?

The seizure of The General and Johnny's subsequent pursuit make up much of the first half of the film. This section is very eventful, challenging Johnny with a wealth of physical tasks whose performance or, rather often, whose misperformance, enable Keaton to define one antipode of his character. The spies pull up rails and litter the tracks with debris in order to impede pursuit, and Johnny must mediate these obstacles in order to continue. The sequence is virtually pure action, providing a comic forum of mishaps through which Keaton projects one side of his characterization of Johnny.

At one point, Johnny reaches a Southern encampment. Troops load onto another train pulled by a locomotive called The Texas. But Johnny, characteristically, forgets to attach the troop car to his engine, and he chugs out of the depot without his army. Nevertheless, the hijackers believe they are being pursued by estimable forces, and so they flee their lonely Fury, Johnny. By the time the Northerners realize that there is only one man chasing them and they counterattack, both trains are in Union territory. Johnny abandons The Texas and makes his way through a dark and rainy forest to a house which turns out to be the Union headquarters. There he learns of the impending Northern attack and of Annabelle's captivity. He must save Annabelle, retrieve The General, and speed South to warn the Confederates of the Union offensive. Which he then does.

Once Johnny has secured both Annabelle and The General, the chase resumes, only this time it is, so to say, in reverse: the Union soldiers are the pursuers, and Johnny is the pursued. Many of the gags from the earlier chase are recycled; however, this time around, most frequently, the Northerners serve as the butt of the humor. Johnny – heaping the tracks with barriers and boobytraps – does unto the Union what it had done to him. Whereas in the first half of the film Johnny had generally shown himself to be inept at or unaware of the tasks set before him, in the second chase, he becomes progressively more adept; his assured, stunningly coordinated and insightful manipulations of the physical world reveal the second side of the Keaton character. For in this second chase, not only has the literal direction of the race reversed, but that reversal itself marks the overall reversal of Johnny's relation to the world around him.

Johnny reaches Southern forces, delivers Annabelle to safety, and is able to warn the Confederates of the Union advance in time for the boys in gray to ambush the boys in blue. A battle ensues in which Johnny distinguishes himself; he is made a lieutenant. And now that he is in a Confederate uniform, his courtship with Annabelle proceeds toward an implied blissful future.

Before turning to Keaton's acting here, it pays to remark upon the extreme elegance and economy of the plot of *The General*. For not only was Keaton the star of the film, but, as was the case with most of his major works, he was effectively a writer and director as well. Thus. many of the qualities that mark the exposition of *The General* – precision, sharp structure, studied reversibility – are applicable, in a different register, to Keaton's performance style. That is, Keaton's character and the fictional world he creates for it are of a qualitative piece.

The first thing that strikes one about the plot of *The General* is its smoothly coordinated narrative logic. The film presents four prevailing narrative questions which it answers with sequentially dovetailing events: will Johnny win Annabelle, which depends upon the question, will he be enlisted? And will he rescue The General and thereby be able to reach Southern lines in time to warn the Confederates? In interlocking order, he recaptures The General and warns the South, for which he is rewarded with a commission which paves the way for a happily-ever-after reunion with Annabelle. Very neat, no loose ends, and tight connections reveal a taste for a clean, logical line of action in Keaton the storyteller, which matches a similar penchant for clear, uncluttered lines of cause and effect in Keaton the performer.

Also, the plot of *The General* is, like that of certain other Keaton films, possessed of a doubling structure.[1] The two chases make for a pattern of theme and variation: first, Johnny derails; then, later, the Union soldiers derail. This gives the film a strong architectonic flavor. Indeed, there is an early scene in which the Union command peruses a map of their attack. It might as well be a diagram of the plot, very linear, but of course reversible. Here one has the sense of a narrative imagination characterizable in scientific and mechanical metaphors. It is a very "geometrical" and "rational" imagination, very linear and likely to be fascinated with erector sets, while the concerns with reversibility and variation suggest an experimentalist mentality. It should come as no surprise that Keaton believed that had he not been a comedian, he would have become an engineer. Moreover, the "mechanical" sensibility expressed by Keaton's narrative preferences is echoed again and again in his gags, which are obsessed with concrete manipulations.

But the doubling structure in *The General* is not only expressive, it is also functional. For it enables Keaton to divide his character into roughly two phases which reflect the two sides of concrete intelligence. Through the first chase, the Johnny Gray character is predominantly, though not always, inept, while from his rescue of Annabelle onward, Johnny perfects his ability to manipulate the physical world. *The General*, like many other Keaton films, offers us a Keaton character split into two strongly contrasting parts, what we might call the inept and the adept, which, in turn, shows us two antipodes of concrete intelligence. The inept character emerges through the physical action of Keaton's "automatism" gags, while the adept character figures in Keaton's "insight" gags.

III. Automatism

To begin to get a feeling for the theme of automatism in Keaton's character, one can look at the first gag proper in *The General*. Johnny is going to visit Annabelle. The gag is composed of a string of six shots. First there is a medium close shot of Annabelle, apparently borrowing a book. She turns to walk toward a gate, her back to the camera. Then there is a medium long shot of Johnny, followed by local town boys, walking past a hedge. The boys imitate Johnny's every move. The third shot is a medium shot which places Annabelle, book in hand, at the end of a pathway that cuts through a hedge. Shot four establishes that the hedge in the previous shot is the one that Johnny is passing. This shot puts Annabelle in the background and Johnny and his entourage in the middle ground. Since Annabelle is just back from the hedge, Johnny doesn't see her. He walks right by and Annabelle, seeing him, falls into step behind the boys. Shot five is a long shot that shows the whole parade turning into Annabelle's front yard, and the last shot establishes the group at Annabelle's door. Johnny adjusts his coat, cleans his shoes, and slicks down his hair. Of course, Annabelle is watching the entire procedure. Thus, if Johnny's last minute touchups are meant to suggest to Annabelle that he is always so precisely presentable, his vanities are exposed, since Annabelle, unbeknownst to him, witnesses his entire ritual. Finally, Johnny knocks; he stands back and sideways, adopting a dignified *contrapposto* stance. At that moment, he is virtually face to face with Annabelle. He looks momentarily ruffled – she's on the wrong side of the door – and his jaw drops in a flustered sort of way. (Parenthetically, it pays to note that this gag is significantly enhanced by Keaton's facial gestures. He is not a great stone face except in respect of not smiling. Otherwise, his face is quite expressive.)

The preceding gag is certainly at the expense of Johnny Gray. What is humorous is what is revealed about his character. As he walks along the street, Keaton portrays Johnny as though he had no peripheral vision. Likewise, when he turns into Annabelle's yard, he is oblivious to lateral presences. What is being represented is a character with an awesome fixity of attention, with acute tunnel vision. His orientation is relentlessly frontal. The character has the idea that Annabelle is at home and that he will visit her. His determination leads him to travel in a manner that suppresses normal perceptual habits, namely he ceases to respond to glimpses on the periphery of his visual field, an impression that Keaton-the-actor reinforces by the rigid way in which he holds his head. The character overvalues the way he thinks things are, and he simultaneously undervalues new input. He's stuck on automatic pilot, so to speak. The result is that he functions almost completely in terms of his idea of the situation without bothering to modify that idea by means of new data. It is this kind of fixity of attention, or rather spectacular inattention, that provokes our laughter.

The courtship section of *The General* concludes with a particularly famous inattention gag. Annabelle has just spurned Johnny unless he joins the army. Dejectedly, Johnny slumps back onto the drive-rod of his engine, completely absorbed in his misfortune. The camera pulls back for a long shot. We see an engineer enter the cab and stoke up the engine. Johnny continues to sit forlornly on his drive-rod. We see that he is out of the engineer's field of vision and that he, Johnny, is ignorant of what is going on in the cab, since his glance is directed at the ground. Suddenly the engine starts. The wheels turn several times; then, just as the train enters a tunnel, Johnny finally realizes that he is lethally balanced on the drive-rod of a moving engine.

Our reaction to this scene is undoubtedly complex. Obviously, the stunt is dangerous – what if the wheels lost traction? But aside from the danger, we can also see that the basis of this gag is two simultaneous acts of inattention. The engineer carries on unaware of what is in front of him on the wheels of his locomotive. He relies on his conception of things, not on the actual situation. Johnny, of course, raises the level of inattention by virtually a quantum leap. For he is initially inattentive to the fact that the train is moving. He is so preoccupied that presumably he fails to respond not only to the sound of the train, but even to his own bodily sensations, which ought to provoke a feeling of rising and falling. This gag is an example of Keaton's "slow burn," i.e., the character's coming to awareness of a (usually untoward) state of affairs over an inordinately long time interval. Here, the "slow burn" is used to bring the theme of the scene to a crescendo by compounding the engineer's initial act of inattention with an almost inconceivable act of inattention on Johnny's part.

So far we have seen that important gags in the first section of *The General* underscore the character's inattentiveness, his inability to register that the world around him has changed in ways that diverge radically from his settled idea of how things stand. How does this connect with the notion of automatism? Well, Johnny is not only inattentive to changes in the environment, but he continues behaving in the way that his preconceptions dictate, often on the way to a pratfall. That is, Johnny behaves automatically or like a preprogrammed automaton, blind to new information. Johnny's path, most often to his chagrin, seems set in stone. Many of the gags of the first half of *The General* rely on this connection between inattention and automatism.

For example, Johnny and four volunteers charge on foot after the hijacked General. We see that Johnny's cohorts give up the chase almost immediately. But until the Union spies subdue Annabelle and sever Confederate telegraph wires, Johnny does not realize that he is alone. Indeed, one feels Johnny would never have turned around, had he not reached a handcar siding. Again, the character's tendency is to adopt a rigid and fixed viewpoint, attending only to what is directly in front of him, assured that the rest of the world is as he supposes it to be. And this, in turn, sends him hurtling forward more like a car without a driver – or a train without an engineer – than a sentient being.

Undoubtedly the most elaborate example of Johnny's tendency to maintain a single track of behavior despite changes in the environment is his entry into Northern territory. The scene begins with the title, "The Southern Army facing Chattanooga is ordered to retreat." There is a shot of Confederate cavalry troops withdrawing. Then a shot of the Union spies shows them crouching in the cab of The General. Finally, we see Johnny, from overhead, cutting wood in the timber-car of the recently acquired locomotive, The Texas. The film then cuts to a shot of the retreating Southerners. Initially it is a long shot. Next, all of a sudden, The Texas pulls into the foreground from screen left. The Texas drives past the camera, revealing that Johnny is still chopping wood with his back to the battle. As the battle continues, the South turns heel and the Northerners take the field. Johnny continues to chop. At one point he breaks his axe handle. But even with this rupture in his work pattern, he remains unaware that he is completely surrounded by Union troops. In all, it takes twelve shots before Johnny realizes his predicament, so absolutely engrossed is he in his work that he never once glances outside the narrow ambit of his wood pile.

In many ways, it seems that the railroad is an appropriate central image in *The General*, for there is a way in which imagery of railroads supplies a source in ordinary language for our metaphors of the type of automatism that is so characteristic of Johnny. We speak of people as having "one-track minds" in order to underscore the fixity of their ideas. The notion of a track in this metaphor emphasizes the rigidity with which the single-minded person maintains his preconceived idea. In this light, Johnny's conceptions of things are analogous to a track. The imagery of the film virtually demands this analogy. And Johnny himself is rather like a locomotive. He travels along his track, oblivious to what the changing environment has placed in his way. Within this context, the recurring derailments and track switchings in *The General* become a kind of objective correlative to the way in which Johnny's "one-track mind" constantly – both figuratively and sometimes literally – derails his schemes and sends him barreling in the wrong direction.

The action of these gags incarnates the automaton aspect of the Keaton character. The acting, i.e., the pretense they require from Keaton, is an impression of utter absorption, a rigidly narrow scope of attention, and a kind of perpetual momentum, often in the service of a repetitive, even mechanical task, such as chopping wood.

The preceding discussion of automatism gags, it is hoped, establishes that there is, in *The General*, a character-based theme of rigidity or inflexibility of behavior patterns, premised on Johnny's inattention to changes in the environment. Of course, inattention, in and of itself, is hardly a theme specific to the Keaton character, but can be found in other comic types. However, within the class of Keaton's automatism gags, we can distinguish a core group which define the special emphasis Keaton exerts in regard to automatism. Those gags are ones that involve physical tasks requiring the manipulation of the natural and industrial environment.

A perfect example of this kind of gag occurs in the first short that Keaton released for distribution. In *One Week*, the Keaton character marries. The newlyweds are given a prefabricated house that Keaton must assemble. A disgruntled former suitor of Keaton's wife vengefully changes the numbers on the crates that contain the prefabricated house. The instructions for assembling the house are based on the numbers on the crates. Keaton persists in erecting the house according to the instructions, despite the fact that the numbers on the crates match up with the numbers in the instructions with outlandish results: second floor doors open onto thin air, and the roof has a valley in it. Obviously, the Keaton character has willfully followed the instructions despite these incongruities. An abstract, preconceived idea, represented by the instructions completely governs the character's mediation with the environment. The madcap house that emerges is a literal monument to the character's single-track mind.

Turning back to *The General*, we see that a large number of central automatism/inattention gags are also involved with the manipulation of the physical environment, for instance, the derailment of the hand-car and the attempt to shunt the box car onto a siding.[2] Of course, most of the gags involving the train chases are obviously concerned with physical manipulations. A particularly emblematic gag in this respect occurs when The Texas, sidetracked by Union spies, nearly runs off an abruptly ending spur. Johnny manages to stop the train at the last minute. He then attempts to reverse the engine. However, the wheels of the engine spin impotently on the track. There is no traction. Johnny leaps from the engine and begins to shovel sand onto the track in an effort to give the wheels something with which to engage. At one point, Johnny turns his back to the engine. He tries to kick loose a clump of grass so that more dirt can be freed to shovel onto the track. While his back is turned, however, the wheels of the locomotive catch on the sand that Johnny previously put on the track, and the train pulls away. But Johnny is too preoccupied to realize his train is gone.

Similarly, when Johnny recovers The General, he and Annabelle stop it to refuel at a corral fence composed of long beams piled carefully on top of each other. Johnny rushes from the locomotive, grabbing the long unwieldy fencing and hurtling it over the tender. Johnny is so utterly immersed in his work that he fails to notice that he has pitched these railings clear over the timber car. All his effort succeeds in achieving is to pile the lumber on the opposite side of the train. At points in the gag, Johnny's behavior is almost robotlike; he works in a preprogrammed manner that takes no account of the actual results of his own actions. It is as though he were devoid of feedback.

All the gags discussed so far involve a duality[3] of viewpoint. There is the situation seen as it actually is – e.g., the train pulling away while Johnny's back is turned – and the situation as the character misconceives it. The audience is privy to both these viewpoints; the gag emerges in the discrepancy between the actual situation and the way the character misapprehends it. To work, such a gag requires a character with a certain type of mentality, and Keaton's acting or action fulfills this requirement by proposing a character who, against the reality principle, fixates on an inflexible mental map of a situation and behaves, with often disastrous effect, in accordance with that mental map.

Though most of Keaton's film acting is a matter of doing, nevertheless, the character that he evolves through his automatism gags is essentially a portrait of a state of mind, of a way of thinking. Rigidity of thought, the incapacity to reevaluate the situation and to modify behavior accordingly, represents a form of dimwittedness or slowness of thought. That Keaton restages these automatism gags very often with reference to manual work, suggests his acknowledgment that such "merely physical" activity requires an intelligence and has a cognitive dimension, cultural prejudices to the contrary notwithstanding.

Through automatism gags, the Keaton character explores the relation of intelligence to physical activity, such as manual work, through a kind of process of negation, viz., Johnny's errors in carrying out physical tasks. By means of this *via negativa*, Keaton outlines his understanding of concrete intelligence through the enactment of gags that exemplify a paradigmatic lack of responsiveness to the environment. To confirm the centrality of the theme of intelligence for the Keaton character, one need only consult one's experience of Keaton's automatism/inattention gags. These gags presuppose alertness on the part of the viewer versus the character's rigidity – a perceptive response versus a virtually blind response. What the audience must do to appreciate the automatism gags is to make up the difference between the rote behavior of characters and an alert, intelligent comprehension of the situation.

The notions of fixation, rigidity, inflexibility, inattention, and automatism deployed in our discussion of the Keaton character so far, of course, are derived from the comic theory of Henri Bergson. Moreover, we have also followed Bergson in holding that the appeal made by such themes is concerned at root with the issue of intelligence. However, Bergson's theoretical machinery is not embraced here in the belief that it is a perfectly adequate theory for all comedy, of which *The General* and the rest of Keaton's oeuvre are but particular examples. Indeed, in the next section it will be shown that as a general theory of comedy, Bergson's approach cannot work, in part because it can't handle certain key aspects of Keaton's comic character. Nevertheless, Bergson's framework is useful for discussing at least that aspect of the Keaton character that is embodied in the automatism gags. For in both Keaton's comic practice and

Bergson's theory, there is a high premium placed on responsiveness to the environment. That is, independently of each other, both Keaton and Bergson construe intelligence in terms of adjustability and adaptability.

For Bergson, comedy performs a social function. Laughter is a corrective. It taunts people away from undesirable modes of behavior. Bergson identifies the most undesirable form of behavior as that which is rote, habituated, or routinized, i.e. "mechanical" in the most negative sense of the term. The absentminded, the inflexible, the unobservant, all these are to be chastized by comedy, thereby driving us to a "wideawake adaptability and the living pliability of a human being."[4] Truly human life, Bergson believes, adjusts itself to the novelty of each situation. In this approach, intelligence, which is very much influenced by Bergson's conception of evolution, is the ability to adapt and adjust to each new circumstance.

Though Keaton appears to lack a view of laughter's role in society, through his characters he seems to share Bergson's conception of intelligence as adaptability, and at least part of his comic practice rests on something very like the Bergsonian connection between adaptability and intelligence. In *The General*, the bulk of the gags involving inattention and automatism all project a picture of mental operations on the part of Johnny Gray that are fixated on a notion of a situation and that are heedless of the need constantly to replenish that idea with fresh details from the environment. Johnny's stupidities, moreover, illuminate what would be a contrary state of affairs, one where the character is intelligent, one where the character behaves as the audience perceives he should; in short, where the character is adaptable.

The importance of the theme of automatism for the Keaton character, and the related opposition of adaptation versus failure to adapt, can be easily identified in Keaton films other than *The General*. Consider the famous projection sequence in *Sherlock Jr.* Sherlock Jr. walks into a scene that is being projected on a motion picture screen. As he goes up to the door of the house in this film-within-a-film, the scene shifts. What is odd about this cut, however, is that the character remains in the same exact screen position that he previously occupied. From the shot of the character before the door, we cut to a garden, and Sherlock begins to sit on a bench in the garden. There is another cut, this time to a city street. Since Sherlock's position and movement remain continuous over the cut, he falls backward into the busy thoroughfare. Sherlock straightens up and starts to walk down the street. All of a sudden, there is yet another cut, and Sherlock nearly walks off a cliff. He looks over the cliff, sticking his neck out. There's a cut, of course; he's in a cage; his neck is invitingly poised in a lion's maw. He backs away from the lion. Cut – he's in a desert. A train just misses him. He sits down and the location changes to a rock surrounded by water. He dives off the rock but a devilishly placed edit lands him headfirst in a snow bank. Standing upright, he reaches out to lean on a tree. A final cut – he is back in the original garden, falling on his head because the tree is no longer there.

This sequence is perhaps Keaton's most delirious exploration of the themes of automatism and maladaptation. Undoubtedly the most frequently invoked example of poor adaptability in the whole evolutionary bestiary is the dinosaur. That dimwitted beast, though suited to tropical climates, supposedly could not survive the rigors of the ice age. The environment changed on him when he wasn't looking. Environmental change is also key to the automatism/inattention gag. And there is hardly a more radical series of environmental changes in all of Keaton than one finds in the preceding sequence of *Sherlock Jr.* Via incredibly precise editing, Keaton is able to draw an image of a character sustaining without modification a set of behaviors appropriate to one environment into another environment where it is inappropriate. This sequence from *Sherlock Jr.* seems to be one of the most symbolic and abstract in all of Keaton, summarizing in almost schematic fashion the Keaton character's underlying tendency toward inadaptability by setting out environmental variations in the most hyperbolic manner imaginable.

Another outstanding automatism gag is the sparring sequence in *Battling Butler*. Here, Keaton, as Alfred Butler, tries his hand at fisticuffs. A professional trainer instructs Butler to watch him. He will make the appropriate countermoves to the thrusts of Butler's sparring partner. Butler need only imitate the trainer, supposedly, in order to protect himself and to win. The hitch in this plan, however, is the time lag between Butler's opponent's punch, the trainer's reaction, and then Butler's reaction. By the time Butler reacts, his opponent's jabs have already landed. The result is a kind of bizarre dance – Butler's opponent throws a punch, the trainer raises his arm in a blocking motion, the punch lands, and Butler, reeling, raises his arm to meet a phantom blow that has already come and gone. The rhythm is repeated again and again until Butler is staggering. As we have seen in *The General*, this is based on Butler's failure to attend to the situation he is actually in. His glance, directed to the trainer, is really a species of deferred attention. Butler is out of synchronization with his environment. Moreover, this notion of being out of synchronization underpins all Keaton's inattention/automatism gags. For synchronization between plan and action, on the one hand, and the environment, on the other, is the very essence of human adaptability.

IV. Insight

Keaton's film acting is primarily a matter of the way in which he acts, in the sense of doing things, most often in the context of gags. It is through these doings that his character emerges. So far it has been stressed that automatism and inadaptability compose a key aspect of the Keaton character, one developed through Keaton's performance of certain types of gags. But this is not the whole story. For the same character who is inattentive, unheeding, and maladapted to some situations can suddenly manifest an awareness, sensitivity, and control over the environment that is nothing short of breathtaking (as well as laughter provoking).

A famous example of this, one concerned with a physical task, occurs during the first chase in *The General*. The Union spies have thrown railroad ties on the tracks in order to derail Johnny. Johnny slows The Texas down and runs alongside the engine. Carefully he slides down the cowcatcher on the front of the engine and runs to dislodge the first tie from the tracks. With great difficulty, he lifts it off the track. Unfortunately, he has not worked fast enough. The Texas has inched up behind him as he struggled with the first tie, and, by the time he picks it up, the front of the engine sweeps him off his feet and lands him on the cow-catcher. The beam that he removed from the track is so heavy that it pins him to the cow-catcher. Suddenly, he sees that there is another tie on the tracks less than ten feet ahead of him. Thus, the locomotive is about to derail with him on the front of it. Yet Johnny sees an avenue of escape. He realizes that the tie on the track is straddling the rails. So if he can hit the overhanging end of the tie on the track, he can knock it out of the way of the oncoming train. He lifts the tie on his chest over his head and hurls it at the one on the track, banging the latter out of the way of the oncoming train, and thus casting two worries aside with a single blow while "inventing" the catapult in the process.

The presuppositions of this gag are quite different from those of the automatism gags. Whereas the automatism gags seem to presuppose a character whose concept of a state of affairs is rigid, this type of successful adaptation involves a character who can rethink a situation and arrive at insights and inventions. Johnny, pinned to the cow-catcher, is able to break out of a single picture of the situation and is able to think of those threatening railroad ties not as mere beams, but as a lever and a weight. He is able mentally to reorganize the elements of the visual field in a new way – significantly, a new way that will save his life. A monkey, given two separate sticks, has an insight when he realizes that he can combine those two sticks into one in order to reach outside his cage and hook onto a bunch of bananas. Similarly, Johnny has an insight when he thinks of the ties not as ties but as elements of a catapult. His state of mind is one that recognizes this picture of the state of affairs. This stands in striking contrast with Johnny's state of mind during the automatism gags, where his mental map of the situation is irremediably frozen.

The sequence of the railroad ties in *The General* is structurally reminiscent of the scene in *Our Hospitality* where the Keaton character, John McKay, struggles to free himself from a rope that binds him to a log which overhangs a waterfall. This rope originally attached McKay to one of the Canfields. For a long section of the film, it has been a bane to McKay's existence. Finally, it binds him to a log which may at any moment loosen and go shooting over the falls, dragging McKay with it. As McKay tugs on the rope, hoping to free himself, he sees his girlfriend being borne to the edge of the waterfall by a swift current. Suddenly, he rethinks his situation. Instead of conceiving of the log and the rope on the model of a ball and chain, he thinks of it as a crossbeam with an attached rope. Seen this way, he can use the former detriment as a device to save his girlfriend. As she crosses the edge of the falls, he swings over and catches her just before she is about to plummet to the bottom of the falls. Again, the character's behavior is predicated on an ability to reorganize his way of seeing and comprehending the situation. In contrast to automatism gags, inflexibility of thought gives way to flexibility.

Another successful adaptation gag in *The General* occurs when Johnny is chopping wood. As The Texas is passing into Union territory, Johnny breaks his ax handle. He desperately needs wood for his engine. He looks at the broken handle forlornly, but only for a second, because, all of a sudden, he realizes that the handle is wood, the very thing he needs to stoke his engine. He dutifully carries this "newly discovered" piece of kindling to the furnace. Here, as before, the character must shed a characteristic way of thinking. He must switch from thinking of the handle as a handle to thinking of it as wood. A process of discovery, a new way of seeing, is called for. Johnny must decenter his concentration on the functional properties of the object *qua* ax handle and shift his way of thinking about the object in terms of its material properties. This involves both cognition and perception. Refocusing the center of attention from functional properties to materials involves a mental reorganization of Johnny's visual field. The moment of recognition of such a shift is the moment of insight.

The gag that concludes *The General* is also an insight gag, actually one that transforms lovemaking into a problem of concrete intelligence. Like so many comedies, such as Chaplin's *The Gold Rush*, *The General* ends with a hero and the heroine united. Johnny has his uniform, so they can run off and romance. Predictably – since that's where all the trouble began – they nestle on the drive-rod of The General. But since Johnny is an officer now, he must salute every passing soldier. And given the way he is positioned vis-à-vis Annabelle, this military ritual means that his every attempted kiss is interrupted. Suddenly, it looks as though the whole army is about to march by. In a flash, Johnny realizes that if he switches positions with Annabelle he will be able to kiss and salute simultaneously. Unlike Chaplin, who would play a final love scene like this for feeling (vide *The Gold Rush*), Keaton treats the kiss as an engineering problem, returning once again to the theme of concrete intelligence. Like so many of the gags in *The General*, this parting joke concerns the manipulation of the right/left operations. Mastery of this basic physical category is the foundation for the comic surprise which accompanies the reversal of Johnny's predicament. Johnny must envision himself as opposite his actual position. He must be able to recognize that in such a position his right arm will be able to negotiate freely his salutes, while his left arm caresses Annabelle. That is, what is required of Johnny is an insight which is based on a mental reorganizing of the constituents of his visual and kinetic fields.

The preceding gags all presuppose insight on the part of the Keaton character, especially in terms of concrete operations. As such they stand in sharp, systematic contrast with the automatism gags examined in the previous section. It is for this reason that I noted earlier that Bergson's theory of comedy was not perfectly general for all comedy nor even specifically for all Keaton's comic invention. Bergson is aligned to a tradition of comic theorizing that associates comedy with stupidity, the nonrational, the irrational, or the absurd. Freud, though quite different from Bergson, also stands in this tradition. However, such approaches to comedy cannot comprehend all the data. In particular, they cannot accommodate Keaton's successful adaptation gags. For these gags involve insight on the part of the character, rather than stupidity. In terms of the audience, such gags involve a shift in our mode of organizing the situation as well. This shift, often abrupt, is surprising. For example, our expectations are brought up short when Johnny comprehends a new way of employing his broken ax handle. Here the Bergsonian idea, that laughter serves to humiliate the character as a behavioral corrective, is completely untenable, because in fact the character's thinking is far ahead of the audience's.

Rather, the audience laughs at these adaptation gags with a variety of laughter that one indulges when a particularly brilliant checkmate is executed or when a tricky mathematical problem is ingeniously solved. Similarly, we sometimes laugh at the intricate movements of a precision machine, or at the solution of a puzzle. That is, there is a category of laughter that is evoked when, so to speak, "things fall into place." This is a kind of laughter prompted by the apparition of pure intelligibility. This is the kind of reaction that greets Keaton's successful adaptation gags. The basis of these gags cannot be given a Bergsonian formulation. For a theoretical framework, one must turn to the kind of configurational theory of comedy proposed by Quintillian and Hegel and by psychologists of the Gestalt tradition in the thirties. From that tradition of psychology, the following characterization is offered of the relevant mental processes of the humorous experience. Note how aptly it describes the Keaton gags of the successful adaptation variety.

Wertheimer has shown that the meaning of elements depends on the configuration of which they are a part. When the configuration suddenly changes, the meaning of the elements suddenly changes as a consequence. . . . Direction is a determining factor underlying the formation of configuration. A problem is always looked at from a certain point of view and this point of view determines what one will do about it (i.e. what direction one's mind will take). A particular direction facilitates certain configurations and inhibits others. Thus, when we are presented with any facts we tend to organize them in a certain way. Usually past experience gives us the point of view; we organize the facts accordingly and consequently miss a new organization or interpretation. A humorous incident is told so as to encourage a certain point of view. Then in the end we are given a conclusion (an organization of the facts presented) which is very different from the one we anticipated. It is like the experience of insight except for certain differences. . . .[5]

Keaton mixes gags that have apparently very different explanations. There are inattention/automatism gags that are based in the presupposition of the character's fixation on a certain idea of a situation, and there are configurational gags that are based on the character's reorganization of his mental map of the situation. Neither the Bergsonian theory nor the Gestalt configurational theory offers an account of all Keaton's gags. Here, we must turn elsewhere for an understanding of Keaton's themes. The obvious place to look, however, is not far off. The intersection of Gestalt theory with Bergsonian theory may provide the location of Keaton's particular subject. Both theories are concerned with thinking and intelligence, but each places different emphasis on the subject. The automatism gags involve failures of thinking, while the configurational gags involve successful thinking. But both are concerned with thought.

Structurally, Keaton seems to counterpoint the ineptness of Johnny's performance of some physical tasks with moments of resourcefulness and quickly calculated judgment that seem to establish new levels of precision in human activity. Thus, through the action of the character, humor of the inflexibility variety is balanced by humor of the configurational sort. Two contrary modes play against each other. Insofar as a task is an amalgam of thought and action, the formal opposition of successfully executed tasks with failures presupposes an opposition of two different aspects of intellectual activity – fixation versus insight. Analysis of major Keaton gags in *The General* constantly leads one to postulate either fixation or insight of characters (Johnny and others) as the predominant focal points of laughter. From this emerges recognition of the locus or subject of Keaton's character, viz. intelligence, especially concrete intelligence, of which insight and fixation represent two poles, positive and negative.

Similar contrastive structures can be found throughout Keaton's work. That automatism gags abound is undoubtedly obvious. But insight gags are also recurrent, especially in terms of physical manipulations. In *Cops*, the Keaton character "invents" a signal arm from a boxing glove and a scissors lamp. Also in *Cops*, the Keaton character evinces insight when he turns the teeter-tottering ladder on which the police have him cornered into a virtual catapult. In *One Week*, Keaton uses the front porch balustrade as a ladder. In *The Blacksmith*, an engine hoist becomes the means to offset variations where the Keaton character was thwarted, through his nonadaptability, in his attempt to manipulate the same kind of objects previously encountered. In *The Navigator*, he is first daunted by the ship's awesome kitchen that was designed to feed hundreds. Disastrously, the Keaton character, called Rollo, tries with a splashing effect to open an outsized can of food, and he fails to boil eggs in a large pot. But the second time around, Rollo has insightfully and humorously adapted to the environment. He uses a crab trap to boil eggs in the enormous cauldron, and he attaches a saw to the wheel of a grindstone to serve as a makeshift can opener. In the scene in *Steamboat Bill Jr.*, where Keaton, as Bill Jr., rescues his father, he has harnessed the objects that earlier bedeviled him – the ropes, throttle and levers – into a mechanism that enables one person to run the entire ship. One can also group the skillful finale of *College* with these "adaptability" performances. Here, Keaton, as Ronald, must run across town to save Mary Haines. There are many obstacles, human and inanimate. Ronald must be especially acute to navigate across parks and landscapes covered with hedges. Nevertheless, he bolts across town at top speed, running around pedestrians like a football player, and leaping over shrubs without missing a stride, like an obstacle course runner. These feats reverse his earlier mishaps with the selfsame academic sports. As he heads toward Mary's second-floor window, he has an insight. Without breaking pace, he grabs a pole that is holding up a clothesline and uses the pole to vault through Mary's window, thereby again reversing his earlier sporting failure. Ronald, in this case, shifts from thinking of the pole's function to simply thinking of it in terms of its length, shape, and weight. Seeing the pole apart from its function enables him to see it as an aid to his jump. Here insight combines with action in a feat of adaptability as the character assimilates the environment to his needs.

The notion of assimilating the environment, of course, applies to key aspects of Keaton's screen action apart from what might be narrowly construed as gags. It extends to feats of superadaptability of the sort that David Robinson has called Keaton's trajectories,[6] i.e., runs such as those at the end of the Roman sequence in *Three Ages*, in *Seven Chances*, and of course in *College*. In these sequences, match cutting facilitates the production of a cinematic image of astounding speed, judgment, and dexterity. Because shot segments of movement are being elided, the composite picture is of sustained continuous movement. It is as if Keaton runs for miles without breaking stride, whereas, of course, he is only actually running for several hundred feet at a time. The appearance is of virtually superhuman alertness and adaptability capable of assimilating every obstacle of the environment into awe-inspiring yet giddy, flabbergasting, unbroken vectors of movement across impossible steeplechases. These feats bespeak and celebrate a bodily intelligence in respect to inanimate things which subsumes them as articles for human use.

In cases such as *Steamboat Bill Jr.* and *College*, the Keaton character becomes possessed of insight and superadaptability at those crucial narrative turning points where he is called to the rescue. In *The General*, insight and adaptability gags are distributed throughout, though with a greater preponderance in the second chase. Obviously, these shifts from inept to adept correspond most often to changes in the direction of the story. However, as to the question of whether these gags are meant to serve the story, or vice versa, I believe that it is the story which functions as the armature for the gags. Keaton's profound theme is not "Love shall overcome," as a purely narratological exegesis might suggest, but rather is an examination of the parameters of human intelligence, specifically bodily intelligence, conceived in terms of adaptability, whose conditions Keaton reveals rather than analyzes through the contrast of automatism and insight which is developed through his actions.

V. Conclusion

It has been the thesis of this paper that Keaton's film acting – i.e., the screen performance elements that shape what is key to our perception of the Keaton character – are his actions, often task-like performances, which occur in the context of gags and his famous "trajectories." Through the contrast of automatism and insight, the Keaton character and his "doings" are preoccupied with the theme of intelligence, particularly bodily intelligence, which is ultimately celebrated in terms of adaptability. In this way, the Keaton character presents us with a reflection upon a dimension of human existence infrequently explored and acknowledged, let alone celebrated, in art: our relation with objects *qua* objects and the special intelligence that that relation requires. Perhaps this can be employed in an explanation of Keaton's ever-rising fortunes in respect to critical and popular response. For Keaton celebrates bodily intelligence with things, a dimension of human skill progressively in diminishing demand in societies where the division of labor and service occupations prevails. Keaton recalls for the salesperson, the clerk, the teacher, the computer programmer, and the journalist a time when the intelligent interaction with things was the fulcrum of a daily life, a time past but not lost.

5

Buster Keaton, *The General*, and Visible Intelligibility

While watching a film the spectator undergoes a variety of cognitive experiences – observing, speculating, recognizing, inferring, interpreting, and so on. The film theorist André Bazin drew a distinction between what he considered the two basic types of cinema viewing. The first, which he associated with editing, seems connected primarily to inference since the spectator must fill in so many unseen details as well as spatial and narrative relations. The second, which he associated with the single shot – specifically, those presented via deep-focus photography – is more a matter of observation. That is, with editing, relations are implied that the spectator is supposed to supply by induction; whereas with the single shot done in the deep-focus medium-long shot (a shot in clear focus throughout with two or more planes of action), the spectator is meant to see and to take note of the relevant relations.

It seems to me that there are more categories of cognitive experience than this in cinema viewing and that they are not necessarily linked to editing versus shot composition in a one-to-one correspondence. In this essay I will use an analysis of Buster Keaton's film *The General* to discuss further, more fine-grained distinctions that need not always be mapped onto an opposition between composition versus editing.

My method will be functional, using the language of goals to describe the cinematic organization of an event and analyzing how formal arrangements facilitate those goals. By the end of the essay we should be able to see a functional equivalence between certain editing patterns and compositional formats.

The primary formal strategy in *The General* is the deep-focus long shot. Penelope Houston has speculated that the recent rise of Keaton's critical stock (in the fifties and sixties) can be accounted for partially by Keaton's use of the long shot, a practice that corresponds to the favored

"Buster Keaton, *The General* and Visible Intelligibility," in *Close Viewings*, ed. Peter Lehman (Gainesville, FL: University of Florida Press, 1990), pp. 125–140.

strategies of the fifties and sixties – including those of neorealism, the new wave, and cinema-verité. Houston writes that Keaton uses the long shot to authenticate the action.

[He keeps] as much of the action as possible within a shot. It started presumably with a natural pride in letting the audience see that those leaps and falls and glissades of movement were all his own work. There could be no cutting because to cut into the action would suggest a cheated effect. He was prepared to risk his neck for an effect which might last twenty seconds on the screen. The camera had to get far enough back to take it all in.[1]

This explanation of use of the long shot is reminiscent of Bazin's thrill when Chaplin enters the lion's cage in *The Circus*. Long shots in such cases vivify the action by establishing that the action performed in the fictional context literally encompasses many of the same risks to life and limb that the represented act entails off-screen.

While the authenticity theory certainly explains Keaton's long shots at least part of the time, it cannot account for Keaton's use of the long shot time and time again in scenes where there are no risks or stunts. A theory that might account for those long shots is that of comic functionality. Much of the humor Keaton employs derives from what Bergson calls the equivocal situation, i.e., one in which two points of view are in evidence – the character's mistaken assessment of the situation and the audience's correct view of how things stand. An example of this sort of gag in *The General* occurs when Johnny Gray enters Union territory. The audience knows Johnny's predicament while at the same time comprehending Johnny's total obliviousness to it as he scrupulously prepares fuel for his engine. The gag, based on Johnny's obsessive inattentiveness, erupts when the audience grasps both the actual situation and another situation, namely the secure one that Johnny wrongly imagines.

One might hypothesize that the long shot is the best way to enact an equivocal situation gag based on obsessive inattention. If this were true, then we would have an adequate comic functionality theory to explain Keaton's use of the long shot, in terms of its being the best cinematic means for articulating his favorite type of gag. And to formulate a comprehensive theory to explain Keaton's use of the long shot we could add comic functionality to authenticity. That is, in this theory, for stunts Keaton uses the long shots to confirm the audience's admiration of his courage and skills, while for equivocal situation gags he uses the long shot to set out simultaneously the character's misperception alongside the correct view of things in the most functionally perspicuous manner available.

The difficulty with the comic functionality approach is that it is simply false that the long shot is the *best* means for representing equivocal situation/inattention gags. Obviously the long shot is one way to do these gags, but it is hardly the only way. Harold Lloyd, for instance, most often favors doing this type of gag by editing, *à la* Griffith. In Lloyd's *The Freshman*, Harold Diddlebock is tricked into giving a public address. As he speaks he holds an épée, whose tip he absentmindedly pushes along the floor. An insert shot of the floor reveals an open light socket threateningly close to the tip of Harold's wayward rapier. One senses that at any moment Harold will unknowingly plunge the sword into the open electrical outlet. Anticipation builds. Clearly the character is unaware of the danger that we, the viewers, know of (thanks to the insert). Suddenly Harold starts dancing frenetically as a shock of electricity courses through the steel sword into his body. Here we have an equivocal situation gag based on inattention. That is, due to his misconstrual, the character believes the situation is safe, while the audience, alerted by the insert, knows it is almost lethal.

The Lloyd example shows that there are ready alternatives to the long shot for representing equivocal situation gags of the obsessive inattention variety. Lloyd uses editing, juxtaposing a detail to a medium shot. Obviously an overhead medium long shot would have turned the trick just as well. Perhaps, were it Keaton's gag, the overhead approach would have been mobilized, with the victim's head in the perpendicular foreground of the shot and the socket, on the floor, in the effective "background" of the composition. However, this means of representing the situation would be no more effective than Lloyd's actual two-shot format, in terms of conveying the information that is crucial to understanding the gag. To respond to the gag, one must know both that the open socket is near the end of the épée and that the victim is unaware of that fact. This knowledge can be communicated by either a two-shot schema or an overhead deep-focus long shot. Regarding the formal requirements that make the gag work as a gag, either format is viable. Thus there is no reason to believe that the deep-focus long shot is the best means for representing equivocal situations, though it is one means.

There is a difference, however, between the two approaches. The Lloyd approach conveys the requisite information synthetically, through editing, without ever visualizing all the elements of the gag in one shot. The gag will work if the audience knows that an event, x, has happened.

But the long-shot approach gives the audience something above just knowledge. In other words, "knowing that x" is sufficient for an equivocal situation gag to work, and – as we have seen – editing can communicate such knowledge. But the long-shot method goes beyond the requirements of comedy in assuring that the audience sees x happening in its totality, i.e., with all its relevant elements visible. Keaton does not opt for the long-shot format simply because it is comically functional but because he has a concern beyond comedy that the audience experience x in a "seeing that x" mode.

"Seeing that x" in the alternative cited above entails "knowing that x." But the "seeing that" modality contrasts with the cognitive state where the audience merely knows x on the basis of inference from the discrete details of montage. Evoking the experiential modality, "seeing that x" can serve as a basis for understanding all of Keaton's long shots. Thus it is more comprehensive in explicating Keaton's use of the long shot than the authenticity theory, the comic functionality theory, or a combination of the two. By explaining Keaton's use of the long shot in terms of a desire to engender the experience of seeing that an event, x, is happening in its totality, Keaton's project may be differentiated from Lloyd's and, for that matter, from Hitchcock's.

So far, distinguishing between "knowing that x" and "seeing that x" hasn't really gotten us much further than Bazin's distinctions that were introduced in the opening of this essay. Also, our explication of Keaton's long shot is too broad. We may be able to differentiate Keaton from Lloyd with these categories, but what of a comic like Tati, who – especially in his later works – also emphasizes the long shot? Both might be described in terms of attempting to promote the same "seeing that x" cognitive state in the audience.

In order to contrast Keaton with Tati a further category will have to be added. In terms of composition Keaton employs far more determinate structures for guiding audience attention than Tati does. These determinate structures include foreground/background play, where one element of the event is in each region with little detail in intermediary regions. Keaton's high and low angulation and his use of diagonal composition also give a highly predictable and compelling direction to the audience's attention.

Tati's composition, at least in a film like *Playtime*, is much more multi-faceted. He often eschews internal structuring devices like the diagonal and angulation, allowing the spectator's eye to wander, to rove, and to savor the kind of ambiguity that Bazin promised as an especially desirable possibility in long shots. This is not to say that Tati shots lack directional devices altogether. Sound and color often direct attention in his films, as they do in all sound color films. But for the sake of a kind of realism, Tati has forgone a battery of visual schemas that move the spectator's eye along preordained pathways. Tati aspires to a kind of neorealist comedy. He attempts to enact the belief that comedy originates in everyday life by presenting comic material in a format somewhat analogous to ordinary perception.

Tati's optimal spectator is one who engages in exploration. Tati decenters his comedies, providing simultaneous comic action all over the shot. He renders the perception of comedy more like the perception of everyday social scenes. We observe comedy in a way that is, from the perspective of comic film conventions, relatively analogous to noncinematic perceptual experiences. This has a thematic significance, of course, as it suggests its own converse. That is, an everyday perspective on the comic complements a comic perspective on the quotidian.

Keaton's composition in the long shot is much more architectonic than Tati's. Attention tends to be directed by the highly determinate structure of the shot. It would be too strong to claim that a diagonal causes the viewer to follow a specific pathway of attention. After all, members of the audience who are locomotive enthusiasts may never take their eyes off the General, no matter how strongly the composition and action suggest that they move from one element of an event to the next. Nevertheless, it does seem correct to suppose that a highly determinate composition, such as one employing a diagonal or angulation, does prompt a certain scenario for attention. One tends to scan to and fro along a diagonal; one tends to follow the trajectory of a high-angle shot much as one follows the sight of a rifle to its target. Such determinate compositions thus can emphasize those objects and actions that are incorporated in the formal structures under discussion. That is, these devices become vehicles for making certain elements of a scene salient. Against Tati's tendency to equalize on-screen elements, Keaton opts for a compositional hierarchy. Given this, it is easy to discover Keaton's program by isolating that which he elevates for attention in his hierarchy.

Here an example seems appropriate. In the first half of the film, when Johnny is chasing the General with the Texas, he stops at a Confederate staging area to pick up reinforcements. Unfortunately, he forgets to attach the platform car loaded with Southern troops to his lumber car. The result is that, unbeknownst to Johnny, he lights out in pursuit alone. The shot I want to consider is the one in which Johnny realizes that he is alone.

It begins as a medium shot. The camera is mounted on the bridge that runs from the cab of the locomotive to the cow-catcher. In the foreground of the shot we see Johnny. He is staring ahead through the window of the engine. We know that the troops are not attached to the train, and we know that Johnny is unaware of this. There is a certain comic reaction to the confidence that Johnny evinces, given its groundlessness. In the screen-left background of the shot we see trees lining the roadway. We can also see a receding line of the tips of the railroad ties that make up the roadbed. But initially we cannot see the track. Because the rails are straight, we also, at first, cannot see behind the train. Given the position of the camera, the locomotive and the lumber car completely block out the track behind. The effect is somewhat like what Keaton achieves in *The Playhouse* when Big Bill Roberts camouflages the entire line of zouaves by standing in front of them with his enormous bulk. Since the trajectory of perception is fixed, since the spectator can't alter her angle of vision, and since the camera can't see around corners, it is easy to interfere with the sheaf of light rays that is being delivered to the audience by interposing objects in that sheaf. Here Keaton exploits the discrepancy between natural vision and cinematic vision – that is, between constantly shifting station points between the subject and the object, and a single fixed station point.

In the shot in *The General* the blocking effect is only momentary. Suddenly the train hits a bend in the track. And as the locomotive and the lumber car snake around that bend, the lumber car jostles out of the camera's path of vision and the open, empty track behind the Texas comes into view, pulling off in a diagonal curve toward the upper screen-right corner of the shot. The audience sees evidence of what it already knew, i.e., that there is nothing behind Johnny.

The foreground/background tension is comically exquisite, with Johnny, confident but ignorant, counterpoised against the devastating absence of the Confederates. Eventually Johnny turns around. Initially pausing, he then pokes his head out of the side window of the locomotive. Pausing again, he then thrusts his entire torso out of the aperture – a full-bodied double take! Then, dismayed, he turns his face toward the camera in a look of disbelief that gradually metamorphoses into a mixture of anger and determination.

The use of deep-focus foreground/background play and the slow diagonal recession of the track are hardly necessary for the gag to be effective. A much easier mode of representation would be to break up the scene into four shots. There could be an establishing shot from the side of the train showing the locomotive and the lumber car with nothing behind them. Then there could be a close shot of Johnny turning around followed by a point-of-view shot with the camera moving over an empty track. Then we could return to another close shot of Johnny in order to catch his comic disgruntlement.

Alternatively, the shot might have been done in a single take from alongside the train. Here the camera would pull up from behind the train, at first registering the absence of the troops and then passing by the cab of the train at just the moment when Johnny leans out of the window and realizes that he is alone. This variation of the shot might end with Johnny turning forlornly to the camera.

In the montage alternative, the audience would know that Johnny was alone. It is well-known about point-of-view shots that though they tell you what a character sees, they often do not supply evidence of how she manages to see what she sees. There is a striking example in Ford's *Fort Apache*. The main character, played by Henry Fonda, is killed in a box canyon. Aided by binoculars, another character, portrayed by John Wayne, sees the death. Or at least this is what the point-of-view shot establishes. One would have thought that, given the distance, the narrowness of the canyon, and all the smoke and fury of the battle, this vision on Wayne's part would be quite spectacular. Given the point-of-view format, we understand that the Wayne character sees the Fonda character die. But we have no idea how this incredible feat is accomplished.

In the alternative single-shot method for shooting the scene in *The General*, the audience does *see* that Johnny learns that he is alone; it does not just *know* that he learns this. However, in the alternative single-shot variation, the audience does not see how it is suddenly physically possible for Johnny to learn what he knows. Keaton's actual approach makes the swerve in the track absolutely salient. Shooting from the side would in all probability flatten out such a subtle curve. But even if the lateral shooting angle did not obliterate the bend, it would still require an extremely thoughtful viewer to make the inferential connection between the curve and Johnny's rude awakening. The viewer would have to reconceptualize the lateral scene frontally. Keaton's approach, of course, begins frontally. To account for why he does this we have to go beyond what is required to make the gag work, for – as previously outlined – there are at least two other formal structures that could make the gag successful: one that relies on a "knowing that x" mode of cognition and another that is a case of "seeing that x." Keaton's choice has more behind it than evoking either of these states.

That "more" is the desire to engender what we may isolate as a third category of audience attention. This new category is predicated on eliciting a cognitive experience in which the audience sees *how* an event happens. For Keaton in *The General*, physical processes provide the basic subject of the film. Engines are stoked, uncoupled, derailed; artillery is loaded, fired, and transported. Keaton approaches this material from a distinct compositional perspective. He employs a battery of highly determinate compositional structures to enable the audience *to see how* the depicted physical processes happened; he uses these compositional structures in order to give visual salience to the key elements in the causal interactions he presents.

From the above we see that there are at least three distinct cognitive experiences that a director may elicit through stylization. To summarize: with regard to depicting an event x, an audience may simply know that x occurs. Here knowledge is based on inference from conventions and on inferences that make the details of the decoupage conform with the information and expectations that the story supplies. Perhaps we should add another distinction here: that of "believing that x" – where the difference between "believing that x" and "knowing that x" might be drawn by claiming that in the former the event truly occurs in the fictional world of the film, while in the latter the event is implied by the editing and the narrative, but it does not occur in the fictional world. An example of this might be one of Hitchcock's red herrings.

"Seeing that x" differs from "knowing that x" in that in the former case one sees the event in its totality, i.e., all the key human and physical elements that make up the event are visible on screen. This in turn differs from the category of "seeing *how* x happens," in that with "seeing how" all the key elements and their interaction are not only presented but also made *salient* by the composition.

To make the contrast between "seeing that" and "seeing how" clearer, consider an extreme case of "seeing that." In Edwin S. Porter's compositions one sometimes finds shots where the shot is so broad, the actors so chaotically arrayed, and the shot so decentered that one can easily miss the basic action. In *The Great Train Robbery* and *The Kleptomaniac* Porter presents strong examples of multifaceted composition, cases where the arrangement of details is so disorganized that one "sees that x" sometimes only in the special sense that the event is imprinted on the viewer's retina. With Porter one can literally fail to recognize an event despite the fact that all the elements are visible. Keaton's composition contrasts strongly with this. Porter approaches an exaggerated case of the "seeing that x" modality. With Porter the viewer may sometimes merely technically see all the elements of the action, but she sees them in such a way that the action is not recognized.

A less extreme case of "seeing that x" is the example cited as the single-shot alternative to Keaton's frontal long shot of the discovery that the Confederates are not behind him. Here all the elements of the event are visible, and the event is recognized. Nevertheless, a contrast may still be drawn between Keaton's method and "seeing that x," insofar as a case of "seeing how x" involves a more directive composition, which not only displays the whole event but also makes the key elements and their significant interrelations salient.

Obviously the range of phenomena that can fall under the category of "seeing that x" is broad and varied. In the Porter cases the entire event is not made salient, while in our proposed single-shot alternative to Keaton's frontal long shot, only the relation between the track and Johnny Gray's perceptual field is obscured. Between these two examples there is a wealth of further variations that might be balkanized elaborately as a continuous set of gradations. Many refinements are possible here, but I will emphasize only one – a distinction between "seeing that x" without recognition of the event and "seeing that x" with recognition. The former, more extreme, case approached by Porter may be labeled "seeing that x"(1), while the other may be given the suffix (2).

Given the above distinctions, we can note the logical relations among some of the categories. A case of "seeing that x" (2) entails that the spectator "knows that x." A case of "seeing how x happens" entails that the spectator "sees that x"(2) and that she "knows that x."

Since "seeing how" is such an awkward locution, it may be better to refer to this phenomenon as "visible intelligibility." This might be understood informally as a case where one comprehends an event at a glance in terms of the interaction of the relevant causal processes.

One value in introducing these categories is their pragmatic value to criticism. The styles of different directors may be characterized in terms of tendencies favoring one or another of these categories. In my research I have found that in *The General* Keaton manifests a commitment to visible intelligibility. This seemed to me especially significant because it suggests a parallel between Keaton's cinematic style and the comic content of the film. That is, many of Keaton's gags involve successes or failures in the mastery of physical tasks. Key here is the question of intelligence, significantly concrete intelligence. An important thematic aspect of the film is Keaton's development of intelligent behaviors vis-à-vis physical processes. On the level of the audience's experience of the film, physical understanding and intelligence are also important for Keaton. He strives for shots that maximize the visible intelligibility of scenes to the audience. For the character, then, concrete intelligence is the theme, while for the audience the visible intelligibility of physical processes is the key cinematic commitment. In both style and content Keaton shows a basic interest in the understanding of the physical world. Perhaps no film is quite as pervasively concerned with the comprehension of physical processes as *The General*.

In employing visible intelligibility as a critical tool certain methodological restraints seem appropriate. In order to corroborate that a given shot is a significant case of visible intelligibility it is advisable to formulate, as I have done above, alternative means of shooting the scene, where the formal arrangement of details would promote either "knowing that x happens" or "seeing that x happens"(2), rather than "seeing how x happens" (i.e., visual intelligibility). The purpose of these thought experiments is to propose that since there are live alternatives to the method actually employed, artistic choice of some sort can be inferred to be operative. In supporting a claim of an artistic concern with visible intelligibility in any film, it is important that one's foils – i.e., one's imagined alternative treatments – be historically plausible in terms of conventions of the context of the film and in terms of the probable aims of the film (given its cultural role). Also, a claim that a shot is a significant instance of visible intelligibility cannot be well supported by using outlandish foils. For instance, shooting a scene from a mile away may supply you with a "seeing that" alternative to your claim of a significant case of visible intelligibility. However, this alternative is so implausible that it is hard to imagine it entering most choice procedures. The degree to which the alternatives to a given procedure are improbable, in general, determines the degree to which a claim of a significant instance of visible intelligibility is implausible.

Discovering cases of visible intelligibility is a matter of intuition. Explicating them is a matter of tracing the compositional variations that make key items in the event salient, once one has a clear description of what event one is dealing with. Confirming a discovery as a significant artistic instance of visible intelligibility involves demonstrating through thought experiments that the given scene could have been one of several plausible alternatives in an artistic choice procedure.

To supply a fuller sense of what is involved in explicating instances of visible intelligibility, let us consider some examples. In the section of *The*

General devoted to Johnny's pursuit of the spies, the Union hijackers disconnect one of the boxcars of the General, hoping it will roll back and impede the progress of the Texas. When he sees the obstacle, Johnny has the idea of pushing the boxcar onto a siding, thereby clearing his path. Johnny stops his locomotive, leaps from the cab, and rushes to pull a device that switches tracks, in order to send the heavy boxcar onto a siding. Next, in an overhead shot, we see Johnny in the foreground of the cab of the Texas; and in the background we see the boxcar in the top screen-left corner of the image. The boxcar is rolling freely on a spur parallel to Johnny's. In the background, unbeknownst to Johnny, the spur the boxcar is on reunites with his spur. While Johnny rushes around the cab, the boxcar slips in ahead of him.

Obviously, if Johnny had been attentive, he would have seen that the tracks converged, and he would have raced his engine so that he would have been far past the point of connection by the time the boxcar slid back onto his track. But he was preoccupied. In a close shot following that shot where we see the boxcar in the lead, we see Johnny framed by the window of the cab. His mouth drops open; he sees the boxcar in front of him. Then he closes his eyes, as if to envision the environment as he had pictured it. Then he turns around – that is where his mental map places the boxcar. Finally, he looks forlorn, as if the entire transaction were incomprehensible, perhaps magical.

The overhead long shot in this sequence seems to me to be a case of visible intelligibility. To explicate it one must attend to the particular strategies or formal articulations in the *mise-en-scéne* that render the key elements of the event salient. The camera is mounted high on the tender. We see Johnny busy in the cab. He is in the center of the foreground of the shot. Off in the background in the upper screen-left corner, we see the wayward boxcar on the parallel track. There is no action in the intermediary regions of the image to avert our natural tendency to scan from near to far. The rectangular boxcar echoes the edge of the frame while the rectangular edge of the window of the locomotive sets up a third resounding formal echo. We move naturally through this formal pattern. Johnny is bending down under the window fiddling with this or that. The high-angle long shot not only shows us the key elements of the situation but also shows us how the boxcar winds up in front of the Texas and why Johnny is insensible to the situation. Here the elaboration of sharply demarcated foreground/background regions, the use of angulation, and the use of rhyming rectangular edges are individual formal articulations that, when coordinated, emphasize how Johnny becomes befuddled by the mechanics of the situation.

The above boxcar gag is followed by another where, unbeknownst to Johnny, the boxcar is derailed when it strikes a piece of debris – a rail-road tie – that the Union spies have thrown there to impede the Texas. The shot that represents this is a low-angle long shot. Here angulation substitutes for editing in terms of selecting the relevant aspects of the situation. The low angulation directs the audience to the track and to the wheels of the boxcar. We anticipate and then understand how the crash has occurred. Rather than starting with a close shot of the tie on the track and then shifting to a standard lateral medium shot of the crash, Keaton employs a single long shot with low angulation. The eye follows the subtly rising trajectory of the low angle to the center of the screen where on the track we find the tie – made larger by the angulation – that overturned the car. At a glance the whole event is pellucid, comprehensible because the low angle immediately gives salience to the tie and thus sensitizes us to the key physical variables of the situation.

The process of explicating a case of visible intelligibility involves an enumeration of the formal articulations of the image whose coordination emphasizes the key causal relations of the depicted event. In our examples, foreground/background play, the diagonal, angulation, and repetitive shapes have been singled out as constitutive elements of the visible intelligibility of the shots discussed. Of course, these are not the only available strategies. Indeed, even in Keaton there are techniques other than these that promote visible intelligibility. In explicating instances of visible intelligibility the task is not to reduce every case to the operation of a handful of recurrent strategies. One would suspect that the list of strategies would grow as filmmakers experiment with new ways of prompting attention.

Though the examples of visible intelligibility so far have been derived from single-shot compositions, since the concept is a functionalist one it may also be applied to editing. That is, visible intelligibility is a goal that can be pursued through or instantiated in a system of editing as well as a compositional system. Here Keaton's variation of the field/reverse field structure is important. In *The General* Keaton reverses the field of a long shot on several occasions. What seems distinctive about this technique is precisely that it is a long shot being reversed. Everyone employs a shot-countershot convention for interpolating close shots in the representation of dialogue. But in *The General* Keaton also uses field reversals with long shots. The reason for Keaton's use of long-shot field reversals seems to be that this particular structure is closely connected with Keaton's use of the foreground/background regions in his single-shot compositions. That is, editing of this sort functions as a means to accentuate foreground/background juxtapositions of elements by systematically rotating those elements in relation to their screen position and prominence. Used in this way editing is an added means of yielding salience, while the use of long shots maintains the constant visibility of all the relevant elements of the scene.

Examples of this use of long-shot field reversal occur in the eleven-shot sequence in *The General* where Johnny narrowly misses blowing himself to smithereens. Keaton begins this sequence with a handful of lateral shots, which include Johnny's priming the gun and getting his foot entangled in a chain between two railroad cars. The mortar is jostled by the roadbed, and the lowered barrel of the gun points right at him.

The fifth shot in this scene is from behind the mortar, with Johnny in the background of the shot. His foot is caught in the chain. He is stuck on top of the ladder on the back of the tender. Our sightline runs along the trajectory the mortar shell will take. Here the foreground/background position aligns all the crucial elements of the scene as well as underscoring the key physical relation, the trajectory of the projectile. In the foreground we see the mortar, its fuse, and its inexorable target. The shot also emphasizes the interrelations of the elements, since the line of vision of the camera is virtually the same as the line of fire of the mortar.

Shot six is a slightly closer version of shot five, in which we see Johnny shake off the chain. Shot seven is a long-shot reversal of shot five. It is a frontal long shot with the camera mounted on the tender. In the foreground there is lumber; in the mid-ground Johnny climbs onto the top of the car; and in the background we see the implacable gun, its fuse steaming and its muzzle lowered directly at the Texas. Johnny throws several chunks of wood at the mortar, hoping to alter its elevation, but to no avail.

This shot is especially important. First of all, it reverses the field of shot five. In this way it frontally underscores the two crucial features of the scene – the cannon and the Texas. The foreground/background juxtaposition of shot five already achieved this. Shot seven further accentuates this formal emphasis by systematically rotating the visual field so that the gun and the Texas exchange the most prominent screen positions. This is a powerful means of giving utmost salience to key elements. This field reversal also gives the audience more perceptual data about the relative positions of the two objects, provoking a refined sense of depth via the systematic permutation of screen configurations. That is, by reversing the screen position more depth cues about the distance between the two objects are supplied, providing a richer comprehension of the space involved.

Last, shot seven alerts the audience to the fact that there is a curve in the track. The curve, of course, is exactly what saves the Texas from obliteration. By emphasizing the track in shot five as a straightaway and then reversing the field in shot seven, where the track curves, the audience is sensitized to the physical fact about the track that accounts for how the Texas is saved.

The most famous shot in this interpolation is the tenth. It is an overhead long shot with extreme depth of field. In the foreground, in the lower screen-left corner of the image, the mortar rolls into the frame. In the mid-ground there is the Texas, and in the background we can see the General. From behind the mortar we can no longer see its fuse smoking. It is about to discharge. Between the Texas and the mortar, however, we see that the track is curved. The Texas is pulled from the trajectory of the volley by the swerve in the roadbed. The gun fires, the shell whizzes past the Texas, and the shell detonates a mile or so away, just missing the last boxcar of the General, deep in the background of the shot. In the foreground, a cloud of white smoke hovers over that part of the track where the mortar fired; it is just before the curve.

Shot ten is certainly composed in a way that maximizes the visible intelligibility of the scene in and of itself. Nevertheless, the earlier field/reverse field alternation of shots five and seven enhances the clarity of the physical situation, not only by emphasizing the basic physical elements but also by emphasizing their alignment – first along a straightaway and then along a curve. The field/reverse field here primes the audience for the basic physical insight concerning the curve in shot ten, thereby facilitating the audience's capacity to see at a glance how the event happens.

Although thus far visible intelligibility has been elucidated in terms of causal relations within events, the preceding discussion of the alternation of shots five and seven suggests a spatial application as well. The systematic alternation of striking long-shot compositions may enhance one's sense of the depth of a shot, specifically in terms of the distance relations between objects. That is, the addition of perceptual cues about the space of the event yields a heightened sense of the distance relations. The data base for the audience's judgment is augmented, supplying a stronger understanding of how pertinent objects stand in relation to each other.

Closely related to the goal of visible intelligibility with regard to its application to spatial relations is what might be described as geographical intelligibility. An example of this occurs, for instance, in the sequence in which Annabelle removes the linking pin from the General so that she and Johnny can hijack the General from the Yankees. There is a frontal shot of men heaving provisions into a freight car. In the foreground a bearded Union officer directs the activities. With Annabelle hidden in a bag on his shoulders Johnny walks past the point where he should have loaded the sack into the freight car. Instead he walks to the lower screen-left corner of the frame, where there is a junction between two freight cars. The Union officer gesticulates. Then Keaton cuts to a lateral shot. This shot is mounted from behind Johnny. The camera looks down the alley between the two freight cars. A hand – Annabelle's – reaches out from the sack and lifts the pin from between the two cars, disengaging them. In the background of the shot, over the top of the sack, we see the Union officer from the previous shot still gesticulating. He orders Johnny to put his sack in the freight car Johnny has just passed. Keaton then cuts back to the frontal long-shot set-up and Johnny throws the sack, with Annabelle and the pin, among the provisions.

The second shot in this chain is crucial. By repeating the officer from the foreground of the first shot in the background of the second shot the spectator can concretely locate the action of the second shot in regard to the action of the first shot. A tighter shot of Annabelle's removal of the pin that did not include the officer would have rendered the geography of the scene more abstract. By *systematically cross-referencing* elements – specifically, the officer – from one shot to the next, Keaton conveys *a concrete sense of orientation* about the relation of the spaces depicted in the disparate shots. The evocation of a sense of geographical intelligibility is not merely a function of the fact that Keaton tends to edit-in-the-round (by which I mean shooting a scene from frontal, lateral, rear, and overhead angles, rather than from a merely frontal perspective). Eisensteinian montage also edits-in-the-round, but it does not evoke a sense of geographical intelligibility, because pains are not taken to perspicuously cross-reference the elements in successive shots.

In the preceding example, geographical intelligibility differs from visible intelligibility in that in the former the audience's strong sense of the directional relations in adjacent spaces is more a matter of construction than of observation. However, even though it is a matter of construction, the spectator has a very concrete and articulate map of the spatial relations between objects because the audience is provided with more visual cues about the relation between the two shots than is usual. And also those cues are saliently composed. As in the baseball sequence in Keaton's own *College* or in the return of Dave Waggoman's remains in Anthony Mann's *The Man from Laramie*, the audience is given an evidential basis for a powerful mental map of the geography; one feels particularly well-oriented to the space. And even though the space is constructed, it is internally articulated well enough with cross-referenced elements that one has the sense that one would know how to move in it.

Though there are differences between our examples of visible intelligibility and geographical intelligibility – especially in terms of degrees of observation versus construction – nevertheless both have the effect of giving the viewer a heightened sense of understanding. In the case of visible intelligibility, that heightened understanding pertains to causal processes and interactions, while in the case of geographical intelligibility it is a matter of spatial orientation. At the level of style, in *The General* Keaton is concerned to portray the physical world and its relations with a clarity perhaps unmatched in the history of film. This interest is of course also reflected in the composition and editing of other Keaton films. And it obviously also corresponds at the level of style to some of the most recurrent themes in Keaton's narratives and gags: the question of understanding and mastering causal relations in a world of things, on the one hand, and the question of precisely locating and correctly orienting oneself within one's environment, on the other hand. The issues Keaton explores in his physical clowning, that is, become central issues of his cinematic style.

6

For God and Country

> The critique of religion is the prerequisite of all criticism.... The foundation of this critique is the following: man makes religion, religion does not make man.
>
> –Karl Marx, *Contribution to the Critique of Hegel's Philosophy of Right* (opening lines)

The critique of competitive capitalism, in Marx, is motivated by a root concern with the topic of alienation, or, rather more abstractly, with the relation between human activity and human accomplishment. Human activity creates a range of "objects" including not only trucks and trains but social systems, values, technologies. Though these "objects" are originally fabricated for the gratification of man, within the historical process, these "objects" become independent of their original function. That is, more concretely, the state or the exchange system evolves from the role of service institution for the needs of man to autonomous entities whose needs must be served by man. Within the historical context, the state comes to presuppose war or the possibility of war as a basic justification of its existence. Hence, conscription. Dialectically, the need of the state has come to supersede the needs of man. The products of human activity come to enslave human activity.

For Marx, this process of inversion, alienation, is paradigmatically represented by religion. For religion is a product of man. Yet, it dominates man not only as a social institution; it inverts the relation of man and god cosmologically. Man made god; yet religion posits that god makes man. Theology bespeaks a primary, philosophical alienation of man from his metaphysical origins. For this reason, Marx depicts reli-

"For God and Country," *Artforum*, vol. 11, no. 5 (January 1973), pp. 56–60.

gion as a paradigmatic and (philosophically) primary source of alienation, and calls for the critique of religion as a prerequisite to the
analysis of other forms of alienation.

It is within the context of Marxist theory that we can appraise the
importance for Eisenstein of the sequence of shots entitled "For God and
Country" in his film *October*. We know that Eisenstein planned to adapt
Capital to the screen. Another way of saying this might be that
Eisenstein envisioned his analytic editing techniques consummating, in
an analogical sense, with the forms of analysis or analytic thought operative in Marx. In this context, the "God and Country" sequence
acquires a special significance. First, because thematically, it initiates the
critique of religion which is propaedeutic to the analysis of other forms
of alienation, and thus prior to *Captial*. Second, because the formal
structure of the sequence is instructive insofar as it represents, in
"embryonic"[1] form, the structure or method of editing Eisenstein envisioned to be analogous to the process of analysis. The relation between
editing structures and ideology was important to Eisenstein. In his own
silent work, there is an aspiration toward analysis and toward the
rehearsal of the analytic process. This represents a political as well as
an esthetic commitment, i.e., a commitment to engendering and exercising the analytic attitude of the worker audience. In other words,
Eisensteinian montage is coordinated with the effort to reshape the consciousness of the proletariat.

Putatively, *Capital* (Eisenstein's), in its structure, would have engaged
any audience in an intense exercise of cognition. But this preoccupation
is already in evidence in the existing corpus of Eisenstein's silent work.
The "God and Country" sequence, an "embryo," is a meeting point of
past and future in Eisenstein. It is on a progressive continuum with
Potemkin and *Strike* while it also yields an inkling of what *Capital* might
have been like. That is, it affords the opportunity for understanding the
way in which Eisenstein's work is not only thematically but also formally committed to Marxism.

The idea of a film based on *Capital* (Marx's) is mindboggling. How
does one represent the labor theory of value? Yet there is reason to
believe that Eisenstein's assumption that he could film *Capital* was not
unfounded. For the "God and Country" sequence takes as its subject
matter not only the depiction of a mode of alienation, but the disproof
of God's existence. These matters are as "purely" conceptual as issues in
Capital. Thus, it is not idle to speculate about the form of *Capital* on the
basis of this sequence.

The "God and Country" sequence is embedded in that section of
October that concerns Kornilov's march on Petrograd. The sequence
begins with titles – "For God and Country," "For God," "God." There is
a church. Then there is a shot of a Baroque statue of Christ, not the cru-
cified Christ, but Christ the King, Christ in his majesty replete with solar
radiations. Christ is intercut with oblique shots of Christian churches.
The image of Christ is repeated. More churches. A relation between the
figure of Christ and the theological-economic-political institution of
Christianity is established through juxtaposition. That is, the Christ is
the Christ of Christianity. The third appearance of the Christ image is
followed by a statue of a pagan god and then by oblique shots of an
Asiatic place of worship. The Christ and the Christian theological system is juxtaposed with a competing theological system. What follows is
a barrage of shots of statues of ten or eleven more and different gods.
This ends the "God" unit of the chain.

The "Country" unit is more complex for its polemic presupposes the
"God" unit. It begins with a series of shots of military medals and
epaulettes. The opening shots of the film, a statue of a czar falling apart,
are recut and projected in reverse motion and intercut with images of
gods from the "God" unit. An incense burner swinging rapidly is also
cut into the sequence. There is a cut to a bishop, then a cut to Kornilov.
Interestingly, both the incense burner and the bishop are shots from
an earlier point in the film where they functioned to celebrate the fall
of the monarchy. In this sequence, they function to endorse the royalist
Kornilov, the man on horseback. There are several shots of Kornilov.
Finally, he adopts a pointing gesture. There is a cut to a statue of
Napoleon, on horseback, similarly gesturing. Kerensky has been previously juxtaposed with a statue of Napoleon, and this particular juxtaposition was also based on a similarity of gesture. So there are two
Napoleons – Kerensky and Kornilov. Eisenstein, using both split screens
and individual shots that emphasize opposite screen directions, faces
off these two Napoleons in a series of nine or ten shots that involve
the physical confrontation of the statues of the two Napoleons. This
is followed by a shot where two statues of gods similarly confront
each other; here the two statues are identical. And they occupy the
same screen space as the opposing statues of Napoleon. Two shots
follow of statues of gods on horseback, gesturing in the manner of the
mounted Napoleon. In each shot, the gods occupy opposite screen
spaces. More shots of gods. Then a shot of Kornilov and a more or less
narrative progression of the march on Petrograd begins, though, of

course, this narrative is often interrupted by short metaphoric bursts of imagery.

It is the "God" unit of this sequence that is the more abstract. Of it, Eisenstein writes

Kornilov's march on Petrograd was under the banner of 'in the name of God and country.' Here we attempted to reveal the religious significance of this episode in a rationalistic way. A number of religious images, from a magnificent Baroque Christ to an Eskimo idol, were cut together. The conflict in this case was between the concept and the symbolization of God. While idea and image appear to accord completely in the first statue shown, the two elements move farther from each other with successive images. Maintaining the denotation of 'God,' the images increasingly disagree with our concept of God, inevitably leading to individual conclusions about the true nature of all deities. In this case, too, a chain of images attempted to achieve a purely intellectual resolution, resulting from a conflict between a preconception and a gradual discrediting of it in purposeful steps.

Step by step, by a process of comparing each new image with the common denotation, power is accumulated behind a process that can be formally identified with that of a logical deduction. The decision to release these ideas, as well as the method used, is already intellectually conceived.

The conventional descriptive form for film leads to the formal possibility of a kind of filmic reasoning. While the conventional film directs emotions, this suggests an opportunity to encourage and direct the whole thought process as well.[2]

Eisenstein suggests here that the "God" unit somehow recapitulates the form of a logical argument, a logical deduction. The sequence purportedly engages the audience's cognition in a manner such that a set of shot interpolations can be read as a disproof of God's existence. The importance of the shot chain is not only thematic ("God does not exist"), but pedagogic in that the editing structure encourages and directs the worker audience to reason through an exercise of analysis.

Though Eisenstein's explication of the meaning and importance of the sequence is clear, it inevitably evokes question. Immediately one asks, how are the shots in this passage anything like steps in a logical deduction? If this sequence is an atheological argument, where are the premises, where is the conclusion?

To answer this question, let us start with a hypothesis, namely, that the premises as well as the conclusion of Eisenstein's argument are made up of a set of inferences we derive from the juxtaposition of certain shots. That is, in any film an audience must make inferences about the connection of two shots. If a shot of a man putting on a jacket is spliced with a shot of that man walking out of a building, we infer the connection between those shots. Generally, the range of connectives one infers need extend solely over temporal, spatial, causal, and psychological relations. However, we may also infer that a concept may afford a shot connection. Griffith's *Intolerance* is a testament to this discovery. Griffith cuts freely between four periods of history; many of the cuts are justified by a concept, namely "man is intolerant." We are presented with a series of scenes from different periods. We infer they are related by a concept. Here, the inference of the shot connective also represents the director's theme. This aspect of editing particularly occupied Eisenstein's thinking. Esthetically, Eisenstein was committed to art that demands that the spectator constantly speculate about the meaning of art objects by analyzing the organization of those objects. Of theater, he writes

...every spectator, in correspondence with his individuality, and his own way and out of his own experience–out of the warp and weft of his associations, all conditioned by the premises of his character, habits, and social appurtenances, creates an image (an idea) suggested by the author, leading him to understanding and experience of the author's theme.[3]

One need not even turn to Eisenstein's theoretical writings to confirm his interest in grounding thematic material on a set of inferences to be performed by the audience in order to render a chain of shots intelligible. The "Guns not Bread" sequence of *October* might be said to begin with a shot of a soldier crouching in a trench. He is seeking safety from an artillery barrage. He looks upward anxiously. Then there is a series of shots of a cannon being lowered by workmen in a factory. The shots of the cannon repeat the downward movement of the gun, from several angles, several times. A figurative relation between the downward movement of the cannon in the munitions works and the crouching soldier is unavoidable. The munitions industry "oppresses" the trooper. The generic reading of the cannon as a representative of the munitions industry becomes explicit as the shot chain progresses. There are cuts from the munitions factory to breadlines. Here, at the very least, one infers that the relation between these shots is a comparative relation that extends over two activities of the same government. The viewer also realizes that this comparison is a contrast between the provisional government's investment in arms rather than relief. To understand the purpose of this contrast, the viewer must infer the moral concept that it is reprehensible to wage war needlessly while the populace is starving. The audience must make inferences to connect these shots; interestingly, at the same time it makes these inferences it rehearses an argument against the policies of the provisional government. Thus, at the same time the shot chain expresses a revolutionary idea, it also educates the audience in a method of argumentation. This process of education is maieutic. The argument is drawn from the audience by setting the task of discovering shot connections.

Likewise, an extended and intermittent set of cuts from the end of the well-known bridge sequence to the beginning of the 'God and Country' sequence is, in part, rendered intelligible by the inference of a moral concept. The bridge sequence ends with a series of shots of the bombed-out Bolshevik headquarters. The cut is to the headquarters of the provisional government in the Winter Palace. Kerensky "ascends" to power. There is a cut to Bolsheviks in prison. There are shots of Lenin's hideout. Lenin's abode, a mere hut, with a fire outside, and a lone teakettle boiling over the fire, is juxtaposed to an elaborate series of shots of the crockery and eating utensils in Kerensky's domicile. These cuts culminate that motif of the cutting, throughout the shot chain, that compares the quarters of the provisional government with those of the prospective government—Lenin's teakettle with an astonishing array of dishes and glasses. Too much against so little (the maldistribution of wealth and power). Again, the set of inferences that the shots evoke, mobilize and rehearse an argument.

Turning to the "God" sequence one can begin to infer a series of premises of an atheological argument. The title gives us the word "God." Then, an image of a Christian church. Next we are given Christ. Since the titles have related God and country (Holy Mother Russia), and there is a shot of a Christian church, we understand that the God this sequence is primarily concerned with is the Christian God. From the Christian God, we move to Christ, a particular instance of the Christian God, iconographically distinct from the Holy Ghost or the Father. The image of Christ, moreover, is not the image of the suffering servant, but more of the nature of Christ the King. Thus, this shot emphasizes a particular aspect of God – his rulership. Furthermore, the idea of Christ's rulership as opposed to the rulership of the Father, suggests the idea of all-benevolence. Shots of churches follow, evoking the idea of Christianity as a theological and social institution. This reference to a theological system, in conjunction with the reference to God, and the image of Christ (who is all-benevolent) grounds the shot interpolation in an expression of theological *doctrine* to the effect that the aspect of God, instanced in the persona of Christ, is an essential characteristic of God. Here, in the juxtaposition of the first ten or so shots, we can locate the first premise of Eisenstein's argument. It is "There is a God such that God is all-benevolent" or "If there is a God, then He is all-benevolent." The range of discourse here is thus restricted to the examination of the idea or denotation of God expressed in the exoteric doctrine of Christianity, i.e., to the God the worker audience is familiar with. This first premise evolves out of both the image of Christ (who is all-benevolent) and its conjunction with the institution of the church (which maintains all-benevolence is an essential characteristic of God).

A series of alternative concepts of God are evoked by the ensuing shot chain. These gods are also related to creeds, in fact, creeds that are incompatible with Christianity. By comparing these images of gods, by comparing shots, new premises result – "some people believe there is a god B," "some people believe there is a god C," " . . . D, E, F . . . ," and "these gods are different," and "the existence of some of these gods is incompatible with the existence of others." To account for these diverse manifestations of divinity one cannot logically argue that they are merely different representations of the same god because Eisenstein has chosen images of gods whose creeds are incompatible. To account for these different beliefs about God, one must postulate that, whichever god exists, he deceives some men about his true nature or he has made some men so that they are unable to know him. This implies the Christian God does not exist. That God deceives men implies he is not all-benevolent. And, since the Christian God is omnipotent, his endowing some men with the inability to know him implies he is not all-benevolent. A set of empirically true premises about various non-Christian faiths leads us to the implication that God is not all-benevolent. The first premise of the argument stated a standard concept of God – "There is a God such that God is all-benevolent." But a contradiction has resulted from the addition of a set of empirically true premises to this original premise. This contradiction can be resolved only by the admission that without the addition of further premises, the argument implies that the Christian God does not exist. Morever, if all-benevolence is regarded as a necessary characteristic of any god, no god exists. ("If there is a God, he is all-benevolent." "God is not all-benevolent." By *modus tollens*, "there is no God.")

The argument, as stated, takes the form of a *reductio ad absurdum*. That is, it assumes a set of premises are true and from that set of premises derives a contradiction. This implies that some premise or premises must be false. The premises that express that there are alternative beliefs about God are all true. The premise that must be false concerns the denotation of God which states that God is all-benevolent. "God," as commonly understood by the worker audience, cannot exist.

At this point it is profitable to recall what Eisenstein says about the sequence.

Maintaining the denotation of 'God,' the images increasingly disagree with our concept of God, inevitably leading to individual conclusions about the true nature of all deities. In this case, too, a chain of images attempted to achieve a purely intellecutal resolution, resulting from a conflict between a preconception [Christian] and a gradual discrediting of it in purposeful steps.[4]

This statement seems to suggest the idea of a *reductio ad absurdum*, for though not stated in terms of logic, Eisenstein has in mind the derivation of a contradiction from the assumption of a standard concept of God, and a set of images of gods of faiths incompatible with Christianity.

The "Country" unit of this sequence further contradicts the idea that God is all-benevolent. Kerensky and Kornilov both oppose one another in the name of God. Both the provisional government and Kornilov have been intercut with the same images of churches and church ceremony. The two personalities, representd by opposing figures of Napoleon, are intercut with an image of two statues of the same god opposing each other in a screen space isomorphic to the screen space of the two Napoleons. Other cuts of gods are also added to the sequence. In the "Country" sequence, then, the topic of revelation is again broached. Both men act according to the will of the same deity. One of them or both of them must be deceived. The opposition of these two crusaders implies the shot of a god in opposition with himself. Either the will of God has been inaccurately understood by someone or someone is deceived. Again, both cases imply that God is not all-benevolent, thus offering a corollary to the previous *reductio ad absurdum*. The "God" unit of the sequence purports to refute the existence of God on the basis of the incompatibility of the revelations of God across various faiths whereas the "Country" sequence suggests that contradictory revelations of God's will within one faith is further evidence that an all-benevolent God is nonexistent.

One objection that this description of the sequence has encountered is that the sequence does not work because the inference that the Christian worker derives from the shots of pagan idols is that these idols are the work of the devil. God is all-benevolent, but the devil deceives men. This interpretation is supported by the fact that a number of the god images in the sequence resemble demons. Nevertheless, this interpretation in no way avoids the general thrust of the argument insofar as the existence of evil is, as well, a putative contradiction to the concept of an all-benevolent God. Thus, the addition of demonic imagery of God by Eisenstein to the shot chain seems to function to introduce yet another argument against God's existence.

Another different though not incompatible reading of the sequence might begin by pointing out that the deities here are all represented by statues. An alternative might have been to represent the various theologies by means of an inventory of culturally divergent ceremonies. Instead, Eisenstein uses statues. The gods, even the Christian God, are man-made objects. This iconography parallels the "Country" sequence, where the state is represented by man-made objects like medals, or braids, or the statue of a czar. (Indeed, throughout the film, there is a tendency to represent the state through objects.) Through this imagery, one may see in Eisenstein a propensity for making literal Marx's notion that religion and the state are man-made things that, through a dialectical, historical process, come to assume mastery over man. Perhaps Eisenstein himself suggests this kind of symbolic reading of the shots when he writes "these pieces were assembled in accordance with a descending intellectual scale – pulling back the concept of God to its origins, forcing the spectator to perceive this 'progress' intellectually."[5] That is, by emphasizing the origin of religion Eisenstein makes reference to the fact that religion which originated out of man's fears and needs, has come to dominate its maker. If such a reading is plausible, one may argue that the sequence not only initiates a critique of religion, but also situates religion as a form of alienation.

At this point, some disclaimers are in order. It is not our claim that Eisenstein has incontrovertibly disproved God's existence or even that Eisenstein invented a new and interesting atheological argument. Whether or not the deduction described is true is irrelevant. What is important is that it is a logically valid argument form. That is, it seems that there is a set of inferences that we may propose in order to explain the juxtaposition or relation of shots in the "God and Country" sequence that suggest a logically valid (though possibly false) atheological argument. These inferences, moreover, can be performed without esoteric knowledge of religions. This evidence, combined with

Eisenstein's description of the scene, enables us to characterize the aspiration of the sequence in terms of an effort by Eisenstein to engage and direct the cognitive processes of the audience in such a way that the audience will perform a logical analysis of the concept of God. Eisenstein takes as the model, for the making of the sequence, a valid argument form, the *reductio ad absurdum*. He supplies a range of shots that will suggest the premises of the argument. The audience in inferring the relations of these shots to one another will evolve a set of concepts that lead to a contradiction. Thus, thematically Eisenstein is engaged in a critique of religion while stylistically he is engaged in a form of pedagogy. The method of making the scene engenders an analytic attitude in the audience viewing it. The method of making the sequence is thus ideologically influenced as is the theme, for the aspiration of technique here is to reshape the consciousness of the audience by exercising the analytic faculty of the mind.

Marx writes "Not only the result, but the road to it is also part of the truth. The investigation of truth must itself be true, true investigation is unfolded truth, the disjuncted members of which unite in the result."[6] This statement, despite its density, makes clear the importance Marx attached to the process of correct analysis. In the "God and Country" sequence, Eisenstein attempts to fully realize Marx's strictures by using a logically valid argument form, a reasoning pattern that preserves truth, as a principle for the organization of shots. The effort is ideological as well in that it attempts to evoke in the audience a rehearsal of the analytic process.

One cannot predict what Eisenstein's film of *Capital* would have looked like. But the "God and Country" sequence does suggest at least one tool that might have facilitated the analysis of abstract concepts, namely, the use of standard argument patterns as models for editing structures.

The sequence is also on a continuum with previous work by Eisenstein. As Eisenstein writes in his description of the sequence, his method grows out of a recognition about conventional narrative films. Cutting demands that audiences make inferences about the relation between shots. To a certain degree, a wide range of shot connections become conventionalized. Nevertheless it is possible to thrust viewers back into a condition of constant inference by an avoidance of conventional cutting patterns, by the use of more complex relations, such as logical or metaphoric relations, as models for editing structures. Cutting the suppression of the workers against an abattoir in *Strike* is a salient example.

Eisenstein's wide use of synecdoche is also a measure of his abiding commitment to a cinema of intense intellectual excitement. He writes

The strength of montage resides in this, that it involves the creative process, the emotions and mind of the spectator. The spectator is compelled to proceed along that selfsame creative path that the author traveled in creating the image (idea). The spectator not only sees the represented elements of the finished work, but also experiences the dynamic process of the emergence and assembly of the image (idea) just as it was experienced by the author.[7]

The "God and Country" sequence is perhaps Eisenstein's most daring experiment along these lines. The juxtaposition of shots evokes a series of inferences which because they are logically incompatible require yet another inference. Here we see a concrete example of an attempt to direct and to exercise the mind of the viewer. For Eisenstein, cinema presupposes inference, which, within a Marxist framework, makes it an eminent pedagogic tool for the reshaping of consciousness.

I have stressed the intent and structure of "For God and Country," leaving open the question of how successful the sequence is in structuring the consciousness of the mass audience. To speculate on how the Soviet audience viewing the sequence in 1929 responded is a question for a master historian-psychologist-statistician unlikely to appear. All that can be said is that there is a way in which the structure of the sequence seems firmly situated in an attempt to evolve not only a theme but a style that is coordinated with the aspirations of Marxism. Nevertheless, one does feel compelled to make some comment on audience response to the sequence. If we can talk about a theoretical (and perhaps dubious) invention called "the sympathetic viewer," it seems fair to claim that, at the very least, that viewer, on first viewing, has the sense that the sequence involves comparison of the attributes of alternate deities and theological systems, and that these alternate deities are somehow incompatible. The speed of projection might not allow *all* sympathetic viewers enough time to reconstruct the argument *during* the first viewing. However, this sympathetic viewer does have a sense of the basic argument pattern and thus should be able to complete the argument either after the first viewing or after subsequent viewings. The fact, moreover, that viewers may have to consider the shot chain for some period of time before they have command of it seems to impute a genuine pedagogic value to the sequence.

The montage style is predicated on the excitation of the inference-making faculties of the audience. To render cuts intelligible the audience must make inferences. Such inferences can be of a highly thematic and conceptual nature. Montage, then, is a way to direct and to engender thought along new lines. The "God and Country" sequence is a concrete example of the restructuring and exercise of the spectator's thought processes. It not only attempts to direct the audience to the recognition that God does not exist; it also, in the maieutic tradition, attempts to draw from and educate the audience in an analytic form of reasoning.

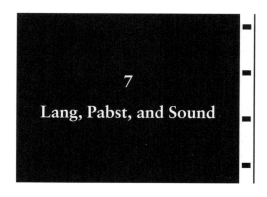

7

Lang, Pabst, and Sound

The coming of sound caused a crisis in film aesthetics. Some theoreticians, notably Arnheim, refused to endorse the shift at all. Sound, for them, was a return to canned theater, a regression to the pre-Griffith era before film had weaned itself from the stage.

More adventurous thinkers, however, embraced the new device and attempted to incorporate it into the aesthetic system of silent film. Eisenstein, Pudovkin, and Alexandrov, in their famous 1928 statement on sound, and Roman Jakobson, in a rarely discussed 1933 article entitled "Is the Cinema in Decline?" proposed that sound be understood as a montage element: aural units should be juxtaposed against the visuals, just as shots should be juxtaposed against shots. Jakobson, ironically, answers someone like Arnheim in the same manner that Arnheim would have answered someone like Clive Bell. Jakobson tells the opponent of sound that his opposition is not based on a thoughtful look at the possibilities of the new medium. Jakobson argues that the sound element in a scene can be asynchronous and contrapuntal, thereby diverging from mere reproduction. This possibility enriches cinema, for added to all the conceivable visual juxtapositions of the silent film are inestimably large reservoirs of sound counterpoints.

The Eisenstein – Jakobson reaction to sound was conservative in one sense. It was an attempt to extrapolate the basic concepts of a silent film aesthetic to a new development, recommending montage as the basic paradigm for dealing with sound. By the forties, another kind of recommendation was evolved by Bazin, one diametrically opposed to the general silent film predisposition toward stylization and manipulation.

In Bazin, the recording/reproductive aspect of film, that nemesis of silent film artists and theoreticians alike, became the center of a theory that made recommendations about the types of composition and camera

"Lang, Pabst, and Sound," in *Film Sound*, ed. E. Weis and J. Belton (New York: Columbia University Press, 1985), pp. 265–277.

movement that would best enable the filmmaker to re-present reality in opposition to the silent film urge to reconstitute it. The formation of Bazin's theory was closely related to the emergence of sound. In the thirties, a filmmaker like Renoir responded to the introduction of sound as an augmentation of film's recording capabilities, and he evolved a realist style that roughly correlated with the notion of film as recording. Bazin described and sought foundations for Renoir's practice, and in so doing defined the predominating ethos of the sound film until the sixties.

The contrast between the reconstitutive response to sound, and the realist's, is much discussed and should not be belabored. But it is important to emphasize that this debate is not merely abstract speculation. Both positions are also artistic dispositions, embodied in the actual practice of important filmmakers. The debate is not only so many words but also many films. Consequently, apart from its dubious theoretical interest, the debate can be historically informative not only about the general directions and transitions in film history but also about the place of individual films within that evolution.

Two films, Fritz Lang's *M* and G. W. Pabst's *Kameradschaft*, are especially interesting in this regard. There are many coincidental similarities between them: both are German; both are by major Weimar directors; both date from 1931; both were produced under the auspices of Nero Films; and both share the same cameraman, Fritz Arno Wagner. Yet, stylistically they diverge greatly. *M* seems to look to the past, to silent film, for its style while *Kameradschaft* presages the future. Nineteen-thirty was the key year in Germany's transition to sound. In September 1929, only 3 percent of German production was in sound. By September 1930, the total jumped to 84 percent. Thus, the 1930–31 period was one of crisis, one where major German filmmakers had to reorient themselves to their medium. Lang and Pabst both did, but each in highly distinctive ways, ways which in fact represent in a nutshell the major themes in the dialectic about the appropriate direction of sound film.

M is what might be called a silent sound film. Other examples would include Dreyer's *Vampyr*, Lang's own *Testament of Dr. Mabuse*, Vertov's *Enthusiasm* as well as *Three Songs of Lenin*, parts of Pudovkin's *Deserter*, Buñuel's *L'Age d'Or*, and Clair's early sound films, especially *A nous la liberté*. Calling these silent sound films is not meant disparagingly. Each of these represents a major achievement. Yet that achievement in each case derives from a penchant for asynchronous sound based on a paradigm of montage juxtaposition as a means to manipulate, to interpret, and to reconstitute pro-filmic events.

The importance of montage for *M* can be demonstrated by a brief look at one of its key scenes, the parallel development of the gangster and government strategy sessions concerning the pursuit of the child-killer. This sequence is not only a matter of parallel, temporal editing; it also involves the articulation of a comparative montage that ultimately equates the police and the gangsters. The two meetings correspond to each other along many dimensions. Both record the same type of event – a search. Both involve similar actions – characters standing and speaking. At this simple visual level, there is a striking resemblance between the behavior of the two groups. Indeed, there is even a similarity in the positions taken in the separate groups, e.g., there are both official and criminal hardliners. At times, the editing almost elides the two meetings; a criminal could be seen as addressing an official and vice versa.

Visual details of the two meetings strongly correspond. Smoke is emphasized in both places. Indeed, cigarettes and cigars lit in the criminal meeting are followed by shots of the smoke-filled police session as if the fumes had transmigrated across the cut. Perhaps this is not only montage but overtonal montage. The elision of the two events is also supported by at least one lightning mix: a gesture begun in one shot by the gangster leader is completed by the Minister of the Interior. This multidimensional comparative montage, of course, is grounded by a thematic point – namely, the identification of the two groups. Lang, here, is critical of the police. Like the criminals, their major concern is self-interest – their "operation" is also being disrupted by the child-killer. They want to catch him in order to get the public "off their backs" and return to "business as usual." Stylistically, in the best Soviet tradition, this pejorative equivalence is emphasized through an elaborate set of comparative juxtapositions.

The commitment to montage shapes Lang's attitude to the sound track. Elsie's death is a good example of this. She is late. Her mother asks people if they have seen the child. Excited, the mother begins calling out her kitchen window. Her voice carries over several shots, including a plate set for dinner, the apartment stairwell, and a yard, presumably in the neighborhood. These are all places where, given the time of day, we might expect to find Elsie. But we don't see her. The mother's poignant voice, audibly dropping as the camera cuts farther and farther away, plus these shots, communicates the idea of danger. This is montage of the most basic sort – a visual idea plus an aural one engenders a new concept. Editing is, in short, the model for sound.

The use of montage in both the visual and the sound editing in *M* does not appear to be a casual technical decision about the best way to solve this or that local problem concerning the most efficient means to represent this or that scene. The montage style of *M* seems consistent. More than that, it seems organic, to use a concept of Eisenstein's.

The most sophisticated versions of the montage aesthetic involved a coordination of style and content. For Eisenstein, the dialectical structure of montage corresponded with the revolutionary subject matter of his films; for Vertov, editing mirrored the modes of thinking of the new socialist society that he celebrated; for Buñuel, montage juxtaposition manifested the irrational by literalizing the primary processes. In each case, the relationship between form and content converged into an organic, functional whole. Similarly, Lang's use of montage in *M* seems of a piece with his theme.

To understand the relation of montage to Lang's thematic preoccupations, we should describe the film's subject. *M* is above all a film of investigation. Extended sequences of the film lovingly dote on the process of gathering evidence. We hear Lohmann's telephone discussion with the Minister of the Interior as we watch the police collecting and examining fingerprints, candy wrappers, cigarette packages, etc. We hear that they have fifteen hundred clues. Throughout the film, Lang returns to the theme of physical evidence. After the raid on the cabaret, not only does Lohmann nab a handful of criminals by careful attention to telltale clues, but his assistants pile up a magnificent assemblage of guns, knives, drills, chisels, hammers, etc. More clues for more crimes. And, toward the end of the film, when Lohmann reads the report about the gang's entry into the warehouse, Lang dissolves from the written words to the pieces of evidence they enumerate. Lang seems visually obsessed with evidence, showing us much more than the narrative requires.

Of course, this visual concern with evidence is integrally related to the plot. The police's interest in evidence is projected onto the audience. In a limited way, we are simultaneously immersed in these clues along with the police. This is especially important at the beginning of the film, where for almost the first third we, like the police, have not identified the killer. He has been kept off-screen, or with his back to the camera, or in a dark place, or with his hat covering his face. Here, our position is strictly analogous to the authorities'. We have clues, for instance his whistle, but we haven't gotten our man. The framing of shots and the narrative conspire to make the spectator's relation to the screen that of a sleuth. Like the police, we base our knowledge of the killer on his traces, e.g., his shadow, his voice, his whistle.

The editing throughout *M* can be seen in light of this first section. Lang often edits actions in such a way that first we see or hear a trace, or a part, or an effect of an off-screen character before we see that character. We see the child-killer's reaction to the blind man at the trial before we can identify the blind man. At the very end we see the criminals raise their hands above their heads before we know the police have arrived. In some cases, we never see the off-screen action, as with Elsie's death; here our knowledge is wholly reliant on traces.

Lang's editing seems predicated on provoking the audience to infer unseen, off-screen presences and actions. Even after the audience knows who the child-killer is, it does not leave off its investigatory role, because by consistently presenting scenes where the audience must infer off-screen agents from their traces Lang continues to make the spectator's relation to the events in the film analogous to a detective's relation to his clues. That is, an investigation involves reasoning from traces and effects to their causes – their agents. Lang's framing and his editing engender the same sort of reasoning – from trace to agent – in many scenes, including even scenes that don't involve off-screen criminals. It is as if Lang's preoccupation with the process of investigation were so intense that he used the process as a general model for framing and editing throughout. A similar point might be made about the large number of overhead shots in the film. These shots mime the posture of investigation, that of the detective bending over a city map or a discarded package of cigarettes.

M is an exemplary case of an organic film. The narrative structure, the framing, the use of sound to present off-screen traces, the overhead angulation, and the order of editing, all seem coordinated to induce an investigatory attitude on the part of the audience – thereby simulating, to a limited extent, the fictional experience of the characters in the viewing experience of the spectators. Montage is the key here. And in the tradition of Eisenstein, Vertov, and Buñuel, it is montage based on imitating modes of thought.

Whereas *M* is a film based on editing, *Kameradschaft* relies far more on camera movement. Since the two films share the same cameraman, Wagner, this difference seems attributable to the divergent conceptions of the sound film held by Pabst and Lang. Pabst and Wagner had begun to use camera movement extensively in the silent period, notably in *The Love of Jeanne Ney*. As the industry changed to sound, Wagner was one of the first Germans to blimp the camera. The mobility this gave him was unleashed effectively in Pabst's *Westfront 1918*, especially in the sequence where the troops crawl along the trenches to mount an attack. *Kameradschaft* marks the high point of Pabst's and Wagner's experimentation with camera movement, not only because the camera movement is interesting in and of itself, but because it is integrated into a complex system of composition that presages the development of sound realism culminating with directors like Rossellini, DeSica, and Ray.

The subject of *Kameradschaft* is a French mine disaster circa 1919. Its theme is blatantly socialist; German miners race across the border to rescue their brother workers. The recent war casts a dark shadow on the action, but the heroic self-sacrifice of the Germans, in the name of working-class unity, dispels French distrust and results in a celebration of proletarian cooperation. This theme is not only stated in the film but also reinforced by the narrative structure, which, in the Soviet tradition, employs a mass hero, thereby democratizing the drama. Instead of a single protagonist or a single set of protagonists knit together by one story, there are several central stories occurring concomitantly.

Kameradschaft is perhaps most interesting in terms of its composition. Like *Battle of Algiers*, but thirty years earlier, *Kameradschaft* builds images that often evoke the impression of documentary footage. Pabst achieves this by intermittently acting as if his camera were restrained in relation to the disaster as a documentary camera would be. For instance, there is a scene of the German rescue crew being given instructions before it enters the French mine. Pabst shoots this from behind the German team. The camera tracks past their backs, as they listen, until there is a break in the line of men. At that point, the camera turns and moves into this space in the crowd so that the audience can see the French official who is speaking. But the camera doesn't dolly in; it remains about ten yards away. What is the significance of this distance? I submit that it is to identify the camera as an observer. It reminds the viewer of a documentary because the camera stays outside the action. In a period before zooms, to move into the action for a close shot of the speaker would interfere with and interrupt the rescue. These men don't have time to pose for pictures. The camera has to stay out of their way. Throughout *Kameradschaft*, documentary distances of this sort are evoked, abetting an impression of a spontaneous recording of the event. This is not to say that all or even most of the shooting respects the "documentary distance." Still, as in Rossellini's *Paisan*, it happens often enough to induce a heightened sense of realism.

The camera's relation to the physical environment is especially interesting. It is important to emphasize that the mines are sets, brilliantly executed by Erno Metzner and Karl Vollbrecht. Yet in a way these are curious sets; often they deny the camera a clear view of the action. In one of the opening shots of the French mine, the camera begins following a character who is pushing a heavy coal bin down a tunnel. Then the camera elevates somewhat and tracks along the ceiling of the tunnel where a diagonal vein has been cut out of the earth and propped up with a veritable forest of short, thick wooden pillars. There are miners digging in this narrow space. You can see them hacking away behind and between the wooden props. The camera then swoops down, picking up the character with the coal bin again. He has stopped at a chute that runs up to the vein where the miners are working. Coal pours into the empty bin.

One thing to note about this shot is that it exemplifies a realist's concern with making the process by which coal is removed and transported inside a mine visibly intelligible – i.e., it enables the audience to see how a mine operates. But more importantly, the shot also demonstrates another realist preoccupation, crucial to Pabst's composition throughout. That is, our view of the miners is obscured by those wooden props; the human element in the scene is blocked by the physical structure of the set. The physical details of the environment restrict the human interest we may have in the characters in favor of details of the environment.

Of course, in a documentary, you must deal predominantly with preexisting environments, which will not always allow you to get clear shots of the action. Pabst and Metzner have built that factor into their sets. Recurrently throughout the film, a tangle of pipes, wires, broken posts, and all manner of debris inhabits the foreground of shots, preventing a clear view of the human action. It is as if Pabst imagined what the problems of a documentary cameraman would be in such a situation, and then had Metzner build a set where Wagner could imitate some of those limitations. In turn, this evocation of documentary elements heightens the viewer's sense of verisimilitude.

Physical elements of the set literally obstruct our view of the drama. When the grandfather drags his grandson into an underground stable, he sets the boy down in an empty stall. This is a charged scene, dominated by the grandfather's emotion. But we cannot see the grandfather's face. A wide board, part of the side of the stall, is in front of the old man, denying a clear view of him at this dramatically important moment.

The significance of this shot should be understood in terms of realism, specifically in terms of the archaeological temperament of many realists.

Whether a Stroheim or a Zola, the realist packs his work with details in an effort to reproduce the particular environment of the event depicted. Pabst does this when he introduces and elucidates the German miners' surprising overhead "locker" system. But Pabst differs from a realist like Stroheim in that he packs not only the background with details but also the foreground. This is an extension of the means at the disposal of the realist. The archaeological realist seeks to increase the weight of environmental detail relative to the dominant human action of the story. This does not mean that the archaeological realist overwhelms the main story, or even that detail has equal weight with the story, but only that the role of detail, as a focus of audience attention, be appreciably greater than one finds in the sparse decors of typical narrative films of the period. Stroheim weighted the background of *Greed* with details, and then used the deep-focus long take to prompt the audience to explore the environment. Pabst does this as well, amplifying Stroheim's practice by often filling the foreground with details, thereby compositionally displacing characters from their privileged position as the first object of audience attention.

Pabst also uses the beginnings or the ends of shots to emphasize physical detail. A shot may open on an object and be held for a second before a character enters. Or, a shot may be held on a detail after a character exits.

Related to Pabst's concern with physical detail is his handling of actors. People often walk in front of the camera. Also, important characters, involved in major actions in the story, are sometimes in the background of the shot behind groups of extras. When the grandfather sneaks into the mine, the camera tracks with him, but between the old man and the lens stands the French rescue crew as well as several imposing steel columns. For brief intervals, the old man disappears from view. What is involved here is a complex compositional acknowledgment of the situation being represented. Standard narrative composition designs its environment and blocks actors so that important characters are at the center of visual attention. The realist deviates from this practice, giving the details of the event and the place portrayed more prominence. The realist acknowledges more complexity in the world, but the realist does not recreate the world. Realism, like standard narrative composition, is a style of representation, not the reproduction, of actual reality. But as a style it acknowledges the complexity of situations by giving detail more compositional attention than does the solely drama-centered narrative.

The realists Bazin endorsed were involved in what could be thought of as a kind of cinematic land reclamation. They repossessed areas of cinematic space, unused in standard narrative composition. Specifically, they resettled the back of the shot and the sides of the shot. They were concerned with depth of field and what Bazin calls "lateral depth of field." Both these preoccupations are central to *Kameradschaft*.

The saga of depth of field is well known. Standard narrative composition, according to Bazin, pays scant attention to background. It either obliterates it by close shots or masks it by soft focus. The background may also be downplayed via abstraction. The background of the standard narrative shot is not so abstract as to call attention to itself, but there is so little visual detail that there is no reason for the eye to dwell there. A table, a chair, a telephone, and a picture are enough. And don't have Mother enter the background to answer the phone while Dad and Junior are having a crucial dramatic conversation in the foreground, because that will divert attention.

Renoir, Wyler, Welles, and the neorealists rebelled against this. The background became an arena of activity; in *Rules of the Game*, sometimes as many as three separate stories are contesting the action in the foreground. *Kameradschaft* similarly upholds this principle of overall composition. Of course, *Kameradschaft* differs from *Rules of the Game*. Primarily, Renoir places interrelated dramatic actions on different compositional planes – Schumacher searches for his wife in the foreground, while the poacher sneaks off with her in the background. Pabst, instead, implodes the frame with the physical and social facts of the situation. Whereas Renoir concentrates on the personal, psychological economy of the drama, Pabst is an anthropologist and an archaeologist. Both rely on depth of field, but they are realists with different types of interests. Pabst is concerned with enriching the environment, wheras Renoir primarily enriches the drama.

Disaster lurks throughout *Kameradschaft*. Explosions, cave-ins, floods, and fires mercilessly erupt. The depth-of-field technique is especially powerful in these scenes. A man will run down a tunnel that is collapsing behind him. Metzner's engineering ingenuity with these catastrophes is overwhelming. Tons of stones are falling within a few feet of the actors playing the trapped miners. Everything is captured in one shot, engendering an awesome feeling of authenticity. Bazin claimed a heightened sense of verisimilitude for depth-of-field shots involving danger. Pabst exploits that effect more than a decade before Bazin conceptualizes it as a central factor in realism.

Of all the ways in which *Kameradschaft* corresponds to Bazin's characterization of film realism, camera movement is the most significant. To
elucidate this, I should start with a brief review of Bazin's interest in
camera movement. He applauds Renoir's tendency toward incessant lateral panning and tracking. Renoir follows his characters, rather than
preblocking the scene in such a way that the camera remains stationary
throughout. Bazin appreciates this use of camera movement for two reasons. First, it imbues the scene with a sense of spontaneity. And second,
it treats the relation between on-screen space and off-screen space cinematically.

This second reason is somewhat obscure and requires comment.
Bazin believes that the stationary, preblocked scene treats the film frame
like the border of a stage or a painting. That is, the picture and the play
are presented as boxes that are spatially discontinuous with their surroundings. The preblocked, stationary scene treats on-screen space on
the box model. In distinction, repeated lateral panning and tracking subvert one's sense of the frame as a self-contained box and affirm the
continuity of on-screen space and off-screen space. The frame is not
analogous to the proscenium arch, which lifts the action out of a spatial
continuum with the wings of the theater, setting it in some virtual realm.
Rather, the film frame is only the viewfinder of the camera as it moves
over a spatially continuous world; lateral panning and tracking acknowledge the presence of that real world and make the on-screen image's
continuity with it a matter of the audience's felt attention.

It is this aspect of realism Bazin dubs "lateral depth of field." Like
ordinary depth of field, this style is realistic relative to a more standard
type of composition. That is, standard practice treats the frame as a theatrical box; the realist repudiates this, thereby acknowledging spatial
continuity by subverting the artifice imposed on the image by standard
practice.

Pabst constantly emphasizes lateral depth of field in *Kameradschaft*.
As in Renoir, there are many slight axial pans in the film. When the
crowds run to the exploding French mine, Pabst includes several shots
that begin with a group of people running in one direction across the
frame. Then the camera pans slightly to the point where two streets
intersect. At that corner, the first group of people turn and join an even
larger group which is running away from the camera. Through the use
of these slight axial pans, Pabst emphasizes the spatial contiguity of all
of the people who are converging on the mine. Throughout the film, this
type of panning recurs in order to articulate the spatial contiguity of

converging action. Pabst often uses panning to represent a character's point of view. Here, the synthetic space of editing is repudiated, resulting in the felt sense of a spatially continuous environment.

Of course, the large camera movements of the film enhance the sense of a spatial continuum as well. Where possible, Pabst knits the different areas of action together with long, snaking tracking shots. I am not denying that there is a great deal of editing in the film. However, there is also a great deal of camera movement, especially for the period. Moreover, much of this camera movement is used in situations where the normal practice of the period would be to fall back on the analytic editing procedures of silent film. Again, to understand what is realist about *Kameradschaft*, it is necessary to consider it as a deviation from standard practice. Much of the film corresponds to the editing bias of the period. But there are also other tendencies, found in the camera movement, which, given the film-historical context, can be interpreted as an acknowledgment of spatial continuity that affirms the role of film as the recorder of a spatially continuous world.

The theme of off-screen space is also inherent in many of Pabst's stationary compositions. When the French rescue crew receives its instructions, the body of one of the miners is cut off by the side of the frame. This type of framing recalls a strategy found in nineteenth-century realist paintings like Manet's *At the Cafe*. The point is to emphasize the continuity of the depicted environment beyond the border of the frame. The innumerable pipes, wires, and tunnels in *Kameradschaft* serve an analogous function; they are the kinds of objects that by their very nature remind the audience that they are part of a larger off-screen spatial network.

Since off-screen space is also important in *M*, it is instructive to consider the different ways Pabst and Lang use it. Lang keeps very specific things off-screen. Examples include: the child-killer, the murder, the gangsters as they break down the attic door, and the police as they raid the kangaroo court. I have already argued that the reason Lang does this is to mobilize an investigatory attitude that corresponds to the theme of detection. But another point can also be made. The agents and events kept off-screen are generally associated with danger. This is especially true of the off-screen agents. They constitute threats to what is on-screen. In my examples, for instance, the gangsters threaten the child-killer, and later the police threaten the gangsters. This is a formal articulation of Lang's theme of paranoia. The off-screen threats are a pictorial means of expressing the paranoid obsession with unseen and invisible enemies. Lang's *films noirs*, like *The Big Heat*, will employ similar strategies. His *1000 Eyes of Dr. Mabuse* takes the theme of invisible danger as its major subject. For Lang, in other words, off-screen space has a symbolic function within his paranoid vision. It has dire connotations as an invisible, menacing empire. In Pabst, off-screen space is just off-screen space, emphasized for its own sake. Of course, in Lang off-screen space is literally contiguous with on-screen space. But that is not its aesthetic point. Lang is interested in developing a subjective world-view, while Pabst is striving for an objective view of the world.

For Bazin, camera movement is also associated with spontaneity. The connection here, I think, must be understood historically. That is, it must be understood in the context of a dominant style based on preblocked stationary compositions that suggested theatrical artifice. The pre-blocked stationary composition gives the impression that the action is preordained and circumscribed. Thus, a style that allows the character to lurch off-screen, forcing the camera to follow him, may have the connotations of freedom and spontaneity. Such camera movement is realist in contrast to a preexisting style that is artificial. It is spontaneous in contrast to a style that gives the action the impression of being controlled.

For Pabst, this sense of spontaneity is central to his attempt to promote the impression that the film is a documentary recording. In some scenes, like the German visit to the French bar, almost three-quarters of the shots contain camera movement. The feeling engendered is that the cameraman is pursuing an unstaged action, shifting his point of view as the event develops. This sensation is induced especially when the German and French rescue teams meet underground. The leaders of the two groups shake hands: the camera dollies in. First, it heads for the Frenchman. But then it turns and moves into a close-up shot of the handshake. This slight change in camera direction is significant. It is as if, mid-movement, the cameraman changed his mind about what was the important element in the scene. I am not denying that all the shots in *Kameradschaft* are preplanned. Yet they often feel unplanned. The shot of the handshake has the look of involving a spontaneous decision on the part of the cameraman. Throughout the film, camera movement has the look of following the action rather than delimiting it. The camera seems to be an observer, with the result that the film projects the impression of a spontaneous recording of an event.

Surprisingly, Bazin does not appreciate *Kameradschaft*. He compares it with *Grand Illusion* since both films employ more than one language. But, he remarks, Renoir gets more thematic mileage out of his polyglot format. Why doesn't Bazin notice the camera movement aesthetic implicit in *Kameradschaft*? One reason might be that there are still vestiges of the silent sound film in Pabst. For instance, there is a fantasy sequence where the sound of a hammer tapping a pipe metaphorically becomes the rattle of a machine gun. Nevertheless, the dominant tendency of the film is toward the sound film style Bazin advocates. Indeed, Pabst not only claims the background and the sides of the frame for realism; he takes over the foreground as well.

The transition from silent film to sound not only involved a question about how sound would be used. It also prompted a reevaluation of the nature of the medium. For Pabst, sound was associated with the recording capacity of film. This led him to a reassessment of the image. He sought and found compositional strategies, including camera movement, which amplified the idea of film as a recording. A whole style evolved in the process of coordinating composition with the commitment to recording. The stylistic system Pabst developed was not the only one available. *M* presents another alternative. But that alternative is based on a very different response to the significance of sound. Steeped in the methods of the silent film, Lang attempts to turn sound into a montage element. The underlying presupposition of Lang's system is that the nature of film is to reconstitute reality, not to record it. In Lang, sound is modeled on preexisting technique whereas in Pabst technique must be remodeled to accommodate sound, specifically to accommodate sound conceived of as entailing a commitment to recording.

Sound caused a major theoretical crisis in the film world. By using the term "theoretical," I do not mean simply that it was a crisis for theoreticians. More importantly, it was a crisis for artists. A framework was needed to understand the aesthetic significance of this new element. Two major ones presented themselves. Sound could function as an element of manipulation as it does in *M*. This is to interpret sound in terms of a silent film paradigm. Or a new paradigm could be embraced, one that responded to sound as increasing film's commitment to recording. In *Kameradschaft*, Pabst accepts this option. It prompts him to develop a highly original camera style, one that presages Renoir. As such, *Kameradschaft* is one of the watershed films in cinema history. I do not mean to use *Kameradschaft* to disparage *M*. *M* is surely one of the greatest films ever made. My point is that *Kameradschaft*, a generally neglected film, is *M*'s peer insofar as it proposes a fully consistent stylistic alternative. In the dialectic between manipulation and recording, both films speak eloquently at a time of crisis and uncertainty.

8

Notes on Dreyer's
Vampyr

I. Introduction

There is a tendency in the recent criticism of Dreyer's *Vampyr* (1931) to assimilate it to the genre of the fantastic, especially in terms of the characterization of that literary species that has been developed by Tzvetan Todorov.[1] I think that this is a mistake. Nor is this mistake a niggling error in classification. It is an error that tends to mislead us about the special qualities and effects of Dreyer's *Vampyr*. Specifically, I contend that *Vampyr* falls squarely into the genre of horror and that its distinctive qualities and effects hinge on Dreyer's variations upon and subversions of certain structural choices characteristically found in that genre. In order to flesh out this claim, I will compare *Vampyr* to Tod Browning's *Dracula* (1931). I choose this foil both because the latter is a film that has been cited as the provocation for Dreyer's production of *Vampyr*[2] and because *Dracula* exemplifies quite nicely a number of recurring narrative structures, strategies, and themes of the horror genre in general and the vampire subgenre in particular. The contrast between *Vampyr*, on the one hand, and *Dracula* and the narrative type it exemplifies, on the other, will, I believe, point us in the direction of what is quite special about *Vampyr* with respect to its large-scale narrative preoccupations. And this in turn may help us understand the probable significance of certain frequently observed features of the small-scale narration of the film, notably, that its story is very difficult to follow.

This essay, then, is divided into three parts: a discussion of *Vampyr* and the fantastic; a contrast between the narrative structure, preoccupations, and plot format of *Dracula*, versus what is found in *Vampyr*; and, finally, speculation on how and why *Vampyr* is difficult to follow. I am especially interested in how its difficulties reinforce what I call the authoritative narrative style of exposition in the film.

"Notes on Dreyer's *Vampyr*," *Presistence of Vision*, no. 8 (1990), pp. 5–14.

II. *Vampyr* and the Fantastic

As is well known, "the fantastic" is the title of a genre that has been explicated by Tzvetan Todorov.[3] Examples of the genre include Sheridan LeFanu's "Green Tea," E. T. A. Hoffmann's "The Sandman," Henry James's "The Turn of the Screw," Thomas Mann's "The Wardrobe," and recent pulp novels like Richard O'Brien's *Evil* or Scott Baker's *Webs*. It seems to me that the genre of the fantastic is practiced more frequently in literature than it is in film, though a well-known film example of it would be *Curse of the Cat People*. Conceptually, the *sine qua non* of the fantastic is an effect instilled in the audience – an effect that involves the audience in the hesitation between two hypotheses about the events in the story. One of these hypotheses is that the events in the story are to be explained naturalistically; the other is that the events are of supernatural provenance. The story, that is, underdetermines its own best explanation. Neither the naturalistic account of the goings-on nor the supernatural account trumps the other. So by the end of James Hogg's *The Private Memoirs and Confessions of a Justified Sinner* we cannot say for sure whether Robert Wringhim has been corrupted by Satan or was just plain mad.

Applying Todorov's conception of the fantastic to film, *Curse of the Cat People* is an example of the fantastic, whereas its predecessor, *Cat People*, is not. *Cat People* is not a case of the fantastic because by the end of the film, the audience knows that with respect to the fiction, Irena is a shape-changer. It's not her mind, it's her body that's acting up. It might be difficult for the characters in the film to prove this to the police, since the coincidental escape of a genuine panther would make such a demonstration daunting. But by the end of the film there can be no question from the spectator's point of view that Irena is a cat-person. And Todorov's notion of the fantastic requires that when all is said and done, we are unable to plump unhesitatingly for a supernatural explanation over a naturalistic one, or vice versa, with regard to the events in the fiction.

Given a strict reading of Todorov's category of the fantastic, *Vampyr* cannot belong to this genre. There is really no possibility at virtually any point in the film that the events portrayed are anything but supernatural. And surely by the end of the film, there are no grounds for the least suspicion that there could be a naturalistic account of what has happened. So, there is no room for us to hesitate over a supernatural versus a naturalistic hypothesis. Again, whether a fiction is an example of the fantastic depends upon whether when all the results are in, we still feel compelled to suspend judgment between supernatural and natural explanations. But such hesitation cannot be plausibly sustained either during or after a viewing of *Vampyr*.

One aspect of the film that tempts interpreters to classify it as fantastic is a worry about the "reality" status of Gray's second putative dream, i.e., the one where he finds himself in the coffin. Here we may be uncertain as to whether Gray is dreaming or whether his ectoplasmic self has become detached from his body and gone exploring. Now I think that this is pretty clearly a dream sequence. But even if there is uncertainty here, it is difficult to understand what this particular uncertainty has to do with the fantastic. Consider the alternatives: dream versus ectoplasmic detachment. If it is a dream, then that affords no naturalistic explanation, for like the earlier dream, concerning the poison, it is precognitive and, therefore, at least anti-naturalistic. Indeed, prophetic dreams are supernatural phenomena. On the other hand, if it is presumed true, in the fiction, that something like Gray's ectoplasmic alter-ego is wandering around, that too can only be regarded as supernatural. So if uncertainty exists here, it revolves around two options, both of which are supernatural. There is no logical room for naturalism nor, therefore, for the fantastic.

Often the dream/reality contrast figures in the fantastic as a device for advancing the natural/supernatural ambiguity. But the dream/reality contrast is not identical with the natural/supernatural dichotomy. It is a possible, but in nowise inevitable, means of provoking the natural/supernatural hesitation, and it is not the mark of said ambiguity. As *Vampyr* shows, there might for some commentators be an ambiguity about whether the detached Gray is a dreamer or an ectoplasmic self. But since the dream in question would be of a supernatural variety, it can in no way serve to block a supernatural interpretation, which of course is the standard function of dreams in fantastic fictions.

Another scene associated with the possibility of the fantastic in *Vampyr* is the visit from Leone's father. Perhaps, initially, there is some ambiguity about whether the father is a ghost, a dream, or a flesh and blood visitor. But that ambiguity dissipates rather quickly. Given what follows, perhaps even in the very scene in question, the visit is explicable naturalistically, though of course this has no bearing on the fact that we must take the film as a whole to demand an unequivocally supernatural gloss.

There is an intertitle in the film which may seem to open up the possibility of taking the story to be a figment of Gray's imagination, although

I think this can be done only by misreading it. The English translation reads:

There are certain beings whose lives seem tied by invisible bonds to the supernatural. They love solitude.... They dream.... Their imagination is developed to such a point that their vision reaches further than does that of most other men. David Gray's personality was thus mysterious.... One night, lured as usual by fantasy toward the unknown, he arrived very late at the inn which is by the river in the village of Courtempierre.

Undoubtedly, this description associates Gray with fantasy, dream, and imaginative vision. But clearly these notions must be understood from a metaphysical point of view, so to speak, rather than from a psychological one. That is, through imagination, dream, and fantasy, Gray literally has access to the supernatural. Dreaming and fantasy, in this context, are not contrary to the supernatural; they are "invisible bonds" or instrumentalities of the supernatural.

Similarly, the hesitation requisite for the fantastic should not be thought to be rooted in a contrast between events in the fiction that are explained versus events in the fiction that are unexplained. Certainly, in *Vampyr*, there are events for which we are given an explanation – e.g., that vampires can command the shadows of the executed – and other events whose causes remain obscure: the apparition of the vengeful father's head, and, according to some, the thresher grinding to a halt toward the end of the film. However, in all these cases, the events are indisputably supernatural. That we do not always get an account of the underlying occult dynamics does nothing to change their preternatural status, whereas the events that are explained are also indubitably supernatural. So, the observation that some events in the fiction are explained and that some are not has no relevance to the issue of considering the film to be fantastic. In Todorov's terminology, it is marvelous. Yet it is not an example of what Todorov calls the fantastic-marvelous, because we never have any cause to doubt the supernatural provenance of the events in the film.

It might be thought that we could change the definition of the fantastic ever so slightly, so that *Vampyr* would fall under its rubric. We might locate the fantastic hesitation that marks the genre in the characters, rather than in the audience. Todorov himself notes that frequently characters in fantastic stories must weigh supernatural explanations against naturalistic ones. However, such a maneuver is of little moment for our purposes, because none of the characters in *Vampyr* convey the slightest doubt about the supernatural origin of the situation. They show no hesitation. They just believe that there are vampires. Moreover, the distinctiveness and significance of this feature of *Vampyr* can be sharply focused by comparing *Vampyr* with Browning's *Dracula*.

III. *Vampyr* and *Dracula*

I have argued that *Vampyr* does not belong to the genre of the fantastic; rather, it is an example of horror. In regard to Todorov's scheme of categorization, horror would be a subcategory of the marvelous. In my conception of horror, which I have defended elsewhere,[4] it is a necessary condition of such a fiction that it concern the existence of a fantastic being, i.e., a being (which I call a monster) not believed to exist by science. In short, horror requires a positive commitment to the supernatural of the sort that we find in *Vampyr*. Insofar as *Vampyr* is a work of horror, its distinctive effects are best isolated through comparison with other works in that idiom, such as *Dracula*, a film that Dreyer, as noted previously, is said to have had in mind while working on *Vampyr*.

Tod Browning's *Dracula*, and the stage play by Hamilton Deane and John Balderston upon which it is based, offer examples of a narrative structure that I call the complex discovery plot. This structure belongs to a family of plots that have at least fourteen primary variations.[5] In the complex discovery plot, the story is organized in terms of four major movements or functions: onset, discovery, confirmation, and confrontation.

That is, a horror story of this sort starts rolling only when the presence of a monster is indicated – when the monster's onset into the realm of ordinary human affairs is signaled. Suddenly, for example, bodies begin piling up on the beaches, or a little girl starts talking dirty and winds up rotating her head 360 degrees. The onset of the monster can be either implied or portrayed directly – as in the recent remake of *The Blob* when we see it attack the old tramp. Quite often, the onset or manifestation of the monster can be a mix of implication and direct portrayal.

Once the monster is abroad, it is available for discovery. Some person or persons, acting on the behalf of humanity, become aware of the presence of the monster, through either inference or direct observation or a mixture thereof. They know, and the audience knows, that there is a monster shark off the coast, or that a demon is in the child Regan. Moreover, something has got to be done about it.

It is at this point that the plot literally thickens in the complex discovery scenario. For our discoverers typically approach some third party – the local government, the Catholic Church, the United Nations, and so on – in order to secure the aid or authority needed to defeat the monster. However, in this plot variation, the people whom the discoverers approach are initially skeptical about the existence of the monster. It becomes the task of the discoverers to prove the existence of the monster to the powers that be. This involves exercises in ratiocination, and it can be quite suspenseful if the monster is gaining in power or dominion while time is being wasted on trying to convince the authorities of the imminent danger. Finally, one way or another, the existence of the monster becomes incontestable within the world of the fiction, and it must be confronted in one or more debacles upon which the fate of humanity (as we know it) hinges.

Clearly, *Dracula* and the play on which it is based are examples of the complex discovery plot, as, by the way, is the core story of *The Cabinet of Dr. Caligari*. In Browning's film, the onset of Dracula is established through his introduction in Transylvania and his reintroduction in London. In the stage play, the onset begins with the strange doings around Seward's sanitorium in London. Van Helsing, of course, is the discoverer. After he has established to his own satisfaction that the problem is a vampire, he must convince Seward and then Harker – whose aid he needs to thwart Dracula – that vampires exist. That is, he needs to prove his hypothesis against skeptical resistance. This allows him the opportunity to indulge in a mixture of lecturing and argument.

This process of hypothesis, explanation, and debate – which I call the drama of proof – threads through the discovery and confirmation movements of the plot and supplies a special sort of pleasure to the viewers of horror films. Undoubtedly, the drama of proof is more elaborate and protracted in the stage play of *Dracula* than it is in Browning's film. But it is still quite evident in the film, and it allows Van Helsing to repeat a famous little speech about the power vampires derive from our refusal to believe in them. Finally, once the existence of the vampire is confirmed, everything is in place for the final confrontation with the Count.

Obviously, one thing that a complex discovery plot requires is skepticism on the part of some characters about the existence of the monster. This skepticism may be evinced by some characters in the process of discovering the monster, and subsequently there must also be some other character or characters who are prepared to say "there are no such things as vampires" to our discoverers. In terms of the vocabulary of the previous section, the complex discovery plot requires that there be some characters who, for a stretch of time, are beset by fantastic hesitation.

Part of the pleasure for the audience in horror stories of this sort is in tracking the debate with the skeptic and in appreciating the mounting superiority of the supernatural hypothesis. My own feeling is that the drama of proof is especially appropriate in horror fictions insofar as the animating donnée of the genre is the impossible being, a monster, i.e., exactly the sort of thing whose existence calls for proof. But even if I am wrong and there is not this deep consilience between the drama of proof and the horror genre in general, it is clear that the defeat of skepticism about the supernatural is a regularly recurring feature of horror fictions.

When one compares *Vampyr* with *Dracula* with respect to large-scale plot structure, it is immediately apparent that what *Vampyr* lacks is a confirmation function. Gray and then the servant read the book *Vampyr* with utter credulity. It is read, understood, believed, and eventually acted upon. Contrast this to the scene in F. W. Murnau's *Nosferatu* where when Harker first encounters the tome on vampires, he casts it aside with derision. But the book in *Vampyr* has absolute, unquestioned authority in the world of the fiction; indeed, it has absolute authority about the supernatural cast of the world of the fiction for the audience as well. There is no third party whose skepticism must be overcome. In fact, there is no skepticism in the film at all.

In complex discovery plots, skepticism about the supernatural is defeated in the story. A scientific outlook is overthrown. However, it is important to note that the way this proceeds actually involves invoking a higher and more compendious ideal of science or rationality against a putatively more narrow variety. Supposing the world of the fiction, Van Helsing really has a more rational and a more scientific position than Seward does. And this is typical of complex discovery plots. The discoverers typically abide by methods of proof, such as observation and the form of induction called hypothesis to the best explanation. They argue dialectically with the skeptics, and, given the world of the fiction, they are generally portrayed as having the better arguments – i.e., arguments that better comprehend the "facts" posited by the story.

Thus, the affirmation of supernatural agencies in such horror fictions should not be thought of as unqualified rejections of the norms of science and rationality. Rather, in horror fictions, given both what is true and what is justified to believe inside the world of the fiction, it becomes rational to accept the existence of supernatural phenomena, and the confirmation movement in such plots could be said to be part of a process of rationalizing the supernatural for the spectator. The confirmation movement does not, of course, convince the spectator that vampires exist outside the fiction but instead rehearses the grounds that satisfy our standards of probability with respect to the story.

Vampyr forgoes the confirmation function altogether. The existence of the vampire is simply asserted by the intertitles and accepted. Commentators have noted the peculiar dominance of these titles in the film as a whole. The intertitles tend almost single-handedly to pull together and make sense of the otherwise difficult-to-follow narrative, and in this they have an uncharacteristic authority. However, another dimension of that authority, from the perspective of the vampire story, is their unchallenged matter-of-factness. They are all assertion and no argument. No doubt is entertained. They have a dogmatic quality. And this, of course, is the important reason that classifying *Vampyr* as an exercise in the fantastic is problematic. For the fantastic must leave room for skepticism, but skepticism is at odds with the special form of address found in *Vampyr*. Moreover, whereas *Dracula* exploits doubt to secure its rationalizing effect, *Vampyr* presumes a kind of faith on the part of its characters that leaves the audience with no alternative save passive acceptance, no matter how incredible or unintelligible the story as a whole appears.

Of course, the complex discovery plot is not the only narrative format available in horror fiction. And the plot structure of *Vampyr* is a very familiar one. I call it the discovery plot.[6] This is a complex discovery plot minus the confirmation function. It comprises three movements: onset, discovery, and confrontation. Sheridan LeFanu's novella *Carmilla*, upon which *Vampyr* is often said to be loosely based,[7] is a famous example of this plot structure. However, when one compares *Vampyr* with *Carmilla*, one notes again that it lacks the kinds of features to which our discussion of *Dracula* has alerted us.

Throughout *Carmilla*, Laura's father serves as the representative of skepticism, rejecting the superstitions of the peasants and the insinuated supernaturalism of the doctor. He even hatches the improbable naturalistic explanation of Carmilla's somnambulism in order to account for Carmilla's disappearance. General Spielsdorf's final revelation of Carmilla's vampirism, though initially met with skeptical glances, does not require a full-scale exercise in confirmation. But on the other hand, it is *explicitly* delivered with the expectation of being doubted, and it takes the form of an elaborate, proleptic proof for that very reason. The reader is swayed by Spielsdorf's argument about "Millarca," a nearly transparent anagram for "Carmilla," because of the otherwise astounding coincidences between Bertha's illness and Laura's. Thus, though there is no confirmation sequence in *Carmilla*, there is a sustained discovery movement, accompanied by a drama of proof, in the context of skepticism.

Skepticism and proof, doubt and demonstration, and the contest for the title of rationality, though perhaps generally more pronounced in complex discovery plots, are also most frequently integral parts of vampire stories of the discovery variety. But unlike most of its near neighbors in the horror genre, *Vampyr* seems unconcerned with the drama of proof. Insofar as the drama of proof invites the audience to participate in horror films at the level of following and filling out the logic of the relevant arguments, the absence of the drama of proof in *Vampyr* renders its audience more passive than usual. Furthermore, where the drama of proof in some sense helps to satisfy the audience's standards of narrative probability, without it, one's relation to what happens in the fiction is unalloyed acceptance, the viewer's analog to blind faith. One does feel that *Vampyr*'s refusal to make any concession to the possibility of skepticism not only denies the audience its customary pleasure in the rational demonstration of the supernatural, but it also eschews rational accommodation in a way that commands a kind of credulity that for many is curious, if not uncomfortable. The existence of the supernatural is asserted abruptly and authoritatively in the film, as if there were no such thing as modern doubt.

IV. Following *Vampyr*

The large-scale narrational style of *Vampyr* is marked by an austere, unaccommodating, authoritative exposition of supernatural events. This seems to me to parallel certain features of the small-scale narration of the film, by which I mean its movement from event to event, and from scene to scene. Specifically, the tendency in the film to reduce the spectator's role, with respect to the vampire's discovery, to one of passive acceptance is related to, indeed it could be said to reinforce, the plight of the viewer with regard to the moment to moment unfolding of the plot.

As has been mentioned already, the small-scale narration in *Vampyr* is generally said to be hard to follow. And this is certainly true. Moreover, the difficulty one has in following the plot tends to compel and to accentuate the feeling of a passive acceptance of the fiction. But in order to say why this is so, we need to say what it is to follow a story, that is, to assimilate a fiction without difficulty.

I think we can posit without controversy that to follow a story is to find it to be intelligible as it unfolds. But what does it take to find a story intelligible as it is unfolding? My hypothesis is that this involves having a sense of where the story is headed. This does not mean that we must know what will happen next, but only that we have some reasonable expectation about the range of things that could, probabilistically speaking, happen or that will happen next.

"Rome was sacked by Alaric in 410; the Normans defeated the Saxons at Hastings in 1066; John Kennedy was assassinated in 1963" is an exposition of a time-ordered sequence of events, but it is not a followable story. This would become even more apparent if we added twenty or thirty more time-ordered, but still disconnected, events. The reason that such a time-ordered exposition would not be a followable story is that for each earlier stage, we have no sense of the range of things that might come next.

On the other hand, if we read that "As Henry removed the jewels from the safe, he triggered the alarm at the police station," we expect that the ensuing narration will inform us, by either exposition or implication, whether Henry was, in consequence, arrested or how he narrowly eluded apprehension. The narrative – "As Henry removed the jewels from the safe he triggered the alarm, but since there was a demonstration at the police station, the cops were unable to get downtown" – is easy to follow because the later event, the failure of the police to arrive in time, falls within the horizon of expectations that the earlier event description delimits or portends.

Following a story, then, requires that the earlier events in the story guide expectations about the *range* of things that will happen next. We have the impression that a story-event is intelligible just in case it is the kind of thing that we expected would or could happen given the earlier events, problems, and projects in the film. The narrative, so to speak, raises certain questions, which later scenes answer. Narratives appear intelligible to the extent that they deliver answers to the questions that they have already engendered in viewers. Narratives are easy to follow – that is, they impart a sense of intelligibility – as a function of the later events in the narrative falling into the range of expectable, alternative outcomes set up in the earlier stages of the narration.

Now if this characterization of following a narrative is roughly correct, then it is easy to say why *Vampyr* is hard to follow. For with a great many scenes in the film one simply has no grounds to intuit the range of things that might happen next. Compare, for example, Renfield's entry into the realm of the vampire in Browning's *Dracula* with Gray's in *Vampyr*. Before Renfield visits the Count, there is a lot of talk about vampires and Walpurgis Night, which Renfield skeptically discounts, as is customary in stories of this sort. But the discussion of vampires primes the audience about the range of what to expect, and the anomalous events – for example, the bat steering the coach – are assimilated within that framework. On the other hand, when David Gray explores the factory, we have no preparatory framework for integrating what he may or may not find, no sense of who's who, nor what's where in the overall scheme of things. We feel at a loss; we feel perplexed.

Similarly, after the poisoning attempt, we have no firm idea of why David Gray is running across the countryside; and, of course, once he falls into his dream, all bets are off about what will happen next. Nor have we been prepared for Leone's sleepwalk nor for the appearance of the giant head at the end of the film. As the film proceeds, our sense of the temporal order of the film is often simply that of one damn thing following another.

Also, the film upsets our standard tendencies to form narrative expectations in a number of ways. On occasion, it will frustrate our expectations. After Gray leaves the doctor's house for the first time, we see a door swing open of its own accord, and we naturally expect someone to come through it. But instead, the vampire enters from an unseen stairwell screen right. Moreover, the languid pacing of scenes, like the activity in the house after the father dies, makes it difficult to form expectations. There is such a clutter of what looks like unnecessary detail that one loses a sense of what might be important and, therefore, a sense of what is at stake and what might come next.

Undoubtedly, there are points in the film where our expectations are in place; when the doctor flees, we expect that either he will escape or, more likely, that he will be destroyed. So the point is not that we have no expectations whatsoever, but only that for long segments we are uncharacteristically at sea in a way that shapes our overall experience of the film. We may characterize that experience by saying that it lacks a strong protentive structure; we are often not in a position to project the direction the story will take because quite frequently there are no cues for anticipation in it. Where a film elicits a strong sense of expectation and where what subsequently happens concords with that arc of anticipation, we have the feeling of participating in its unfolding. But in *Vampyr* that feeling is generally unavailable, reducing us to the role of passive acceptance.

Vampyr is hard to follow, but it is important to emphasize that *Vampyr* is not hard to understand. We don't find it difficult to say what happened after the film is over. In retrospect, everything falls into place. But following a film is not simply a matter of retrospective understanding. It involves the active, protentive projection of the directions the story is likely to take as it unfolds. And this is what it is hard to do in response to *Vampyr*.

One might be prone to think that a major source of this problem with narrative expectation involves the often cited spatial dislocations within the film. However, I am tempted to think that this reverses the order of things. Where a spectator has a strong protentive sense of the story, she is, I believe, less likely to notice spatial anomalies. When Dracula comes onto the deck in Browning's film, we get an impossible point-of-view shot of him watching the crew battling a sea squall. But I think few are jarred by this just because we know protentively what is going on. Dracula is sizing up his next meal. However, we are more prone to notice cinematic incongruities and to be perplexed by them when it is already the case that we are not following the story.

The difficulty in following the small-scale narration of the story in *Vampyr* parallels the tendency in the large-scale narration to forgo the drama of proof. In the latter case, we are denied the customary pleasure of following an argument, i.e., of anticipating, projecting, and rehearsing its moves. In the former case, it is following the story that is problematized. Horror films, indeed films in general, that employ the drama of proof and followable stories, in the sense in which I use those terms, impart a feeling that one is participating in the evolution of the narrative. But in *Vampyr*, one feels that the story, so to say, is being projected *at* us rather than *with* us.

This feeling of diminished participation or exclusion from participation is key to the distinctive effect of *Vampyr*. And this is why classifying the film as an example of the fantastic is so misleading. For the fantastic requires a participatory spectator, whereas *Vampyr* leaves little room for one. It tends to reduce the spectator to passive acceptance – passive acceptance of what often seems virtually unintelligible both in terms of narrative expectations and in terms of the canons of rationality operative in the genre.

Of course, when I speak of the spectator's role as one of passive acceptance, this is a term of art meant to characterize the qualities of our experience of *Vampyr* in contrast to the specific levels of participation typically found in the horror genre. By talking of passive acceptance, I do not mean to imply that the spectator accepts the existence of vampires or that there is no cognitive processing going on. I merely want to give a name to the role that *Vampyr* imposes on its viewers and to the dominant affective qualities of the film. However, though my use of the notion of passive spectatorship here is contextually stipulative, it is not entirely disconnected from the realm of genuine belief and real-life acceptance. For one has the sense that Dreyer has designed the large-scale and the small-scale exposition of *Vampyr* in order to set up a homology between the fiction and its passive acceptance, on the one hand, and the supernatural and faith, on the other. Thus, by constraining the spectator's role to that of passive acceptance, Dreyer secures the structural wherewithal to express his own conviction that the response to the supernatural should be faith.

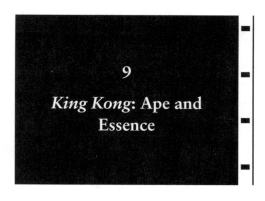

Because its basic subject matter is fear, the horror film is a popular-genre vehicle that is prone to manifesting the specific anxieties that dominate the cultural context in which it was made. For example, horror films of the late seventies and early eighties – e.g., *Alien* (1979), *The Thing* (1982), *Dawn of the Dead* (1979), *Halloween I & II* (1978 & 1982), the *Friday the 13th* series, *The Evil Dead* (1983), and so on – emphasize the recurring theme of survival at a time in American history when economic circumstances have transformed the mere "bottom-line" commendation that "he/she is a survivor" into the highest badge of achievement that one can hope for. Likewise, the thirties' theme of the unjustly alienated monster, such as Frankenstein's progeny, signaled the depression anxiety of being cast out of civil society due to impoverishment; the fifties' invasion obsession reflected internal politics and the apprehension engendered there; and the early seventies' infatuation with possession and telekinesis announced a complex fantasy of powerlessness combined with infantile delusions of omnipotence during a period when it was a common experience to be enraged at being at the utter mercy of the seemingly unpredictable shifts in the national and international economy. The purpose of this article is to examine the social anxieties submerged in the classic horror film *King Kong* (1933), which, interestingly enough, literalizes survival metaphors that bear a noteworthy relation to those found in contemporary tales of terror.

King Kong is one of the miracles of cinema, beguiling audiences of all ages and every intellectual pretension. It is a film that abounds with interpretations. These come in many shapes and sizes – Kong as Christ, Kong as Black, Kong as commodity, Kong as rapist, Kong enraptured by *L'amour fou*, Kong as Third World, Kong as dream, Kong as myth, Kong according to Freud, according to Jung, and even according to

"*King Kong*: Ape and Essence," *Planks of Reason*, ed. B. Grant (Metuchen, NJ: Scarecrow Press, 1984), pp. 215–244.

Lacan. The 1976 version of *King Kong* selects a few of these interpretations – notably Kong as Third World, Kong as commodity and *L'amour fou* – and makes them explicit; the helicopters seem to sweep in from the Mekong Delta and the swooning heroine suggests that Kong is not always alone in his madness. Yet the remake seems so much the worse for its clarification. For certainly part of the fascination of the original was its openness to interpretive play.

What I wish to explore here is an aspect of *Kong* that has been given scant attention heretofore – what I call its evolutionary theme. I am not offering this theme in order to reject previous interpretations but because it seems to me that this theme can be used to answer certain questions about *Kong*. Some of these concern the incessant repetition of visual and narrative motifs, especially in the second half of the film. Some examples of these repetitions include: the sacrifice of Darrow on a platform with her arms splayed/the visually similar "crucifixion" of Kong in New York; Kong fights a snake-like reptile/he attacks a subway; Kong climbs to the summit of Skull Mt./Kong climbs the Empire State Building; Kong fights a pterodactyl/Kong fights the rickety bi-planes. There are more of these repetitions and I will discuss them later. Even the 1976 remake of *Kong* acknowledges them, though characteristically in an all-too-conspicuous way when, in a flashback, we catch on to Kong's interest in the World Trade Center. The repetitions in the original function to equate the island with Manhattan and this raises questions not only about why the equation is forged but also about what significance it could have for its audience. I will try to answer both these by reference to an implicit theme of evolution in *Kong*. Specifically, *Kong* can be seen as a popular illustration of Social Darwinist metaphors which, in turn, were and to some extent still are generally held articles of faith of the American *weltanschauung*, shared by every class. In this light, the equation of the city with the jungle is perfectly fitting – almost "natural." What seems like an incongruous, surrealist metaphor is really a literalization of a banal but persuasive American belief about the nature of society.

To appreciate the basic elements of the evolutionary theme in *Kong*, it is helpful to examine its sources. One might think that this is a monumental task, requiring us to go back to the earliest tales of heroes and dragons. But this is not the case. For though *Kong* is packed with dinosaurs and though dinosaurs appear to be our best cues for identifying the subgenre that *Kong* inhabits, *Kong* is not even peripherally a dragon story. The reason is simple: dinosaurs do not belong to the same symbolic species as dragons. Dragons, from Egypt onward, are fusion figures, condensing metaphysical forces such as earth, air, fire, and water into one composite entity. The recent *Dragonslayer* (1981), for example, carries on this tradition; its dragon walks, crawls, and lives underground (earth), it flies (sky), belches flame (fire), and sleeps underwater, as well as compounding biological parts of different genera, a tendency most pronounced in the dragonelles, which look like bulldog-lizards. Dinosaurs, on the other hand, are not composite creatures and the ideas we associate with them are inextricably bound up with our ideas of the pre-historic. Thus, as symbols, dinosaurs and their fictional lost world are rather modern, i.e., as modern as our concept of pre-history.

There is no ancient literature concerning dinosaurs because our knowledge of dinosaurs is only two centuries old. Fossils, mostly imprints of sea life, were familiar in the Middle Ages but few persons, save da Vinci, had any glimmering of what they were; many thought that they were the residues of abortive trial runs that God had made at creation before he succeeded. The first significant fossil find of a dinosaur occurred in 1780 in a gravel-pit at Pietersberg, near Maestricht in Holland. The skeleton was shipped in 1794 as a trophy of war to Paris where it was analyzed by Georges Cuvier, who, on the basis of this find plus his analyses of the American mastodon, a Siberian mammoth and a small Bavarian pterodactyl, declared that the earth had once been populated by creatures now extinct.

The name "dinosaur" (*deinos* – "Terrifying"; *sauros* – "Lizard") was coined in 1842 by Sir Richard Owen, a man who was quite instrumental in implanting the creatures in the popular imagination. In 1852, Joseph Paxton's Crystal Palace was dismantled and reconstructed in Sydenham, where it was to be a permanent display for the achievements of art and science. Owen, at the suggestion of Prince Albert, was asked to decorate the grounds with life-sized models of his dinosaurs. Here we find the popular prototypes of all those lumbering movie monsters. The models were executed by Benjamin Waterhouse Hawkins in 1853 and they are referred to in Dickens' *Bleak House*. The next fifty years witnessed a lively and at times extremely competitive proliferation of models and paintings of dinosaurs, many produced for museums and universities. Working under Willis O'Brien, Marcel Delgado used such paintings by Charles R. Knight from the American Museum of Natural History in New York as models for the creatures in *The Lost World* (1925). By that time the visage of the dinosaur and the "look" of the prehistoric world – including dinosaurs locked in an archetypal clash for survival – had been etched graphically in the popular mind.

There could be no fiction of the prehistoric world variety until the scientific conception of it had taken root. The earliest significant appearance of dinosaurs in literature occurs in Chapter 33 of Jules Verne's *Journey to the Center of the Earth*. Professor Lidenbrock and his nephew watch from afar as two sea monsters struggle. They are not victims of the beasts but rather observers, which is much in keeping with the rest of the book – Verne's work is not presented as allegorically satiric in the manner of forerunners such as Ludwig Holberg's *A Journey to the World Underground* (1742) and the anonymous *A Voyage to the World in the Center of the Earth* (1755); instead, Verne's is a heuristic device for propagating the most recent science.[1]

In *Journey to the Center of the Earth*, adventure is less important than detail and description; if you ever need to know about the equipment you'll need to explore caves, read this book. Verne's characters catalogue the stratas of the earth and even spy a human leading a mastodon in the distance. But unlike later exercises in this genre, to which *King Kong* is indebted, *Journey to the Center of the Earth* is written from a pre-Darwinian point of view and its heroes steer clear of direct confrontation with these prehistoric creatures.

The prehistoric world genre was most popular from the 1880s to the 1930s. At first, the earth's poles were favored locations for lost worlds but Southeast Asia also was a draftable locale, perhaps as a result of the growing dissemination of information about the discovery of Angkor Thom. In some cases, the prehistoric motif was conjoined with the Atlantean, as in Cutcliffe Hyne's *The Lost Continent* (1900). Such novels continued to be written after WWI: Karl zu Eulenburg's *Die Brunnen der Grossen Tiefe* (1926) and Owen Rutter's *The Monster of Mu* (1932) are two examples. The subgenre of the missing link, which is relevant to *King Kong* since the anthropomorphized gorilla may be seen as one, was also active at this time and included entries like Gouverneur Morris's *The Pagan's Progress* (1904), Carl Edward's *Two-Legs* (1906), and F. Britten Austin's *When Mankind Was Young* (1926). Throughout this period a number of plot elements – which are essential to *Kong* – as well as their cultural associations were in the process of being established .

The best known and probably the best written – at least the wittiest – prehistoric creature story is Sir Arthur Conan Doyle's *The Lost World* (1912). It begins with a rollicking satire of academics and proceeds to a plateau in South America that is swarming with dinosaurs. Among other adventures, Prof. Challenger and his confreres help the savage humans of the lost world to overcome their more ape-like foes.

Since Challenger is mistaken by the ape types as one of their own, it seems fair to say that Doyle is turning something that could be treated as intra-species tribal warfare into inter-species warfare for territorial dominance. The prehistoric world is presented under the metaphor of war at the same time that war is cast as inter-species competition. It is hard to resist seeing *The Lost World* as an apology for colonialism. Anglo-Saxons arrive with their superior technology and know-how and aid the "human" population to gain its rightful place by defeating its subhuman competitors. This is achieved against a backdrop of clashing dinosaurs – the paradigm or associated picture in the popular imagination of, indeed the icon for, "the survival of the fittest."

The combination of dinosaurs with the biologically charged characterization of battling nation/tribes (in which the "humans" are aided by Europeans) is a recurring motif in prehistoric tales; it registers the application of intrinsically nondramatic biological concepts like "competition" and "survival" to social contexts where the biological concepts become particularized, dramatized, and literalized. Fictional interracial warfare replete with a background of battling dinosaurs is not really so far removed from political polemics like the American Rev. Josiah Strong's *Our Country: Its Possible Future and Its Present Crisis*, wherein the confrontation of Anglo-Saxon ideals with other races is envisioned in terms of the survival of the fittest. This tendency to translate the terms of pure biological theory into vivid, combat-oriented metaphors for picturing society was rife at the turn of the century and prehistoric tales may, therefore, be seen in conjunction with the currency of Social Darwinism .

The man who was most responsible for crystallizing the motifs of the prehistoric world adventure – undoubtedly because he wrote so many stories in this genre – was Edgar Rice Burroughs. Burroughs' lost world, Caspak, is elaborated in three novels: *The Land That Time Forgot*, *The People That Time Forgot* and *Out of the Abyss*, all copyrighted in 1918.[2] Caspak is located somewhere in the South Pacific, near the Antarctic; it is uncharted; its towering cliffs make it impenetrable . Also, the layout of Caspak recapitulates Burroughs' idea of evolution. One end of the island is completely prehistoric. As one progresses inland, life reaches higher and higher grades on the evolutionary scale. Most of the fully human people of Caspak, the Galu, have undergone complete primate evolution during their own lifetime. They are "cor sva jo," or "from the beginning," which means they were spawned as apes at the far end of the island; each day they wade in revivifying puddles; and at times some of them hear the call, and walk to the next stage of evolution, biologically transformed. One day you're an ape-man, an Alu, and suddenly you are changed and you travel to the next, more human, niche in evolution; you join the tribe of the club-men, the Bo-lu. Next you become a Sto-lu (hatchet man), a Band-lu (spear-man), a Kro-lu (bow-man), and so on. These are not just tribe/nations but tribes that are also differentiated as distinct species. Where Verne depicted the spatial concept of the earth's stratification by means of time, i.e., a journey that is somewhat like a tour, Burroughs visualizes the temporal concept of evolution through space – the map of Caspak is a fictional evolutionary time line.

All of Caspak is at war; the modern visitors arrive only to be immediately attacked by dinosaurs. The Darwinian struggle for survival, complete with giant reptiles, begins as soon as their submarine surfaces. Caspak is an almost Hobbesian state of nature: "It is the way in Caspak. If you do not kill, we shall be killed, therefore it is wise to kill first whomever does not belong to one's tribe ," To-mar tells Tom Billings in *The People That Time Forgot*. To be caught outside one's tribal/species territory is certain death, even though all the primates are at least dimly aware that they are connected through Caspak's strange biological design. Caspak is not only a microcosm of evolution but a microcosm of social relations as seen through a Social Darwinian optic, a jungle where the law of every living thing is strife.

The smartest species on Caspak is not exactly human. Called Weiroos, they are all male and winged. They kidnap Galu women in order to propagate their species. It is understood in Caspak that whichever intelligent species is first to procreate viviparously will dominate Caspak. Two themes of evolution – breeding and dominance – are thus conjoined in a rough, symbolic, popular mechanics sort of imagery that also gives an added significance to Burroughs' favorite plot device, the abduction of human women by nonhumans.[3]

Burroughs was an extremely repetitive writer, which probably accounts for the massive number of novels he produced in such a short time. Certain formulas are repeated with unnerving frequency – heroes are often described as never-being-what-you'd-call-a-ladies'-man just before romantic scenes, and the hero's prowess in this or that kind of collegiate athletics is adduced just before the performance of some incredible physical feat. Certain plot situations also appear almost mandatory in the Caspak series, and in the vastly similar Pellucidar series – for example, the escape from the enemy capital. Indeed, the overall plot structures of these books are strikingly similar. In each of the Caspak books, the male protagonist, in the course of the adventure, falls in love with a woman and the plot unravels as the hero and heroine are separated – often the female is abducted by a nonhuman – and then rejoined. Each of the novels climaxes with the final reunion of the lovers. In the first two Pellucidar novels, David seems to make a habit of rescuing Dian the Beautiful from Phutra, the Mahar capital. Burroughs undoubtedly uses this structure because it is an easy way to generate scenes, resolutions, and sequels, and it occurs in his non-prehistoric novels, such as *Princess of Mars* and *Tarzan of the Apes*, as well.[4] But the pattern is especially interesting in his ersatz Darwinian chronicles where the abduction of the potential "wife and mother" occurs in a context where procreation is an explicit element in the battle for species survival. Burroughs, of course, was not the only American writer working in a Social Darwinist vein; Theodore Dreiser, Jack London and Hamlin Garland each mobilize a Social Darwinist perspective derived from Herbert Spencer. But Burroughs not only crudely applies "Darwinian" principles in his fictional characterization of society; he also creates a world – a paleontological nightmare where humans and dinosaurs coexist – populated by what the popular mind would associate with the basic characters of the theory of evolution.

King Kong owes much of its narrative structure and several of its plot elements to the prehistoric story as it was popularized by Burroughs. The military/war theme is introduced in the beginning of the film with a discussion of the excessive amount of munitions that Denham has loaded onto the ship; the mention of "gas grenades," in particular, seems to allude fleetingly to WWI. Denham's group, in the tradition of the prehistoric story, is a technologically savvy team, and Driscoll, pursuing Kong with only a knife, stripped, so to speak, of his technology, is also in the Burroughs lineage – it is as if modern man must prove his superiority in primitive terms before he can reap the benefits of his technology. Also, at least initially, Kong, the King, is presented as a tyrant who exacts merciless tribute; he holds the natives in a reign of terror and, in this, is like the Weiroos, and the Mahars of Pellucidar. On the other hand, he is also akin biologically to the various, partly sentient ape-men that populate many prehistoric tales. Though nothing is made of it, the technologically superior whites do liberate the human natives. This is not the crux of *King Kong* nor is it a theme that receives any emphasis. Yet one can still see submerged in *Kong* the structural elements of the species liberation plot.

Kong generates action much in the manner of Burroughs. The second part of the film is organized around two abductions of Ann Darrow by a nonhuman, eventually followed by two rescues. Kong performs the function of the tyrannical, nonhuman races à la Burroughs. Also, Kong seems to be a race of one, which effectively makes that race, like the Weiroos, entirely male. *Son of Kong* (1933), aside from being an occasion of lewd jokes and speculation, may, in part, seem so misconceived because it tampers with the implied myth of the earlier film – that King Kong is absolutely singular and unique, the only one of his kind, profoundly alone, and ultimately a fit object of pathos for that reason – like the Frankenstein monster. Of course, the fundamental structural device of abduction/rescue in Kong diverges from its use in Burroughs because first, rather than follow the exploits of the rescuer, *Kong* stresses the *heroic* exploits of the abductor; and second, the virtues of the abductor – not only courage but gentleness, and certain ingratiating anthropomorphic traits, including childlikeness, confusion and even timorousness with regard to Darrow – overshadow the abductor's earlier identification as a cruel tyrant, as a force of pure evil. Nevertheless, large chunks of the film derive their narrative coherence, their pretext and resolution, from the abduction/rescue structure whose internal logic resembles the relation of a question to an answer.

Moreover, *Kong*'s primary method of filling in the actions that transpire between pretexts and resolutions – its plot complications, in other words – is also straight Burroughs: viz., a series of rough and tumble confrontations, hair-raising battles between Kong and various other contestants, often undertaken to protect the heroine. These are very repetitive and to hold our interest they depend to a large extent on how inventive the narrative is in finding more and more outrageous sparring partners for *Kong*. And, of course, *King Kong* is quite amazing in this regard.

But perhaps *King Kong*'s most important debt to Burroughs is its tendency to mold the prehistoric tale in such a way that it suggests itself as an exemplification of a Social Darwinist *view* of our society. In Burroughs, Caspak and Pellucidar are literalizations of Social Darwinist metaphors as applied to politics. Burroughs' American readers could have assimilated his imagery unblinkingly; they had already been accustomed for decades to hearing politicians, clergymen and popular lecturers, like Edward Livingston Youmans, invoke Darwinian rhetoric to describe civil society.[5] *King Kong* does not refer its Darwinian imagery to politics; yet its portrait of ill-tempered monsters struggling tooth and claw for survival does relate to another aspect of society – the economy.

The third scene of the film – Denham's search for a starlet (even if he has to marry one) – makes this reference unavoidable. Denham sadly peruses a queue of women at a soup kitchen; he saves Darrow, caught pilfering fruit, from the law, and the Depression looms large in their subsequent discussion, which not only dwells on her unemployment but which intentionally (though finally fallaciously) suggests that Denham's proposition is just that, an offer of prostitution or white slavery to a woman at the mercy of a depressed economy. For all the ensuing sound and fury, it is hard to shake the memory of these early scenes; the detail makes the Depression an unforgettable character in *King Kong*. Also, the plot of *King Kong* is subtended by the same fantasy that one finds in early thirties' musicals; like *42nd Street, Gold Diggers of 1933* and *Footlight Parade* (all 1933). *Kong* holds out the prospect that a show, in this case a movie, is just the panacea the characters need to chase the Depression away. The presence of the Depression in the film thus leads one to connect the jungle imagery to the economy. That is, the breakdown of the marketplace brings up the issue of the marketplace, which, in Kong, is juxtaposed with (later collapsed into) the prehistoric world. And the marketplace, as represented by that great emporium, New York City, is identified with the jungle.

The use of the Social Darwinist idiom to describe the economy and the operation of the marketplace was established by the late nineteenth century. Darwinian metaphors provided an attractive argot for robber barons.[6] Nor is Social Darwinism simply the language of financial giants. Small businessmen and free agents still attempt to glowingly excuse, at least to themselves, mercantile improprieties on the grounds that in the jungle anything goes; surviving is what counts.

At the same time, Darwinian metaphors could and can still be used pejoratively; business and the marketplace may be excoriated as a jungle or as ruled by the law of the jungle, as it was by Upton Sinclair in 1906. Of course, Protestant America had a pre-Darwinian prototype for condemning business via bestial imagery in Martin Luther's maledictions on usurers, who, he said, ". . . oppress and ruin the small merchants, as the pike the little fish in the water, just as though they were lords over God's creatures and free from all the laws of faith and love." And another negative, though not morally strident, use of the jungle metaphor is that of an anxious, dispirited mood which accepts the competitiveness, heartlessness and treacherousness of the marketplace as a necessary but bitter fact of life. In this sense the jungle metaphor is a sign of resignation that acquiesces to the pronouncements of the robber barons not with jubilance but with a twinge of lost innocence. The jungle is perilous, exhausting, with potential tragedy on every side (not only for others but for oneself), a battlefield on which the bottom line, survival, is the most one holds out for. This possibility of the jungle/business metaphor is, of course, most serviceable in times of economic crisis when "survival" comes to feel like a characterization of everyday life. That this jungle/business metaphor can be either honorific or horrific is less important for an initial understanding of *King Kong* than the fact that the Darwinian jungle was a readily accepted figure for the market in the culture in which *Kong* was made. For this is what makes the otherwise oxymoronic combination of the prehistoric jungle and the entrepot of world capitalism so singularly appropriate. Kong carries the battle for survival, with all its prehistoric trappings, to the heart of New York.

The leisurely pace of the first part of *King Kong* – i.e. the ocean voyage – is actually quite deceptive. A great deal of thematic work is being done throughout this section, even if the narrative seems to be merely lolling about. From the very first scene, with the guard and the theatrical agent, the audience's expectations are thrown in gear. At first, this is done through unexplained incongruity. The watchman says the voyage is crazy, that Denham is crazy and that the crew is three times larger than the ship requires. Why? Our questions are intensified in the very next scene. More unexplained incongruities are introduced in the captain's cabin when, in the course of discussions about insurance, possible government inspection and Denham's inability to acquire a starlet, we learn that these difficulties stem from the fact that the ship is carrying enough ammunition and gas bombs to blow up the harbor, and that even the skipper doesn't know where they're headed. Denham's secrecy is used to explain why Denham must find his own actress but the secret itself remains unexplained, pulling the audience ahead along an arc of anticipation. Throughout the introduction, the theme of the secret continues, the careful escalation of the mystery distributed in such a way as to periodically revitalize our flagging interest by reminding us of the secret that the film promises to reveal. At first, Denham is coyly vague about the secret; Darrow asks their destination and he liltingly says, "a long way off." Then he becomes evasive: when Driscoll asks what they're going to do when they reach the island, Denham retorts, ". . . How do I know, I'm not a fortune teller." At the same time, Denham suggests that he knows more than he cares to say. He keeps harping on the "Beauty and the Beast" slogan; indeed, he even remarks to himself, at one point, "I'm going right into a theme song here." The allusion to "Beauty and the Beast" supplies only a hazy forecast of things to come but it gives us just enough information to prime expectancies.

Denham ups the ante somewhat in the scene where he discloses the location of the island. It is as if his previous vagueness were getting a little threadbare, and, to remedy the problem, a few more details are added to tweak the spectator. The information is, however, still vague and only suggestive. Map in hand, he ominously points to the wall of the island: "The natives keep that wall in repair. They need it." Somewhat elliptically, he moves to the subject of why the natives need the wall by asking if the captain has ever heard of Kong. The captain thinks it's a native god and Denham defines Kong teasingly and obscurely, mostly through negation: "Well, anyway, neither beast nor man. Something monstrous, all-powerful, still living, still holding that island in a grip of deadly fear," and "I tell you there's something on that island that no white man has ever seen." When Driscoll sarcastically observes that Kong might not like his picture taken, Denham has a smart-aleck answer prepared, one he delivers with know-it-all nonchalance: "Well, now you know why I brought along those cases of gas bombs." This partially answers one of our earlier questions but at the price of an even greater mystery: what in the world could Kong be?

This mystery is first raised in the dialogue but is then accentuated visually in the next scene, the screen/scream test. This sequence is virtually a template from which much of the rest of the film will be struck. Darrow, in medium shot, stands in a satiny medieval outfit, her eyes downcast, fiddling with her fingers like Lillian Gish. Following Denham's offscreen directions, she, prophetically, looks higher and higher, and finally starts screeching repeatedly, at the timbre that has earned Fay Wray a reputation for having the greatest lungs in the history of film. This one shot is the germ of numerous similar ones in the second half of the film, though at this point we don't realize that Denham, figuratively speaking, is shooting much of the film to be. Denham's directions heighten our curiosity but supply us only with affect rather than details. He says, "Now you look higher. Still higher. Now you see it. You're amazed. Your eyes open wider. It's horrible, Ann, but you can't look away. There's no chance for you, Ann – no escape. You're helpless, Ann, helpless. There's just one chance. If you can scream – but your throat's paralyzed. Scream, Ann, cry. Perhaps if you didn't see it you could scream. Throw your arms across your face and scream, scream for your life." As the peals of terror still echo in our ears, the camera cuts to Driscoll, who asks our question for us: "What's he think she's really going to see?" Diabolically, the camera dissolves to a low-angle shot of the ship swathed in fog – so we can barely see anything. Imagery of fog or mist recurs throughout the rest of the film with gray-miasmic connotations of obscurity, primordialness, fantasy, dream-likeness, and ghostly presence. At this point in the film, it coincides with the approach to the island, capping off the theme of mystery, the major narrative motor thus far, with the fog as a visual correlative for the unknown, the faintly perceived, the vague outline wrapped in uncertainty.

The ship approaches Kong's island in a thick fog that marks the threshold or passageway into a new realm. The pace of the ship seems slow and gliding. The tone of this imagery, if not downright supernaturalist, is that of quiet, pregnant danger, as the adventurers float, virtually blind, into the unseen/unknown. The visual opacity in and of itself raises apprehensions; the dialogue about what they will see quickens its banefulness. Asked how he will know the right island when he sees it, Denham says that it has a mountain shaped like a skull. Death lurks in this soup. Next, the sense of unknown menace – menace, in large part, *because* it is unknown – jumps a notch when Denham resolves the ambiguity of some offscreen sound effects: "It's not breakers, it's drums." The traditional horror film makes a special moment of the approach toward unseen danger – e.g., the doorways in *Psycho* and *The Exorcist*. The threshold, and the unseen/unthinkable thing beyond it are perhaps the prime, interrelated themes of the classical horror film. In *Kong*, the island itself is made into the object of this anxiety; instead of an unseen chain clanking in the night, drums beat in the fog; it might be the wind, it might be the breakers. Instead of preparatory ghost legends, we are told that the island itself is the image of death.

Another major theme that is broached in the opening sequences is that of self-advertisement. Through the conceit of the film-within-the-film, *Kong* constantly informs us about how we are to take it. *Kong*, more or less, writes its own reviews, telling us what to think about it as it goes along. Denham's comments about the film he's going to make, and Denham's remarks about the adventure he's engaged in rebound, so to speak, from inside the film and stick to *King Kong* itself. No other film has ever been as self-congratulatory as *Kong*. It is a swaggering, arrogant film that spends much of its time telling us how great it is, yet its blustering, gigantic view of itself is not off-putting; somehow it accords with the circus-exaggerated energy that is its most distinctive quality.

Denham starts the proceedings with "I'm going to make the greatest picture in the world. Something that no one has seen or even heard of. They'll have to think of a lot of new adjectives when I get back." Played by Robert Armstrong with the manner and gusto of a carny barker, Denham convinces Darrow to be his star by saying, "It's money, adventure and fame. It's the thrill of a lifetime. . . ." Denham is the epitome of the advertising huckster; his obsession with "Beauty and the Beast" is that of a salesman trying to find a tag-line for a new product. What Denham manages to advertise most is *King Kong*. Arriving at the native ceremony, he reminds us, "Holy mackerel, what a show ," while Darrow asks us, "Isn't this exciting?" *Kong* is the quintessential American film – its self-image is so enormous. Denham can only speak in superlatives; Darrow is "the bravest girl"; or, to Capt. Englehorn, "I tell you, this Kong is the biggest thing in the world." It is, of course, very difficult to separate our reactions to Kong and to *King Kong*, a fact that their titular identification only enhances. Thus, when Denham abandons the film project for something more ambitious, viz. Kong, it has the effect of praising the movie he (Denham) is in – "We came here to get a motion picture and we found something worth all the motion pictures in the world." Denham hatches the ultimate ad for *King Kong* immediately after he gasses the beast into submission – ". . . in a few months, it will be up in lights on Broadway: *Kong, The Eighth Wonder of the World*." And, naturally, it is, just as quick as you can say "dissolve."

King Kong is the sort of film that is apt, in current critical parlance, to be designated reflexive. It not only contains the film-within-a-film conceit, but it could be argued that it bares its own devices – the screen test as metafilmic gesture – and it displays, indirectly, the hysterical cadences and hyperbole of Hollywood advertising. Undoubtedly, the element in *Kong* that most tempts us toward a reflexive interpretation is the fact that so much of it is devoted to the subject of putting on a show. The film begins as the story of a movie and turns into the story of a theatrical. Also, the film-within-a-film conceit turns the native dances into the kind of exotic, ethnic extravaganzas that were popular in the thirties and forties and date back at least to the Chicago World's Fair, and to the San Francisco Fair of 1893, while the procession leading Darrow to the sacrificial altar strikes the viewer as pure, staged spectacle. The capture of Kong reminds one of the culture hero Frank Buck, whose *Bring 'em Back Alive* was published in 1931; Buck, of course, was famous for supplying zoos and circuses with wild animals for exhibition, and the Kong-show at Madison Square Garden is of the nature of a circus feature – one recalls Ringling Brothers Barnum and Bailey's famous gorilla Gargantua, billed as the largest ape in captivity . Also, there is the surge of media-hype throughout *King Kong*, and one feels that had Denham completed his own film its potentially prurient content could have turned it into an exploitation vehicle following in the footsteps of Congo Pictures' *Ingagi* (1930), a film that promised "documentary" footage of a woman being sacrificed to an ape.

Yet for all the references to cinema and show business that one can find in *Kong*, it seems mistaken to identify the film as a significant example of reflexivity. Its primary function is not to make us aware of the processes of filmmaking. Rather, the show business topics and allusions function expressively, supplying a mood and an energy, an increment of brashness and excitement and shameless vulgarity. If *Kong* were not so profane in its handling of myth, so boisterous in its self-advertisement, it would not be so perfect a reflector of its time and place. Its celebration of naive, unselfconscious opportunism and of an imagination at once grandiose and shallow, fantastical and pragmatic, presents a mirror of pre-WW II America, and not an unflattering one. For in its vulgarity – just like an American to crucify a god and then sell tickets to it – there is strength and vitality. And it is that quality or feeling of an admixture of hokum and enthusiasm, superficiality and profound energy, that the movie and show business motifs serve to project. The show business razzmatazz and self-advertising serve to incarnate the *geist* of unsophisticated American dynamism .

The character of Denham is central to this effect. In a number of senses, it is his story. It is Denham who persistently embellishes and editorializes on the action. He is a hustler and a loudmouth, sanctimonious but pragmatic, a P. T. Barnum type. And though, at times, we are meant to resent him – why does he take these risks? why doesn't he leave well enough alone? – he emerges positively because he is driving, manic, an artist/businessman, a dreamer/doer whose conceptions – outlandish, insensitive, sensational in the most trivial way, awesome, enterprising, and empty-headed – consume every ounce of his estimable energy. He is a sincere confidence man, an American *par excellence*, a rapacious innocent. We can view Denham nostalgically, overlooking the horrible things he does, and admire his untroubled, ignorant vitality, his arrogant energy. The show biz hoopla is as much an end-in-itself as it is a means for the Denham character. Promotion becomes a way of being-in-the-world, if not introspective, at least intense and active, something which *Kong*'s first audiences could recognize as a source of American pride and a behavioral model, though not one exactly strong on morals. Denham predates The Ugly American. He is just an American, aspiring, noisy, crude but alive.

Denham is a combination of two familiar thirties' movie figures: the newspaperman à la It Happened One Night (1934) and The Front Page (1931), and the show business artiste à la Twentieth Century (1934) and myriad backstage musicals. Denham is related to the newspaper image not only because he is a documentary filmmaker of sorts, and, consequently, some kind of purveyor of facts, but because he thinks and talks like a movie newspaperman – e.g., the journalists at Madison Square Garden "stumble" on the "Beauty and the Beast" routine and Denham hurriedly okays it as if he'd never heard it before. Denham is also cut from the same cloth as someone like the Jimmy Cagney character in Footlight Parade. Both the newspaperman and the show person (whether actor, actress, impresario, or director) in thirties' movie iconography stand for a special race of people who think (and speak) faster than mere mortals. Their diction is slangy, rapid, rhythmic and sarcastic, and they represent a wise-acre, cynical view of the world that sizes up and sees through things, that lays it on the line with jazzy candor to the everyday types in the films. Show business and journalism, in the movies of the period, at least, give one a special purchase on the truth; they are ways of being-in-the-world which can be described under the rubric of knowingness. That Denham combines the iconographic movie authority of the journalist and show person, of course, gives the self-advertisement of King Kong all the more weight.

A third major theme is also set in motion in the captain's cabin in New York – that of a defensive attitude toward women, enunciated in almost boyish extremes of contempt. Denham mewls questioningly whether anyone thinks he wants to "haul a woman" along on his adventure and whether there isn't adventure in the world "without a flapper in it." This theme of disdain for women is developed during the ocean voyage. One part of the theme unfolds apace with the budding Driscoll/Darrow romance which begins when Driscoll accidentally cuffs her – Darrow should have known enough to abandon ship right then and there – and then tells her to stay below for the duration of the journey. Initially Driscoll informs Darrow that merely by being around, she causes trouble. With a manifestly adolescent fear of sex, Driscoll says, "You're alright, but women can't help being a bother – made that way, I guess." Driscoll's resistance gradually turns to ambivalence and then into infatuation. Finally there is a mutual profession of affection, sealed by a kiss, followed by Darrow's abduction, which sends the story hurtling into the primal jungle of Kong. The latent fear of sexuality, of its being *unleashed*, of its darkness and danger, is more or less confirmed by the plot. Once sexual attraction is acknowledged, the film goes on a Dionysian rampage; the forest functions as a metaphoric primal scene conjoining sex and violence, rape, rage, death and clawing frenzy, just as our adventuresome boys subconsciously suspected it would from the start.

The second half of the fear-of-sex theme is developed through the "Beauty and the Beast" motif, which holds the rather unlikely proposition that sex is unmanly and unmanning. Denham's favorite metaphor in his "Beauty and the Beast" myth is "going soft." Denham explains to Driscoll that it's "the idea of my picture. A beast was a tough guy. He could lick the world. But when he saw Beauty she got him. He went soft. He forgot his wisdom and the little fellows licked him." When Denham catches wind of the Driscoll/Darrow romance, he equates Driscoll with the beast in his forthcoming film ". . . You're a pretty tough guy, but if Beauty gets you. . . ." Again, the "going soft" metaphor predominates: "What's the matter, Jack, you going *soft* on me?" – "you have gone soft on her, huh?" – and, "I've never seen it fail, some big hardboiled egg gets a look at a pretty face and bang, he cracks up and goes *sappy*." Considering the Driscoll/Kong equation, we can retrospectively hear Driscoll's outraged protest – "think I'm gonna fall for any dame?" – as a baleful prediction, since Kong does take the plunge in the biggest and most lethal way.

After the discussion with the theatrical agent in the captain's cabin, Denham decides to find a leading lady on his own. There is a long shot of Times Square, a fitting choice for a film redolent with show biz and movie imagery. There are dissolves to a cab, then Denham debouching from it, and a cut to what Denham sees – a flashing neon sign, "Women's Home Mission." Denham overhears the best the women can expect here – soup at night, and coffee and sinkers in the morning. The women speak with joking bravado, which amplifies the ruefulness of the scene. As they kid about their lack of basic necessities, the Depression intrudes in a particularly forceful way. Basic necessities also weigh heavily in the next two scenes. Denham pays for the fruit that Darrow attempted to steal, and we get our first view of her opalescently, angelically lit face, looking up, predictably enough. He brings her to a drugstore/coffee shop. The camera pans along the counter, noting the well-packed shelves of goods – everything Darrow needs/wants – and Denham brings her a cup of coffee. She is unemployed and her complete destitution generates its opposite, voiced by Denham: a dream of fortune, riches versus rags. The Depression details of privation anchor and call forth, so to speak, the Depression fantasy of wealth and fame.

In the captain's cabin, Denham attempted to compare the dangers of New York with the dangers a woman might encounter working in his film. The subsequent "Depression" scenes make the dangers of New York apparent – life at the level of economic necessity and powerlessness at the hands of monied males. The invocation of the Depression and unemployment elicits metaphors of the cruel marketplace. Darrow is struggling for existence, for survival. The economic circumstances are of the desperate, competitive variety which the common, pejorative metaphor of "the jungle" describes. The film does not state this metaphor outright at this point, but with these "Depression" scenes, it hovers on the horizon, awaiting the lavish, figurative jungle/city condensation of the second, "island" half.

Darrow's sacrifice on the island bears a number of strong formal relations to Kong's exhibition in New York. Darrow is tribute paid to the local tyrant; Kong is a product to be marketed. Both are exchange commodities. Kong, especially, recalls the imagery of a slave being auctioned. Darrow is presented to Kong as a novelty (remember Denham's racist "Yeah, blondes are scarce around here") just as Kong is presented to New York. Both presentations are preceded by elaborate ceremonies. And the presentations have strong visual correspondences with each other – both have raised platforms, bonds, "crucifixion" imagery, and audiences. The massive gate on the island is matched by the massive curtain in the theater. The torches on the island become the flashbulbs in New York. If Darrow is a white speck on a dark field, then Kong is a black figure on a white ground. Thematically, in both these rituals, the sacrificial hosts are displaced and thoroughly alienated characters.

The equation of Kong, who is introduced as the ultimate rapist, with Darrow, an archetypal victim, is not as perverse as it first appears. Both are proper objects of Depression pathos. Darrow has been brought to the brink of this fate worse than death by unemployment. Kong is the victim of the modern jungle. I say this not only because Manhattan is a place we are wont to refer to as a jungle but also because it bears certain resemblances to Kong's homeland. Both are islands, a fact about Manhattan that is underlined in one of the shots of the planes taking off from New Jersey. Manhattan, like Skull Island, also once had a barricade at its foot, commemorated as Wall Street. Kong, enslaved by the market and sold for the price of a ticket, is conquered by the modern jungle. His bewilderment at its machinations is palpable in his last moments. He falls as precipitously as the economy had in the world outside the film. By the end of *King Kong*, he garners our sympathy because he is exploited as a commodity, displaced for the sake of business, befuddled, and smashed to a pulp in the modern jungle as the result of the antics of hucksters. Kong is not only the biggest country bumpkin ever to be crushed by the city. He is also a metaphor for the Depression Everyman, lowered in the course of Denham's promotional bid for the show biz pot of gold.

The rescue party reaches the gate just as Kong carries Darrow off. Driscoll, recoiling, catches sight of the beast from behind. The whites split up and a heavily armed platoon trails Kong into the jungle. We get our first view of the primordial world along with this martial-looking rescue squad. In the initial shots, the jungle is in soft-focus, grayish in a way that suggests a misty background. The flora dwarfs the men; it's everywhere, huge, enveloping. The forest is primeval and wild enough – in the sense that it is dense – but it is more mysterious than it is physically forbidding. It is soft and seems darkly comfortable, a feeling accentuated by the relaxed jungle march music. If not exactly Edenic, it nevertheless has some seductive power.

The animals in the forest are another matter. First, the rescue party comes upon a grazing stegosaurus which they polish off handily with their gas grenades. The monster's charge is back-projected in front of the resolute humans. One can't avoid feeling aware of this back-projection – i.e., can't resist some awareness of a screen within a screen – in this scene and many succeeding scenes. Despite Willis O'Brien's skill, the space of many of the shots sporting battling, back-projected behemoths in the background and tiny humans in the foreground seems curiously disjunct. The monsters inhabit tangibly different spacial zones than the humans. They appear, at times, like visions, imbued with an aura of irreality, which, in the long run, works in *Kong*'s favor as yet another dimension of dream-likeness.

The rescue party loses its mastery of the jungle quickly. They stay on Kong's heels until they reach a steamy swamp. They hear Kong sloshing across but cannot see through the fog. The jungle has suddenly become less inviting. The thick mist reminds one of the impenetrable haze that surrounded the island. The swamp is desolate and murky, the shoreline forebodingly strewn with broken logs . Like the earlier fog, this mist is also a threshold, the entry into the real terrors of the island. As the tiny raft poles across the water in a gray long shot, the theme of invisible menace oozes quietly from the image. The sea serpent one might have anticipated earlier appears: a brontosaurus rises slowly from the milky slime, water dripping from its jaws almost obscenely. The brontosaurus provokes the same kind of terror as the denizens of the deep in such films as *The Creature from the Black Lagoon*, *Jaws*, and *Shockwaves*. It stalks its earth-bound prey under a watery cloak of invisibility. It is most fearsome when it disappears; it can strike from any direction. From this point on in *King Kong*, danger can come from anywhere.

After overturning the raft, the brontosaurus chases the crew ashore, periodically chewing their heads and casting the bodies aside like play soldiers. The dinosaur's gait is noticeably abrupt and jerky, a characteristic of O'Brien's animation technique inherited by his epigone Ray Harryhausen and still apparent in the fantastical beings of *Clash of the Titans* (1981).[7] However, the visible unnaturalness of the monsters does not make them any less persuasive. Rather, it accents their otherness, a more appropriate effect for this type of film than a smoother, flowing naturalism would offer. When the cinematic seams show in *King Kong*, they fortuitously fit the overall expressive scheme of the film. The deviations from a norm of convincing realism in the special effects do not distract. We are, of course, aware of them, but integrate them as elements of the overarching strangeness of the film's fictional world.

The rescue party emerges from the twilight, dreamlike swamp into a nightmare, discovering that the island is nothing so much as a treasury of phobias. Giant snakes curl underfoot and dinosaurs swoop from the sky. Men are decapitated, eaten, crushed, hurled, and dropped from deadly heights, not to mention what the creatures of the island do to each other. Kong is strangled, pecked, burnt, gassed, stabbed, slashed, speared, and machine-gunned. The dazzling range of brutality in *King Kong* as well as the scale of the carnage make it quite a ferocious film. But its ferocity is as much a function of its pacing as it is of its individually brutal sequences. From the swamp onward, the narrative is basically a relentless series of fierce battles with few lulls in between. And these battles are basically stations amidst three different chases. The longest pause between violent actions is Kong's unveiling in New York. Most of the rest of the dialogue sets up functionally and efficiently for the next (action-packed) scene: no sooner does Driscoll vow that Kong will never get Darrow again than we hear Kong's resounding leitmotif on the soundtrack; a split second after the radio announces that Kong is on the

Empire State Building, Driscoll recites his plane plan, and then we dissolve to the airfield. The story moves breathlessly in a series of flabbergasting adventures paced at a velocity that has few if any rivals. From the abduction on, the narrative, often preceded and ably fleshed out by the subliminally informative leitmotifs, skyrockets ahead (again like a dream) with little or no time for explanatory exposition – so what are these battling dinosaurs doing here in this day and age? The intensity of each fray on its own is raised exponentially by their tight conjunction along the pullulating trunk of the narrative. If the studied conflicts of prehistoric beasts define the world of *King Kong* in terms of the law of the primeval jungle, then the pacing of the film implies that the battle for survival is ceaseless, uninterrupted, and without quarter.

What little time is spent on character nuance in the second half of the film is given over to Kong. At first, he is simply grisly, arriving offscreen in order to allow time for the vague suggestions we've heard previously to come to a boil. In the intentionally darkened American prints,[8] we see his silvery outline, and his eyes and teeth pop out of the blackness like the front of a car at night. Kong looks something like the devil in Gustav Dorés illustrations for Dante's *Inferno* (and in unexpurgated prints of the film, he munches on humans just as Dante's demon snacks on Judas). Initially, Kong's glistening white maw is the most striking thing about him in his first close-up, but the camera quickly moves in on his eyes; it is hard to tell whether the rapidity of the camera movement is meant to register Darrow's shock at first seeing Kong or vice versa. This is the first step in Kong's anthropomorphization.

Kong growls at the natives and pounds his chest to assert his majesty. But most of the scene is spent revealing other attributes of Kong. His reaction to Darrow is questioning and quizzical. Rather than tearing her off the altar, he undoes the bonds like an awkward child with a delicate toy. You want to say he's gentle, in his clumsy way. He picks her up with two hands – carefully? – and he looks like a delighted though slightly confused kid with a doll. This image, Kong as child, is the film's first lever on the audience's sympathies toward Kong, its first appeal for an endorsement. The image is used later for comic effect. Driscoll stabs Kong in the finger and the big bruiser sits like one gigantic lump of a crybaby trying to find the pinprick. The mood shift involved in this scene is quite radical since this spate of comedy comes right after one of the most violent and harrowing incidents in the film, the sequence where Kong rolls the rescue party off the log bridge. In a matter of seconds, the film moves from Kong at his most vicious and threatening, a mountain of thundering anger, to Kong playing cat-and-mouse like a curious infant with Driscoll in the cave. The child image of Kong also grounds his adoring attitude to Darrow – Kong seems just the right age for a case of puppy (ape?) love. And, out of necessity, Kong's passion is pregenital, restricted to adolescent petting, stroking, and sniffing.

Kong's heroic stature is developed in his battles with the island's dinosaurs. Through these contests, we come to regard Kong as Darrow's protector. While Kong is nursing his finger, Darrow is beset by a Tyrannosaurus Rex. She unfurls a volley of bloodcurdling screams. Kong rouses and there is a shot of him leaping over a fallen log – the animation is done in the style of countless movie heroes "coming-to-the-rescue." Kong and the dinosaur circle each other before the clutch. Kong's manner of fighting is more than simply anthropomorphic; it is undeniably Anglo-Saxon. Kong lobs round house punches at the reptile as well as slapping a headlock on the beast and flipping it. Willis O'Brien's experience as a sports cartoonist and his early animated films of clay boxers undoubtedly come into play here. Admittedly, Kong bites the Tyrannosaurus Rex and, in the end, cracks its jaws apart. Nevertheless, Kong's generally humanized, "Americanized" fighting style invites us to side with him, whereas the reptile, who only kicks, scratches, and bites, is clearly the very image of a "dirty fighter." Kong comes off as a gentleman and a sportsman compared to the dinosaur.

Kong goes on to defend Darrow from the snake and the pterodactyl. If Kong is childlike in some cases, he is a child's fantasy of a male mate, a muscular superhero for whom sexual relations are a series of strenuous exercises in which the big fella (Superman, Tarzan) snatches his beloved from the jaws of death. Perhaps the reason why *Kong* postulates a sexually impossible liaison is because its reference is not to adult sexual relations but to a son's overweening affection for his mother. Darrow is Kong's bride since every son wants to marry his mother, and their life together is as any twelve-year-old might imagine – he protects her and vanquishes all the enemies. Kong is as big as the island is egocentrically his; he is the king, the head of a monarchy, the easiest form of government for a young child to understand. Kong is the king a child might wish to be or fantasize that he is.

At the same time, *King Kong* is self-pitying. Darrow never stops screaming, no matter how many lizards Kong stomps. One function of this shrieking obbligato is to give the film a sense of unrelenting horror; Darrow never lets us forget how ghastly the situation is. But the screams also become significant as a rejection of Kong. Kong comes to symbolize, through magnification, the child's feelings of ugliness, and Kong embodies the fantasy that the ugliness is unjustly held against him despite the (contradictory) fact that he is transpicuously noble. And there is Driscoll, the miniature father figure who will win the woman back, though Kong is stronger and greater.

One might think that a better interpretation of the film would see Driscoll as the son-figure and Kong as the tyrannical father, outfoxed by his cunning, much smaller opponent. But this does not square with either the childlike image of Kong in the film or the pathos of the ending. Kong's size stands for a child's perception of himself as an emotional giant and an emotional powerhouse. Kong clutches the small white Darrow as the "motherly" Brobdignagian monkey does Gulliver in the illustrations of "Book II" of Swift's masterpiece, by such as Granville and Pierre Bailly. Yet despite Kong's proportions and the possible iconographic reference, Kong is not a domineering parent but the adoring, rejected son. That he does not understand Darrow marks him not only as an object of pathos, but as an uncomprehending babe in the woods.

The portrayal of Kong as a child-lover provides the psychological foundation of Kong's most significant attribute, his rage. Above all else, it is the uncontained and uncontainable quality of Kong's fury – as he tears apart the native village and, later, midtown Manhattan – that rivets us to our seats. Nothing can hold Kong, not even chains of chrome steel. Nothing can halt him, not even the gigantic gate on Skull Island. When his beloved is filched, he goes on a rampage, tossing midget humans to and fro. His is the terrible rage of the child frustrated – frustrated when the mother-figure Darrow is taken away. If the diminutive humans stand for the child's contempt for adults, then the gargantuan scale of Kong is the objective correlative of the infantile belief in the omnipotence of the will. The film seduces us by rehearsing a fantasy. The absent mother, according to the fiction, *has been stolen*, and the fictional creature, Kong, is physically capable of wreaking the apocalyptic havoc that the ordinary child can only imagine. Anyone blocking Kong's path becomes a weightless beanbag, effortlessly crumpled, hurled or torn limb-from-limb. Kong-as-god can be glossed as an infantile delusion of grandeur.

Though the mechanics of this imagery are primarily psychological, it is also possible to discern an associated social fantasy telescoped in the action. Darrow-as-mother represents a plenitude that has been taken from Kong which is analogous to the well-being and promise of prosperity that the Depression had snatched from the audience. Perhaps it was the pressure of the Depression that made the audience susceptible to the regressive myth in *Kong*. In any case, that myth itself can be turned on the Depression as an emotional organizing device. Denied Darrow, denied plenitude, Kong's rage appears boundless . He becomes a one-ape revolution, momentarily venting the pent-up fury and indignation of a frustrated audience, their feelings of powerlessness relieved in an orgy of power, as if indulging infantile flights of pandemonium were their only option.

But in the end, Kong's power is limited. As with the final oedipal tragedy, Kong cannot possess the mother. Forces he cannot understand destroy him. If our commiseration with Kong is more maudlin than for Oedipus, it may be because the emotions *Kong* stirs up are more regressive. *Kong* is a cautionary tale. But like many cautionary tales, *Kong* offers two bonuses along with its admonition. First, before we are warned of the dangers of an infantile world view, that view and our affection for it are given a run for its money – two islands shattered by the scorned child. And second, even death, the putative warning, has lost its unattractiveness since Kong's fall, because of its combination of inevitability, alienation, hopelessness, and bravery, becomes admirable if not glorious.

I have already noted that the events on Skull Island and those in New York bear strong similarities to each other: the sacrifice/the show; the snake/the subway; the mountain/the skyscraper; the pterodactyl/the bi-planes. Other correspondences include: Kong's breaking down the gate/Kong's breaking down the theater wall; rolling the crew off the log/tumbling the passengers in the subway; punching reptiles/punching the subway. Kong tosses native huts into the air, they sail upward off-screen, and then come crashing back into the frame. Exactly the same technique is employed when Kong demolishes the canopy, torn off a building facade in New York. Kong reaches into a cave carved into a vertiginous precipice to ferret out the obstreperous Driscoll; just as Darrow complains that with Kong loose in New York, it's like a horrible (recurring?) dream – "It's like being back on the island again" – Kong's paw smashes through the hotel window, clobbers Driscoll, and grabs Darrow. The crew's fall – stated with excruciating thuds – is echoed by Kong's plummet from the top of the Empire State Building, which, in turn, strongly contrasts with the lovers' leap to freedom from the promontory (Driscoll does fall for a woman, though quite successfully). The repetition of musical leitmotifs also serves to identify disparate places on the two islands. For example, the same musical theme is played both when Kong examines Darrow in his lair and at the pinnacle of the Empire State Building, thereby equating the sites of the highpoints of Kong's bewilderment. Throughout the second half of *Kong*, a feeling of *déjà vu* pervades; it is the *déjà vu* of a persistent, haunting nightmare.

The basis of much of the doubling in *Kong* is the idea of transporting a prehistoric creature to civilization where it escapes, a motif derived from Doyle's *The Lost World*. In Doyle's book, this gambit is played for comedy . A baby pterodactyl flaps out of the window of a science convocation and nestles with cathedral-top gargoyles, probably mistaking them for relatives, before winging it back to South America. Willis O'Brien's version of *The Lost World* raises the dramatic stakes by replacing the pterodactyl with a brontosaurus who tramps disastrously about London before falling into the Thames. Kong is a descendant of *The Lost World*, and the relation between the prehistoric world and the modern world is developed with much greater complexity in *Kong* than in its forebear. Most of the comparisons between the two islands in *Kong* are done stylistically through the repetition of visual and narrative motifs. Furthermore, this equation has particular expressive power because it animates certain pejorative societal metaphors at a time of great economic crisis, and in a way that encourages the audience to see the allegory as a characterization of their adversity which depicts the situation of civil (market) society as immoral and implacable, and which shows defeat in the modern jungle as tragically heroic.

Kong is not only a cautionary tale with regard to psychological matters; it is also a cautionary tale with regard to economic behavior. In films like *Little Caesar* (1930) and *Scarface* (1932), pop tragedies with a rise-and-fall rhythm, thirties' audiences were treated to an ethnic warning about the danger of leaving one's place in society for the sake of ambition. As soon as the gangsters don ritzy airs, replete with laughable *nouveau riche* manners, they are headed for their downfall. They are out of their class in more ways than one and they will be brought low. Likewise, once Kong leaves his domain and penetrates the gate, the boundary between nature and culture, he is out of his element and, therefore, doomed. His final bafflement is thick enough to cut with a knife. On one level, *Kong* warns: stay on your own turf or the bastards will drag you down. Life in the modern jungle, exactly because it is a jungle, is precarious, even for a Kong – a piece of perennial American folk wisdom distilled to a higher proof by the experience of the Depression.

Kong is not just a conservative warning about individual behavior, it is also a reflection of an enduring American attitude toward civil society that is readily intensified by conditions of economic anxiety. The prehistoric imagery (especially the clashing dinosaurs) and the condensation of the jungle and the city draft the Darwinian metaphor of the struggle for existence as the sign of modern, competitive, urban (read "economic") life. But in *Kong*, the battle – marked as such by the use of warplanes – does not have the triumphant connotations it had for the robber barons. Rather, it suggests that the city as a jungle is a source of bitterness and sorrow that at the very least reveals regret over the loss of innocence modern civil life entails as well as fear concerning what feels like slim prospects for surviving in such an environment. As a child, I remember my father trying to explain business to me. He wanted to impress me with how difficult, dangerous, and horrible it was. Though at the time neither he nor I was aware of it, his tropes were all Darwinian. I barely understood his lecture beyond gleaning that business was a terrible place and that it was wearing him down. But the reference to jungles, competition, survival, teeth, and claws made me think, irresistibly, that business must be a lot like the world of *King Kong*.

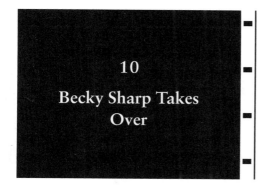

10

Becky Sharp Takes Over

Becky Sharp is a film that warrants a place in world almanacs; it was the first feature-length movie to be shot completely in three-color Technicolor. Unlike other historic firsts of the medium, such as *The Jazz Singer*, *Becky Sharp* (1935) is not marred by the awkwardness of an experiment. Its use of color is various and assured. Its director, Rouben Mamoulian, had already completed seven films. He was brought onto the project in January 1935, after the film's original director, Lowell Sherman, died while just beginning work on the production.[1]

Ostensibly the film is based on Langdon Mitchell's 1899 stage adaptation of W. M. Thackeray's *Vanity Fair*.[2] But examination of Mitchell's play quickly reveals that scriptwriter Francis Edward Faragoh, though using some of Mitchell's lines and ideas, returned to Thackeray's *Vanity Fair*, reinstating many of the scenes that the play had deleted: this is understandable since the pace of a 1930s film allowed for far more scene changes than a play did. The film owes more to Thackeray than to Mitchell and is rather an adaptation of the novel than of the play.

Adaptation

Thackeray's *Vanity Fair* (1847) is a novel on a scale and of a style that present imposing problems for film adaptation. Not only does it run over six hundred tightly printed pages of packed incident, but its emphasis is on comedy of manners rather than on visual description. The prospects for condensing all its dramatic (often digressive) details within the time frame of a standard-length feature film seem hopeless. *Becky Sharp* is only eighty-four minutes long. Obviously it involves a simplification of *Vanity Fair*. The important questions that this process of

"Becky Sharp Takes Over," in *The English Novel and the Movies*, ed. M. Klein and G. Parker (New York: Ungar, 1981), pp. 108–131.

143

adaptation raises are: What is the nature of each of the major simplifications in the film adaptation? Are the kinds of simplifications we find
systematic? And, if they are systematic, what do they imply about the
thematic, commercial, and ideological stance of the film?

A significant index of the type of simplification favored in *Becky Sharp*
is the title itself. The move from *Vanity Fair: A Novel without a Hero* to
Becky Sharp suggests that the novel without a hero has become a film
with a heroine. Becky is certainly a prominent figure in the book, indeed
the most prominent. But she appears only intermittently. She is first
among a cast of equals, which includes Amelia, Dobbin, the elder
Osborne, and others. In the film, Becky, played by Miriam Hopkins, is
the central character, putting in an appearance in almost every scene and
dominating most of them. The other characters are uniformly secondary
and vaguely defined. If some strike us as particularly vivid, it is because
several of the actors have produced witty, eccentric character studies.
Generally, attention is focused on Becky and her motives, plans, attitudes, and adventures. In this respect the film is individualistic, rooted in
a central character with whom the audience is invited to align itself,
whereas in Thackeray there are numerous characters, each of whom
makes a play for our allegiance at different times. The use of shifting
allegiance is part of what can be called Thackeray's perspectivism – his
ability to represent situations from numerous points of view. By anchor-
ing the film in Becky, not only is the ambiguity and complexity of the
original reduced, but Becky and her associated values gain added rhetorical power since they are no longer in a context where alternative values
seriously challenge them.

When Thackeray called his book *Vanity Fair*, the allusion to Bunyan
marked it as a piece of social criticism. *Becky Sharp* is a title that befits
the story of an individual. The novel is a description not only of social
manners but of a social system. Through its wheel-of-fortune structure,
it produces a multitude of repetitions and variations that suggest the
relation of individual behavior and major narrative events to an underlying social system in which money and rank are coveted above all else.
The narrative structure requires the reader to engage in a constant
process of comparison and contrast that impresses us again and again
with the recognition that what most people say and do in *Vanity Fair* is
predicated on what they believe they stand to gain or lose in terms of
wealth and prestige.

Becky's marriage to Rawdon Crawley and Amelia's marriage to
George Osborne both meet strong opposition because both women are

penniless. These marriages are implicitly contrasted to the unquestioned suits of George Osborne's sister and Rawdon Crawley's brother, which are sanctioned by large dowries. Society's reaction to Amelia once she regains guardianship of little Georgy (the legatee of his grandfather's estate) contrasts with the way she was ignored when impoverished.

The structure of repetition and variation enables Thackeray to generalize his social criticism. He consistently treats his characters as admixtures of good and bad qualities while reserving the brunt of his moral judgment for the social system as a whole. What is monstrous about Becky and George Osborne, for instance, becomes intelligible within the context of the acquisitive society that spawns and nurtures them. The novelist is less concerned with the notion of individual villains as such than with the social institutions that produce them.

Becky Sharp, in the main, omits the comparative structure of *Vanity Fair* and in so doing brackets not only Thackeray's specific social criticisms, which admittedly by 1935 were out of date, but, more importantly, abandons the systematic viewpoint with which any serious social criticism begins. The result is that Becky's roguishness, or what remains of it in the film, is presented as an individual character trait rather than as the product of a social system. Likewise, the hypocrisy and vanity that typify so many of the characters are proposed as personal vices rather than as consequences of social ills.

The way the adaptation simplifies *Vanity Fair* is to recast its social criticism as questions of individual morality. Some characters are stupid, like Miss Julia Crawley, and some are willful, like Becky. But why the characters are as they are is ignored. The adaptation could have been otherwise. Perhaps, in the fashion of *Wuthering Heights* (the film), only half of the story could have been told, keeping the comparative structure intact. But since that is not how it was made, we must try to find some motive for the version we have. What is missing is Thackeray's emphasis on the ways that personal habits, attitudes, and decisions are determined by larger social forces. Note how the relation between parents and children is absent in the film. Mr. and Mrs. Sedley and Mr. Osborne, for example, have disappeared. This removes the action from the context of a social process. In *Becky Sharp* the fictional society is a collection of individuals, not a function of social institutions like the family. This, it seems to me, indicates part of the ideology of the film. In the mid-1930s *Becky Sharp* projects a view of society which obscures the potential for systematic social criticism in favor of a conception of the social world as fundamentally individualistic. Insofar as fictions can act as models for thinking about human events, *Becky Sharp*, unlike *Vanity Fair*, offers its audience history as a spectacle of individual effort, achievement, vice, and virtue. Although this was probably not the conscious intention of any of the makers of the film, the approach to society embodied in *Becky Sharp* does function to deflect the possibility of social criticism in a way quite common in Hollywood film, and at a time when the need for systematic social criticism had particular urgency.

The adaptation also forgets several of Becky's worst deeds. In the novel Thackeray strongly suggests that Becky kills Joseph Sedley for his money, while in the film they seem destined to remain together playfully ever after. In the novel there is every indication that Becky conspires with Lord Steyne (Sir Cedric Hardwicke) in Rawdon's (Alan Mowbray) arrest so that the two can spend the evening together; nor, in the novel, does this seem to be their first tryst. But in the film, Steyne alone is responsible for the attempted arrest. Moreover, Becky's part is scripted to suggest that she hopes to charm her way out of Steyne's embrace. She is presented as a wife who is playing with fire but who is committed to staying out of the flame. In a way, her rendezvous with Steyne is connected with her dedication to Rawdon since it is the only way she can get the five hundred pounds that he needs. She is visibly and audibly depressed by her predicament. Listen to how her singing changes when Steyne places the money in her lap. And she attempts to turn the table banter about wolves and sheep into a plea for Steyne to release her from her promises. Not only is she not an adulteress, but she is working hard to avoid becoming one. This is not Thackeray's Becky but one laundered for an upright family audience.

In the novel, Thackeray spends a great deal of time establishing that Becky is a horrible mother. Her son hates her and her behavior is contrasted incisively with Rawdon's, Lady Jane's, and Amelia's (Frances Dee) attitudes toward parenthood. Becky pays attention to her son only when she believes it will impress people she is interested in winning over. But the whole mother/son relationship is dropped from the film. This is part of the overall tendency of the film to deemphasize Becky's ruthlessness. The omission of the murder, of Becky's callousness toward her child, and of her calculating infidelity makes her an easier character with whom to align oneself.

This is basically a matter of empathy, grounded in an audience's recognition of the moral values that it shares with the characters. For an American family-oriented audience to identify with Becky, it was imperative to excise her crimes against the family, specifically her adultery and inattention to her son. What remains of her character is positive moral virtue – intelligence, drive, wit, and the joy of living. In Thackeray, Becky, as the symbol of selfishness in an acquisitive society, is the enemy of the family. But in the film, her selfish drive is framed in a way that the threat to the family (which would also constitute a threat to the audience) is hidden. This suppression does not merely soften Thackeray's point but rather negates it by making the attractiveness of selfishness stand out, without suggesting that it also has more destructive effects.

In the film, Becky's character is tinged with a blatant streak of dishonesty which may appear as a negative moral quality. Yet, for a 1930s audience, much of Becky's larceny may be excused because Becky is presented as a class heroine. Becky lies and cheats, but to a certain extent this is justified as the only means a member of an underprivileged class has for dealing with an unjust society that respects only money and rank, merit notwithstanding. The film begins with Becky's deflating Miss Pinkerton, whose pomposity marks her as extravagantly upperclass, ridiculous, and hypocritical. Note that the film lacks the Miss Jemima episode, thereby muting Becky's propensity toward cruelty. Instead, the image is of a brazen, clever, lower-class girl unafraid of her oppressively self-satisfied ''betters.'' Characters like Miss Crawley, Pitt Crawley, and Joseph Sedley's offscreen parents similarly suggest that to a degree Becky's chicaneries are exculpable in the light of the exigencies of the conflict between rich and poor. Becky's loaded dice and thirst for success are chided within the film and duly punished. But these transgressions are not nearly as extreme as those in the book, and Becky remains essentially an exemplary figure, an emblem for members of aspiring social classes.

Previously it was claimed that the film's removal of Thackeray's comparative structures presents the values associated with Becky almost uncritically and, therefore, with more rhetorical seductiveness. What are those values? Clearly they are indomitable drive, the ability to "live by one's wits," and selfishness. As a class heroine, Becky gives value to enterprise and individualism. By downplaying her ruthlessness and by not contrasting her with fully developed moral alternatives, like Dobbin, the film effectively endorses her *modus vivendi*. Acquisitive self-interested individualism, exactly what Thackeray disdained, is presented as a positive moral virtue. More than that – as a role model for members of aspiring classes, Becky exemplified the attractiveness of individualism at a time in American history when individualism implied individualism-rather-than-collectivism. Needless to say, collectivism has nothing to do with *Vaniy Fair*. But it was an issue that was relevant in the 1930s. And in this context it is possible for us to assess the unity of the simplifications in *Becky Sharp* as an ideological projection of a class heroine for a family-oriented audience – a heroine who celebrates spirited, self-interested individualism as the model for behavior in the conflict between rich and poor.

Stylization

As a Hollywood film of the mid-1930s, *Becky Sharp* is a very stylish production employing visual symbolism, clever scene transitions, a great deal of camera movement, and a deft manipulation of color. Some of this stylization is in the service of adapting *Vanity Fair*, whereas other elements are independent of the task of adaptation and contribute to the effect of the film as film.

Undoubtedly, Mamoulian's background in theater, as well as that of production designer Robert Edmond Jones,[3] are major factors behind the graceful, creative handling of color throughout the film. The range of ways color is used is quite rich. It directs attention – at Lady Richmond's ball our eyes jump ahead to the cluster of red uniforms from which Becky will emerge. It builds decorative patterns – the reds and the alternations of blacks and whites at the ball. At other times, it formally stresses dramatic contrasts – Becky in blue versus Amelia in pink; or it makes metaphoric comments – Miss Pinkerton costumed in the colors of Mademoiselle Harlequin. In the often cited flight from Lady Richmond's ball, color is coordinated with montage in order to express and release mounting tension, while on a purely formal level Mamoulian often composes medium long shots of British soldiers in which arresting, almost abstract, designs of redcoats leap at the spectator. Though these uses of color were not unprecedented in theater, their appearance in this first film of its kind established a high standard of sophistication for those who were to follow in Mamoulian's footsteps.

One key theme in the visual adaptation of *Vanity Fair* is that of theater, and especially acting. A central concept in Thackeray's vision of *Vanity Fair* is "artifice," a word he repeats innumerable times. In the film, this notion is visualized through constant references to theater. Throughout, there is a recurring use of drapery as an allusion to theater curtains. The action begins with the girls at Miss Pinkerton's school opening a curtain – the same curtain that figures prominently in the series of shots in which Becky hurls the *Dictionary* at the Grand Dame.

Becky hangs on the blue satin drapery at the end of Lady Richmond's ball like a nineteenth-century diva. And in the scenes of the midnight dinner with Steyne and its discovery by Rawdon, the silken, diaphanous drapes at the entrance of the boudoir are stressed again and again. The curtains are a synecdoche for theater, which in turn stands for artifice and illusion – the hallmarks of Thackeray's *Vanity Fair*.

The theme of theater is also evoked in terms of overt acting, especially on the part of Miriam Hopkins as Becky. Thackeray suggests acting as a central metaphor for Becky in a number of ways. Becky's mother was an actress; Becky's ability to charm is based in large measure on her ability as a mime (as well as a singer, a musician, and an actress); and she briefly becomes a professional actress when her amateur standing in society fails her. Thackeray associates Becky with the arts of illusion, among which acting is her forte. Mamoulian takes the metaphor of Becky as actress and makes it the basis of Hopkins's role, directing her to adopt a very theatrical style when she is involved in deceiving other characters. Kneeling next to the trunk with plaintive, outstretched hands when defending her mother's memory to Rawdon's aunt is one of the many examples in the film of intentional overacting. This is meant to signal to the audience that Becky is playing a part and to represent her as an "actress" in the moral sense of the word.

Throughout, Mamoulian is careful to use Hopkins's gestures so that they convey rich connotations. She is a seductress as demonstrated by the almost supine positions she strikes when talking to men (for example in the couch scene with Joseph Sedley). Becky is as determined and as disciplined as a soldier in her quest for success – see how she marches to the balcony, strutting to the beat of drums at the end of the Waterloo sequence. Mamoulian repeatedly uses the hurling of objects as an act of defiance – including books, flowers, and a scrub brush – as a visual epithet for Becky's proud, rebellious mode of being-in-the-world. But of all the gestural symbolism, that of Becky's discernible acting is the most important. Other characters also display this tendency to a certain extent, and Mamoulian directs some scenes so that the characters make what look like stage entrances and exits that are quotations of theater, rather than merely stagey, due to camera movements that constantly reframe the action.

The overriding significance of the metaphor of acting in the film is borne out by the addition of the scene of Becky's ill-fated performance, which is only a line in the book and which does not appear in the play at all. At one level this scene functions to complete the previous one since it fulfills Becky's dolorous prediction that "they'll laugh at me." This, of course, is what happens during the performance. Symbolically, Becky's failure on the stage also stands for the temporary dislocation of her ability to influence other people by acting. But that failure is only momentary, and in the final scenes – with wringing hands and feigned faints of virtually pantomimic dimensions – Becky is able to wrap Pitt Crawley and Lady Jane around her little finger. We leave Becky, the actress, triumphant.

Related to but distinguishable from the emphasis on theatrical acting is the use of fast transitions in character throughout the film. We see Becky contemptuously throw Joseph's rose away, while in the next shot she is graciously accepting another one from him and vowing that she presses all his flowers. The transition from crying to laughing, often marked by a cut, is an important motif; examples include Becky's exit from Miss Crawley's sitting room and the cutting that links Becky's interview with Dobbin to the one with Pitt. Becky changes her attitude with breathtaking speed. In the Waterloo sequence Becky moves from contempt for George, love for Rawdon, financial opportunism with Joseph, sympathy for the soldiers, casual compliance with Steyne, and hunger in the spate of a few minutes. The inconstancy of her character, her changeability, communicates her insincerity by representing her as an actress through contrast, that is, by juxtaposing her many different roles one on top of the other. This fast character transition captures part of the flavor of the novel where in one paragraph, as in the description of the early history of Becky's acquaintance with Miss Pinkerton and Jemima, Thackeray is able to change our moral perspective on Becky three or four times. Of course, in the film we are never completely appalled by what Becky does. However, her chameleonlike behavior does retain a residue of Thackeray's penchant for shifting, contradictory perspectives while at the same time supporting the central portrayal of Becky as the consummate actress.

Becky Sharp is an example of 1930s stylishness. The film employs a great deal of symbolism. Objects are given added meaning in order to make visual comments on characters and actions. The translucent dressing screen between Becky and Amelia, for instance, not only marks the contrast between the two, but Amelia, in silhouette, recalls a figure on a piece of bone china, thereby evoking connotations of refinement. At the same time, the screen also functions as a symbol of Amelia's blindness since George and Becky are flirting on the other side. The scrubwoman's brush is made to stand for the destiny of an adventuress so that when

Becky hurls it out the door, the act visually expresses Becky's rejection of a fate similar to the char's. The book that beans Pitt at the end of the film recalls the one flung at Pinkerton (and, by extension, at her euphuistic elocution) so that the objects and actions become emblems of the refusal to be taken in by hypocrisy.

Mamoulian's treatment of objects is comparable to what is called, in another context, the Lubitsch touch – a talent for visual expression by means of the symbolic use of objects. The most elaborate example of this involves the exchange of flowers. The cut between Becky spurning and then accepting Joseph's roses signals her duplicity. Becky's compact with Steyne is sealed by the exchange of a flower which coincides with the exchange of the five hundred pounds – the passage of the flower amounting to a metaphor for prostitution. Finally, Becky's darkest hour, her disastrous performance, is represented by a battle of bouquets with Becky and the audience hostilely lobbing flowers back and forth. In each instance, an exchange of flowers indicates the state of Becky's fortunes.

The tendency toward visual symbolism extends to every aspect of the film. For example, camera movement at times functions metaphorically: the opening pans between Becky and Amelia present the opposite sides of the hall as spatial symbols of class. Mamoulian uses dissolves not only to make temporal transitions but to mount metaphoric asides. Through superimposition, the popular political metaphor of a dictator's specter or shadow falling over the land is literalized when Napoleon's shadow lingers and then fades out over the image of Lady Richmond's ball.[4] In terms of editing, Mamoulian transforms the flight from the ball into a symbol of frenzy by building the montage to the shot where the billowing red cloaks of the hussars predominate, provoking a chain of associations of excitement as the reds flap in the wind.

Besides symbols, Mamoulian uses emphatic juxtapositions, often achieved through editing, to make cinematic statements. Becky's and Amelia's reactions to Napoleon's escape are sharply contrasted in a lightning cut. Likewise, the aftermath of Waterloo is presented in terms of two rhyming dollies-back – the first from George's gravestone and the second at Becky's festive table. The similarity in the mode of cinematic articulation in these shots underscores the comparative disparity of the consequences of the war for honest Amelia versus ambitious Becky.

Becky Sharp, despite its theatrical trappings, is a very "cinematic" film: Mamoulian often underlines basic themes of the plot visually, rather than relying exclusively on their outright statement in the dialogue. By using the term "cinematic," however, I do not mean to argue that the film has a specific, transhistorical, quality-making feature that renders any film of any period good. Rather I mean that inscribed in *Becky Sharp* is an esthetic stance that is extremely relevant to films of the 1930s, when the advent of sound raised the danger of films that merely reproduced (or recorded) plays. Against this threat, directors like Mamoulian employed assertive visual stylization as a means of defending what they took to be the integrity of the film medium. *Becky Sharp* is a cinematic film by the standards of 1930s filmmaking; as such it bears the traces of an esthetic proclivity for strong visual stylization as an attempted hedge against canned theater.

Becky Sharp is not only very expressive visually; it also strives to be simply visual wherever possible. Mamoulian consistently dollies in and out of many of the talkier scenes not only to emphasize certain lines of dialogue but to inject some dynamism into the otherwise static theatricality. One can also see the clever scene transitions – the dissolve from the picture of the Prince Regent to the Prince in the flesh, or the tilt from the auction notice to the playbill – as gestures that stress cinematic articulation as part of a commitment to the esthetic of film as film. Of course, to the eyes of a 1950s or 1960s filmviewer, whose prejudices about what is cinematic lean more toward realism, these effects may appear quite contrived. But in the 1930s, when the memory of the international style of silent film was tantamount to a yearning for a lost golden age, Mamoulian's stylization counted as an attempt to remain true to the medium through visual assertiveness.

At the same time, the artifice and stylization in which the film luxuriates has a holistic expressive effect on the audience. Its visual grace, wit, contrivance, and opulence appropriately correspond at the level of form to properties we associate with the *haute monde* the film represents. Like Lubitsch's *Trouble in Paradise*, there seems to be a fitting correlation between the panache, cleverness, and taste for splendor of both director and heroine. Becky's élan, for better or worse, is seductively incarnated in an "artful" cinematic idiom.

11
Interpreting *Citizen Kane*

Citizen Kane is a film that has engendered a classic conflict of interpretation. That is, there are at present two leading views of its thematic point, and these two views appear, on the surface, to be incompatible. These two interpretations can be called the enigma interpretation, on the one hand, and the Rosebud interpretation, on the other. Each interpretation is quite simple, and, I shall argue, its simplicity is important to the function it *actually* plays in *Citizen Kane*. The enigma interpretation says that *Citizen Kane* illustrates the point that the nature of a person is ultimately a mystery; a person is all things to all persons, and, correspondingly, a multiplicity of selves. The Rosebud interpretation says that Kane's personality is finally explicable by some such notions as those of "lost childhood" or "lost innocence." I hasten to add that many commentators may, strangely enough, fail to see that these interpretations of *Citizen Kane* are incompatible. But they obviously are: if human life is inexplicable in the way the enigma interpretation says, then a life like Kane's cannot be explained in terms of a clue like Rosebud. Or, alternatively, if Rosebud yields a convincing explanation of Kane's life, then Kane's life, and, by extension, human life in general is not inevitably inexplicable, i.e., not unavoidably enigmatic.

A recent defense of the enigma view, one that is aware of its incompatibility with the Rosebud view, can be found in Ian Jarvie's *Philosophy of the Film*. He writes:

The newsreel narrator suggested that Kane was all things to all men; to the right he was a communist; to the left a fascist; a man of the people who consorted with the rich and powerful; a foe of corruption who was himself corrupted by power; an amiable man with a stubborn and ruthless devotion to his own views. The successive stories embroider on this dual aspect of Kane; depending on who is talking he can be seen either way; his best friend finds him corrupted by ego-

"Interpreting *Citizen Kane*," Persistence of Vision, no. 7 (1989), pp. 51–62.

tism; his business manager sees him as a creative and dynamic boss; his guardian as a dangerous and headstrong ne'er do well; his valet sees him as a man with feet of clay.[1]

Jarvie goes on to hypothesize that these disparities indicate that "*Citizen Kane* is to be read as a critique of the naive theory of human identity, namely that there are clues to it which can be deciphered and so make sense of much of what a person does. . . ."[2] Jarvie pushes the enigma approach so far as to suspect that the film is explicitly anti-Freudian; he says:

One could then read the film as a criticism and repudiation of the very idea that there are deep childhood and sexual clues to a person. That rummaging round in people's memories of Kane does not turn up some vital clue to what makes him tick. That he eludes the best efforts of an investigative reporter. That a person is an enigma. The only real clue they have, "Rosebud," is nothing more than a sled, which is perhaps a random memory on a dying man's lips.[3]

This view, minus Jarvie's putative perception of the rejection of psychoanalysis, is quite familiar. Borges writes: "We understand at the end that the fragments do not have a hidden unity: the unhappy Foster Kane is a shadow, a mere chaos of appearances."[4] Borges, then, invokes the metaphor of a labyrinth, presumably one with no center.

Of course, the biggest problem with the enigma view is what to do with the final appearance of Rosebud. After the mystery of human life is intoned for the last time, the mystery appears to be cleared up. One way to try to get rid of the incongruity is to insult it, as Welles did by calling Rosebud "dollarbook Freud," and saying it was Herman Mankiewicz's fault anyway.[5] Jarvie's response is more civil but equally dismissive:

It [Rosebud] seems at the centre of things but it is actually irrelevant. This makes for a better defense of *Kane*. The alleged mystery of what makes Kane tick may be merely a McGuffin, a plot device to enable us to follow this reporter back into various people's memories. The interaction of the people on screen, the events that happen to them, become the point of the movie, and the hunt for the McGuffin slips into the background: then, in the incinerator scene, it is rounded off neatly, but *cynically* (emphasis added). For we see the smoke pouring out of Xanadu's chimneys, scattering this albeit meaningless clue to the winds.[6]

In this quotation, we see that Jarvie, more than any previous commentator, is aware that the Rosebud finale seems logically to contradict the enigma interpretation. Jarvie tries to remove the contradiction by making Rosebud a matter of irony or cynicism. However, there is very little to support this interpretation. Admittedly, the ending is tricked out with Gothic conventions. But this cannot be interpreted as irony or cynicism. For these conventions are evident throughout the film; if they are to be recognized as ironic in the last instance, they would have to be ironic in earlier instances, which would make virtually any interpretation of the film, including an enigma interpretation, unintelligible. Clearly, Jarvie's main defense of this reading of the last scene is that it gives us the most satisfying interpretation of the film. But that is to defend the enigma interpretation as the best interpretation by saying it is the best interpretation. The attribution of cynicism or irony to the last sequence is not motivated by the film and it seems little more than an *ad hoc* attempt to save the theory in the face of contravening evidence.[7]

Of course, if one takes the final apparition of the sled seriously, one is apt to have a very different view of the theme of the film. The sled becomes the emblem for a loss. By whispering "Rosebud," André Bazin surmises, "Kane admits before dying that there is no profit in gaining the whole world if one has lost one's own childhood."[8]

One difficulty with this line of interpretation is that, insofar as we know almost nothing about Kane's childhood or his enduring reactions to being uprooted, Rosebud might be thought to function as an explanatory placebo. In fact, the Rosebud interpretation runs the risk of being embarrassing. The idea of childhood nostalgia is about as vapid as you can get, while the Rosebud device verges on hokum. The latter criticism is, indeed, the basis on which commentators, like Parker Tyler, deride the film.[9] So a liability of the Rosebud interpretation is that, however accurate, it has the net effect of making *Citizen Kane* sound pretty dumb. Thus, a critic who favors the Rosebud interpretation is likely to accompany it with a defense of the intellectual credentials of this way of explaining Kane's behavior. James Naremore provides this service when he argues that:

Some of the psychoanalytic ideas in *Kane* might have come straight out of a textbook. According to Freudian terminology, Kane can be typed as a regressive, anal-sadistic personality. His lumpen-bourgeois family is composed of a weak, untrustworthy father and a loving, albeit puritanical mother; he is taken away from this family at a pre-pubescent stage and reared by a bank; as an adult he "returns" to what Freud describes as a pre-genital form of sexuality in which "not the genital component-instincts, but the *sadistic* and *anal* are the most prominent." Thus, throughout his adult life Kane is partly a sadist who wants to obtain power over others, and partly an anal type, who obsessively collects zoo

animals and museum pieces. His childhood . . . seems far from idyllic; nevertheless, it is a childhood toward which he has been compulsively drawn.[10]

Both the enigma interpretation and the Rosebud interpretation are
well supported by the dialogue, the narrative structure, and the visual
elaboration of the film. The basis for the enigma interpretation is amply
set out in the "News on the March" sequence. Rhetorically, this
sequence is structured in terms of oppositions and catalogues. The oppositions invoked run the gamut of logical types from oxymorons and
binary reversals to what are meant to appear as contradictions. Kane is
described as a communist, a fascist, and an American; he starts one war
and opposes another; he speaks for millions and is hated by millions;
few private lives were more public; he supports and denounces public
figures, often supporting and then denouncing the same person; Kane
made history, but then he became history; and, of course, in short order,
we see a man who loves public attention and who preens for the camera
become a recluse who shuns cameras. Many of these oppositions are not
very deep; they are rather the artifacts of a catchy journalistic style.
Nevertheless, this introduces Kane to us as "a mass of contradictions" –
in the argot of newsspeak – or a bundle of opposites. Kane, in other
words, is not presented as a coherent identity so much as a collision of
contrasting figures.

The catalogues in the newsreel also articulate this sense of opposition
both verbally and visually. These breathless catalogues stress heterogeneity. Introduced to Xanadu and its holdings, what principle of taste
could accommodate that jumble of styles; the best the commentator can
do is to call it a *collection of everything*. Similarly, when we learn of the
extent of Kane's businesses, the meaning of the word "conglomerate"
strikes home; Kane owns newspapers, radio stations, forests, paper
mills, factories, mines, apartment houses, grocery stores (why grocery
stores?), and ocean liners (why not?). What seems to hold this list
together is a simple principle of acquisition rather than a coherent plan;
his holdings are an analogue for Kane himself – a collection of activities
rather than the stuff of a coherent project.

These interrelated themes – of the multiplicity and heterogeneity of
Kane – recur throughout the film. Kane tells Thatcher that he is speaking
to two persons – ones indeed with contradictory purposes; the idea that
Kane is more than one person is also supported metaphorically in the
imagery. Not only do a multiplicity of photographic images of Kane pro-
liferate throughout the film, but Kane speaks before a giant image of

himself at the political rally.[11] And, summing up the multiplicity theme, as Kane leaves his wife's room and passes the mirrors at the end of the valet's story, at least six images of Kane are on the screen, and an infinity of others is suggested.[12]

At the level of action, Kane's behavior is often contradictory in a way that on the face of it, at least, indicates that it issues from a divided self. He finishes Leland's review in a manner that is *at odds* with his own interests, *but then* he fires Leland, *but then* he sends Leland a check for $25,000. And, of course, as Jarvie points out above, the narrative device of the interview advances the notion of a multiplicity of selves in the sense that Kane's identity *may seem* relative to whomever is telling the story.

Throughout the film, the heterogeneity of Kane's collections continues as an objective correlative of Kane's personhood. The scenes in Xanadu's living room mix classic, medieval, and baroque artworks.[13] And there are the massive, high-angle shots of crated artifacts that, to my mind, recall the piles of the fragmentary, unassembled pieces of Susan's puzzles – which puzzles, of course, are proffered, quite explicitly, as the visual equivalent to the narrative investigation. The reporter, Thompson, prompted by the appearance of one of Susan's puzzles, equates his investigation with it, calling Rosebud a piece in such a puzzle and going on to say that it cannot explain a man's life. Kane's life, in other words, remains a mystery, a puzzle, an enigma – a congeries of fragmentary parts that do not finally cohere.

Nevertheless, the Rosebud interpretation is *also* extensively grounded in the film. To see this, however, more has to be said about what this interpretation involves. The film offers a portrait of Kane, one in which he is shown to have great difficulty sustaining what might be thought of as reciprocal love relations. His relation to the underclasses, of whom he is a self-appointed champion, is paternalist, and his relation to his second wife is domineering and patriarchal. Kane's view of love, as he explicitly admits, is that love is something to be had on one's own terms.[14] Kane does not adjust his affections to the purposes, rights, and desires of his love objects; he does not, or he does not easily, brook, so to speak, negative feedback from these love objects. When they fail to bend to his fantasies, his responses are rage and/or retreat. Confronted by reversals of expectation, he becomes reclusive. He hides away with his collection of art objects and his zoo.

Interestingly, the art objects he seems fondest of accumulating are statues, – "people" who can't talk back to him[15] – while his animals are completely under his control; indeed, the first specimens of these that we see are his monkeys, exactly the sorts of creatures Leland predicts Kane will lord it over after the love of the people fails him.[16]

This behavior, which the film presents as self-destructive, also has a ready explanation. Kane has been separated from his family at an early age. That separation, of course, is one in which the sled called Rosebud is an important accessory;[17] it cannot be satisfactorily replaced by the fancier sled, the Crusader, which Thatcher offers Kane in an ensuing shot. So, though we are unaware of its name, the Rosebud sled figures in Kane's separation from his family, most importantly in his separation from his mother. And, significantly, Kane utters "Rosebud" for the second time in the film, when he picks up the glassy snowscape after Susan[18] – with whom he fell in love during a discussion about mothers – has left him.

This second separation – which is recounted twice – closes the investigation which itself was initiated by Thatcher's recounting of the original separation of Kane from his family, with which the second separation seems to be identified as a tragic replay. The saliently posed theme of separation, which organizes the central plot structure in the film and which is emblematized by Rosebud, in turn, can be worked into an eminently plausible explanation of Kane's behavior. Specifically, separated from a family – that is, from an at least structurally congenial context where the potential for developing a capacity for reciprocal love relations has a running start – Kane is emotionally disadvantaged in a profound way. And that disadvantage is the root of his self-destructiveness – of his inability to act within the bounds of reciprocity. In short, deprived of a certain form of family life, Kane apparently has trouble with love, specifically in terms of reciprocity.

Of course, much of this interpretation is available on the surface of the film. Basically, I have arrived at it by paraphrasing what Leland and Susan say of Kane while interpolating some quasi-technical, though not arcane, notions such as reciprocity and separation. Both Leland and Susan Alexander return to the issue of love several times, emphasizing Kane's inability to love, especially in terms of the way in which Kane confuses love relations with those of ownership[19] and monetary exchange. Leland says Kane did everything for love but that this failed because Kane could only love himself (and, he adds as a perspicuous afterthought, his mother). Susan complains that Kane is essentially domineering – a point underscored by at least two particularly stunning, low-angle shots during her interview – and, in the course of the argument in the tent, where the tune "It Can't Be Love" suggestively blares in the background, Susan charges that Kane confuses loving with buying (an especially poignant accusation since one infers that Kane is doing unto others as the bank did unto him).

The accounts that Leland and Susan offer of Kane are pivotal to any audience understanding of Kane's behavior because they are the only attempts at explaining Kane that are found in the film. That they dovetail is important as well as the fact that they are not contradicted by anything else that is said of Kane.

The latter observation undoubtedly sounds as though it flies in the face of received wisdom about the film; for it is commonplace to note that the various interviews stake out different views of Kane. However, it is crucial to note that these differences really have to do with varying evaluations or assessments of Kane's character. The interviews do not conflict on factual matters. *Citizen Kane* is not, as David Bordwell points out,[20] like *Rashomon*; the descriptions, as opposed to the character evaluations, are internally consistent.

That each narrator has an opinion of Kane does not appear to affect his or her reporting; Thatcher hates Kane, but his picture of the young editor is of as ebullient a figure as Bernstein's. Similarly, what Leland and Susan say by way of summary descriptions of Kane's problems with love and reciprocity fit with everything else that is presented, and, insofar as they represent the only, as well as an unchallenged, explanation of Kane, they have *prima facie* authority as a statement of certain general facts of Kane's life.

The sequence which does the most work in connecting these general facts about Kane's life with the theme of separation is the first scene in Susan's apartment, where, as already noted, we see for the second time, in an insert shot, the glassy snowscape (which earlier occasions the word Rosebud) on Susan's vanity table. Kane talks of the death of his mother, his search for his youth, their mutual loneliness, and his trip to a warehouse, where, one infers, the sled awaits. Susan also speaks of her mother and her mother's operatic ambitions for her.

This affects Kane audibly, and one feels that it is at that moment that Susan's operatic career is born. The psychological structure, here, seems to be that Kane attempts to recover the loss of his relation to his mother by reinstating a mothering relation with Susan, one in which he will carry out the project that Susan's mother – against Susan's better judgment – elected for Susan. Their relation, then, begins under the aegis of a fantasy that denies the existence of Susan's goals and rights, but which is concocted as a way for Kane to recover his own psychic debits. That is, the lack of reciprocity in Kane's relation to Susan is a causal consequence of Kane's separation from his family. Kane's failure is an attempt to re-establish a family, which is something he is bound to botch since he was torn from his own family.

Expanded in this way, the Rosebud explanation does a nice job of explaining a great deal of the film. It illuminates why Kane attempts to find love by taking command, and it renders intelligible the reasons his projects auto-destruct. It also suggests a psychic rationale for the theme of acquisition so vividly underscored in the photography. For in amassing these collections of statues and animals, Kane creates a world of beings that he can control, a world of love on his terms.[21]

The Rosebud interpretation of Kane's behavior is not directly stated; but the various elements that compose it are set forth saliently, and the audience is prompted to put the pieces together with the apparition of the sled. This inference is not hard to come by – though it is aesthetically gratifying to do so – not only because it is a rather simple explanation, but, more importantly, because it is a commonplace, or what might be called folk-psychological, explanation. This is not said to disparage it. This sort of explanation is perfectly adequate and acceptable; it rests on the acceptance that there is a generalization, of some marked probability, of a connection between separation and the inability to form reciprocal love relations. That there is such a generalization, and since there are not other rival explanations of Kane's behavior, makes the Rosebud explanation preeminently sound. And, since the correlation between separation and the inability to love is also generally endorsed in our culture, audiences are likely to fill in the Rosebud interpretation when they see the sled.

But again, the Rosebud interpretation contradicts the enigma interpretation, which is not only well grounded in the film, but also rather simple and accessible, and rests, as well, on a cultural cliché. So which one is the correct interpretation of the film? They can't both be true since they contradict each other.

The problem here may be simply that we are beginning with the presupposition that the point of the film is to offer an interpretation of Kane's behavior. An alternative interpretation of the *film* – in contradistinction to an interpretation of *Charles Foster Kane* – might be that the film is about staging a conflict of interpretations about Kane's life in particular and lives in general. Here, of course, I do not have in mind a conflict between the perspectives of Thompson's various informants; for, as I attempted to argue above, there is no real disagreement at the level of description and explanation there. Rather, the film advances two readily accessible, though incompatible, interpretations of Kane's life.

What remains of primary importance in this respect is that these interpretations are, for the most part, in the film; the enigma interpretation belongs to Thompson and, perhaps by extension, to the media. The Rosebud interpretation, in full, does not belong to any character, although most of it is put in place by Leland, who, at least, has a glimmering of the importance of Kane's mother, as does Kane himself to some degree. Or, perhaps it would be better to assign the Rosebud interpretation to the ever-probing camera. In any case, like the enigma interpretation voiced by Thompson, the former is an interpretation of Kane's life that is to be found in the film.

There is no need, however, to think that the interpretation of the film must be an interpretation of Kane's life. The film, that is, may contain interpretations of Kane's life without it being necessary to identify the film with either of those interpretations. Instead, the film may be about setting the life interpretations it contains in opposition.

Another way to get at this point is to note that the output of a film interpretation need not always be a statement of what a film *means*. We might also interpret a film in terms of what it *does*. In this light, I am trying to dispel the pressure of deciding between the enigma and the Rosebud interpretations of *Citizen Kane* by suggesting that an interpretation of this film does not reduce to a decision about its meaning (vis-à-vis the meaning of Kane's life). Instead, we should interpret the film as an attempt – similar in purpose to many philosophical dialogues – to animate a debate. Specifically, it is designed rhetorically to draw the audience into a consideration of the conflicting claims of two commonplace views about human lives. That is, *Citizen Kane* is structured in such a way as to afford the opportunity for the general audience to interrogate prevailing cultural views of the nature of human life by setting them forth in competition.

This is not to say the film holds that there is no possible interpretation of a human life – that would effectively be a way of re-instituting the enigma view. Rather, the film leaves it to the audience to determine whether lives like Kane's can be explained or whether they are enigmatic. That is, the film invites further reflection, discussion, and re-viewing, rather than closing the topic unambiguously. And, as well, in considering the conflict of the common conceptions of life the film projects, the viewer comes to reflect upon those conceptions as they figure in life as well as art. Indeed, I think that where a viewer feels pulled toward one of these views over the other, it will be in virtue of reflecting on lives in general.[22]

Of course, maintaining that there are two determinate, though incompatible, interpretations of Kane's life in the film does not imply that the film is an open text, redolent with an infinite play of meanings. The film is structured around two intricately motivated interpretations which, however inconsistent, are both thoroughly grounded in the dialogue, narrative, and visual elements of the film. And although the film has two interpretations of *Kane's life*, the *film* can be characterized in terms of one interpretation which attributes to it a unified purpose.

The primary virtue of treating the film in this way is that it explains why two obviously contradictory views of Kane's life are so forcefully posed in such close proximity. It also accounts for the way in which the film is so carefully structured in support of each of the prevailing interpretations of Kane's life. Moreover, this view of *Citizen Kane* seems to me more in accordance with our intuition of its singular importance than would tying the film to either of the alternative themes we have discussed. For, surely, activating the tensions between two standing cultural conceptions is more aesthetically engaging than opting for one in favor of the other.[23]

I have often stressed that the two leading interpretations of Kane's life – the enigma interpretation and the Rosebud interpretation – are simple as well as culturally well entrenched. This is appropriate for the role they play in the dialogical structure of the film.[24] For if I am right, the point of the film is to involve the movie audience in a conflict of views about life. And in order to be functional in this respect, the views must be relatively simple, somewhat commonplace, and near or on the surface of the work. That is, they have to be accessible. Recondite or complex views of life would lack the salience required for a movie audience to pick up and enter into the debate. And, indeed, a well-structured debate is obviously more accessible to a movie audience than would be an infinite play of signification. Thus, one advantage of postulating an interpretation of *Citizen Kane* as a staging of commonplace views of life for the movie audience is that it shows how it is possible for the film to remain so popular for movie audiences. At the same time, maintaining that the debate remains open indicates one reason that it may be pleasurable to re-view and to re-engage the film again and again.

Furthermore, what I have called a dialogical interpretation of *Citizen Kane* also has the asset of fitting together with and expanding upon some of the best observations of the film's style that we have – viz., those of André Bazin. As is well known, Bazin believed that elements of the visual style of *Citizen Kane* made possible a distinctive level of audience participation. Through shots where the action is articulated on multiple planes, Bazin observed, the viewer might be said to discover dramatic meanings on her own and notice telling details as she actively scans the image. Not all or even the majority of the shots in *Citizen Kane* are of this sort, though many important ones are – enough, in fact, that this type of shooting influences the overall feel of the film significantly. Of course, the multi-planar shots that Bazin thought encouraged audience participation were not unstructured. Rather they had a structure that facilitated and rewarded the spectator's active search for significance.

Similarly, what I have identified as the dialogical structure of the film's narrative also makes possible a level of audience participation with the film – this time, however, by articulating, in a manner of speaking, multiple planes in the film's conceptual space. There is no guarantee that every spectator will be sensitive to this play of interpretation and engage it, just as there is no guarantee that every spectator will see everything there is to see and to reflect upon in the film's visual space. Nevertheless, the structural modifications are there, and they allow, rather than mandate, a level of, albeit limited, audience participation of a sort rare in Hollywood filmmaking.

One difficulty, of course, in attempting to align our interpretation with Bazin's approach is that Bazin, as mentioned earlier, explicitly advocates the Rosebud interpretation of the film rather than a dialogical interpretation. In this regard, I am forced to say that Bazin did not take advantage of the best interpretation that was available to him. For surely the notion that *Citizen Kane* has a dialogical structure accords best with his intuition that what is important about Welles is the issue of choice for the spectator.[25] It is true that Bazin generally speaks of choice in terms of camera style; but he is also aware, as his remarks about Stroheim indicate,[26] that the camera style is part of an overall narrative approach. So in advocating a dialogical interpretation of the film, one abides by the spirit rather than the letter of Bazin's writings.[27] Moreover, in pinpointing the overall significance of *Citizen Kane* in virtue of these expanded opportunities for audience participation, one is in a position to situate the importance of the film for the cultural politics of the Thirties and Forties in a way that has been hitherto overlooked.

In order to appreciate the cultural significance of *Citizen Kane*, it is useful to recall Clement Greenberg's extremely influential 1939 article entitled "Avant-Garde and Kitsch."[28] It is a meditation, a professedly Marxist one, about the direction art should take in modern mass society. This article might be regarded as a clarion call for postwar fine art and its cinematic fellow-travelers. Effectively, Greenberg argues, the rise of mass society has sundered the traditional foundations of art. Industrial society produces a demand for highly consumable art, easy art, art that does not engage reflection, but which counterfeits the patina of the great artistic achievements of the past. This is kitsch. Kitsch is the hallmark of fascist and Stalinist art. Likewise, a magazine like *The New Yorker* is kitsch as is any art that is designed to elicit the "spectator's unreflective enjoyment." It is art that demands no effort. Though Greenberg does not discuss film, I would surmise that Hollywood movies, such as John Ford's films of the Thirties, would be preeminently kitsch. Moreover, the upshot of this article would appear to be that any attempt at addressing a mass audience – and, in consequence, any attempt to make a mass movie entertainment – will result in kitsch.

In opposition to kitsch, Greenberg recommends avant-garde art because it has detached itself from industrial society at large, and because, in concentrating on problems internal to art, it will preserve the great accomplishments of Western culture through dark times. Avant-garde art, by definition, enjoins reflection, effort, and participation from the spectator. It is difficult. It depends on the spectator adding something to it as a result of reflection, thereby enshrining the high premium the Kantian tradition puts on the play of perception and cognition. And, obviously, Greenberg maintains, in a gesture of immense significance for the direction art and (avant-garde) film art will take, that ambitious art must be detached from mass society in order to secure this sort of reflection on the audience's part. The choices are: kitsch versus the avant garde, mass consumption art versus isolationist aesthetics, and unreflectiveness versus audience participation. Furthermore, the way in which Greenberg has stacked the deck makes it look as though any attempt to engage a mass audience by means of movies will be illegitimate from the perspective of genuine art.

But in this context, of course, a film like *Citizen Kane* represents the possibility of a middle road. Its dialogical and visual structures – including the montage structures that Bazin often (but not always) ignores – propose a way of coming to terms with mass culture that is neither kitsch nor avant garde. *Citizen Kane* is a mass popular entertainment which sustains the availability of participant spectatorship. It suggests a way in which mass art can accommodate the strictures of traditional art while also welcoming mass audience participation. It is not kitsch but rather satirizes Hollywood's penchant for kitsch by way of magnifying Charles Foster Kane's colossal bad taste. As Michael Denning has argued, the project of the Mercury theater was to bring art to the people.[29] In *Citizen Kane* that commitment is connected to encouraging participant spectatorship – putatively one of the highest values of traditional art – in a mass format not divorced from questions about life. *Citizen Kane* is an example of a mass popular entertainment that is also art in the *demanding* or *honorific* sense that it abets reflection. With respect to what I submit is Greenberg's still influential but by now clearly unsatisfactory dilemma – either kitsch or the avant garde – *Citizen Kane* proposes a third way, a way that encourages rather than discourages the ambitious artist to attempt to make movies for the general public.[30]

12

The Moral Ecology of Melodrama: The Family Plot and *Magnificent Obsession*

In the late 1970s, Hollywood film production is increasingly reliant on traditional genres. The exhumation of old formulas – from the 1950s especially but also from the 1930s and 1940s – is becoming more and more pronounced. Programmatic, albeit often high-budget, horror, sci-fi, war, and sports films dominate the current fare of domestic releases. To a certain extent this is a result of Hollywood's innate business conservatism: Nothing succeeds like something that succeeded before; old genres never die, they merely await rebirth in another decade. But Hollywood had been more daring in the range and types of films it experimented with from the late 1960s to the mid-1970s. The retreat to genres is not completely an industry initiative; it is also a response to the growing conservatism of the period, which, in turn, is reflected in the films.

Melodrama is among the genres presently being recycled. Two 1978 releases – *International Velvet* and *Uncle Joe Shannon* – are particularly interesting because of the similarities of their structures. Both concern the symbolic reconstitutions of families; lost parents are replaced by loving parental figures who, concomitantly, gain surrogate children. In certain respects, these films can be seen as in the lineage of the melodramas of kidnap and restoration that are so important in Griffith's Biograph work. They also recall the Dickensian ploy of an orphan who is rediscovered by a relative. Of course, in Griffith and Dickens, a family is literally reunited, whereas in *International Velvet* and *Uncle Joe Shannon* the reconstitution is symbolic. Nevertheless, the narrative structures in all these examples are predicated on the "rightness" of the nuclear family. Indeed, that "rightness" underlies the esthetic "fitness" of the plot; i.e., narrative closure is achieved through the restoration of nuclear family relations.

"The Moral Ecology of Melodrama: The Family Plot and *Magnificent Obsession*," *New York Literary Forum*, vol. 7 (1980), pp. 197–206.

International Velvet is a belated sequel to *National Velvet*. In it, Velvet, who is now in her forties, has a niece whose parents have died in some unmentionably gruesome accident. The resentful orphan is shipped from Arizona to England to stay with her aunt who has a writer boyfriend. The child is sullen not only because of her parents' death and her abrupt resettlement, but, more importantly, because she has never felt loved. We ruefully note that the only reason the child did not die with her parents was that, because they always ignored her, they did not take her on their last, fateful trip. The child is described in the film as lacking an identity, as living a cardboard, cut-out existence with no depth of feeling. And this is associated with the lack of parental affection.

The child's lack of a real family (in both a literal and psychological sense) is paralleled by a similar lack on Velvet's part. We learn that Velvet tragically lost her own child as the result of a miscarriage during a riding accident. Both Velvet and her niece are depicted as psychologically "incomplete"; they both need families to make them "whole."

The niece's alienation first begins to ease when riding and caring for Velvet's legendary stallion, Pie. Her eyes glow while she watches the birth of Pie's last foal. As the colt gambols with its mother, the editing connects the maternal scene with the niece, symbolically defining the child's yearning as not just for the horse but, more broadly, for a family. When Velvet buys the niece the horse, the girl rides it day in and day out, becoming even more obsessive about riding than Velvet had been in the earlier film. Years pass as the child, now a teenager, evolves into Velvet Junior. However, she is so preoccupied with the perfection of her equestrian art that she forgoes boyfriends and a social life. Thus, though somewhat fuller, the character is not yet complete. For that we wait until the final reel when as a member of the British Olympic riding team she "miraculously" wins a Gold Medal while also learning the meaning of teamwork. With the medal comes the sense of personal identity she lacked all along and this is connected with her marriage to the captain of the American riding team. Returning to England, the niece introduces her new husband to "her parents," finally acknowledging the family bond whose denial has caused all the emotional tensions in the film. The act is further commemorated when the niece gives Velvet her Gold Medal; this compensates for the award that Velvet didn't receive, for technical reasons, in the earlier film. Thus, from one horse race, we get two generations of families whose constitution neatly solves all the emotional problems presupposed by the rest of the plot.

The melodramatic elements of *International Velvet* – including the emotional extremes, coincidences, and improbable complementary plot symmetries – are even more exaggerated in *Uncle Joe Shannon*. Released as a "Christmas" film, it underscores its use of the "family plot" with all the imagery of the Yuletide season. Christmas is the day on which our culture celebrates the completion of its mythic first family. Because Christmas exists in large measure as a mass fantasy – inextricably bound up with childhood associations of the warmth, generosity, and security of the family – the holiday is one of the most potent symbols in Hollywood's arsenal. In the hands of a master propagandist like Frank Capra, a Christmas carol at the right moment becomes a veritable national anthem, instilling a wave of irrational fellow-feeling that makes Capra's nebulous populism seem almost plausible. The mechanics of this effect are simple – Christmas imagery induces regression, rekindling childlike beliefs in social stability and community that grow out of ideal-izations of the family. In *Uncle Joe Shannon*, the ideological use to which Christmas is put is not in the service of a broad political stance like pop-ulism but as a reaffirmation of the family and its role as the central and natural form of human relation.

The film opens with the eponymous Joe playing his trumpet at a recording studio. The camera pans around him, the circular movement suggesting that he is complete as well as at the center of his harmonious universe. It is his son's birthday and Joe gives the boy a trumpet like his, only smaller. Joe is at the height of his career, but the film makes it clear that fame is less important to him than family. Joe is unremittingly uxo-rious, touching and kissing his wife at every turn. He ignores triumphant curtain calls after his concert at the Hollywood Bowl in order to be home in time for his son's birthday party. But disaster strikes; his home is aflame as he pulls into his neighborhood. The film dissolves, and seven years later we see Joe – a skid row wino desperately clutching his horn. He has lost both his family and his art. These are the two losses the plot must recuperate.

Joe visits a prostitute, but she is out. Her son, Robbie, who calls all her clients "uncle," demands that Joe tell him a story. Joe and Robbie fall asleep. Next morning, the police awaken them at gunpoint. Robbie's mother has run away and the boy must go to an orphanage. He revolts and hides in Joe's car, convinced he can make something (namely, a father) out of this bum.

In the tradition of Chaplin's *The Kid* (a particularly interesting film in terms of the family plot), Robbie comes to idolize Joe. Christmas is approaching so Robbie steals a Santa Claus outfit from a department store, and the duo plays street-corner renditions of "Jingle Bells" to earn their keep. At this point Joe does not yet understand that Robbie is his salvation. He slaps the boy for playing with his own dead son's trumpet, tries to send Robbie away, and finally puts the boy in the orphanage. Joe's inability or, perhaps more aptly, his refusal to acknowledge Robbie as his symbolic son is an example of a key device of melodrama for engendering suspense. We know the boy is exactly what Joe wants; when will he realize it?

Joe attempts to commit suicide after he puts Robbie in the orphanage. This is the symbolic turning point in the film. Director Joseph Hanwright floods the scene with metaphors. As Joe sinks to the bottom of the bay, he looks up and sees a ball of light shimmering on the surface. Having "seen the light," he struggles upward, no longer "drowning in self-pity." He kidnaps Robbie from the orphanage. In subsequent scenes, his music begins to improve. The opening symbol of "harmony" continues; each station in Joe's progress is reflected in his playing. Insofar as the etymology of "melodrama" is drama plus music, *Uncle Joe Shannon* is at least notable for making Joe's solos an explicit index of each phase of his moral growth.

Though Joe acknowledges his paternal affection for Robbie, a catastrophe (the favorite type of plot complication in melodrama) erupts. Robbie has cancer. Joe convinces him to undergo surgery. But when Robbie's leg is amputated, the boy feels Joe has betrayed him. He refuses to talk to his surrogate father. He won't practice using his wheelchair or his crutches. The doctors fear that he has lost the will to live.

The plot becomes perfectly symmetrical. Now Joe must redeem Robbie. He gives Robbie his son's trumpet, a gesture whose phallic significance is no harder to decipher than the horse symbolism in *International Velvet*. But Robbie still won't budge. Joe tries to infuriate him back to life. Joe plays his horn at a Christmas party for the other hospitalized children. He has never played better. Hearing the music, Robbie struggles downstairs to reclaim his "father." Unsteady on his crutches, he glowers at Joe; but hatred and pride give way to love. The boy hangs on Joe's neck while Joe plays mellifluously with one hand. The camera circles them, echoing the opening shot. Both have become complete again. The father has a son, and the son, a father. The music, the camera movement, and the Christmas iconography heighten the effect of this "family reunion." The esthetic "unity" and integration of elements here not only correspond to but mirror the theme of emotional symbiosis between father and son.

Coming on the heels of a decade of radical and/or feminist criticism of the nuclear family, melodramas like *International Velvet* and *Uncle Joe Shannon* are somewhat surprising. In their particular use of the family plot, they project and unquestioningly endorse the family as the right structure for human relations. Parent-children relations are posed as inevitable – something characters are irresistibly drawn toward (for their own good). Emotion is engendered in the audience by means of characters who, for a given period of time, fail to see or refuse to acknowledge the rightness of the symbolically reconstituted family proposed by the plot. The idea of the family, as it is shared with the audience, makes these stories possible. But, at the same time, the existence of these stories reinforces prevailing beliefs in the idea by symbolically rehearsing a faith in the family through fictions that train, or, at least, further inculcate audiences in this particular way of ordering everyday human events.

A sense of *déjà vu* accompanied my encounters with *International Velvet* and *Uncle Joe Shannon*. I knew I had seen their basic plot structures in operation before, and I set about trying to remember where. The answer came quickly; it was *Magnificent Obsession*, a 1953 adaptation of a Lloyd Douglas novel of the same title, directed by Douglas Sirk. Sirk was, among other things, a highly successful director of film melodrama whose critical currency shot sky-high in the early 1970s. Part of the reason behind this reevaluation is the fact that new German directors, like Rainer Werner Fassbinder, who are interested in parodying or extending the melodramatic form, honor Sirk as a major forebear, including, for example, homages to his style in their films. Sirk is now considered a central exemplar of film melodrama. In some cases, especially with reference to *All That Heaven Allows* and *Written on the Wind*, favorably disposed critics argue that Sirk uses melodramatic formats in order to subvert regnant values and preconceptions. Historically, melodrama has at times provided a vehicle for social criticism. Yet, though I am not sure whether *All That Heaven Allows* and *Written on the Wind* merely appear subversive, I am certain that *Magnificent Obsession* is conformist in terms of form and content, and form as content.

Whereas in previous examples, the symbolic transformations of the family plot involve the replacement of parents and children with surrogates, in *Magnificent Obsession* the plot works to substitute a lost husband with a new one. Like many melodramas, the film begins with a tragic accident. Millionaire playboy Bob Merrick overturns his speedboat; an ambulance rushes to the scene with Dr. Wayne Phillips's resuscitator. At the same time, the venerable Doctor Phillips has had a stroke, but without his resuscitator, he dies. His young wife, Helen, is informed. Several characters pointedly remark on the irony of the situation. A great humanitarian and surgeon has been lost so that a wastrel like Merrick can live. They presuppose an injustice or imbalance in the way Wayne Phillips died, something that will in fact be rectified in the way the plot unravels.

Merrick is introduced as reckless, arrogant, brash, discourteous, and selfish – the very opposite of the saintly, always thoughtful-to-others Helen Phillips. Merrick, hospitalized in Wayne Phillips's clinic, barks at the doctors, diagnoses himself, and lectures on medicine; he announces that he once was a medical student – a fact that will become important shortly. The clinic staff treats Merrick aloofly and he sneaks out of the hospital. In the tradition of melodramatic coincidences, he hitchhikes a ride with none other than Helen Phillips. He tries to make a pass at her until he learns that she is Mrs. Phillips and that he is connected with her husband's death. He gets out of the car but faints. She returns him to the hospital, learns who he is, and vows to avoid him. Yet their fates have already been intertwined. His desire for her continually grows while she resists each of his advances.

Another story line develops parallel to the romantic interplay between Merrick and Helen. Just as these two characters "discover" each other's identities, so Helen gradually "discovers" who her husband, Wayne Phillips, really was. People write to, and visit, her with stories of mysterious debts owed to Dr. Phillips. At crucial points in their lives, Phillips helped them with money, advice, and influence. In each case, he swore them to secrecy. When they attempted to repay him, he said it was already "all used up." We learn, primarily through a painter named Randolph, that Phillips practiced a bizarre, quasi-religious faith. He believed that helping others gives the benefactor access to "power." One could achieve whatever one wanted through this cosmic power. Strained analogies with electricity are offered to explain how this moral-metaphysical mechanism works. For example, the secrecy is like insulation. Great men "ground" themselves in this power. In fact, their greatness "flows" from this power. Christ is cited as one of the founders of this system of self-interested altruism. Randolph's career as a painter floundered until he mastered the method under Phillips's tutelage.

Randolph explains Phillips's religion, his "magnificent obsession," to Merrick, who, despite warnings against trying to "feather one's own nest" with it, attempts to apply the power in his pursuit of Helen. He helps a parking attendant whose family is in trouble and suddenly he sees Helen. He rushes to tell her about this "miracle" and about his allegiance to her husband's faith. She grows increasingly annoyed and, in her efforts to escape from him, is hit by an oncoming car. As a result of the accident, she is blinded. Along with her widowhood, this is another tragedy the plot will commutate.

Merrick, moved by the consequences of his actions, begins to practice Phillips's doctrines in earnest. He secretly helps the Phillips's family by buying their house at an exorbitant price. He also enrolls in medical school again as the best means to help others, and predictably he specializes in surgery. Quite clearly, he is becoming Wayne Phillips. Helen refuses to allow him to see her, but he takes advantage of her blindness and visits her at the beach daily. He tells her that his name is Robbie Robinson. His whole manner is changed. He is no longer brash but humble, self-effacing, other-directed, and reassuring. He emotes all the cultural cues of being a "concerned" person – a visible altruism has supplanted his earlier selfishness. He secretly pays for Helen to travel to Switzerland where she is examined by a battery of the world's most renowned specialists. When they tell her that a cure is impossible, he flies to her side to lend support. He takes her to a peasant festival to distract her, and after they dance all evening he confesses his love as well as his real name. She says that she knew he was Merrick (the theme of identity again) and that she loves him. But the obvious denouement is blocked, enhancing melodramatic suspense. She runs away; she is afraid that he will marry her out of pity.

He goes on to become an internationally famous doctor. His sideburns turn gray. He repairs patients' private lives, demanding secrecy and refusing future repayment on the grounds that by that time "it (the power) will be all used up." As he rushes about the hospital corridors, we assume that this is what Wayne Phillips must have looked like. In short, during this interlude, both Merrick and Helen prove they are "good," which, in this context, means "self-sacrificing." They are ready to reap their rewards.

Randolph tells Merrick that Helen is ill in New Mexico. He arrives and the local surgeon asks Merrick to perform the operation. Merrick is afraid he is not skilled enough, though we realize he has stored up a surfeit of "power." After some reluctance he operates, hoping to restore Helen's eyesight. He spends an all-night vigil at her bedside. She awakens; she can see; they will marry. The injustices and imbalances, the disequilibriums in Helen's life, introduced earlier in the plot, are adjusted by means of the practice of Wayne Phillips's "magnificent obsession," and homeostasis returns. Helen regains her husband in the form of Merrick, who has been molded according to the Phillips prototype. The original family has been reconstituted with a kind of narrative symmetry that portends "destiny."

Sirk's *Magnificent Obsession* differs from Lloyd Douglas's novel in many respects; a large number of plot details have been changed, dropped, or added including Randolph's occupation, Merrick's age, Helen's blindness, etc. Also, Sirk's film avoids Douglas's banking metaphors for the power, relying only on the electrical one, while also deleting Douglas's notion that religion is a science. According to Sirk, his script, which was prepared by Robert Blees, was primarily based on the screenplay for the 1935 adaptation of *Magnificent Obsession*, directed by John Stahl. Nevertheless, the Sirk film remains true to the essential tenets of Douglas's mysticism. As in Douglas's *Disputed Passage* and *Green Light* (also films directed by Frank Borzage in 1939 and 1937 respectively), *Magnificent Obsession* promotes an ethic of service and sacrifice, devoted to systematic selflessness which is connected to impersonal, moral powers that have causal efficacy in the world of everyday events. That is, Douglas and Sirk present a viewpoint where morality is treated as part of the basic structure of the universe. Facts and values are not strongly demarcated; moral disequilibriums are reflected in events.

In the film, Merrick's wasteful existence and arrogant manner "cause" Phillips's death and, later, Helen's blindness. His melodramatic regeneration, through a hodgepodge of metaphysics and popular mechanics, results in redressing these tragedies. In this sense, what I call a moral ecology is presupposed by the plot. That is, the plot is structured as if there were a strong causal interdependency between a fundamental moral order (which is geared toward producing self-sacrifice) and everyday events. A violation of the moral order, an imbalance like Merrick's selfishness, causes a repercussion which, in turn, causes further events until the imbalance in the system is adjusted and equilibrium again obtains in the relationship between the moral order and human affairs. Melodrama, in general, emphasizes strong dichotomies of good and evil as well as exact correspondences between moral conflicts and dramatic ones. In *Magnificent Obsession*, the metaphor of "the power" is a device that conflates the moral order and everyday events into one synchronized (ecological) structure.

The values and virtues in all variants of *Magnficent Obsession* are "other-regarding." They include some elements that are not normally thought of as "moral," but more as matters of etiquette. In Sirk's film Merrick is initially marked as "bad" because he is rude, impatient, and domineering. Politeness and courtesy-to-all rather than the proverbial white hat is the most important sign of the good guy in American film. Merrick is the villain until he learns the power – a form of cosmic sensitivity (and good manners) to others – at which point he is virtually a demigod.

Stoicism, in terms of both physical and emotional sufferance, is also lauded. Both Helen (vis-à-vis her blindness) and Merrick (in his love of Helen) evince it and are duly rewarded. This stoicism, especially in Helen's case, is other-regarding; she does not want to burden her friends and companions. Humility and generosity, of course, are the prime ingredients of "the power." Thus, the film projects a seductive fantasy, cathecizing receptive audiences in courtesy, stoicism, humility, and charity. A constellation of values is ideologically reinforced by promising that that precise ethos is connected with, is even constitutive of, 'the source of infinite power."

The moral order, or at least the moral order being valorized, is presented as part and parcel of the nature of things as a causal force or as a regulatory force with causal efficacy. In this respect, the particular moral order is represented as natural, namely, as part of the nature of things. The nuclear family – the favored form of human relationship in this ethos – is also part of the cosmic order. If damaged, it restores itself. This process is given as natural in a context where to be natural is right and vice versa. The family plot in melodramatic fiction structures human events in a way that exemplifies and endorses the ideology or ethos it presents as natural.

In *Magnificent Obsession*, the family is not only associated with the structure of the universe (unfolding itself), but also it has connotations of being curative, both psychologically and physically. By the end of the film, Helen is no longer alone and she is no longer blind. Both the sicknesses of the heart and those of the body have been cured by Bob Merrick's becoming Dr. Phillips. This notion of the curative power of the family is implicit in the family plot. Though *International Velvet* and *Uncle Joe Shannon* lack the metaphysical trappings of *Magnificent Obsession*, they too rely on the idea that the (figurative) restoration of the family is "restorative" in a broad sense, namely, a remedy for existential maladies. The family plot is a narrative structure with strident ideological implications; it portrays the family as part of some underlying order and as having naturally revivifying powers.

Sirk develops the theme of order in *Magnificent Obsession* visually in a way that buttresses the family plot with consistent metaphorical imagery. Throughout the film, there is a recurring motif of nature. Large windows look out over landscapes; one of the many examples is the forestry outside Randolph's house which we see when he opens the blinds. The Phillips's home is surrounded by compositionally emphatic, well-kept lawns and trees. We see many tranquil, picture-postcard vistas around the lake. Nature is presented as quiet, serene, and harmonious. That these specific connotations are the relevant ones for the imagery in *Magnificent Obsession* is established in the opening shots. Merrick's white speedboat with its red stripe plows through the placid lake. Sirk stresses its speed and its intrusiveness as it cuts a high, vertical wave through the water. Merrick's recklessness, symbolized by the boat crash (and later the car crash outside Randolph's house), is set against the order and calm of nature. When nature reappears, as it does often, it stands not only for beauty but for organic unity. Though the idea that the natural order is providential or divinely appointed is never made explicit, it hovers in the background. The "harmony" of the landscapes functions as a visual correlative to the moral ecology of the plot.

Another major motif is that of floral arrangements. There are flowers of all kinds everywhere in the film. Sometimes these flowers satisfy a simple compositional need, drawing the audience's attention to what will be a dramatically pertinent sector of the screen. Sometimes the flowers play a symbolic role; when a despairing Helen, who believes she is incurably blind, accidentally knocks a pot with a rose in it off her Swiss balcony, we remember an earlier rose, associated with Dr. Phillips's death, and the pathos of the scene is magnified by correlating her blindness with her other major tragedy. But over and above the local effects of flowers in a given shot or scene, the sheer statistical volume of floral arrangements in the film as a whole is expressive. They connote beauty, nature, and design, a cluster of attributes that summarize the sentimental order of the family plot.

Of course, the use of color throughout the film serves a similar end. Image after image can only be described as color coordinated. The compositions resemble those of a department store catalogue. Everything is new and matches everything else in the most balanced and symmetrical way. For example, in the first beach scene there is a green and white striped tent in the background and a matching chair in the foreground.

As the camera pulls back when Helen arrives in her pink dress we see two matching, low, symmetrically disposed, red beach chairs. Later she has a green beach blanket to go with her green swimsuit. These color coincidences can be quite insistent. Helen hands a lilac bouquet with a white spray to a companion wearing a lilac-colored suit with a white collar. We see a close-up of Helen's farewell letter to Merrick; it is written in lilac colored ink and it is held in front of a floral arrangement with lilacs visible in the background. Not all of the color coordination is as aggressive as some of these examples but it is never understated either. We feel that both the manmade and natural environments are incredibly designed. That sense of design is educed through visual clichés of harmony and order that associatively bolster the concept of design and destiny (the inevitability of the family) in the narrative.

The concurrence of the style of composition and choice of iconography with the narrative theme in *Magnificent Obsession* is an example of a variation of the pathetic fallacy, though the technique is really more of a donnée than a fallacy when it comes to film melodrama. Sirk began his artistic career (in theater and film) in Germany in the 1920s. In certain respects, the stylization of *Magnificent Obsession* recalls some tendencies of the expressionist-neoromantic films of the Weimar period. His color symmetries, for example, are reminiscent of the black and white, architectural symmetries of Fritz Lang's *Siegfried's Death*, where the composition also has connotations of "design" and "destiny." Another expressionist device – the use of height to signal authority – comes into play in one of the key scenes in the film. Just before Merrick operates on Helen, he has a crisis of nerve. He looks up; there is a cut to a low-angle shot of Randolph standing behind a plate of glass and observing Merrick from the gallery of the operating theater. The soundtrack blares the "Ode to Joy" theme from Beethoven's *Ninth Symphony* (which has been the leitmotif of the "magnificent obsession" throughout the film). The low camera angulation plus the "celestial choir" render Randolph as a fatherly, godlike figure suddenly come to earth to dispense courage, strength, and assurance. This notion of (secret) providential intervention inflects the significance of the stylization throughout the film – all the various visual orders and designs are ciphers of a supranatural system which works through characters, casting them in terms of a specific ensemble of "other-regarding" virtues and quite literally "sanctifying" the family. Stylization functions as a virtual hierophany in *Magnificent Obsession*, expressing a religious faith in the subservience of the visible world to deeper principles.

Neither *International Velvet* nor *Uncle Joe Shannon* traffics in theology as overtly or as systematically as *Magnificent Obsession*. Their idiom or rhetoric is psychology rather than religion. Both assume an extremely broad notion of a psychological economy that has the capacity to adjust to the loss of beloved objects through processes of symbolic replacement. This somewhat general principle is then put in the service of the nuclear family. The psychologically wounded characters find replacements for lost relatives who actually play the social (not merely the psychological) role of their lost family. The films begin with a valid enough (though vague) psychological principle but employ it to construct plots that celebrate the inevitability of the nuclear family. Undoubtedly, the use of psychology is more palatable to audiences of the 1970s than the theology of *Magnificent Obsession*. But the effect is the same.

13

Mind, Medium, and Metaphor in Harry Smith's *Heaven and Earth Magic*

A work of art often implicitly offers a definition – and sometimes a redefinition – of its medium; through the way in which its materials are manipulated, it reveals presuppositions about the kind of object it should be understood to be. For an example from early film, Georges Méliès treats cinema as an analogue to theater, using the frame as a proscenium arch, and employing the full paraphernalia of the nineteenth-century theatrical apparatus in his magical feats. Méliès's conception of film as theater made possible the kinds of films he made, and prevented him from conceiving others.

Harry Smith's film no. 12, called *Heaven and Earth Magic*, is a work where a quite different vision of the nature of the cinematic medium performs a constitutive function in the organization of the whole film. No. 12 has a story of sorts. According to Smith.

The first part depicts the heroine's toothache consequent to the loss of a very valuable watermelon, her dentistry and transportation to heaven. Next the film follows an elaborate exposition of the heavenly land in terms of Israel, Montreal, and the second part depicts the return to earth from being eaten by Max Muller on the day that Edward the Seventh dedicated the Great Sewer of London.[1]

This humorous and evasive description has been rendered less obscure through the admirable research of P. Adams Sitney. *Heaven and Earth Magic* is a work of painstaking animation; many of the figures in the animation were garnered from a nineteenth-century periodical that was published on the day that Edward the Seventh dedicated the Great Sewer of London.[2]

"Mind, Medium, and Metaphor in Harry Smith's *Heaven and Earth Magic*," *Film Quarterly*, vol. 31, no.2 (Winter 1977–78), pp. 37–44.

In terms of the narrative, a woman, after chasing a dog that stole her watermelon, goes to the dentist where, under the influence of a powerful anesthetic, she experiences a series of oneiric fantasies. These fantasies were often inspired through Smith's reading of the Canadian neurophysiologist Penfield (hence, the reference to Montreal), and of the Kabala (the reference to Israel).[3] The anesthetic wears off (this is the descent to earth). Despite this rudimentary story line, Smith's creative energies are not devoted to the development of the narrative. Rather the narrative serves as pretext for the almost autonomous proliferation of imagery – a rapid, energetic succession following its own principles. These principles derive from a conception of cinema not based on narrative models like the epic poem, or the short story, or the novel: they model cinema on the mind.

I mean that the simile of cinema as mind provides a context in which the imagery of *Heaven and Earth Magic* becomes intelligible. On the most immediate level, the film employs everyday metaphors about states of consciousness as sources of imagery. For example, we often describe the state of reverie in terms of images floating into consciousness. In *Heaven and Earth Magic*, this phenomenological metaphor is embodied in a number of ways. Items descend at a stately pace from the top of the frame in defiance of the laws of gravity. Also, the image of floating is mined by the use of the sound of lapping water on the aural track, sometimes suggesting that on-screen objects are suspended in a liquid solution.

The popular tendency to anthropomorphize faculties of the mind is literalized. The film is dominated by the figure of a little man, a miniature gymnast, who seems to direct much of the action. He is a sort of executive homunculus, a personalized mental faculty, a little man within the mind who makes it work.

The psychological arcana of the drug world is also apparent. The woman's consciousness literally "expands" – her head gets larger after she is injectd. Drugs purportedly strip away our ego disguises; as her head explodes, a mask flies out. The idea that a drugged state induces a "high" is embodied in the upward heavenly movement of the imagery; as the drug wears off, the heroine not only comes "down," she "crashes" – her landing accompanied by a smash-up on the sound track. The befuddlement of the sense of time under drugs is suggested by images of floating clocks. And, on the sound track clocks with different cadences count out time at different intervals, suggesting in a symbolic way the possibility of divergent experiences of time.

This generally humorous mimesis of the drug experience doubtless derives from Smith's documented use of drugs. This concern extends to much of the imagery of *Heaven and Earth Magic*. Repeatedly, Smith searches for images of the experience of the ego under drugs. In some cases the border between inside and outside becomes ill-defined – there are images where a stomach is attached to an arm. There are constant references to the fragmentation of the self through visual images of persons splitting apart, through visions of dismemberment, and through aural images of glass shattering and splintering. These motifs serve as literalizations of the everyday clichéd expressions of the "breakdown" of the ego.

Apparently, Smith originally wanted to carry even further the notion of the ambiguity of the border between self and other, under drugs, by designing a special theater for the film in which spectators would sit in seats that repeated the recurring objects of the film. Ensconced in upholstered watermelons and eggs, the visual differentiation between screen and auditorium would be slightly less complete than usual, that incompleteness serving as a symbol of the unsteady boundary of the ego under stress by means of continuing the motif of the blending of supposed contraries (i.e., internal is to external as screen is to audience).

But *Heaven and Earth Magic* ultimately is involved with more than the mimesis of states of consciousness. Rather the film presents itself as an image, or better, as a set of images of consciousness, of the mind itself. This is made explicit in the iconography of the film during the ascent of the heroine to heaven. The dentist's chair transforms itself into the outline of a head. The head, in turn, is inscribed in a box, the very sort of image that John Locke evokes when he analogizes the mind to a cabinet,[4] a closet, a dark room, and a *camera obscura*.[5] Two standard images of the mind, the head and the box, encompass the action, functioning as two frames within the cinematic frame, and thereby suggesting that the third frame in the rhyme, the cinematic frame, is to be understood on a par with the head and the box as yet another figure for the mind. Here the frame is demonstrably proposed as a correlate to consciousness. The rest of the film, as well as what went before, is devoted implicitly to deepening this explicit metaphor.

Of course, to analyze *Heaven and Earth Magic* as a metaphor of cinema as mind involves a number of complexities, not the least of which is the fact that "the mind," itself, is an elusive term, indeed one that we often attempt to characterize by means of metaphors like the *tabula rasa* or the spotlight. Coleridge thought of it as a vegetable,[6] to mention an eccentric case. Cinema, itself, has even served as a figure of consciousness – questioning the empiricist concept of the mind as a darkened room, the late Aron Gurwitsch wrote: "Hume expressly likens consciousness to a theater, but it is so to speak a theater without a stage. In modern terminology, one could compare consciousness with a perpetual succession of kinematographic pictures. . . ."[7] Thus, in discussing the cinema/mind analogy we are in a thick soup where metaphors play on metaphors, sometimes doubling back on themselves. Yet, it is important to note that it is the very fact that the mind is often thought of in metaphors, indeed most often in terms of concrete visual metaphors, that allows Smith to propose and to develop the identification of cinema with thought.

This is not to say that in the course of *Heaven and Earth Magic*, Smith evolves a consistent, original philosophy of mind. Rather, the film is a series of poses, identifying with this or that metaphor of mind, trying on different and not always evidently harmonious images of thought as the basis for the genesis of imagery. The screen is a mindscape; sometimes it is the mind as darkened room, and sometimes it is the mind as machine. The coherence of the film is not derived via a consistent perspective on the nature of thought, but instead coherence emerges through the succession of imagery that proposes different images of the mind, though not manifestly reconcilable ones. *Heaven and Earth Magic* interests us for aesthetic, not philosophic, reasons; it evokes the sense of an organic totality unified by the theme of mental metaphors.

One source of the mental metaphors in *Heaven and Earth Magic* is the language of British empiricists. The initial contents of the film are introduced by being emptied from Egyptian mummy cases. This is reminiscent of Locke's idea of the mind as a cabinet or closet, full of simple impressions of perception. In Hume's *The Treatise on Human Nature*, it is held that ". . . what we call a mind is nothing but a heap or collection of different perceptions united together by certain relations. . . ."[8] The notion of the heap, of course, occurs vividly toward the end of the film when the heroine's descent is marked by a pile of disparate objects, the details of her fantasy, crashing in front of a carnival arcade.

The notion of a person as a bundle[9] of perceptions is evoked in the beginning of the film when the heroine appears as a package with a head. That self-identity is nothing more than a congeries of percepts is proposed visually when, in an introductory scene, a woman is created through the metamorphosis of a pile of objects including a barrel, a valise, a hatbox, and a handbag. Here it is important to emphasize that the objects of *Heaven and Earth Magic* are patently magazine cutouts; their rather stiff pictorial quality is unabashed, making them easy analogues to the empiricist's simple percepts and discrete sense-datums.

Throughout, the mind as collection is a dominant motif. The very dated quality of the imagery suggests some kind of antiquarian collection while the way in which the various items are juxtaposed on-screen often affords a kind of combination of elements that can only be described fittingly by as neutral a word as "collection." Locke's metaphor of the train of ideas,[10] Hume's of ideas gliding across a stage,[11] as well as the common empiricist metaphor of the stream or torrent of consciousness, all emphasize a phenomenological experience of thought as a partially ungovernable succession of the discrete objects of sensation. Such a characterization correlates to the incessant, intrusive manner in which imagery invades the frame in *Heaven and Earth Magic*.

It is not my contention that in *Heaven and Earth Magic*, Harry Smith has evolved an illustrated history of British empiricism. Many key empiricist metaphors, such as the *tabula rasa*, do not appear in the film. I am not even claiming that Smith acquired the empiricist metaphors from reading the empiricists; these metaphors are deeply embedded in our culture and are available without studying Locke and Hume. Smith has developed only a selection of the culturally available metaphors of mind, employing those chosen generatively; i.e., the heap, the closet, the flow of ideas each in turn serves either as a pretext for the appearance of a certain image or as a means of combining or organizing discrete images.

Empiricist conceptions of the mind also seem to influence Smith's imagery in terms of its mechanical motifs. At times, the insides of the heroine's head are portrayed as a set of spinning gears, with a jack hammer and other machine noises synchronized on the sound track. Of course, empiricism is allied with mechanism in a very specific way, because of its conception of the operations of thought in terms of the processes of the association of ideas. Associationism, the empiricist's vision of thinking as the combination, dismantling, and recombination of simple ideas, is at the root of the empiricist's identification with mechanism. Moreover, associationism also seems relevant to Smith's *Heaven and Earth Magic* because various categories of association seem to supply the best descriptions of the step-by-step articulation of imagery in the film.

Classical associationism proposes the building up of complex and abstract ideas out of simple ideas or sensations. This sort of artisan's view of thought recurs in *Heaven and Earth Magic* through various repetitions of tools including pliers, a saw, a vise-grip, a mattock, an ax, and an engineer's hammers. These repeated elements suggest a theme of construction. The engineer's hammer is especially important because it is a major device for transforming one element of the heroine's fantasy into another. Either when in the hands of the miniature gymnast, the ringmaster of the film, or while floating free, the engineer's hammer need only touch an object, and, with an accompanying crash, the object metamorphoses completely.

The emphasis on a sense of the composite or of assemblage in associationist imagery is also in evidence in *Heaven and Earth Magic*. There are strange flying figures that stalk the heavenly realm. Sometimes birds, sometimes insects, they are made of cut-outs of shells, gears, wires, and whatnot. They, like the assemblage of the cyclops in the first half of the film, remind one of the associationist claim that the fantastic beasts of mythology are recombinations of elements previously experienced in perception.[12]

The mechanical tone of associationism is captured in a number of ways. Often on the sound track there is the whirr of machinery. As well, an array of objects, putatively the kind of heap of perceptions that constitute the mind, spins around, and in the process becomes transformed into thirteen wheels, cogs in the mind machine. At another point, these machine gears turn so fast that they are transformed back into objects: a hammer, a fan, a gramophone, a dog, a hand, a skull, an enema, a bird, a light bulb, an urn, a mortar. Here, the transformation suggests that the machine image and the ensuing collection are in some way equivalent, perhaps two faces of the same view of the mind.

The mechanical metaphor of the mind is also developed by Smith through iconography that represents items of the heroine's fantasy being produced by a huge, mysterious machine. All sorts of entities are fed into the machine – fish, eggs, umbrellas. And out come effigies of the heroine – the machine of consciousness collating percepts into personal identities.

I have already emphasized that one does not encounter a consistent philosophy of mind in *Heaven and Earth Magic*. This is especially evident in Smith's use of associationism. For though he does employ several empiricist images of the mind, the type of associationism Smith most favors is not empiricist but psychoanalytic. For Hume, simple ideas were related to each other in virtue of resemblance, continguity, or cause and effect. In *Heaven and Earth Magic*, typical cause and effect relations are often suspended. Instead of creating images generally in accordance with the "commonsense" empiricist schema, Smith, perhaps intuitively, relies more on the primary processes of the unconscious for the provenance of associations between his various images.

Harry Smith, himself, has pointed to his reliance on the psychoanalytic conception of free association in the organization of his imagery. He said

I tried as much as possible to make the whole thing automatic rather than any kind of logical process. Though at this point Allen Ginsberg denies having said it, about the time I started making those films he told me that William Burroughs made a change in the Surrealist process–because, you know, all that stuff comes from the Surrealists–that business of folding a piece of paper: one person draws the head and then folds it over and somebody else draws the body. What do they call it? The Exquisite Corpse. Some one later, perhaps Burroughs, realized that there was some kind of what you might call God. It wasn't just chance. Some kind of universal process was directing these so-called arbitrary processes: and so I proceeded on that basis: try to remove things as much as possible from the consciousness or whatever you call it so that the manual processes could be employed entirely in moving things around. As much as I was able I made it automatic.[13]

Here the automatic process gives rein to the free association of the disparate objects of the film. Undoubtedly, Smith's penchant for free association is somewhat overdetermined. It derives not only from a surrealist concern with psychoanalysis, but also from Smith's preoccupations with the Kabala insofar as the psychoanalytic process of free association is akin to the Kabalistic form of meditation known as skipping, wherein one writes out a random set of letters or words, and then lets the eye jump from one to another, changing the original order in the hope that one of the recombinations will provoke a powerful insight. In both skipping and free association, a play of juxtaposition is set in motion that unites disparate items in ways that defy straightforward rational ordering. As Smith suggests, there is a universal process at work. That process, of course, is the unconscious.

Throughout *Heaven and Earth Magic*, one detects the presence of unconscious processes operating in the association and organization of the disparate elements of the film. One such process is what Freud called condensation in his discussion of dreams.[14] An analogue to verbal metaphor, condensation is a visual means through which disparate elements come to be identified. Condensation functions by the construction of composite or collective images, through the construction of one object out of aspects of several different objects, thereby suggesting a relation of identity.

In *Heaven and Earth Magic*, the relationship between sound and image often seems to be primarily condensatory. Many of the transformations in the film are accompanied with the sound of a crash or a crack-up, yoking together or associating the aural event with the visual in a way that characterizes metamorphosis as a violent process, emphasizing the destructive component by identifying the process with mayhem. At one point in the film the gymnast is leaping from one pedestal to another until he comes to a place where a row of small couches continuously passes across his path to a larger couch. The smaller couches descend from the top of the frame at a steady pace. The sound cue changes several times. One moment it is the sound of wind, coloring one's perception of the image so that the space between the gymnast and the larger couch can be experienced as a gorge. Another moment the cue is moving water, projecting a sense of the moving objects as a river or a stream. Then the sound cue changes to honking horns, affording a view of the scene as a street full of traffic, each couch seen as a car. The effigies produced by what I earlier called the machine of consciousness are assembled while carnival noises play in the background, suggesting that these mannequin figures are shooting-gallery targets. Thus, disparate elements of sound and image are combined, yielding metaphoric identifications, though not all the identifications are as easily readable as these examples.

Another process of the unconscious mind that appears consistently in *Heaven and Earth Magic* is what Freud calls dramatization,[15] through which imagery is organized in such a way that it evokes a word or concept. For instance, Eisenstein explains to us that his motive in animating the stone lions in *Potemkin* was to literalize an old Russian epithet for indignation that describes appalling events as those with the power to make the very stones roar. We many presume that Eisenstein is a conscious master of this technique since we know he was familiar with Freud's *Jokes and Their Relation to the Unconscious*.[16] Dramatizations recur throughout silent Eisenstein, especially in the first half of *October*. Indeed, as a film instructor, Eisenstein asked his students to find verbal solutions to the problem of visualizing scenes as he did when in *Potemkin* he transformed the notion of "flight" into the stone flight of the Odessa stairway.

As has already been suggested, *Heaven and Earth Magic* abounds with this sort of literalization. "Being high" and "crashing" are immediately accessible dramatizations. Likewise, the idea that the heroine's mind is in conflict during her descent from heaven is literalized through visual imagery of boxing and wrestling as well as through aural imagery of fight arenas with bells ringing and crowds shouting. That the heroine's experience is one where ideas and memories are "stirred up" is represented by the constant appearance of spoons (which also have drug connotations). This literalization would have been even more apparent in Smith's original plan for the film where Smith envisioned a scene in which "everyone gets thrown in a teacup which is made out of a head and stirred up."[17]

The important point is not simply that condensation and dramatization appear in *Heaven and Earth Magic*. These forms of symbolism function in many films, and not, for that matter, only in historically enshrined art films – popular sound films, as critics like Parker Tyler have often elucidated, are full of these forms of expression. Nevertheless, the way in which condensation and dramatization appear here is distinctive, for rather than being virtual figures of speech, as they are in Eisenstein's cinematic vocabulary, in *Heaven and Earth Magic* they are, as it were, the very subject matter of the film. This is borne out by the large number of vaguely decipherable condensations; it is difficult to say exactly what these expressive structures communicate, yet it is still possible to identify them as expressive structures, albeit ones that are often merely displayed rather than functioning. That is, often symbolic devices in the film are not experienced as vehicles conveying a legible subject matter, but instead they constitute the subject matter – they become the signified, not the signifiers, in contradistinction to their usual role in film.

Smith's version of baring the device aligns him with the surrealist project, because the types of signifiers revealed and displayed have psychic prototypes. Of course, the correlation between *Heaven and Earth Magic* and surrealism does not hinge simply on this single correspondence. Smith himself has made clear his attempt to transcribe the surrealist's use of automatism into cinematic practice. As well, the concern with extreme wanton violence – a fantasy manifestation of the destructive power of the id – provides another common ground between Smith and surrealists. Also, there are iconographic congruities. In his use of nineteenth-century engraving and in conjoining objects of disparate scale, Smith recalls aspects of the work of Max Ernst. And the correlation of the work of art with the box of consciousness wherein memories are juxtaposed allusively suggests the elegiac collages of Joseph Cornell.

A surrealist film text, *Le Chien Andalou,* sheds light on *Heaven and Earth Magic.* Just as Smith much later was intrigued by the idea of the Exquisite Corpse, Buñuel and Dali attempted to devise a kind of automatic editing akin to Breton's notion of automatic writing. Wherever they detected a conceptually intelligible connection between shots, they broke the splice and recombined their materials until what resulted struck them as arbitrary. In place of normal narrative connections, they arrived at dreamlike associations, modeled on the psychic prototypes of the structures of the primary processes. For instance, dramatization structures imagery – the underarm hair of a woman migrates to the face of a man, recalling Magritte's painting *La Viol,* where, as well, a pun between the sense of "figure" as both face and body serves as the elementary motive of the imagery.

Buñuel and Dali, like Smith, rely heavily on dream structures. The most famous example of this sort of coordination of condensation and dramatization in *Le Chien Andalou* occurs when a man who has been chasing a woman suddenly picks up a rope and drags two priests and two grand pianos (filled with two dead mules). The whole style of analysis in *The Interpretation of Dreams* is predicated on the supposition that the primary processes express conceptual relations by physical connections. Thus, that the man's lust is repressed by religion and culture is depicted by his literally being restrained by the rope and burdened by the priests and that great symbol of nineteenth-century bourgeois artistic pretensions, the grand piano. That Buñuel and Dali view religion and culture as asinine is expressed by dumping dead asses in the pianos.

There is a sequence of shots in *Le Chien Andalou* where a shot of ants dissolves into one of an armpit which fades into a sea urchin which fades out into a head. Here, the process of association condenses these disparate elements via superimposition, one of the very metaphors that Freud employs when he refers to Galton's composite photos as a means of describing the mental process of condensation.[18] The surrealist use of transformation as a means of identification, as when buttocks turn into breasts,[19] or when books turn into guns, also occurs in *Heaven and Earth Magic,* where Smith, a self-professed alchemist, makes transformation the major recurring motif of the film. To a large extent, the identifications in both *Le Chien Andalou* and *Heaven and Earth Magic* remain ultimately opaque; it would require long hours of psychoanalysis with the filmmakers to decode the precise significance of these images. However, that processes of identification are operating can be intuited – one recognizes familiar processes of thought in action. *Le Chien*

Andalou abounds with strategies later found in Smith. There is the constant repetition of visual elements – the recurring diagonal stripe design, the image of the nun's habit, and the anaclitic relation between the first man and his tormentor. Here repetition functions as a cue of significance, though the exact signification eludes us. Repetition serves the same function in Smith where various permutations of the same action intimate sense without conveying it. Thus, a woman hits a dog, and the dog hits a woman who hits a bull, etc. Motifs repeat in a way that suggests that they are likely bearers of messages. The viewer is primed by the presence of regularities to suspect significance because some system appears manifest though its messages remain undecoded. The shapes within Smith's images also echo each other – watermelons and eggs, for instance, seem to suggest some psychic equivalence through their visual similarity, recalling Buñuel's anti-sentimental rhyming of a cloud drifting across the moon with a razor slicing an eye.

The surrealist motive behind the display of the expressive mechanisms of the unconscious was to force into public consciousness an acknowledgment of modes of mental experience ignored by a bourgeois culture attentive only to utilitarian and rational processes of thought. Bourgeois culture emphasized only a segment of experience, sweeping under the rug that realm of experience encountered in the incessant play of thought, which constitutes a major part of everyday life. That realm, the Surreal, involves the experience of dream, of reverie, of slips of the tongue, of humor, and of the constant evocation of past memories through association. The strategies of surrealism were predicated on triggering, through artworks modeled on psychic prototypes, a recognition of universally operative but rarely acknowledged dimensions of experience. Here, it was important to emphasize the modes or forms of irrational experience because it was the operation of these modes to which attention had to be drawn. It was the signaling system rather than the particular signals which required recognition. If the signals were clear, the operation of the irrational would be experienced from a rational perspective; the mechanisms of the unconscious would appear as just another foreign language; the qualitative divide between rational and irrational would be co-opted. Attention would be drawn away from the unconscious modes of experience and drawn toward a preoccupation with the assertions of the unconscious, rewritten in the intelligible language of wishes and demands. Thus, it was essential to the surrealist project that its display of the operations of the unconscious remain partly inscrutable. Through the hermeticism of *Heaven and Earth Magic*,

Smith engenders this provocative inscrutability, intimating sense through the presence of unconscious expressive processes, thereby making the unconscious manifest, eliciting its recognition by displaying its universal modes in such a way that the audience gasps as a mirror is held up to its repressed mental life. And, as with Buñuel and Dali, that gasp is often accompanied with a burst of involuntary laughter as the boundary line of rationality is transgressed.

Smith read Daniel Paul Schreber's *Memoirs of My Nervous Illness* while working on *Heaven and Earth Magic.*[20] Schreber was an important Austrian justice in the late nineteenth century. He experienced two mental breakdowns which, in his memoirs, he described as visionary experiences. Schreber believed, among other things, that he was being transformed into a woman in order to be impregnated by God. Schreber's memoirs served as the only case study Freud devoted to paranoia, which Freud analyzed as a disavowal of homosexuality.[21] *Heaven and Earth Magic* is not an illustration of Schreber's memoirs; however, certain elements in the film parallel the memoirs. Both involve the construction of a woman. Moreover, given that the primary mental faculty in the woman's mind, the homunculus, is male, there seems to be a theme of sexual confusion in the film. Were one to identify Smith with the heroine, then one might postulate that Smith is, at least intuitively, miming Schreber's metamorphosis. This hypothesis could be motivated by the fact that it is through Smith's automatism that the film progresses. The constant imagery of dismemberment suggests castration. As well, recalling Schreber's relation to God, the motifs of enemas, the tinkering with innards, and the skeleton's penetration of the watermelon indicate a preoccupation with rape. The significance of these correspondences with Schreber may lead one to propose that Smith, perhaps intuitively, is working out a consistent paranoid fantasy of homosexual denial; a syndrome of mental illness is providing a model for the design of the film.

Initially *Heaven and Earth Magic* appears both confused and confusing. Its moments of narrative intelligibility are even rarer than those in *Le Chien Andalou.* Yet the film ultimately reveals a remarkable degree of coherence. The explicit identification of the frame with the mind provides the pretext for further elaboration. The bit-by-bit articulation of imagery as well as the overarching paranoid structure develop in detail the explicit mental metaphor, literalizing empiricist and psychoanalytic theories of the mind, identifying basic structures and techniques of film and of animation with mental processes. Smith presents one with an exemplary instance of aesthetic organicity, the parade of diverse objects reconciled and subsumed through a consistent view of the film as a mind. Smith has a definition of film that is implicit within the film itself. It is a definition that is a function of its use in Smith's cinematic practice.

14
Welles and Kafka

Films adapted from important novels almost always suffer unfavorable comparison with their literary sources. This is the line often adopted when discussing Orson Welles' 1962 adaptation of Kafka's *The Trial*. However, it seems to me that Welles' film is, in fact, a brilliant adaptation – a point that I will now try to elucidate especially in terms of the ways in which Welles treats those aspects of Kafka that revolt against the processes of mystification fostered by mass, modern bureaucracy.

Welles is a director noted for his manipulation of cinematic space. Hence, a likely first step in analyzing Welles' film is to examine Kafka's use of space in order to compare it with Welles' organization of film space.

Space, in terms of geography, constitutes an explicit element of at least one important plot motif in Kafka's *The Trial*. This motif involves a related continuum of events including K.'s being lost or K.'s being confused or disoriented geographically. For example, K. is literally lost when he enters the law court offices for his first interrogation. He adopts the ruse of "the joiner Lanz" in order to find the Examining Magistrate, but to no avail. In addition, on K.'s second trip to the law court, he is unable to find the way out of the building. Here, Kafka spends a third of a chapter on the matter of K.'s confusion, and on the sensation of sickness that that confusion engenders.

The motif of disorientation does not always involve K.'s being lost. K. often discovers things located in geographically surprising places. K. is surprised,on his first interrogation, to discover the law court offices in a slum. He is even more surprised and disoriented when he realizes that Titorelli's painting studio adjoins the law court offices.

Corresponding to the notion that K. is often spatially surprised, in terms of his geographical assumptions, is the fact that he occasionally

"Welles and Kafka," *Film Reader*, no. 3 (February 1978), pp. 180–188.

fails to take initial notice of items of his visual field, only to be caught off-guard, as the narrative ensues, by their presence. The appearance of the Chief Clerk of the Court in Huld's apartment, as well as the belated recognition of the second door at Titorelli's studio, are examples of this motif of unexpected appearances that disrupt K.'s sense of what is where.

The point of this discussion is that in *The Trial* Kafka elaborates a narrative theme of spatial disorientation that is embodied in numerous narrative events of different sorts, all of which presuppose K.'s uncertainty or unfamiliarity with the terrain that he is operating on. Furthermore, and most importantly, this theme is also embodied in the general style of writing that Kafka adopts. That is, there is an explicit narrative motif of spatial disorientation that involves K.'s being lost or geographically confused. In addition, there is also what might be characterized as a stylistic theme of spatial disorientation that involves the use of a set of writing strategies that keep the reader "lost," or at least confused and mystified about the terrain of the narrative. In this respect, the experience of K. is paralleled by the experience of reading the novel.

That, in general, in *The Trial*, there is a doubling or parallel between the narrative (embodied in K.'s experience) and the style (embodied through the reader's experience) is straightforward. For instance, the reader is as confused as K. about the legal system of the book because of the style of reportage that Kafka employs. In this light, I propose that K.'s occasional spatial disorientation is also replicated in the reader's experience because Kafka's style is such that the reader is almost always at a loss to speculate on the geographical coordinates of narrative action. Moreover, this inability on the part of the reader is not unnoticed, but rather engenders a global sense of uncertainty about the tale.

The stylistic origin of the reader's uncertainty might be called Kafka's tendency toward abstraction, specifically toward geographical abstraction. By using the term "abstraction," I don't intend to contradict commentators who remark that Kafka's great attribute is his concreteness. For what is meant by "concreteness," in regard to Kafka, is that Kafka refers to objects without describing them as part of an elaborate geographical setting. The reader is introduced to the object abruptly or incidentally. This strategy is described in terms of concreteness. It is consistent with this, of course, to claim that the context in which the object or detail appears is abstract insofar as it is barely set out or minimally sketched. That is, what I call Kafka's tendency to abstraction amounts to an avoidance of articulating a detailed environmental framework. Perhaps the Old Testament, if one accepts Auerbach's analysis, provides a source for this tendency.[1]

Not only does Kafka refrain from offering a physical description of K.; he also omits mention of the city or country in which the action occurs. When an author names the location of a narrative, the reader can use his knowledge of the location to have some sense of the spatial movement of the characters. Of course, this sense may be very inexact. Yet, at least, if the city is London or Paris, or the country is Russia, one feels that the characters' movements are plottable because they occur in an established context. Even if the reader is unfamiliar with the location, he still assumes the action can be mapped if the location is an existent one. Such an assumption is unwarranted in *The Trial*, resulting in a feeling of uncertainty. This is not to deny that a novel may have a fictional location. But such a location must be introduced and established by the conventional types of description employed to depict existent locales. In this respect, I am claiming that *The Trial* engenders geographical uncertainty through suppression of cues that would establish the locale either as an actual place or as a fictional place described by the decorums employed in establishing action in existent environments.

In short, to map the space of *The Trial* is impossible. Reference to an established context like Prague or Berlin is suppressed, making mapping on the basis of an existent city obviously impossible and thus cancelling one's presupposition that the space of the novel is coherent. Moreover, in terms of conventions of fictional location, the geographical descriptions in the book are too unrelated and stylistically opaque to suggest a map of the overall context. A sense of geographical uncertainty emerges from the lack of specification of any overarching geographical framework, existent or fictional. Georg Lukacs, writing on Kafka,[2] claims that Kafka's style involves what, from his prespective, is a flagrant deletion of information about the political, social, and cultural context of narrative action. The same point can be made in regard to the geographical context of the book. We have no idea of what movement across the city involves. Scenes materialize and disappear, unconnected by even a suggestion of a broader geographical totality.

In what is considered the first chapter of the book, "The Arrest," there is no preparatory description of K.'s house. We have no inkling of the spatial context. We learn only incidentally that the house has at least two stories when we read that K. is descending a staircase. This method of handling space is a striking contrast to the realist technique employed by someone like Zola. Consider, for comparison, the opening of *La Bête Humaine*.

The room was stifling hot. Old Victoire must have put too much slack on the stove before she went out to work that morning. As soon as he got in, Roubaud put the bread, the pâté, and the white wine on the table, opened the window and leaned out.

The house was the last one on the right in the small Paris street called the Impasse d'Amsterdam. It was a tall building used by the railway company to house members of its staff. The room was an attic on the fifth floor and from its mansard window you could see into the great railway terminus, the Gare St. Lazare, which seemed to cut a great slice out of the heart of Paris. That afternoon the houses in the Rue de Rome beyond looked nebulous and insubstantial in the fitful gleams of February sunlight. To the left was the vast station-roof with countless panes of smoky glass. On this side were the main lines and on the other, separated from them by the post-office building and the store-room where the footwarmers were kept, were the suburban lines serving such places as Versailles and Argenteuil. To the right a bridge, the Pont de L' Europe, flung a network of iron across the vast chasm which extended beyond it up to Batignolles tunnel. Immediately below the attic window the three double lines that ran out from under the bridge split up and fanned out into countless metal ribs which disappeared under the station roof. (Translation by Goodyear and Wright.)

Zola and Kafka virtually constitute a polarity in terms of spatial representation. In this sense, Zola is admittedly an extreme, yet he is extremist on that end of the pole which most novelists occupy. Kafka's style, in contrast, is unusual insofar as the reader is at a complete loss to place the context of action or to speculate about the geographical framework of events. Of course, it is true of many novels that one cannot exactly plot the movement of characters. Nevertheless, it is also true that most novels suggest geographical contexts. *The Trial* brackets such suggestions, thus making spatial ambiguity an issue for the reader's felt experience of the text not only because of straightforward epistemological problems about inferring the geographical coordinates of a fictional place, but more importantly by means of a suppression of writing conventions devoted to outlining or to describing, in a limited way, the spatial context of narrative development. The absence of such descriptions promotes an unsettling experience.

The spatial ambiguity of the narrative is also made an issue by Kafka for the reader through scenes that involve surprising the reader by revealing the presence of hitherto unexpected spaces in the geography of certain scenes. Consider the following description of K. and his uncle approaching Herr Huld's house.

The taxi stopped before a dark house. His uncle rang the bell of the first door on the ground floor; while they were waiting he bared his great teeth in a smile and whispered: 'Eight o' clock, an unusual time for clients to call. But Huld won't take it amiss from me.' Behind a grille in the door two great eyes appeared, gazed at the two visitors for a moment and then vanished again; yet the door did not open. K. and his uncle assured each other that they really had seen a pair of eyes. 'A new maid, probably afraid of strangers' said K.'s uncle and knocked again. Once more the eyes appeared and now they seemed almost sad, yet that might have been an illusion created by the naked gas jet which burned just over their heads and kept hissing shrilly but gave little light. 'Open the door!' shouted K.'s uncle, banging upon it with his fists, 'we're friends of Herr Huld.' 'Herr Huld is ill,' came a whisper from behind them. A door had opened at the other end of the little passage and a man in a dressing gown was standing there imparting this information in a hushed voice.[3]

What passageway? Where did it come from? The mode of description here is quite disorienting. This passageway is not set out in the initial description of the front of the house. The passageway virtually materializes in an unexpected manner.

K.'s experience of space (the narrative motif of disorientation) and the reader's experience of space (due to stylistic manipulations that make the terrain of the book vague, abstract, and at times perhaps even incoherent) are parallel expressions of the same point in Kafka. The best way to elucidate that point is by reference to Freud's concept of "dramatization." Dramatization is the process by means of which the unconscious expresses ideas by literalizing metaphors employed in language about said ideas. For example, in language we discriminate between gradations of authority through metaphors of altitude; thus a general is said to be higher than a captain. The primary processes might pictorially dramatize this idea by literally portraying a general standing above a captain in the dreamwork. Of course, this technique is also common in art. In Kafka's *The Trial,* we find space being used as a means to represent or to literalize the spatial metaphors applied in ordinary language to legal and other bureaucratic institutions. In English and in German, the law can be referred to as a labyrinth; it is something one may get lost in. Think of how we employ the metaphor of getting lost in red tape. One attempts, in this example, to characterize one's experience of the legal code or bureaucratic procedures in terms of spatial disorientation. Likewise, the notion of the labyrinth of law evokes a sense of displacement or disorientation in terms of being placed in a new and strange environment. There is a propensity in ordinary discourse to describe bureaucratic institutions through metaphors of spatial disorientation. One of the many themes in Kafka's *The Trial* is to represent literally the metaphor of being lost in the labyrinth of the law. Thus, in the narrative, K. is sometimes literally lost and often spatially disoriented. Furthermore, the reader is very often spatially disoriented and something akin to lost as a result of Kafka's writing style. Geography and the law are associated in language. One can be lost in a legal system as in a labyrinth. What Kafka does by means of the narrative motif of spatial disorientation and by means of the stylistic transformation of geography into spatial opacity is to dramatize, literalize, and represent metaphors of 'the labyrinth,' of 'being lost,' and 'disoriented' that ordinary language applies to the law and other bureaucratic institutions. K. is lost amid the procedures of the court; he is literally lost in the law court offices; the reader finds it impossible to follow the thread of legal argumentation; the reader is lost in (disoriented by) the space of the novel. Critics often allude to the labyrinth of law that *The Trial* evokes. This feeling of intellectual complexity is mirrored and indeed represented by a theme of spatial opacity and complexity.

The attribution of the use of the technique of dramatization to Kafka, in *The Trial*, seems consistent with his other works. For instance, in *Prisms*, Adorno points out that the central image of *The Metamorphosis* is motivated by an ordinary German expression which equates traveling salesmen with insects.[4] The case of *The Penal Colony* offers another example. There, Kafka constructs a diabolical pun which transforms a legal sentence (in the sense of a verdict) into a linguistic sentence.

Of course, spatial disorientation, as a metaphoric characterization of the experience of bureaucracies, is not the only thematic concern in *The Trial*. Nevertheless, the narrative and stylistic themes of disorientation do constitute an important element in the ideological dimension of the work. Kafka's deprecation of bureaucratic procedures is more horrifying for the compression or conjunction of the experience of bureaucracy with the biological experience of spatial disorientation. Kafka's technique is to recall the original wisdom and horror embedded in ordinary expressions like the labyrinth of the law by representing the biological basis of the metaphor in terms of geographical confusion. The narrative and stylistic themes of being lost or spatially disoriented are ideologically motivated attacks on the experience of bureaucracy. These attacks derive their impetus and rhetorical power through the dramatization of ordinary language about bureaucratic and legal institutions.

This is not to suggest that Kafka introduces into the text all the metaphors his style plays off, though sometimes a specific metaphor does occur in the novel. K. says "The higher officials keep themselves well-hidden."[5] This metaphor is incarnated several times. For example, the Chief Clerk of the Court hides in the darkness of Huld's apartment. Likewise, the unexpected placement of the law court offices in the unlikely attics of slums is another dramatization or representation of the metaphor that court officials (and the law) are 'hidden.' Still, not all the metaphors of ordinary speech that Kafka dramatizes are found in the text. This does not weaken the novel; it enriches one's aesthetic experience of it.

Turning from Kafka's novel to Welles' film, it is easy to detect an ideological tendency in Welles. For example, the idea of free-floating guilt in Kafka is partially anchored in terms of society in Welles. Iconographic references to Nazi concentration camps and to the atomic bomb are made, suggesting guilt as a repercussion of life in the modern state. This imagery expands the Kafka text rather than adapting it. Nevertheless, it is Welles' concern for an ideological inflection of the text that predisposes him to an ingenious adaptation of the more ideological components of the novel.

Welles, as a film-maker, turns his attention to what is potentially cinematic in Kafka, i.e., to Kafka's use of space. Moreover, Welles seems unfailingly to grasp that an adaptation of Kafka's treatment of space would accord with the ideological thrust that Welles was interested in. Of course, somehow evoking Kafka's treatment of space through film had no obvious or easy solution, for, as was noted, Kafka's geography is disorienting because of its lack of detail and because of its vagueness, whereas a film image, whenever standardly composed, is a clear and distinct record of objects and their spatial relations.

Welles adapts Kafka to the screen by means of a highly disjunctive editing style. The film and, indeed, individual scenes within the film are composed of shots taken at various locations. These shots are then interpolated in a way that makes the film look like a Kuleshov experiment writ large, spanning locations from Zagreb to Paris. Unlike the Kuleshov experiment, however, in Welles the viewer cannot help but remain acutely aware that the space of the film is a composite space, one made up of disparate places and about to fragment. The purpose of Kuleshov editing is to homogenize space. In Welles' hands, the purpose of this editing is subverted, for the spaces that are putatively linked by cutting are often too incongruous to give the sense of constituting a unified and intelligible space. Movement in the film becomes, at times, impossible to map. The sense of synthesis proposed by Kuleshov's creative geography is aborted. And the viewer of Welles' *The Trial*, like the reader of Kafka's, is constantly disoriented spatially.

Welles employs a gamut of editing strategies to render his film an emblem of spatial disorientation. These include some that are more obvious than others. For instance, in the sequence that depicts the usher giving K. a tour of the law court offices, the shots of interiors are from the Gare d'Orsay. When K. leaves said offices, he exits through the facade of an Austrian palace. Creative geography implies that the Gare d'Orsay is in the palace. But the architectural mismatch here elicits a sense of geographical confusion. This confusion is heightened by ensuing shots of K. in the courtyard of the palace because K.'s movements from one shot to the next do not appear consecutive, adding further to the viewer's sense of spatial incoherence.

Another example of spatial inchoherence occurs in regard to the attorney's house. An exterior shot of the house shows it to be at least three stories high whereas the interior shots, replete with abundant sky lights, imply that the building is only one story.

In the first sequence of the film, the shot of Frau Burstner arriving home from work situates K.'s building on a paved street directly across from another apartment building. Later, however, when Frau Burstner's crippled friend drags her trunk from the apartment building, there is no street; the building is surrounded by an enormous vacant lot.

A critic steeped in the tradition of Hollywoood editing might be tempted to dismiss these editing patterns as clumsy mismatches. But there are several reasons why such a move is suspect. First, there is a non-Hollywood tradition of disjunctive editing. Some examples of this tradition include French surrealist films such as *Blood of a Poet* and *The Andalusian Dog*. Given Welles' iconographic references to surrealism, e.g., his use of very deep space and of images that recall Dali and Ernst, it seems that what are called mismatches are better described as disjunctive cuts influenced by surrealism. A second reason to abandon the mismatch hypothesis is that the film is too intensively organized around the principle of disjunctive editing—so much so that virtually the entire film would have to be written off as an error if the preceding scenes were. At the very least, adopting a hypothesis that forces us to interpret a film by a major director as an error from beginning to end seems imprudent. Lastly, the clumsy mismatch dismissal overlooks the fact that the disjunctive editing of *The Trial* results in a uniform experience of the film object. The idea of a clumsy mismatch explains anomalies in our experience of a film. But one's experience of the space of Welles' *The Trial* is uniformly disjunctive and fragmented to such an extent that it is most plausible to assume spatial disjunction as the norm rather than as the anomaly.

One sequence that exemplifies the stylistic theme of spatial disjunction in Welles' *The Trial* begins when K. is summoned to his first interrogation. K. is in the auditorium of the opera. A note beckons him to the lobby. When K. enters the lobby, on a cut, the viewer is struck by the fact that the lobby by its structure and by its degree of disrepair cannot be part of the opulent opera house. On a series of cuts, K. moves through a maze of putatively adjacent rooms that are sometimes at odds with each other structurally and all of which are at odds with the architecture and repair of the opera house to which creative geography implies the rooms belong.

The interrogation hall constitutes a similar problem. The rooms which editing suggests are immediately adjacent to the hall seem much too small to function plausibly as an approach to the huge hall. The spatial irrationality here is further exacerbated by the fact that the door that K. enters at the beginning of the scene is different from the one that he exits from, though every directional cue leads us to surmise that he is supposedly exiting and entering through the self-same main door. Yet, on entering, the door is much smaller than on exiting. Indeed, the door K. exits from is gigantic, symbolizing his diminished power in relation to the court. The sound cue here further compounds the viewer's difficulties in rationalizing the space. For when K. exits the hall, and closes the door behind him, the sound cue is the sound of the door closing in the parable told at the beginning of the film. This repetition of a sound from earlier in the film can be explained via the Freudian notion of condensation. That is, the composite of the sound of the door of the parable and the image of the door of the interrogation hall identifies the two metaphorically. Beyond this metaphoric identification, however, in the context of an intermittently disjunctive sequence, the yoking together of a disparate sound cue with a different place serves to heighten and reinforce the viewer's overall sense of spatial confusion.

The way in which the portrait of the judge inexplicably moves from one room to another in the attorney's home is also a constant source for the disruption and perturbation of the viewer's sense of location.

More confusing still is the Titorelli sequence. K. visits Titorelli, the painter. Titorelli's apartment is rather like a large machine crate perched atop some kind of enormous heating unit. Somehow (actually by editing) this crate is attached by a door to the law court offices, though such a connection is structurally imponderable for several reasons. Why, for instance, would a door be placed in a wall so many feet away from any available floor? Also, it is hard to imagine the modern offices of the law court as connected to the older building that Titorelli lives in, let alone as connected to Titorelli's ramshackle box. K. enters the law court offices from Titorelli's room. There is only one door here and only one room to which the door connects. Yet, when K. flees from the law offices, he passes through the self-same door he entered but he does not re-enter Titorelli's apartment. Titorelli's room seems to have disappeared. The door now seems connected to a series of different passageways including, fittingly, a sewer. Initially, the scene is set on the top of a building. As it progresses we find ourselves in a sewer with no acknowledgment in the editing of a movement from upstairs to downstairs. It is impossible for the viewer to divine the geography of this sequence. How K. manages to move from one space to another is felt to be incalculable because K.'s movement appears palpably incoherent.

Welles makes quite explicit the fact that he is involved in "dramatizing" or representing spatial metaphors. For instance, the attorney says he moves in "legal circles." Immediately after this, the attorney walks around a column in his bedroom. Also, at the end of the film the notion that the law is inaccessible is represented in spatial terms. K. walks toward the projected door of the slide parable. He will obviously never enter that door. It is two-dimensional, while he is three-dimensional. To digress, it is interesting to note that somewhat akin to visualization of the idea that the law is inaccessible is the way in which Welles represents the idea that the law is incomprehensible. Welles, playing the attorney, mumbles, speaks with a towel on his face, speaks with a cigar in his mouth. These devices make his words, words about the law, quite literally incomprehensible. The aural image of incomprehensibility provides the justification for much of the sound recording which some critics attack as inaudible. Welles clearly had control of much of the post-synched dialogue. Its distortion is meant to reflect back upon the incomprehensible messages that the language conveys. Moreover, this device is precedented in Kafka's text where K. has great difficulty understanding the dialect of the Italian businessman. That is, difficulty in hearing a language is one element Kafka introduces in his overarching image of K.'s lack of comprehension.

Turning back to Welles' editing, its disjunctiveness seems to function to disorient the viewer spatially. One often does not understand how K. moves from one space to the next. More importantly, one is aware of this lack of understanding. The incoherence and unconventionality of the matching make the viewer aware that he or she has little or no idea of the geography of the whole film, and, very often, also aware that he or she has no convincing idea of the geography of various sequences. Like Kafka, Welles introduces into the style of his work conditions that eventuate in the spatial disorientation and confusion of the spectator. This is by way of an attempt to evoke a cinematic image of "being lost." Through editing Welles subverts the viewer's naive preconditioned convictions about the homogeneity of narrative space. *The Trial* is a film that bursts into a thousand disassociated images of geographical confusion. The seamless, soft-cutting devices of *Citizen Kane* are eschewed by Welles not because he has forgotten them but because they would not be functional in *The Trial* where editing technique aims at making the viewer aware of his inability to map with any conviction (especially with the conviction of convention) the terrain of the narrative. Like Kafka, Welles is attempting to use space to dramatize ordinary metaphors about the law and bureaucracy in order to identify the biological terror of being lost and the experience of bureaucracy.

I am not claiming, of course, that Welles is either the first or the only film-maker to employ dramatization for the production of cinematic metaphors. The practice emerged in the silent film period. Indeed, there is probably no better theoretical description of Welles' procedure than that offered by the formalist critic Boris Eikhenbaum. He writes:

Film metaphor is entirely dependent on verbal metaphor. The viewer can understand it only when he possesses a corresponding metaphoric expression in his own verbal baggage. Of course it is possible that as cinema develops further it will create its own semantic patterns which can serve as a basis for the construction of independent film metaphors, but this will not change anything in principle.

A film metaphor is a kind of visual realization of a verbal metaphor. It is natural that only current verbal metaphors can serve as material for film metaphors; the viewer quickly grasps them precisely because they are already well known to him and because they are easily recognized as metaphors.[6]

Admittedly, not every sequence of Welles' *The Trial* is as spatially disorienting as some of the previous examples. Yet, scenes of radically felt disjunction seem to engender a kind of spatial skepticism about other sequences in the film, so that on continued viewings more and more sequences seem outright disjunctive or probably disjunctive. That is, one becomes skeptical about the spatial implications of the cutting in general. Moreover, this seems crucial since insofar as the system or code of editing is associated with the legal system or code, the breakdown of the one stylistically implies or connotes the breakdown of the other. ("Breakdown" or "collapse," of course, is, as well, a constantly developed theme through images of architectural deterioration.)

That Welles shoots the same scenes with different angled lenses also causes spatial confusion in that the scale and curvature of given locations become variant. Likewise the dubbing in the film elicits a feeling of disturbance. Voices are often dubbed at high levels so that there is an incongruity between the visual distance cue and the aural one. Also, Welles, himself, dubs the voices of other characters thereby escalating the spatial disorientation. That is, we hear Welles' highly recognizable voice without seeing his equally recognizable body anywhere. Dubbing in general engenders disorientation in that it disembodies the voice. Dubbing at high sound levels accentuates this spatial confusion, while dubbing at high sound levels with the same voice virtually demolishes any sense of a natural space continuum. The claim here is not that the only reason for the dubbing is to subvert spatial cues. Rather, the claim is that the various dubbing techniques of *The Trial* are consistent with a more generalized aspiration which is the confusion of the viewer's spatial sense by means of the subversion of cinematic cues of spatial homogeneity.

Here, one last disclaimer is in order. Welles' use of creative geography is not adopted only because it serves his vision of Kafka. Certainly production exigencies also motivated his decision. However, after creative geography was adopted as the basic method of editing, Welles, perhaps intuitively, seized upon the possibility of emphasizing the disruptive potential of linking disparate places rather than relying on smooth cutting.

Thomas Kavanagh, in an article entitled *"The Trial* as Semiology,"[7] offers an interpretation of Kafka's novel which represents K. as a semiologist attempting, without success, to decode a series of systems including not only the legal system but also codes of gesture, custom, and, in the case of Titorelli, painting. Kavanagh argues that the degree to which these systems or codes are incomprehensible indicates the degree to which they have broken down. Perhaps one might postulate that Welles' editing presents the viewer with conventions that are in the process of deteriorating, thus recapitulating, at a metaphoric remove, K.'s experience of a legal system in a state of collapse.

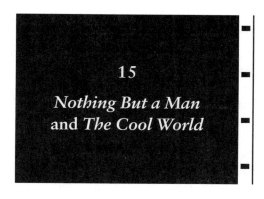

15

Nothing But a Man and *The Cool World*

Egalitarianism was one of the greatest, if not the loudest, concerns of the 60s. America, it was discovered, was an unequal society. The recognition of this fact came as a shock to many, and served as a rallying point for innumerable social, political and personal agendas of the period. Along with general recognition that not everyone was treated equally, there was also a specific recognition that not everyone was heard equally. That is, the established culture – TV, movies, indeed the whole complex of what came to be called mass media – did not represent the whole compass of the American experience even-handedly. A typical TV series – more likely than not – would have as a central character a white, middle-class male, though many viewers were neither white, middle-class nor male. Gradually, in the 60s, such phenomena came to be regarded as exclusionary, and as a form of cultural domination. As the decade wore on, the battle for representation had not only a political dimension – as blacks struggled for voting rights – but a further cultural dimension as different groups aspired for equal representation not just in the legislatures but in the media as well.

Much of the activity of the American independent film movement is best comprehended within the context of the mounting battle for cultural representation. It strove to confront the dominant cinema on a series of issues, in terms of both style and content. It presented subculture, counter-culture, beat-culture and minority culture versions of the American scene, presupposing the necessity of representing these viewpoints as a crucial means of enfranchising other-than-mainstream variations on our national experience. This process is unmistakably in operation in the cases of *The Cool World* and *Nothing But a Man*, both "problem"-oriented films that try to depict aspects of the black experi-

"*Nothing But a Man* and *The Cool World*," *The American New Wave*, ed. Melinda Ward and Bruce Jenkins Minneapolis, MN: A Walker Art Center/Buffalo Media Study Traveling catalogue, 1983, pp. 41–47.

ence with more realism and more of an "inside" understanding of black life than would be found in even the ambitious, socially conscious ventures of the dominant media such as *To Kill a Mockingbird*. That film, for example, grapples with the problem of racism in a way that filters the issues through the point of view of a white girl-child and the heroic actions of her Lincolnesque father.

The black civil rights movement was the first of the great, post–World War II egalitarian revolutions; in many ways it was the model for the movements to follow. In the early 60s, the civil rights movement was marked by the nonviolent tenor sounded by Martin Luther King, and it was devoted to achieving equality between blacks and whites through due process of law. The rhetoric of the movement was grounded in simple justice, claiming for blacks only that which most whites already had. Both *The Cool World* and *Nothing But a Man* bear the pre-Watts and pre-Black Power stamp of this stage of the civil rights movement. Their form of address is not that of the firebrand or the revolutionary; neither film threatens retaliatory black violence. Unlike a film such as *The Harder, They Come*, both works are underwritten by the hope that the documentation and explanation of injustice will move people of good will to eradicate it. These films suggest neither revolutionary upheaval nor violent apocalypse but instead try to show, in the case of *The Cool World*, how discrimination leads to the needless waste of lives mired in brutality and violence, and by showing, in the case of *Nothing But a Man*, how racism causes conditions in which self-destruction and cruelty flourish.

Both *The Cool World* and *Nothing But a Man* are "theme" films, dedicated to expounding an idea by means of a dramatic narrative. The particular idea, which both films explore, is the notion that racism creates a set of circumstances in which blacks themselves inflict a great deal of the misery they suffer upon themselves; part of the invidiousness of racism is that it turns the victim into his own executioner. In *The Cool World*, this thesis is worked out through the experience of the adolescent, would-be gang leader, Duke, whose limited world view – the product of segregation – is dominated by the belief that to be a man and to gain respect is to have a gun and to be a real, cool killer. Pursuing this mythic ideal of selfhood, of course, has the direct consequence of harming other blacks. Duke's violent ethos guarantees suffering for other blacks, and, ultimately, for himself. In *Nothing But a Man*, the indignities of racism force the central character, Duff, to turn inward and to sour. His frustration turns into self-hatred and begins to smolder into cruelty toward his saintly wife, Josie.

Though *The Cool World* and *Nothing But a Man* are propelled by simple ideas, neither feels like a tract nor veers into the self-explanatory preachiness or staged dialectics of a *Guess Who's Coming to Dinner*. Both films avoid overt, summary statement – thereby distinguishing themselves from the facile, Hollywood, race-problem film – and they elaborate their message by dramatic implication. They try to capture a sense of the psychological processes that bring about some of the generic phenomena that shape the contours of everyday black existence. The films achieve this by means of their plot structures. Both films are developmental in design; both chart the evolution of the consciousness of their central, male characters. In both films, this involves the characters' awakening to the fact that they are enmeshed in self-destructive psychological traps. In *Nothing But a Man* the process of awakening is gradual, distributed evenly at several stations along the way of the plot's progress. In *The Cool World*, the awakening comes abruptly, hitting Duke like a ton of bricks in a series of untoward events that erupt back to back as the film hurries into its finale. In neither film is it clear what practical value these awakenings will have for the characters in question. At the end of *The Cool World*, Duke is manacled in a police car, on his way to another beating and probably a jail sentence, though he is now suddenly aware of the futility of the macho-gunman creed. In *Nothing But a Man*, Duff and Josie embrace; Duff knows he must not alienate himself from Josie; but there is no answer to the question of how he can work with dignity for The Man. Neither film advocates a definite program for responding to the problems of racism. Both concentrate their energies on revealing the psychological traps racism conjures up for blacks. The awakenings that the films dramatize are, in a manner of speaking, necessary preparations for confronting racism, but they are not themselves such confrontations. The awakenings Duff and Duke undergo are the fictional correlatives to the audience's emerging understanding of some of the psychological straits blacks are caught in under racism.

Of the two films, *Nothing But a Man* is the more classically narrated. It builds to its crisis and quasi-resolution by carefully setting out Duff's character against a background of studied foils and contrasting characters. The credits roll by over a stunningly photographed scene of a group of black men laying tracks for the railroad somewhere near Birmingham. These men are gandy dancers. Relatively high paid, they lead a nomadic existence, shuttled to and fro by the railroad wherever repairs are needed. They are a rootless, all-black, cloistered male group, living together for weeks on end until they complete each job. Like soldiers, the workers brag of their freedom, yet to outsiders their nearly monastic way of life appears exploited, oppressive and claustrophobic. The opening scene in their battered bunkcar is one of edgy tedium; the men loll around with nothing to do but get on each other's nerves. Duff is singled out for special attention when the railroad men head to town for a night out. Rather than taunt a local B-girl in the manner of his friend Frankie, Duff buys her a beer without expecting any sexual favors. Thus, Duff is marked off as someone different from his fellow workers – someone with a sense of nobility and a commitment to decency which makes him an immediate locus for the audience's allegiance. He leaves the bar and wanders into a church service which presents an alternative style of life – one based on family, responsibility and religion. Though the very opposite of his own, rough *modus vivendi*, Duff is attracted. He meets Josie, a school marm and the preacher's daughter, and he wants to see her again.

Their courtship is initiated by symmetrical scenes of disapproval. Duff's friends ridicule him, suggesting that his prospects for sexual fulfillment with the likes of Josie are pretty low, and worrying that Duff wants to give up the freedom of the road for the half-life of domesticity. In suit, Josie's parents warn her of the dangers of the wild, no-account sort of man that gandy dancers are reputed to be, and her stepmother snidely insinuates that there's just one thing that could interest Josie in Duff. Josie and Duff obviously see each other as natural complements. Josie is an antidote for Duff's rootlessness while Duff has vitality and courage, uncommon virtues among the house-broken, middle-class black males Josie knows. The two want to forge a new kind of life, one that falls between the options of either the footloose loneliness or repressed domesticity that surround them. But it is not clear that society-at-large will allow blacks to survive outside these two stereotypes.

The love affair is beset with difficulties from the outside. The impossibility of reconciling domesticity and dignity becomes increasingly frustrating to Duff, and his only recourse appears to be to regress into rogue malehood. As his anger grows, it spills outward. Isolated, Duff can only assuage his pain by hurting Josie; but that is only another way to hurt himself. Duff is aware that racism is effectively dehumanizing him, and, concluding that he is "no longer fit to live with," he leaves in a gesture that seems meant to explain the break-up of many black homes. He goes to Birmingham where he visits his father for the second time in the film. Will's deterioration since their last meeting has been precipitous. The old man is in an interminable drunken stupor, shouting at Duff to leave while his mind founders. He has become a mass of human wreckage and waste, even more pathetic because much of the torment is self-made. Duff tries to rush his father to the hospital, but the old man dies in the car. While making funeral arrangements, Duff is brought face-to-face with the testament of the rogue male. No one knows when or where Will was born, or what work was his specialty when he was alive. In the book of life, Will was a desolate, blank page. Reading this as a premonition of his own fate, Duff is once again quickened into action by his father's negative example. He retrieves his own son, James Lee, and returns to Josie, their final clutch symbolizing Duff's determination to give himself roots through the family. The camera holds on Josie's tearful face. She is, at first, crying for joy. But there is anguish too, perhaps because she realizes that though Duff promises that everything will be allright, they have still not discovered a way of really reconciling Duff's role of domestic breadwinner with his righteous desire for self-respect. Indeed, if there were one criticism that might be leveled at the plotting of *Nothing But a Man*, it would be that the emotionally satisfying reunion of Duff and Josie blurs the audience's recognition that the major problem developed by the narrative – the incompatibility of sustaining a black household and maintaining one's self-esteem – has not been resolved. Nevertheless, on the asset side, the film does clearly demonstrate how racism causes frustrations that can turn one against oneself and those one loves. And this certainly is the sort of knowledge that can be emancipatory.

The classical plotting of *Nothing But a Man* is matched by its generally conservative cinematic style. This, however, is not a criticism since, though often conservative, the cinematic qualities of the film are of an especially high caliber. Shot in black and white, at a time when this had come to connote serious intent, the filming stresses strong contrasts rather than softly mapping the gray scale. This prompts a feeling of austerity and even harshness which coincides appropriately with the bare settings, underscoring the sense of indigence. Producer-cinematographer Robert Young has a special flair for shooting work and machinery. Using low-angle shots and often capturing action simultaneously on two visual planes, Young monumentalizes labor, imbuing the track laying, the trip to town on the handcar and the milling with heroic stature. One derives not only a sense of the physicality and communality of work from Young's brief portrayals, but a sense of strength and definition as well. Group acting is also handled scrupulously though not perhaps with understatement. Many scenes require – in the same shot – shifting attitudes from the players: Rev. Dawson, for example, smiles when the white school superintendent makes a dubious witticism, but then signals displeasure when the man turns his back. These dramatic touches are framed perspicuously, and the overall strategy of handling dramatic ensembles in this way is an effective means for conveying the disparity in perspective between what the generally insensitive whites think is going on and what we know the blacks think of them.

For the most part, *Nothing But a Man* is an independent film that shows little of the influence of the formal innovations of the French New Wave, or of the vibrant American experimental movement of the early 60s. Except for its stylistic asceticism – which I tend to think its creators still would have imposed for expressive purposes even if they had had a bigger budget – *Nothing But a Man* is not constructed that differently from a studio film. It is basically composed of dramatic scenes which are set out efficiently, sensitively, but classically. However, in what might be thought of as the film's interstices – the material *between* the dramatic scenes (e.g., Duff's travels to and about Birmingham) – one does see evidence of the new styles of 60s filmmaking. Primarily, this involves the use of documentary-type shooting – including apparently hand-held cameras – of the sort associated with cinema verité. A good example of this is the panning of the congregation when Duff comes upon the church meeting. The shooting, because of its style, looks like an extract from a nonfiction film of the period (and, undoubtedly, the black and white photography enhances this effect). This imitation of documentary forms in a fiction film format not only evinces a 60s interest in what was thought of as mixing documentary and fictional modes, but also performs a useful rhetorical function in this film of social criticism since it operates to claim some kind of documentary "authenticity" or "honesty" for itself by dint of its cinema verité look. This expropriation of the connotations of the ostensible veracity of nonfiction technique continues to this day with famous examples such as *Battle of Algiers* and certain scenes in *Mean Streets* and *The Deer Hunter*.

Whereas *Nothing But a Man* limits its forays into vanguard documentary stylization to its interstices, Shirley Clarke's *The Cool World* has a rough, spontaneous-looking, cinema verité appearance throughout. The camera is hand-held, the black and white film stock is fast, scenes are obviously shot on location rather than on sets and the boys are nonactors playing themselves with a nod to Italian neo-realism. As well, a great many details of Harlem street life, which have little direct bearing on the narrative, are packed into the montage, giving the film an undeniable aura of being steeped in – being in the thick of – its subject. Again, the documentary look and putative direct-cinema spontaneity that this fiction film imitates give it an expressive purchase on the kind of veracity and contemporaneity that cinema verité promoted. Of course, any spectator looking at this film for more than a few minutes can figure out that it is not an unstaged documentary. Nevertheless, in its exploration of the use of documentary techniques in a fiction format, the film betrays an early 60s obsession with realism, one that held that cinematic virtue, if not truth, lay in recording the way things were as closely as possible. In retrospect, we see that much of the conceptual foundations of this ethos were misguided – there is no correlation between wobbly camera movement and epistemological certainty. However, at the same time, it is hard not to catch the urgent feeling, and desire to capture the moment that is anxiously inscribed in the improvisatory mannerisms of cinema verité (especially when that style is contrasted with that of either the contemporary TV documentary or studio drama of the 60s). In adapting the cinema verité style, *The Cool World* makes itself appear hip, in touch with its subject, savvy, up-to-date, intimate and in-the-know while speaking directly. You could call it a case of virtue by association.

Apart from the qualities of "authenticity" that its style projects, *The Cool World* is also notably consistent in engendering a feeling of abruptness. Many shots end with flash-pans. In all probability, this was done to make editing easier. But it prompts an atmosphere of nervous tumult and of rapid, chaotic transitions. It makes this brutal world feel even more unsteady, full of wrenching changes that can come at any time. As well, the film often straight-cuts from scene to scene rather than fading, thus enhancing its abrupt quality. If the classical style of *Nothing But a Man* is appropriate for its rural, Southern setting, *The Cool World* is a nervous, jagged, Northern urban nightmare, tossing fitfully from shot to shot and scene to scene. The musical score, hard jazz that punctuates the film in often short jabs, heightens this feeling as does the narrative, which does not prepare the audience for what comes next but drops us into many successive scenes as if we were *in media res* time and time again.

Before preparing this essay, I had not seen *The Cool World* for fifteen years. Upon re-seeing it, I was very much impressed by its formal rigor, and its brilliant editing and sound mixing. The film is an intricately crafted artifice which is designed and minutely controlled to provoke the impression that it is an artless slice of life. Its tempo is magnificent, blending the directionless pulse of hanging-around time – the unemployed boys are on vacation – with the sharp transitions, across several dimensions of the exposition, which mirror the contingency of the boys' social world, a place where violent and abrupt changes are the order of the day. One technique that recurs throughout the film seems to me especially distinctive. Often when Duke is wandering around the street, even when we hear his voice-over thoughts, the editing includes cut-aways to everyday street scenes: couples, children, dogs, storefronts. These shots are often very difficult to fit into the story. They don't seem to be point-of-view shots, i.e., shots of things Duke is looking at; nor are they simple establishing shots in the normal sense of the term. Unconnected directly to the narrative, they seem to almost float into the film, shards of facts related to, but unfettered by, the story. At first, you might think that their function is to universalize the story – to imply that what is being said of Duke could apply to all of Harlem. But the images seem too fugitive and disparate to add up to a general comment. They provide atmosphere, of course. Yet, it is the way they are situated in the film that makes them special. For these "floating facts" seem randomly placed, accentuating the slice of life effect, and, perhaps more importantly, conveying a feeling of aimlessness (where "aimlessness" is a specific condition in the narrative that gives rise to the self-destructive life style of boys like Duke).

The film begins with three incisive scenes stressing the segregation of blacks in American society. First we see an abrasive close-up of an incensed black orator – a man as angry as Ras The Destroyer in *The Invisible Man*. As the camera pulls back, giving us a wider, shaky, cinema verité catalogue of street scenes, often connected by flash-pans, the imagery – with inserts of policemen and a plaster-cast Jesus – bears out the preacher's claim that whites are an intrusive, invasive force in Harlem. In the next scene – after Duke meets Priest, who offers to sell him the gun that obsesses the boy for the rest of the film – Duke and his friends pile onto a school bus for an educational tour of Wall Street on which their cranky white teacher badgers them every inch of the way. The camera details the trip downtown at length. It is impossible to miss the gradually emerging contrast between the tattered poverty of Harlem and the increasingly grander appointments of the white sections of Manhattan. This scene is not just a travelogue of New York. It literally measures the distance of Harlem from the financial center of the city which, needless to say, also comments on the "distance" of blacks from

the white center of power. The scene establishes that Harlem is unequivocally separated, physically and economically. These high school kids
are crossing a geographical border into a foreign land. In the third scene,
the boys' distance and segregation from the American Dream is given
pictorial embodiment. In the background of a shot, we see the statue of
George Washington in front of the Treasury Building; the white teacher
pronounces a civics lesson in front of it. But in the foreground of the
shot – palpably on a different, lower, visual plane – we see Duke and his
friends chattering away, oblivious to the teacher. They are not part of
the world that belongs to Washington, Wall Street and the teacher. They
are outside, in a realm of their own, divided, segregated and apart, not
merely in space, but, as the film comes to emphasize, in consciousness as
well.

Suddenly, on an abrupt cut, the film leaves the white world and
plunges into Duke's. Compressing time and space, the film presents two
hectic scenes: Duke snatches a purse which, in turn, he loses to a rival
gang, the Wolves, who beat him insensate on his own stairway. Both the
action and the cinematic presentation define this new world as violent
and full of threat from every direction. Duke is carried up to his parents'
apartment, but he staggers to his feet and sneaks out as soon as they are
asleep. This is an important moment in the film because it underlines
that Duke is separated not only from the white world but from the
world of adults in general. This point is most strongly stated when
Duke's friend, Littleman, drives his own father from his apartment with
a knife, and the boys turn the flat into a clubhouse. From then onward,
though Duke returns at times to his parents' home, Duke lives essentially in a world of adolescent ritual and fantasy, unchecked by any adult
reality principle. Part of the power of *The Cool World* is its deft recording and close observation of the rituals and ambience of the adolescent
gang. Had the film been made in the era of Black Power, it might have
attempted to turn the street folkways of these boys into black virtues, in
the manner of, say, *Sweet Sweetback's Baadasss Song*. But, as it is, the
insularity of the boy's world, instead, is developed as a crucial factor in a
cautionary tale of self-destruction.

Though the plot seems stitched together episodically – with what follows what in time as its only organizing principle – two questions are
woven through the narrative in a way that pulls the story forward.
These are Duke's preoccupation with securing a gun for the rumble, and
his desire to overthrow Blood, the ineffectual junkie who leads The
Pythons, the gang Duke belongs to. As Duke stalks the streets, selling

joints and shaking people down, to get the $50 for the gun, we often attend his thoughts, which he speaks in voice-over commentary. His fantasies are extremely repetitive; we are struck by the limitation of his imagination, fixed upon the gun, the gang and getting "fame" by becoming a real, cool killer. His inability to come up with $50 is a poignant enough comment on his limitations. But ultimately more distressing is his compulsive, fixated, incantatory, comic-book take on the world, which, though it first scares us, finally becomes a sign of Duke's helplessness. As we are uncomfortably locked into listening to Duke's myopic monologues, Duke is locked into the threadbare myth it espouses. We realize that this sort of macho-fantasizing can survive only as long as it remains contained in the world of adolescent ritual; as soon as it crosses into the space of the real world, however, there will be trouble. The "cool" in the film's title is fraught with pessimistic irony.

The film offers Duke very few options. The only positive alternatives he has are represented by a friend of Duke's, a basketball player presumably headed for a scholarship, and Blood's brother, a freedom rider. But these characters are sketched too briefly to seem like real alternatives for Duke. Instead, his options are narrowed to Blood, who Duke says taught him what he knows, and Priest, who also adopts a mentor role toward Duke. But his is a choice between the devil and the deep blue sea. Blood is a wasted drug addict, and the dapper Priest gets a bullet in the head for all his smartass shenanigans, as Duke appears to realize in an agonized moment toward the end of the film.

Duke almost recognizes in time that he is on a disaster course. These murmurings of self-knowledge come through his affair with LuAnn, a child prostitute who services the Pythons. She has poetic dreams of escaping her sordid surroundings which seem to move Duke, albeit incoherently. The couple goes to Coney Island, but LuAnn disappears inexplicably. The psychological effect on Duke is marked but unclear. It, at least, takes his heart out of the upcoming rumble. He's on the verge of giving it up. But events move too quickly upon him. The rumble ensues, and he is involved in the meaningless killing of one of the Wolves. Duke runs to the clubhouse, only to find Priest dead there, a harbinger of his own fate. Duke runs home, but the police grab him, beat him and drag him off in a furiously paced, inescapable and brutal exercise of real world justice.

The overall sense one has at the end of *The Cool World* is that of needless pain. In some ways, it could be compared to *Raging Bull*, a film in which the central character destroys himself because of his lack of understanding and his adherence to an obsolete, ethnic, macho creed that comprehends the world solely in terms of fast fists. *Raging Bull*, like *The Cool World*, is the story of self-destruction through monumental ignorance, through living in a fantasy that has little connection with the actual, surrounding world. *The Cool World*, however, differs from *Raging Bull* by locating Duke's adolescent view of the world and his lack of a reality principle in a social context. For Duke's self-destructive fantasies, which all but guarantee a wasted life for him, are the product of *de facto* segregation, and the insularity it creates. If Duke lives in a dangerous psychological dreamworld, the economics of the actual world has brought this about. As the film ends, there is mention of the Constitution, a document we often associate with equality. But in this context, the allusion is bitter. For it comes at a moment when we recognize that America, a country that literally brags about its egalitarianism, is in fact anything but an equal society. Yes, Duke is given a certain legal equality under the Constitution. But when it comes to what could be significantly called equality of opportunities, *The Cool World* has shown, through its combination of anthropological observation and psychological insight, that those equalities are something that Duke has not got.

16

Identity and Difference: From Ritual Symbolism to Condensation in Anger's *Inauguration of the Pleasure Dome*

Though we are quite willing to approach commercial, narrative films as reflections of cultural themes that dominate the milieu of their making, we tend to treat avant-garde works differently – i.e., apart from their social and historical contexts (as one might, for example, treat certain philosophical positions). The initial reason for this is understandable. Since the perspective that a new avant-garde film presupposes, illustrates, or alludes to is one that many of its viewers either inhabit or are coming to share, they do not readily see it as a particular perspective bound to a specific place and time. Yet, in retrospect, we can note sharp correspondences between the projects of the New American Cinema and preoccupations pervasive in surrounding cultural and intellectual neighborhoods.

For example, Brakhage's concern with "alternate" aspects of perception accrued special significance during a decade in which, from acid to anthropology, a great debate about the validity of different modes of experience (and living) rocked American social institutions. The formal articulation of the theme of presence in Brakhage likewise correlates with the emphasis on the lived moment – on the intensification and enrichment of experience – that was a rallying cry in the 60s and early 70s. Part of the importance of Brakhage's untiring effort, looked at through the optic of history, is his creation of symbol systems that served as emblems expressive of vital issues and interests in the culture from which they emerged.

A recurring theme of the American avant garde has been personal identity. But one can detect a change in attitude toward this subject over time. In her recent film, *Journeys from Berlin/1971*, Yvonne Rainer presents the self as fragmented, as a layering of discrete purposes (notably

"Identity and Difference: From Ritual Symbolism to Condensation in Anger's *Inauguration of the Pleasure Dome*," *Millennium Film Journal*, no. 6 (Spring 1980), pp. 31–42.

private and political) that need not cohere or fit together neatly. The presumption that the self is divided has been central to the New American Cinema at least since *Meshes of the Afternoon*. But at various junctures – such as *Inauguration of the Pleasure Dome* – the acknowledgment of the self's multiplicity has been conjoined with the wish or desire for wholeness, for the subsumption of multiplicity in some "higher" unity.

In contrast, Rainer appears to propose the disunity of various levels of personal experience as an existential condition, as an effectively inescapable fact. Rainer's attitude somewhat correlates with – though I do not think it is caused by – a growing interest in filmworld and artworld circles with the conception of the self popularized by Lacan-inspired intellectuals. In this respect, it is a benchmark (one among others) of a transition not only in the direction and presuppositions of the avant garde, but, as well, a reflection of the increased sobriety, sense of limitation and lowering of expectations of the present period.

The purpose of this essay is to analyze the overall structure of the Sacred Mushroom version of Kenneth Anger's *Inauguration of the Pleasure Dome* (henceforth often called *Inauguration*). The film was originally made in 1954 while the Sacred Mushroom edition, in which the superimpositions of the last third were added, was first screened in 1966.[1] Particularly because of the use of the superimpositions – to merge the various personae (ultimately) with the character called Lord Shiva – the Sacred Mushroom version of *Inauguration* seems to me to be highly indicative of the intellectual climate of the 60s.

Whereas Lacan's work is becoming the preferred reference of contemporary artistic and literary cognoscenti, in the 60s in America, the prevailing vanguard view of the self was represented by writers like R. D. Laing and Norman O. Brown. Though I don't claim that Anger read Brown's *Love's Body* (published in 1966), I think it is telling that the conclusion of Brown's chapter "Boundary" could be read as a paraphrase of some of Anger's major themes in *Inauguration*. Brown writes

Dionysus, the mad god, breaks the boundaries; releases the prisoners; abolishes repression; and abolishes the *principium individuationis*, substituting for it the unity of man and the unity of man with nature. In this age of schizophrenia, with the atom, the individual self, the boundaries disintegrating, there is, for those who would save our souls, the ego-psychologists, 'the Problem of Identity.' But the breakdown is to be made into a breakthrough. As Conrad said, in the destructive element immerse. The soul that we can call our own is not a real one. The solution to the problem of identity is, get lost. Or as it says in the New Testament 'He that findeth his own psyche shall lose it, and he that loseth his psyche for my sake shall find it.[2]

This clarion call to utopia finds visual articulation in the multiple superimpositions of *Inauguration*. What Brown spoke of Anger showed, celebrating cinematically those sentiments Brown verbalized to and for a very receptive audience. Brown's notion of the abolishment of the *principium individuationis* and its substitution by more encompassing unities provides a tantalizing correspondence with Anger's use of superimposition. For that superimposition, in terms of the symbolic work it does in the film, is one of the most sustained cinematic instances of the dream process of symbol-making called condensation. And condensation, in turn, in its formal operation, is involved both with ignoring the boundaries of given identities and with forging new ones.

The basic structure of the Sacred Mushroom version of *Inauguration* is simple and direct, though perhaps not immediately apparent. Considering the choice of symbols employed, we can chart the trajectory of the film as moving from the use of ritual symbol-making processes to dream processes – specifically from rites of incorporation to condensation.[3] And there is a definite kind of psychoanalytic "logic" in this movement, namely, the rituals are of a propitiatory sort whose wishes, appropriately enough, the cinematic dreamwork fulfills.

Though *Inauguration* could be segmented meaningfully in several (slightly) different ways, for present purposes I will look at it as having three major sections: the preparation for the ritual, its enactment, and, finally, the "magical" realization of the desires inherent in the ritual. The overall structure is highly evolutionary because each section propones or brings up the matter of the next section in such a direct way. For this reason, it is difficult to analyze the film except by narrating its unfolding in time.[4] This is not to imply that *Inauguration* is a narrative film, though it may bear some family resemblances to such films. I point to this feature of *Inauguration*, not to apologize for the detail of the ensuing exposition, but because there may be something significant here since many (most?) avant-garde films can be easily analyzed without recourse to narration.[5]

The film opens as the camera tilts up the title – florid, gold lettering on a field of black. The camera reaches an obscure, glittering object – suddenly recognizable as a necklace when the camera racks focus. The chain is pulled into clear view by the figure of Shiva, dressed in red satin and lying on a bed. He wraps it around his hands. There is a dissolve to a slightly closer position. Shiva's hands wave languorously; one moves to the right and the camera pans to a table packed with ornate paraphernalia. The image dissolves to a close shot, the table strewn with rings, a pipe, and a statue of Buddha. This recalls the dresser-top regalia in *Scorpio Rising*. Shiva picks up two rings. There is a cut to Shiva – every finger has a ring and the necklace festoons his hands. Then another dissolve, this time to a low angle of Shiva reclining, feet-first in the foreground. We watch him swallow the necklace.

Visually, this series of images sets forth a number of recurring themes. The hot colors, the attention to fabric, and the tendency to bedizen continue throughout the rest of the film. In retrospect, we also realize that the objects used here – the rings and necklace – have symbolic portent. Van Gennep, in another context, has identified them as ritual elements that function as signs of incorporation.[6] We might speculate that the necklace is an ideal symbol for identity in difference, for the adjunction of disparates. That Shiva swallows it is a straightforward gesture of oral incorporation, presaging the major mode of symbolism in the ritual section of the film. Thus, through ritual objects and gestures, the desire for some sort of "unity" is pronounced in the opening shots.

The camera pulls back to a longer view of the room; Shiva is rising. On the left, there is a red rug on the wall and red chairs; on the right, a yellow lamp and, behind it, a golden-winged figure. The image dissolves to a mirror and then cuts to a pair of scissors which Shiva picks up. He walks from this room to a corridor with two flaming orange doors. The scene dissolves to a room with three mirrors toward which Shiva bends. There is a cut to a new character, called 666, who, in fact, is played by the same actor portraying Shiva (Samson De Brier). 666's face is painted yellow with lines of green; he has a black beard and his eyes are surrounded with rouge. The angle of the shot of 666, plus its juxtaposition to Shiva before the mirror, strongly suggests that 666 is what Shiva sees in the mirror. Shiva daubs on makeup with a red cloth. He leaves the room of mirrors, returning to the orange corridor with a silken, billowy scarf thrown around his shoulders. He stops on the threshold and, in what appears to be a point-of-view cut, the camera tilts up the body of a standing figure, the Scarlet Woman. She has short hair, and is suffused in warm, pink light. The previous cut to 666 and the way the camera examines the Scarlet Woman tempts me (perhaps rashly) to think that this persona is another mirror image of Shiva.[7] This cut also marks the end of the preparatory section for the ritual.

The symbolic elements in this last group of images include the scissors, the mirror, and the doors or thresholds. Each articulates the theme of separation or splitting. In the film, the scissors are probably the least salient of the three. Yet they correlate with the mirror and threshold insofar as they are a metonymy for cutting, and cutting usually plays a part in rites of separation.[8] Anger's emphasis on the threshold is obvious. The corridor is a "liminal" space, a symbolically charged divider between two realms, but more importantly, between two stages.[9] The symbolism of the threshold and of the doorways acknowledges the existence of some division, while crossing the threshold is traditionally preparatory for ceremonies of incorporation.

The mirror is the most important symbol in this constellation. When Shiva peers into it and "sees" 666, we recognize the creature as some sort of *doppelgänger* for Shiva. Since the monster's demonic name is not included in the film, we do not, I think, identify him as an evil facet of Shiva. His curious comic/monstrous appearance – looking like a squashed Satan – gives few clues to the uninitiated as to what dimension of Shiva 666 stands for; yet the symbolic use of the mirror is so familiar that we understand 666 as a counterpart to Shiva. This use of the mirror is well-precedented in literature and film where the mirror, like the shadow and the portrait (things that in common parlance are "reflections") often becomes a metaphorical vehicle for projecting doubles that in turn can stand for a range of alternate aspects of the self – including that which is repressed, hidden, opposed or merely unacknowledged or potential. In terms of what is on the screen, *Inauguration* is not perspicuous about the exact relationship of Shiva to his multiple *doppelgängers*. But through the use of the mirror in the introduction of 666 we are able to understand these figures as parts or facets of, or selves within Shiva.

The visual symbolic structure that underpins the operation of the mirror/*doppelgänger* association is decomposition, which itself has two major forms – one spatial and the other temporal.[10] Temporal decomposition is a favorite trope for the construction of the creatures of horror films, e.g., werewolves. There, the violent and the civil selves are *divided in time*. By day the moral self presides and, by night the bestial. In the case of spatial decomposition, the fission of the self is depicted by *multiplying it in space*, e.g., Dorian Gray's portrait or the perambulating *doppelgänger* in Dostoevsky's *The Double*. Through the use of "mirror cuts" in the first section of *Inauguration*, Anger mobilizes spatial decomposition, physically multiplying Shiva's counterparts. Whereas the immediately preceding section of the preparation for the ritual, centered around Shiva's divan, invokes symbols of incorporation, the second half, with its room of three mirrors, develops the theme of the fragmentation, separation, and splitting of the self. Both the wish for unity and the pre-supposition of disunity appear in the preparation for the ritual. The ritual, of course, will attempt to resolve this conflict.

The cinematic space in which the ritual is about to occur is mysterious to us in terms of its location vis-à-vis the previous shots. Shiva stands on the brink of it and, as the cutting implies, he sees the Scarlet Woman. But what is the spatial relation of her position to Shiva's bedroom (which one might have guessed was immediately adjacent to the corridor)? The effect of this spatial disjunction leads us to speculate that the space of the Scarlet Woman is some magical or oneiric realm. This interpretation is further abetted by the composition of the initial, individual shots of this new realm. They are abstract in the sense that they are so dark that only the characters – 666 and the Scarlet Woman – are visible, surrounding details lost in the blackness. This is, of course, among other things, a the-atrical convention for the allegorical, the psychic, and the supernatural. Undoubtedly, interpreting this space as a special realm is no great news. But I think we can hazard a more specific account of the kind of realm it is. Since 666 and the Scarlet Woman are introduced through "mirror cuts" their realm is modalized as a "looking-glass" world, populated by *doppelgängers* of Shiva.

The shot of the Scarlet Woman dissolves to one with her and 666. In a series of cuts and fades, she brings her hand to her face, opens it, and reveals a tiny horned figure. She hands it to 666, whose robe has a visage like his own painted on it (another *doppelgänger?*). 666 takes the statue and it bursts into flame; the Scarlet Woman lights a joint with it and an image of Aleister Crowley, bluetinted (is Crowley the smoke from the joint?), with a pipe, is superimposed. This scene establishes the two major themes of the first part of the ritual – gift-giving and orality, enact-ed through offerings meant to be ingested.

The double image of smoking sparks (so to speak) the next exchange. Associated with the motif of burning, a shot of fire fades-in; there is a blonde woman, called Aphrodite, in a white toga superimposed in the flame. The superimposition identifies her with the fire, and as she walks closer, she grows larger. On a cut, she walks past the brazier and on a dissolve she meets Shiva, also garbed Roman style, and she gives him a golden apple.

The following transaction, mediated by the glance of the Scarlet Woman and presaged by the *golden* apple, finds Shiva costumed as a golden mummy. A woman, Isis, dressed in harem attire with gold trimming, feeds Shiva a golden snake, recalling the preamble where he swallowed the necklace. Shiva has a sort of spasm and Isis does a quasi-Egyptian dance. The Scarlet Woman turns again and there is a dissolve to a room of candles. Another woman, Lilith, emerges and presents Shiva with a glass bauble. He is wearing a magnificent red rug and a Cossack hat. Shiva swallows the gift and a hat like a halo rises around Lilith's head.

After the Lilith exchange, the pace of the film slackens momentarily. We see Shiva against a dark field bathed in yellow light, wearing a steep, pointed peruke. He turns and we take up what we surmise is his point-of-view of a balustrade. For some time the characters pose, sometimes in silhouette, on this balcony. The ritual action of exchange no longer organizes time. Our experience of the goings-on becomes durative. The characters' seemingly undirected or unmotivated posturing and lolling about feels languid. This apparent break from the tight ritual structure is really the first of a couple of similar interludes that represent the fruition of the rites of gift-giving and oral incorporation. Joined to Shiva by these ritual gestures, the guests disport themselves in an ideal "communitas," the durative sense of time suggesting "timelessness." Through a series of communions, they have achieved a kind of social communion, ecstatic because it is not manifestly structured.[11]

More guests arrive and the exchange pattern begins again. First, there is Pan. He gives Shiva grapes. His approach is cinematically complex, intercut with a similar action by Isis. Also there is a flashback to Lilith's giving Shiva the Jewel. Both these devices associate and identify Pan with previous guests. When Astarte appears, we see shots of her feet, echoing Pan's entrance. As with the rhyming shots of Isis, this juxtaposition of repeating motifs urges us to regard the different characters as in some way "the same." The underlying desire of the rites of oral incorporation, in brief, is already being actualized by cinematic tropes of identification, though it is not until the final segment that the machinery of this cinematic wish fulfillment asserts its total dominance.

Astarte, like the others, brings Shiva a gift – a pill. She passes it outside the frame twice and each time it returns to view it is larger. A crescent is superimposed on it, metaphorically linking it with the moon. Astarte gives it to Shiva; it metamorphoses into a pill again and he pops it. With a cut, Shiva grows wings and puts on an angelic smile reminiscent of Harry Langdon with a cold. This shot ends the first half of the ritual with the only guaranteed laugh in the film.

On different occasions, Anger has described what goes on in *Inauguration* in different ways, changing the names of his characters. This supplies one reason for avoiding an analysis of the film that searches for the allegorical meaning of the imagery – i.e., an exegesis where one rifles volumes of magical lore for the hermetic significance of such items as Wormwood Brew. The eclecticism of Anger's descriptions, both in terms of the religious traditions he mixes and in his alternate versions of Who's Who, indicates that the film does not comprise one single, historical myth but a mythic structure upon which more than one set of characters can be grafted. Consonant with this is the fact that one can grasp this myth structure – as it is ritualistically performed – without foreknowledge of the characters' names. We recognize the characters as coming to a place that in some sense "belongs" to Shiva, and as performing a rite of territorial entry, joining themselves to Shiva through offerings that he incorporates orally.

The extreme concentration in *Inauguration* on orality correlates with a theme in Coleridge's "Kubla Khan," the source of Anger's title. That (incomplete) poem breaks off with

For he on honey-dew hath fed
And drunk the milk of Paradise.

One commentator has speculated "that the 'he' of the end of the fragment... prefers the oral satisfactions of the pleasure dome to the imagined coldness of vaginal 'caves of ice.'"[12] In this light, the orality of *Inauguration* may be an index of sexual choice. But whether or not there is submerged significance in Anger's use of oral imagery, the motif has an overt, easily decipherable meaning. The offer of orally charged gifts is a standard ritual gesture of union. If we identify the creatures of this "looking-glass" realm as aspects or *doppelgängers* of Shiva, then the gifts symbolize the desire to incorporate or to reincorporate these parts in a new unity.

The second movement of the ritual begins when the Scarlet Woman and 666 beckon a figure called Caesare from the darkness. They dispatch him on an errand that takes him through a room full of candles and into a hidden closet where he meets a woman, Hecate, veiled in black, who gives him a ceramic cannister. Crowley's head, with a pentagram on the brow, is supered over the door as if to suggest metaphorically that this space is somehow in his mind. The blocking and editing of Caesare's journey give us a strong sense of directionality and spatial location, unlike most of the rest of the cutting in the ritual sequence. This leads us to perceive Hecate's closet as separate and apart from the rest of the action.

Caesare, it turns out, has obtained some kind of magic elixir from Hecate. He returns to the gathering and pours Hecate's powdery substance into the crenelated goblets of the assembled "gods," starting with the Scarlet Woman.

The ritual that began with oral offerings now appropriately develops into a kind of feast whose significance is described by Van Gennep when he says "The rite of eating and drinking together... is clearly a rite of incorporation, of physical union."[13] This repeats the earlier imagery in a new key. In the previous rites, Shiva himself was the recipient of the gifts. Now it seems that he – as the bewigged Shiva – is reciprocating in kind.

Several pages ago, I claimed that the progression of actions and events in *Inauguration* is not strictly narrative. I hope that it is clear now what I meant by that. Namely, the relations between "scenes" – like the arrival of the gods – are not based on causation. The structure of ritual – in terms of repetition (and finally reciprocation) – provides the temporal order of the film rather than the rhythm of cause and effect. The last segment of *Inauguration*, however, relies on yet another type of connective.

As the revelers toast each other, Anger begins to introduce superimpositions of various sorts. The faces of different guests are placed atop each other so that they begin to merge visually. Also, masked figures – like a skull and a horned bear – are superimposed over the characters. Earlier scenes, as well, are straticulated into the array. At points, the motif of splitting – of the scissile ego – intervenes. For example, there is a shot of opposite profiles of the Scarlet Woman superimposed over Aphrodite and Shiva (in his Roman outfit). Yet, despite the occurrence of division, the overwhelming tendency is toward constructing composite images.

Hysteric episodes erupt. Hecate does a convulsive dance, full of pelvic thrusts – part Graham but mostly the Jerk. The motion suggests both copulation and parturition, thereby signaling the imminent birth of the new self. Pan is set upon and beaten with feathers. Sitney identifies this as ritual *sparagmos*,[14] undoubtedly because that type of sacrifice correlates with the other sorts of ritual symbolism used. I am a bit hesitant to agree with Sitney in this case since we do not see anything that resembles cannibalism on the screen.[15] But I do think that the oral imagery is still important in this section.

Anger includes red-tinted images from *Dante's Inferno* by H. Lachman. This affords a blazing red backdrop for the layers of superimposition. The motivation for this choice, I believe, is not simply the literalization of metaphors of excitement, smelting and sexuality by means of fire, but also the notion of fire as "consuming."[16] The oral imagery of the ritual has, in part, been metamorphosed into an "all-devouring" conflagration.

The superimpositions continue. Gradually the wigged figure of Shiva becomes more and more dominant. The film ends with a shot of him alone. His head is in the upper left quadrant of the frame, his face green-hued. His off-center position on the top of the frame literalizes the idea that he has reached some "higher" unity, putatively through his assimilation of his other facets in the preceding superimpositions.

The major formal device in the last segment is superimposition, primarily the superimposition of heads. Also, past and present are overlaid. In this use of superimposition, we see Brown's call for the obliteration of distinctions – self and other, past and present – cinematically and fictively achieved.

The specific symbolic structure that the superimposition exploits is condensation, one type of which involves the creation of metaphoric identities through the composition of collective figures. In *The Interpretation of Dreams*, Freud discusses an instance of dream condensation that reminds us of Anger's strategy. Freud remembers that he dreamt of a figure that had his Uncle Josef's elongated features and yellow beard but also features of his friend R. Freud explains that part of the meaning of the image was to metaphorically equate Uncle Josef and R.

Interestingly – for film theory – when Freud attempts to describe this dream image he resorts to an analogy from photography that has equal relevance to film. He writes

The face that I saw in the dream was at once my friend R.'s and my uncle's. It was like one of Galton's composite photographs. (In order to bring out family likenesses, Galton used to photograph several faces on the same plate.)[17]

Freud also notes,

What I did was to adopt the procedure by means of which Galton produced family portraits: namely by projecting two images on to a single plate, so that certain features common to both are emphasized, while those which fail to fit in with one another cancel one another out and are indistinct in the picture.[18]

Freud, in short, is using superimposition to describe one kind of condensation. This suggests that perhaps one type of superimposition has condensation as its psychic prototype. In film history this variety of condensation is known, but, I think, statistically uncommon. We recall the introduction of the spies in *Strike* and the machine/Moloch in *Metropolis*, but this use of superimposition is not as frequent as that of superimpositions that depict the memories or thoughts of characters, or otherworldly apparitions. Looking at the avant-garde tradition, of course, we see that the use of superimposition as condensation is more prevalent than it is in film history at large. One thinks of Brakhage immediately, for example. The last section of *Inauguration* is one of the most spectacular examples of the use of superimposition as condensation in film. However, its point should not be semantically unpacked by "Shiva is like his *doppelgängers*" but by "Shiva is his *doppelgängers*," or better still, "Shiva becomes the amalgamation of his divided selves," thereby reaching the kind of *higher* consciousness and unity that was the desperate yearning of the 60s.

Moreover, Anger's use of condensation accords adroitly with the overall aesthetic structure of *Inauguration*. I have already mentioned that the correlation of the movement from ritual symbol to dream symbol is homologous to the movement from wish to fulfillment. But the relation between rites of oral incorporation and condensation is also grounded in another respect. Both symbolic formations postulate the identity of disparates through an act of physical union. The ritual symbols correspond to the dream symbols, therefore, not only in the way that a question leads to an answer but as two structures that can operate nonlinguistically to imply identity via physical connections.

17

"Text of Light"*

The films of Stan Brakhage are exceptionally rich in their themes. This is certainly true of his new work, *Text of Light*. Yet, at the same time, there is a simple and straightforward way in which this film relates to the main preoccupation of Brakhage's overall aesthetic program. To a certain extent, Brakhage's work might be considered as an epistemological meditation insofar as Brakhage initiates, through his art, what might be thought of as an investigation of the relation of the way men see to the nature of the world. Specifically, Brakhage uses the relativity of perceptual systems as a starting point for artistic creation. He writes in "Metaphors on Vision":

Imagine an eye unruled by man-made laws of perspective, an eye unprejudiced by compositional logic, an eye which does not respond to the name of every thing but which must know each object encountered in life through an adventure in perception.

Quite literally, *Text of Light* is such an imagining. It is a film shot through a glass ash-tray. This uncommon lens generates an equally uncommon image of the world. The density and shape of the glass subtracts linear perspective from the visual field. In this respect, the ash-tray takes up part of the function of rapid camera movements and zooms in other Brakhage films insofar as the ash-tray demolishes perspective. As well, in *Text of Light* objects lose their individuation, their outlines blurred in masses of light and color. Brakhage films the world without reliance on habitual perceptual categories like individuation and perspective. In short, the world can be seen differently; it is a matter of "lenses." In this, *Text of Light* represents an elaborate counterexample

---

*Co-authored with Bruce Jenkins, "Text of Light," *Film Culture*, nos. 67/68/69 (1979), pp. 135–138.

to the naive realistic viewpoint that posits the way 20th century Americans see as somehow inevitable.

To be more precise, the normal camera lens interprets the world by organizing received light in terms of a system of rational perspective. Thus, focusing is interpreting insofar as it is a rendering of the world according to cognitive schema. Indeed, focusing a camera is a form of intellectual work. Perhaps this is why in ordinary language we use the metaphor of "focusing" for selecting important aspects of a field of study. Yet, in *Text of Light*, the normal lens is opposed by the ash-tray lens. Perspectival focusing becomes impossible. Focusing becomes primarily a mechanical rather than an interpretive operation, a simple adjustment of the lens, palpable as a transformation of light values, but not as a schematization.

At the same time that Brakhage subverts the "normal-lense" view of things, he does not present the ash-tray view as ultimate. In image after image, for instance, Brakhage plays with his light sources in order to emphasize the flaws in the ash-tray, which shine like gems from the screen. The normal lens is interpretive but the ash-tray view is also subject to the physical conditions of its production. Brakhage acknowledges the relativity of the mode of vision employed in *Text of Light* by making the structure of the lens an active element of imagery. In this, Brakhage's point does not appear to be that there is one, privileged vision of things but rather that the world is generous in affording a multiplicity of points of view

Often, Brakhage speaks of the importance of natural visual phenomena such as closed-eye vision, i.e., the phosphenes that appear in your visual field when you close your eyes. Similarly, Brakhage is concerned with all the sorts of visual "noise" that occasion normal sight but which we block as a result of social training which ignores such phenomena by not calling attention to it. Brakhage films serve as a corrective in this respect. Often he contrives cinematic images that imitate normal but ignored aspects of perception. In *Text of Light* there are images of white light tinged with blue that recall the kind of perceptual effect that might be achieved by squinting into the sun, and focusing into the distance in such a way that your unfocused eyelashes act as a haze in the foreground of your visual field. Brakhage presents such images to underscore the exclusionary dimension of normal vision. This move is made, it seems, not in the name of another system of perception but in the spirit of a kind of pluralism.

Of course, to write in such a baldly thematic vein does *Text of Light* a great injustice. For the film is not a treatise but a cinematic experience.

At best, the preceding notes are merely a partial summary of aspects of the film. The dryness of such notes contrasts poorly with the richness of the aesthetic experience. In *Text of Light*, the tension between one's normal mode of perception and its subversion is a matter of personal experience. The film leads one to observe the way one sees. The abstract, nonfigurative imagery may suggest clouds at night, an aurora, or perhaps a landscape swathed in a glaring yellow light. Such "suggestions," however, are projections, testaments to our indefatigable drive to make the images comprehensible on our own terms. Landscapes appear to emerge when an image presents two bands of color, the top band lighter, and the bottom band darker. On this slender evidence, one postulates a horizon. One postulates depth. Brakhage may later include an image that reverses these tonal values. This reversal then can function to reveal the conditions of our original postulation. One is virtually forced into an awareness that we have brought to the screen notions of up and down and of sky and earth. We assimilate the screen into our experience, assuming the top of the screen is, in some ultimate sense, up. The landscape is our projection. Reversing the tonal values serves to make us reflect on the ways in which we structure our perceptions. In this respect, one recurring locus of attention in the film is a dynamic tension between one's natural tendency to project depth into images that are not only literally flat, but which assert their flatness and pure optical nature by virtually exclusive reference to secondary properties of light and color rather than to substances or bodies. Indeed, one can be constantly astounded at one's capacity for projecting depth on the slightest cue into this environment of pure light. In this way, the mechanics of our effectively involuntary perceptual habits are laid bare.

Undoubtedly, much of the history of cinema is modeled on the idea of the screen as some kind of window to the world. In a sense, *Text of Light* diabolically literalizes this metaphor, but with an important hitch. The window-pane, though glass, is an ash-tray which resists one's attempt to see through it. Successive attempts to map images in familiar schemas give way to apperceptive contemplation of processes of visual organization. Brakhage is a major filmmaker, one who can be unblushingly compared to Eisenstein and Renoir at the peak of their achievements. Like those other masters, Brakhage presupposes audience participation of a very special sort. Brakhage's concerns with the nature of vision emerge in the process of viewing. The investigations of the filmmaker, so to speak, are echoed by the viewer's critique of his own responses to the image.

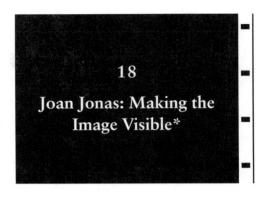

18

Joan Jonas: Making the Image Visible*

The recent, untitled video/performance piece by Joan Jonas is more striking for its video than for its performance elements. Theatrically, the video imagery dominates the spectacle insofar as the live performance is most interesting in terms of the way it is reconstituted on video. This enables Jonas to focus on what might be thought of as an esthetic interrogation of the conditions of representation in video. Her video imagery is predominantly representational, but her treatment of it bypasses a concern with the referential or representational significance of the imagery in favor of a preoccupation with the representational power or scope of that imagery. That is, Jonas seems less concerned with what the imagery represents and more involved with how much it represents.

The piece begins with the audience assembled in an area defined by the presence of three television monitors and a camera. Two of the monitors face each other on a slightly diagonal north – south axis. Initially, these monitors determine the lateral limit of the audience. Spectators, seated on cushions, cluster around these monitors. Both the spectators' distance from the monitor and the spectators' posture are highly evocative of the everyday, home viewing of television. The third monitor is in front of the audience on the set of the performance. A camera, placed in front of the performance area, keeps the audience back from this third monitor, assuring that each spectator will have at least two, and in some cases three, distinct vantage points on the video imagery.

The first section of the piece is all video. The monitors click on. The image is black-and-white; a group of people are surveying land. The images are representational, but there is no narrative, or apparent, continuity from image to image. The dialogue adds little that is not obvious from the picture.

* "Joan Jonas: Making the Image Visible," *Artforum* (April, 1974), pp. 52–53.

The fact that there are three monitors unavoidably invites the spectators to scan from one monitor to the next in order to reassure themselves that each monitor has the same image. That it turns out that the monitors are synchronized, however, does not abate the motivation to scan from monitor to monitor because in the process of checking the synchronization of the monitors one is struck by the apparent degree of abstraction in the monitors farthest from the viewer.

Because the content of Jonas' imagery seems to have neither narrative nor allegorical significance, attention is directed to the image itself. In this respect, the function of the three monitors is to give the audience several perspectives on the same image. The front monitor, in this context, is important for the way it contrasts with the monitors on the sides. The image on this monitor is recognizable, but at the same time the extreme degree of schematization of information involved in the black-and-white video transmission is placed in relief by the distance of the monitor. This distance predisposes one to look "at" the front monitor rather than "into" it, making the physical structure of the image as much a matter of attention as the content of the image.

What is striking about the physical structure of the video image is its minimalization of information. One proceeds from the farthest monitor to the nearest, scrutinizing the image for detail. That the subject matter of the piece is land surveying makes the impression of depth an important issue. There are many compositions employing strongly articulated diagonals. Strings lead from surveying markers in the foreground to the background. Yet one is still struck by the fact that it is exceedingly difficult to judge distances between objects. Sometimes it is difficult to differentiate objects on the landscape. Distance cues, like texture and tonality, and details are diminished in the black-and-white video process. Jonas takes this fact as the esthetic ground for her piece using the disparity between natural vision and black-and-white video recording as a means to promote a variety of perceptual discoveries on the part of the audience. In the opening sequence of land surveying, she succeeds in establishing the central theme of her piece as the active exploration of the limitations of the video image.

Images or land surveying give way to an image of a woman running in place. Her head is cut off by the top of the frame. As she runs, one of her knee-socks falls down, and she moves out of the frame. She is succeeded by a wooden beam which swings into view. The camera pans to the right on the motion of the beam revealing Jonas and a woman. These two move behind the wooden beam making the forward/backward orientation of objects the salient feature of the composition. The camera holds the women and the beam in medium close-up. The area behind them is uniformly white and presumably solid. But it is impossible to get an idea of the distance between the foreground objects and the background. This spatial ambiguity is emphasized when Jonas walks behind her partner, and stands on her left side. Whereas the land surveying images had proposed the problem of distance in the video image in terms or long shots, this second sequence states it in terms or closer shots.

The third sequence of images that follows on the monitors involves special effects. The basic, initial motif of the mixing here is a loft, different views of which are superimposed over each other. Unfortunately, this sequence has nowhere near the conceptual clarity of the preceding sections. Here and there interesting images evolve that suggest that different layers of superimpositions are in the same spatial continuum. Yet this general display of video pyrotechnics seems, on the whole, uninventive, perhaps because the possibilities of special effects are so well known through television advertising.

This unhappy lull in the piece is not effectively broken until the end of the section that is exclusively video. In this last sequence, an image of two women appears. One, Joan Jonas, is wearing a kimono. She sits in the foreground while the other woman sits in the background. The camera switches to a closer shot of Jonas. As she caresses herself the camera zooms back. Jonas stands up and walks around a screen in the back of the set, and the woman in the background walks forward to Jonas' chair. Jonas reenters, and walks toward the woman seated in the foreground. The camera zooms in. The sequence ends with a tight shot of a postcard held over the eyes of the seated woman. The basic strategy of this section involves the play between tight framing and medium shots. Since the sequence is nonnarrative, the alternation of the frame by zooms does not function ostensively, it merely includes or excludes objects and performers. Here, Jonas juxtaposes the bracketing aspect of the frame with the screen, behind which she passes, identifying the two, in order to define the frame functionally as a visual barrier.

The tight shot of the woman with the postcard over her eyes ends the exclusively video segment of the piece. The side monitors switch off, and attention shifts to the monitor in the front. This monitor is on the left-hand side of the performance area. On the right is a school desk. Between the desk and the monitor, but farther back, is a white cardboard cone that is about three feet high. The image on the monitor is that of the performance area.

The structure of the situation clearly dictates comparison between one's natural perception and the video recording. The discovery of the differences between the two supplies a powerful motive force and source of pleasure. For instance, the lighting of the performance area is somewhat behind the desk and the cone. Consequently, the white cone appears as a dark silhouette on the monitor as does the desk. Through the recognition of such relations, the basic material conditions of the video image become occasions for an absorbing play of attention that is primed by an intellectual curiosity in isolating and investigating the limitations of the video image.

As if to assert the disparity between the video image and natural perception even more strongly, the video image goes negative when Jonas walks into the performance area and sits at the school desk. Jonas takes a rabbit out of the desk. Then she toots on the cardboard cone. For the most part, these actions are unrecognizable on the monitor. One moves from the live action to the monitor on an insistent arc of attention searching for momentary glimmers of correspondence between the two.

Shortly following this, Jonas begins to work with a series of images that dramatically elaborate themes of the earlier all-video section of the piece. There is a screen behind the cardboard cone. Jonas begins to raise and lower it. On the monitor, the white cone appears black. At points, one can read the image of the cardboard cone as a shape drawn on the screen that Jonas is lowering. The depth between the cone and the screen is incalculable. The theme of loss of detail is also reexplored when Jonas enters the performance area completely wrapped in a blanket. On the monitor, the blanket is a dark abstract shape. No differentiation of tonality or texture of the blanket is registered, so that Jonas is an unidentifiable black figure on the monitor.

Jonas' trump card in this piece is the audience's familiarity with television. That familiarity includes the recognition that the television image is mediated by directors, often for ideological purposes. But such familiarity is still naive in that it grants or assumes that the video image is the visual equivalent of what it records. The fact that the image is mediated by a specific technology rarely becomes the focus of one's attention. The image is used as a proxy for the event it records. Consequently, the active presence of video technologies is bracketed from perception. Jonas has organized a situation where the use value of the image is undercut by the copresence of the event it records. As a result, Jonas is able to remove the brackets from the physical structure of the image in a way that proceeds through alienation and reflection to a rediscovery of video. This is not to suggest that her work is didactic. Rather, its sources of gratification are intensely perceptual, grounded in seeing afresh a familiar object of everyday life.

A good example of the way that Jonas subverts one's ordinary experience of the video image occurs in a sequence where Jonas, snapping a leather belt in time with a recording of "Sans Souci," walks toward the audience. On the monitor, there is a chiaroscuro effect to the lighting that might be characterized as moody. The video image might easily be read as some expensive patio where yet another sultry star emotes world weariness. This familiar image, however, when compared to its natural source loses its affective connotations, and becomes the locus of an intellectual evaluation of its technique.

Unfortunately, the "Sans Souci" number is followed by a routine involving Jonas' improvised responses to letters written to her by her friends. In a way, this routine seems to attempt to reverse the general format of the piece in an effort to give live performance precedence over its video representation. The mild humor of the performance, here, seems to be a play for undivided attention. This move, however, is highly unsuccessful because it involves a palpable lowering of perceptual tension. There are moments of interest in this segment. But predictably these involve reactivating interest in the monitor.

For instance, when Jonas steps slightly outside of camera range and doesn't appear on the monitor, one moves from the monitor to the camera, and inspects the camera's angle of incidence. In this way, the camera suddenly is made an active focus of attention, thus rounding out the reflexive structure of the piece. Drawing attention to the angle of incidence of the camera also evokes a metaphoric correspondence which suggests the origin of the cone-shaped forms in the performance area.

Despite such moments of clarity, the improvisations diffuse the intensity of the rest of the piece. Luckily, it does not end here. Rather, Jonas concludes with a bravura image that sums up the more interesting concerns of the piece. She sets two beams swinging, one behind the other, and she begins to rotate a huge, metal rim that had been concealed behind a curtain throughout the performance. The beams swing slowly as the metal rim turns, and a recording of calliope music supplies a musical cadence that emphasizes the rhythmic movement of the objects. On the screen of the monitor, it is difficult to judge the distance between these objects. Intermittently, it is possible to read the heavy objects as flat patterns, thus underscoring the two-dimensionality of the video image.

On the whole, this untitled piece is satisfying. Jonas is fairly consistent in structuring perceptually provocative situations. In this respect, she is expertly supported by Babette Mangolte, her camerawoman, who has a sensitive and intelligent command of the aims of the piece. It is impossible to overlook the rough spots in the work. Nevertheless, one must also admire the economy of the piece, which succeeds in making the representational video image interesting by finding a context that makes the image itself "visible."

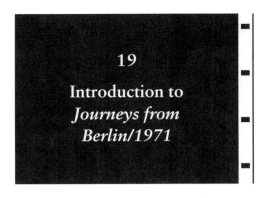

19

Introduction to
Journeys from
Berlin/1971

The period in which Structural Film (as distinct from Structuralist–Materialist Film) dominated the American avant-garde scene appears past. Attacks by sentimental humanists, on the one hand, and professorial marxists, on the other, are not causes of the decline of Structural Film but symptoms of what is already a fact. Structural Film is retiring from the field not because it lost the battle of ideas – if such a mishmash of amateur theorizing can be so called – but, more seriously, because it no longer crystalizes the attitudes, values and fantasies of the avant-garde intelligentsia. The image of the filmmaker as part cognitive psychologist, part mathematician, part chessplayer – the epitome of rarefied intellect – is no longer compelling, perhaps because the qualities it mimes and projects – including professional coolness, expertise with systems and technologies and controlled experimentalism – cannot, for all sorts of reasons, be regarded heroic in the way they were in the early seventies. The revived interest and attention given to documentaries and autobiographical film, as well as the appearance of the punk/no wave, indicate the displacement of Structural Film from the center to a corner of the American avant-garde arena.

If the tempo of anticipation and discussion at major New York strongholds of avant-garde film bears any resemblance to reality – a proposition many non-New Yorkers may greet with a hearty harumph – then the tendency pretending to or contending for the throne is what we might call The New Talkie (All Talking, Some Singing, Some Dancing). *Riddles of the Sphinx*, *Argument*, *Dora*, *Thriller*, *Our Hitler* and *Journeys from Berlin/1971* are examples of this "direction" (rather than genre). As the title suggests, The New Talkie emphasizes language – specifically, in this sort of film, language is more important than image. Of course, Structural Film also often made language its topic –

"Introduction to *Journeys from Berlin/1971*," nos. 7/8/9 (Fall/Winter 1981–82), pp. 37–42.

e.g., *Rameau's Nephew*, *Poetic Justice*, *nostalgia*, etc. But Structural Filmmakers seem primarily interested in the possibilities of language (e.g., the polysemy of words) and its limitations, whereas practitioners of The New Talkie are preoccupied with this while at the same time with "saying something." Undoubtedly, it is the urge "to say something" that accounts for the rise of The New Talkie as well as for its energetic if not always admiring reception so far.

Though I am writing about the American scene, The New Talkie, as the preceding list evinces, is not essentially home-grown. Its origin is largely European, seasoned in some cases with devices garnered from American Structural Film. Nor is the grouping homogeneous. *Riddles of the Sphinx*, *Dora*, *Argument* and *Thriller* go together as espousals of a cluster of interwoven ideas drawn from marxism, feminism, psycho-analysis and semiology. *Our Hitler* is in a class unto itself; it is an eccentric working through of a poetic/imagistic idea about the rise of Nazism – that it was a case of art (bad art) becoming life – and about its significance – Nazism is a major moment in the Americanization of the Twentieth Century – that is utterly idiosyncratic. *Journeys from Berlin/1971* (henceforth, *Journeys*) is closer to the other films cited – it shares related subjects and sources (Godard, Straub/Huillet) – but it is not of their ilk either. It does not so much allude to antecedent theories as represent, in the broadest sense of that concept, the contesting claims of politics, feminism, morality, psychoanalysis, and personal needs, desires, fears and myths, on an individual perplexed by urgent decisions about how to live and what to do. The film does not answer these questions nor does it recommend a theory with which to attempt to answer them. Rather, it is a highly stylized imitation of the tugs, conflicts and texture of the inner and outer debates such questions prompt.

Journeys is Yvonne Rainer's fourth feature-length film. The primacy of language has always been key to Rainer's cinema, but what can con-veniently be called "content" has never before concerned her as forcefully as it does in *Journeys*. The major influences on Rainer's film-making are twofold, yet converging. Of prominent American avant-gardists, Rainer is the one whose work is most analogous to European film modernism of the Godardian variety. In the first half of the seventies, for instance, her use of quasi-narratives (*cum* distantiating devices) distinguished her from most of her compatriots (though, of course, this is no longer quite the differentia it used to be). American avant-garde dance and performance of the sixties – of which Rainer her-self was a pioneering figure – is another source of her film style. Both influences predispose Rainer to her favorite formal strategy – radical juxtaposition.

Juxtaposition defines both the gross and fine structures of *Journeys*. In terms of the gross structures, *Journeys* is a dialogue of dissonant and at times contradictory voices discoursing on topics like political and psychological domination (and oppression) and the interrelation of the two. There is no overt framework – like a narrative or an authorial commentary – that organizes the various debates. Rather the film is a species of free-floating forensics with voices antiphonally adding information and opinion to a breccia of neighboring issues. The voices include: an exposition of the Baader – Meinhof saga of German terrorism (mostly in printed titles); selections from Rainer's teenage diary concerning her emerging moral consciousness; a stylized psychoanalytic session in which a psychiatrist, played by three actors, listens to an attempted suicide, played by Annette Michelson and called "the patient," who grapples free-associatively with a skein of psychological "knots" involved with the nexus between self-loathing and relations with The Other; an off-screen exchange between two disembodied voices – a man and a woman – arguing about the propriety of personal (read psychologically compensatory) motives for political action, particularly about the relation of displaced vengeance and terrorism; memoirs by Russian anarchists; an interview with Rainer's nephew; and a videotaped "letter" of Rainer, as a character, addressing her fictionalized mother.

These voices follow and even interrupt each other in an apparently desultory manner but, in fact, they are not rambled together. Most often the speeches are linked by correspondences in subject matter or analogies between thematic issues from categorically different registers. For example, the man in the offscreen debate compares the Russian anarchists' cognizance of oppressed classes with the blindness of German radicals to the plight of foreign workers. Then suddenly we hear the young diarist discuss her moral unease when confronted by a tired saleswoman. Likewise the Russian anarchists' violence is explicitly compared to the Baader – Meinhof Gang's while the patient's attempted suicide implicitly stands as worth considering in relation to Meinhof's death. Along with these correspondences in subject matter, there are thematic correspondences such as the covert connection between the problem of equality and interpersonal acknowledgment in the analytic sessions and the revolutionists' concern with social equaity.

But no sooner is a similarity bruited than it is dissected. Nineteenth century Russian terrorism and seventies German terrorism are not on a par – the Russians were more in tune with history. The two suicides are not the same; Meinhof's did have some political significance as an act against a patently repressive state whether or not her actions in general were somewhat compromised by her personal motivations. For every position in the film, its opposite appears. Though the patient derives benefit from psychoanalysis, Meinhof shows how it can be a harmful regime. When several characters realize the unreliability of trusting one's feelings – contra pop-psychology – and the imperfectibility of human nature, Jean-Jacques Rousseau chimes in with a contrary word or two. The spectator is turned into a dialectician, in the classical sense, weighing arguments and noting both shades of difference and telltale correlations in the evidence marshaled.

Journeys can be viewed as an inner dialogue, the various voices portraying radiations of a single consciousness at sea, pondering related questions from multiple, incongruous angles. Or, the controversies may be the product of several distinct disputants. In either case, the intellectual and emotional tensions are the same. And it is those tensions and their sources that Rainer aims to depict.

The bristling debates and the lacunae between different perspectives open onto deeper chasms. For at the heart of *Journeys* is the intimation that some of the debates are irresolvable, that certain fundamental perspectives about human life are irretrievably disjunct. For example, the contentious couple continually return to the issue of whether the possibly vindictive motives of terrorists should count in the evaluation of their acts. If personal motives are to be considered, the acts will be assessed more negatively than if they are not. That is, we can judge either the terrorists' actions (a form of deontic judgment) or their characters and motives (aretaic judgment), and the results from these two perspectives may not be the same, signaling a potential incommensurability between certain of the most rooted moral perspectives at the core of the concept of value. This, in turn, portends an inevitable discontinuity between the political realm and the personal (at the level of theory rather than practice, I hasten to add).

Rainer observes other, putative, profound disjunctions; she stresses a gap between what one feels to be right and what one knows to be right. She acknowledges the possible dissonance between the two while also sympathetically conveying the basic human intuition that things "ought" to be otherwise. The repeated shots of Stonehenge metaphorically bear testament to this "mystery." But unlike a philosopher, Rainer attempts neither to reconcile the preceding antinomies nor to prove that they are necessarily irreconcilable. Instead, she animates them, embodying and projecting the experience of fragmentation in an aesthetic form.

Politics and psychoanalysis are the ostensible subjects of *Journeys*. But I cannot help sensing that they are ultimately means for exercising an underlying preoccupation with moral questions. This is clearest in the political discussions where the political/historical consequences and effectiveness of the various assassinations and bombings itemized are less a matter of concern than their possible ethical impropriety. The analytic session is a way for exploring the fragmentation of the self, its multiplicity of contradictory motives and desires. But in Rainer's treatment, the analytic session takes on a strong normative dimension. It is a positive process of self-discovery and, I take it, of emancipation. It is a way of rectifying behavior if only by slackening the demands of absolute perfection enunciated by the super-ego. If *Journeys* is a journey through a mind, the mind is that of a moralist.

The fine structure of the film – its moment by moment articulations – is grounded in intricate word/image associations. Objects mentioned in the dialogues are arrayed along a recurring mantelpiece or in the background of shots of the analytic sessions; we see an image and recall an earlier word, or we hear the word and remember the earlier image. There are verbal images or literalizations. For example, when the therapist, played by an adult male who is taller than the patient, is presiding, the desk and chairs are mounted on a platform so that the camera "looks down" at the patient, but when the boy therapist appears the platform is reversed, emphasizing his "smallness" vis-à-vis the patient; and these features of the image refer to the power relations between the patient and the therapist. At times, the soundtrack literalizes what is said; the patient remarks that "some members of the family don't say anything," and then the audio goes dead; we watch her lips move, but we hear nothing. In other instances, the language/image relations are more attenuated. As the patient snaps at the therapist "You always seem to be talking out of the other side of your mouth," there is a cut to a flipped image where what was previously on the left of the shot is stationed on the right.

These word/image associations abet a sort of cognitive and perceptual play; the mention of objects and their apparition is particularly important in this respect because of the way that it engages the spectator's memory. *Journeys*, in other words, is the kind of film that makes a space for audience "participation." At first glance, this type of "participation" seems merely equivalent to the implied invitation to participation found in many Structural Films (i.e., an invitation to participate in a formal game, e.g., recognizing the rubato schema of the "Interval" section of Joanna Kiernan's *Trilogy*). And yet, due to the context of *Journeys*, Rainer's avowal of participation accrues expressive overtones. This initially formal concept appears to take on moral significance, as it did, in different ways, for both Eisenstein and Bazin. That is, the participatory style itself operates as a metaphor of value, proposing the spectator as a "free" agent involved in the active application of "judgment" as he/she partakes in the "democratic" construction of the film. This theme of participation in the fine structures is, of course, strictly analogous to the position of the spectator in regard to the gross "dialectical" structures where the viewer (or perhaps more aptly, the listener) weighs countervailing arguments, judges them and above all *chooses* – not only what is relevant to what, but also a stand on the issues. "Choice," like "participation," is morally charged; the form of *Journeys*, in short, appropriates thematic connotations of vital importance to Rainer. As she has said of other matters, "Choice is something I believe must be consciously and repeatedly engaged in."

20

The Future of Allusion: Hollywood in the Seventies (and Beyond)

One rootless man, driven by an illicit passion for another man's wife; a murderous bargain with the siren; fateful destruction. It's an old story. Or, to be more exact, it's an old movie – shades of *The Postman Always Rings Twice* ('46) and *Double Indemnity* ('44). And yet, of course, it is also a new movie – *Body Heat* ('81), directed by Lawrence Kasdan, coauthor of such other historical pastiches as *The Empire Strikes Back* ('80) and *Raiders of the Lost Ark*('81).[1] Nor does *Body Heat* merely rework an old plot. It tries to evoke the old films, films of the forties, that the plot was a part of. *Body Heat's* costumes are contemporary, but of a nostalgic variety that lets us – no, asks us – to see the film as a shifting figure, shifting between past and present. The lighting extensively apes the *film noir* style of the forties, thereby enhancing its mood of pessimism-cum-destiny by citing the approved cinematic iconography for fear, lust, and loathing. We understand *Body Heat's* plot complications because we know its sources – in fact, because, through its heavy-handed allusions, we've been told its sources. Without this knowledge, without these references, would *Body Heat* make much sense? Even its eroticism requires our explicit association of the female lead with certain movie myths – for example, the woman-as-devil/temptress archetype – in order to be really forceful.

Though recent commercial film is too diverse to capture in a single formula, there is a tendency, of which *Body Heat* is an example, that distinguishes the seventies and eighties from every other decade in Hollywood's past – viz., allusion. Indeed, this tendency is so pervasive that it has already trickled down to TV advertising. There is an ad for women's blue jeans in which a long-legged, long-haired model strikes a pose of James Dean's (in a convertible, against a prairie mansion) that is a straight imitation of a shot from *Giant* ('56). Of course, allusionism as

"The Future of Allusion: Hollywood in the Seventies (and Beyond)," *October*, no. 2 (Spring 1982), pp. 51–81.

it is practiced in the new Hollywood is generally more motivated than it is in this ad. Allusion, specifically allusion to film history, has become a major expressive device, that is, a means that directors use to make comments on the fictional worlds of their films. *Allusion,* as I am using it, is an umbrella term covering a mixed lot of practices including quotations, the memorialization of past genres, the reworking of past genres, *homages,* and the recreation of "classic" scenes, shots, plot motifs, lines of dialogue, themes, gestures, and so forth from film history, especially as that history was crystallized and codified in the sixties and early seventies.

During that period, a canon of films and filmmakers was forged. An aggressive polemic of film criticism, often called auteurism, correlated attitudes, moods, viewpoints, and expressive qualities with items in the putative canon. These associations became available to contemporary filmmakers, who were able to lay claim to them by alluding to the original films, filmmakers, styles, and genres to which certain associations or assignments were affixed in the emerging discourse about film history. Hence *Body Heat,* a film based on references to film history, a film that tells us that for this very reason it is to be regarded as intelligent and knowing, a film that demands that the associations which accrued to its referents be attributed to it and that it be treated with the same degree of seriousness as they were.

The strategies for making allusions are various. They include the outright imitation of film-historical referents; the insertion of classic clips into new films; the mention of illustrious and coyly nonillustrious films and filmmakers in dialogue; the arch play of titles on marquees, television screens, posters, and bookshelves in the background of shots; the retreading of archaic styles; and the mobilization of conventional, transparently remodeled characters, stereotypes, moods, and plots. I am grouping all these practices and strategies under the rubric of "allusion to film history" because the new films in question are structured by pertinent strategies and practices in such a way the (1) informed viewers are meant to recall past films (filmmakers, genres, shots, and so on)while watching the new films, and that (2) informed viewers are not supposed to take this as evidence of plagiarism or uninspired derivativeness in the new film – as they might have in the works of another decade – but as part of the expressive design of the new films. The force of *supposed to* in this formulation is conventional; it is a rule of seventies film viewing, for example, that a similarity between a new film and an old film generally can count as a reference to the old film.[2]

Furthermore, such allusions by seventies filmmakers are expressive devices; they are a means for projecting and reinforcing the themes and the emotive and aesthetic qualities of the new films. By referring to a film by Howard Hawks, contemporary filmmakers assert their possession of a Hawksian world view, a cluster of themes and expressive qualities that has been(ever so thoroughly and repetitiously) expounded in the critical literature; by such an allusion, the new filmmakers unequivocally identify their point of view on the material at hand and thereby comment, with the force of an iconographic symbol, on the ongoing action of the new film. Observing the same phenomenon from the opposite side of the screen, we can say that the invocation of the Hawksian world view serves as privileged hermeneutic filter for informed film viewers, who can use it to bring into sharp focus the filmmaker's attitude or ethos.

Not all or even most films of the seventies and eigthties employ allusion; and certain major filmmakers, like John Cassavetes and Michael Ritchie, seem altogether immune to it.[3] Nevertheless, the large number of prominent contemporary auteurs who do indulge in allusion, and allusion's appearance in so many works both major and minor indicate that it is the symbolic structure that most distinguishes the present period from the past.

The boom of allusionism is a legacy of American auteurism, a term that I intend to adopt, for better or worse, to denote the frenzy for film that seized this country in the sixties and early seventies. Armed with lists from Andrew Sarris and incompatible aesthetic theories from Eisenstein, Bazin, Godard, and McLuhan, a significant part of the generation raised in the fifties went movie mad and attacked film history. They passionately sought out films they had missed, returned obsessively to old favorites, and tried to classify them all. At times, this orgy of connoisseurship degenerated into downright film buffery. An unprecedented awareness of film history developed in a segment of the American film audience. A common vocabulary developed, including catch phrases such as "Langian paranoia" that were used both to describe past films and to categorize new ones – "x (some new film) has a Fordian view of history, a Hawksian attitude toward women, an Eisensteinian use of montage, and a Chuck Jones approach to the body."

Among those engaged in this discovery of film history – particularly American film history – were some people who would become filmmakers. Like their confreres, they were caught up in the whirl of discourse and discovery. They, too, used the nascent critical categories as a crude taxonomy for understanding film, for labeling it, and, most importantly, for fixing standards of seriousness and accomplishment. In their study of film history, they learned the exemplary themes, styles, and expressive qualities as these had been selected and distilled by American auteurism. These filmmakers predictably attempted to incorporate the budding film-historical sensibiltiy – the central intellectual event of their youthful apprenticeships – into their works. Filmmakers began to appear who equaled, and in some cases surpassed, the erudition of the film-historically conscious audience – Paul Bartel, Peter Bogdanovich, John Carpenter, Michael Cimino, Bob Clark, Francis Coppola, Jonathan Demme, Brian DePalma, Monte Hellman, Tobe Hopper, Dennis Hopper, Philip Kaufman, George Lucas, Terence Malick, John Milius, Dick Richards, George Romero, Paul Schrader, Martin Scorsese, and Steven Spielberg.[4] A number of these directors were trained in film schools, and many who were not were autodidacts of an almost monastic bent, worshipping film classics at local revivals. Some wrote about film; some taught it. Their command of the quasi-academic film lore of the sixties is estimable. Moreover, as indications of that knowledge surfaced in their works, each was recognized by the film-historically conscious audience as a secret sharer in the movie mania. Their works were greeted by an expanding cinema-learned coterie, constantly reinforced by the influx of film-school critics and college-bred, film-appreciation and film-society audiences. The proliferation of these film-history credos allowed emerging directors to presuppose that at least part of their audience was prepared to look for their allusions to film history and to see in them signals of the expressive commitments of their films. The game of allusion could begin; the senders and receivers were in place; the necessary conditions for allusionistic interplay were satisfied.

*

In a nutshell, the language of sixties film connoisseurship and criticism has become associated with certain genres, compositions, lighting styles, plots, and so forth, so that a new film that evokes an old film (genre, lighting style,and so on) refers not only to its own fictional world but also to a web of interrelated ideas previously introduced by film criticism and then recycled as reflections or commentaries on the fictional world of the new film. The film-historically conscious directors and viewers grew up together. They encourage each other by a reward system based on reciprocal recognition. Each side of the exchange abets the other's view of itself (that is, reinforces the criteria for serious film viewing, on the one hand, and for serious filmmaking, on the other). The result of this situation is a cinematic style that is subtly changing the nature of Hollywood symbol systems.

A Hitchcock, a Hawks, a Ford, or a Fuller employed certain shots, cuts, genres, or plots in a way that critics and aficionados came, over time, to isolate as crucial to the work of these directors. In formal analyses, these devices were seen to function as parts of organic aesthetic wholes that communicated specific themes and expressive qualities. These organic correspondences of forms and contents were dubbed Hitchcockian, Hawksian, Fordian, Fulleresque . . . , and once these connections were established and disseminated it became possible to use knowledge of them as a shorthand. Allusions to Hitchcock, Hawks, Ford, and Fuller became a means by which directors following these masters could pretend to the same preoccupations and to the same intensity as the originals. What had been organic expression for a Hawks was translated into an iconographic code by a Walter Hill or a John Carpenter. A similar story can by told about stylistic epithets like *film noir.* For example, dark lighting in an urban setting is, in virtually dictionarylike fashion, now a telegraphic transmission for anxiety and a "descent" into "existential angst," even if that mood is not exactly borne out in the film's own specific dramatic development.

Though the college-educated provide an important portion of the regular movie audience, neither they, nor the cognoscenti in their ranks, constitute the bulk of Hollywood's loyal constituency. The queue at the box office is dominated by teenagers seeking a hearth away from home. These consumers know what they want and Hollywood has listened to them; after the experimentation of the early seventies, genres have once again become Hollywood's bread and butter. And the viability of genres is what makes allusionism a practical option. The film-historically conscious director can deftly manipulate the old forms, satisfying the adolescent clientele while also conveniently pitching allusions to the inveterate film gnostics in the front rows. At many late-seventies premieres, one frequently had the feeling of watching two films simultaneously. There was the genre film pure and simple, and there was also the art film in the genre film, which through its systems of allusions sent an esoteric meaning to film-literate exegetes. For example, in *Halloween* there is the Grand Guignol at ground level, and then, at another remove, the meditation on the atavistic, irremediable nature of irrationality that is broached almost exclusively through references to *Forbidden Planet* ('56) and *Psycho* ('60). It seems that popular cinema wants to remain popular by developing a two-tiered system of communication which sends an action/drama/fantasy-packed message to one segment of the audience and an additional hermetic, camouflaged, and recondite one to another. Taken as a proposed solution to the problem of Hollywood's aesthetic survival, however, this is far from ideal, because there is a remainder of the audience that the two-tiered system ignores and that is nonplussed by what it perceives as films that are, paradoxically, at once intelligent, sophisticated, and just plain dumb. Annual excursions in deathly sincerity like *Kramer Versus Kramer* ('79), *Ordinary People* ('80), and *The Four Seasons* ('81) are appeals to the backlash instincts of these disenfranchised, college-educated movie lovers.

It may appear specious to make generalizations on the basis of films like *Halloween*, admittedly a flagrant example of the seventies film-school film. But it is important to keep in mind that such films are the direct beneficiaries of a widespread, eager, contemporary willingness to endorse an explicit film-historical consciousness as a hallmark of ambitious filmmaking and film going. Indeed, serious American commercial filmmakers have come to require serious film goers – that is, those well enough versed in film history to note references and delicate variations, and sufficiently committed to the pretensions of Cinema to bother to decipher such self-conscious gestures – as a prerequisite for anything approaching a full appreciation of their work.

One common practice reveals the measure to which the contemporary director presupposes a shared film-historical consciousness with the audience; it is the genre reworking in which a traditional schema – that of the western, the thriller, the horror film, or the mystery – is changed in its rhythms, characters, plot structures and so forth. For informed viewers such deviations mark the personal stamp of the new auteur.[5] This practice is more complicated and generally less objectionable than the one-to-one allusions of *Halloween*, but it obviously presumes an extremely knowledgeable spectator who will interpret the new film – the reworking – against a backdrop of the accepted associations of the appropriate genre. That is, the reworking evokes a historical genre and its associated myths, commonplaces, and meanings in order to generate expression through the friction between the old and the new. The reworking of genres has become one of the major career focuses of contemporary directors. The filmmaker proceeds from one genre to the next, revising each one so that a personal vision shines through. The progress in recent years of Robert Altman, Stanley Kubrick, Romero, Bogdanovich, and Scorsese approximates this program to varying degrees.[6]

To state the point in greater detail, consider the case of Altman: *McCabe and Mrs. Miller* ('71) and *Buffalo Bill and the Indians* ('76) rework the western; *M*A*S*H* ('70) unpatriotically plays off the army comedy somewhat in the manner of what one might imagine would be SDS an adaptation of Phil Silvers's TV series *You'll Never Get Rich; Thieves Like Us* ('74) is a gangster film of the "road" variety that comments on predecessors like *Bonnie and Clyde* ('67) and its prototype, *They Live by Night* ('47, released '49); *A Wedding* ('78) is a farce, although one that owes more to *Rules of the Game* ('39) than to any American genre.[7] *Countdown* ('68) and *Quintet* ('78) are science fiction; *That Cold Day in the Park* ('69) is a melodrama; *The Long Good-Bye* ('73), a detective film; *Popeye* ('80), a cartoon; *California Split* ('74), a gambling film; *Images* ('72), a thriller psychologized between fantasy and reality à la Resnais; *Nashville* ('75) is a cross between show-biz biographies and a backstage musical. *That Cold Day in the Park* and *Countdown* are probably best assessed as pedestrain genre rehearsals rather than as ironized reworkings. And, of course, some Altman films are not easily pigeonholed as genres: *Brewster McCloud* ('70) and *Three Women* ('77). My point is not that Altman works only in genres. I want to direct attention to the surprising extent to which his creativity hinges on genres (and their subversion) for its energy and the concomitant degree to which such a project assumes an audience ready, willing, and able to follow and savor every self-conscious modification of received formats.

McCabe and Mrs. Miller launches it broadside against American individualism by tampering with the character stereotypes, among other things, of classical westerns, particularly those of the forties. McCabe is a founding father, the builder of a town. At first, he appears a likely heir to the resourceful and strong Clark Gable or to the more beautiful but still resilient Errol Flynn. Gradually, after evoking such associations, he is revealed to be a bumbling loser – weak, ultimately ineffectual, and not very smart (a fact developed in large measure through another stereotype reworking, the person Mrs. Miller). We might say, metaphorically speaking, that Altman is talking to us through genres; we have to grasp the fact that his film makes reference to certain prototypes and their connotated values in order to understand that *McCabe and Mrs. Miller* is about the discounting of the myth of the rugged individualist and not just about some poor, dead slob in the snow. *McCabe and Mrs. Miller* is an example of the revisionist western which dates back at least to *The Wild Bunch* ('69), a film that introduces its darkening view of America

by presenting townspeople, the community, as the lunatic fringe, simultaneously chanting and besmirching John Ford's beloved "Now We
Gather at the River" (was ever an allusion so cruel?). The revisionist
western[8] lives off the classical western,which it criticizes by decisive
subversions of set genre plots, locales, and/or characters (whose intelligence, competence, and, at times, sanity are often intentionally and
severely limited). The revisionist western assays these alterations for the
sake of projecting a broad sentiment of social disenchantment by demys-
tifying national myths and registering a sense of loss. One could watch
McCabe and Mrs. Miller and other revisionist westerns heeding only the
drama and the ever flashier gunplay. Yet surely this sort of spectatorship
would miss the discursive implications of these films.

But how can these films have discursive implication? By referring to
genres that have a large body of established meanings, by using genre
itself as a symbol, *McCabe and Mrs. Miller* requires a viewer informed
of the fact that the western takes American values as its general subject,
and that changes in elements between westerns of an earlier period and a
new western are indexes of changes in attitude toward certain American
values. An expressive system so strictured on self-conscious, stylistic
change, of course, presumes a great deal of historical knowledge, since
the allusions can be quite arcane. Nor is the western the only terrain on
which this genre-banked mode of expression has flowered. Altman's *The
Long Good-Bye* derives its ironic tone through its systematic contrast
with the moral universe of 1940s private-eye films. Examples like
this – remember *Chinatown* ('76) and *Farewell, My Lovely* ('75) – are
easy to multiply. *The Late Show* ('77), as its title suggests, also derives
its expressive flavor through explicit contrast with vintage detective
films.[9]

It is not my contention that contemporary genre reworkings are automatic successes. In fact, they are dangerous risks at the box office at
times when audiences are looking for old-fashioned entertainment.
Precisely because reworkings are constituted through strategic subversions of fixed genre elements, reworkings are likely to frustrate the
audience's expectations in a way that makes the audience nasty and
bitter. Kubrick's *The Shining* is a recent example. His property was a
popular novel, and his advertisements promised the scariest horror film
ever. But what he offered was a reworking, one that jettisoned Stephen
King's carefully built rhythm of tension and replaced a number of King's
smoothly timed shocks (in the center of the plot) with an abyss of lan-
guor. Audiences were confused, bored, and angered. Defenders of the

film quickly pointed out that what Kubrick had done was to substitute one horror – the loneliness of the nuclear family – for another. I have no quarrel with this analysis. But, in addition, I would hold that *The Shining,* like many other reworkings, was designed on the two-tiered structure of communication described earlier and that only one of its meanings, the esoteric one, reached its target.[10] Scorsese's genre reworking, *New York, New York* ('77) – perhaps the most intricately cross-referenced film of the new Hollywood – shared a similar fate.

Another practice within the perimeter of the genre-as-symbol is memorialization, the loving evocation through imitation and exaggeration of the way genres were. *Star Wars* ('77), both parts of *Superman* ('78, '81), and *Raiders of the Lost Ark* are some of the most extravagant examples. For one part of the audience, ostensibly the youngsters, these are rousing adventure sagas. But the more seasoned among us are asked to view them also as remembrances of things past, of comic books and serials, and of times of which it is said that good and evil were sharply cleaved. A film like *Raiders of the Lost Ark* is not a perfect replica of a B cliff-hanger; for one thing it is too lavish. Rather it is the filmmaker's reverie on the glorious old days; if it has more action and adventure than Tim Tyler ever saw, then memory has worked its magic, heightening the excitement of *Raider's* potboiler prototypes so that they are finally as breathtaking as we want to remember them. The plot implausibilities – Indiana Jones hops on a submarine without worrying whether it will submerge – and its oxymoronic, homemade surrealist juxtapositions – the Nazi Army led by the Hebrew Ark of the Covenant – are not forsaken but defended as homage duly paid to the very source of charm in the originals. Despite all the thunder and fury, *Raiders* uses its allusions to produce a sense of wistfulness and yearning. Like Borges's Pierre Menard, the producers of *Raiders* can't stifle the acquisition of new expressive properties in the process of putting old wine in new bottles. Nor, probably, do they want to, since these qualities can be cashed in on as nostalgia. A genre reworking like *Popeye* defamiliarizes its source (by humanizing it) in order to reveal the strangeness of this thing, Popeye, that we once accepted unblinkingly. There is no irony, however, in *Raider's* reminiscences. Its message to the informed viewer is that of paradise regained, also the selling point of Lucas's first big box-office triumph, *American Graffiti* ('73). The aesthetic risk of *Raiders* is that the line between a genre memorialization and a tawdry genre rerun, like the difference between the new Hollywood and the old, may become all but invisible.

Not only genres but specific films are singled out for reworking. *Blow-Up* ('66) has already been twice reincarnated, once as *The Conversation* ('74) and more recently as *Blow-Out* ('81). The mime at the beginning of Coppola's film and the title of DePalma's unmistakably allude to Antonioni as do the repetitions of Antonioni's core plot structure, that is, the accidental recording and discovery of a crime. Via allusion we are instructed to interpret both of the newer films as concerned with the theme of the artist's relation to reality. That is, it is through the allusion to *Blow-Up*, a film that dealt far more directly with the topic than do either of the reworkings, that Antonioni's groundwork enables us to gloss *The Conversation* and *Blow-Out* as their respective auteur's attitudes to their vocations. We note that both Coppola and DePalma have changed their protagonists into soundmen, a transformation that befits the high-tech self-image of the seventies director and the shift from film-as-chemistry to film-as-electronics. We also note that the plot machinations and dramatics of the newer films suggest that neither Coppola nor DePalma is as reconciled as Antonioni and his surrogate were at the end of *Blow-Up* to the relation between art and life. Both *The Conversation* and *Blow-Out* also sharpen their reflexive edges through their central theme of voyeurism. The significance of this cannot simply be explained as something they found in *Blow-Up*, though, of course, it was there to be found. Rather the importance of voyeurism in the newer films also rests on the fact that voyeurism was one of the premier themes (watch-words?) of the movie-crazy sixties, the time when Coppola and DePalma came of age artistically. For obvious, undoubtedly narcissistic reasons, film connoisseurs of the sixties (and beyond) loved voyeurism – I mean as a theme. They looked for it everywhere and showered great attention on it wherever they found it; Hitchcock particularly benefited from this. Moreover, voyeurism as a dramatic element in the fictional world of a film, like *Rear Window* ('54), could always work overtime as a symbol for the conditions of filmmaking and/or film viewing as far as film connoisseurs, critics, and buffs were concerned. Both Coppola and DePalma chose to allude to a popular theme and to an influential film of their youth as a means to articulate their perhaps only fashionably pessimistic view of their art in films that without the cross-references might slip past as nothing more than thrillers with, at most, some touches of political topicality.

Allusions to *Psycho* in recent film are ubiquitous – let mention of *Sisters* ('73), *Texas Chain Saw Massacre* ('74), *Dressed to Kill* ('80), *Funhouse* ('81), *The Exorcist* ('73), and *Halloween* suffice. *Rebel*

Without a Cause ('55) stands behind the race in *American Graffiti,* while *Badlands* ('73) engenders much of its aesthetic static – that persistent feeling that something is missing – through its complex use of the James Dean image in a figure who retains his mentor's glamorous romantic isolationism but also repulses sympathy by being an unlovable, dumbly opaque, irredeemable sociopath.

The Searchers ('56) is another bible of the new Hollywood. Allusions to it appear in *Who's That Knocking at My Door* ('69), *Mean Streets,* ('73), *Taxi Driver* ('76), *Dillinger* ('73), *The Wind and the Lion* ('75), *Big Wednesday* ('78), *Star Wars* ('77), *Ulzana's Raid* ('72), and possibly *Close Encounters of the Third Kind* ('77) and *The Deer Hunter* ('79). The film that most ruthlessly repossesses *The Searchers* is incontestably Paul Schrader's *Hardcore* ('78). The Indians become West Coast skin merchants; the wilderness, the underworld of pornography; the searcher is no longer an obsolete frontiersman but one of the elect of the Protestant ethic, a real pilgrim; if he was on the inside of the door that shut John Wayne out, he is now on the outside, traveling across a landscape that is stylistically constructed like Ford's – all California seamlessly blends into a homogeneous continuum until it seems like one undifferentiated symbolic arena. Ilah Davis has sidekick and a scout; his daughter is a (possibly kidnapped) concubine and she likes it. Through these allusions (and others) Schrader borrows *The Searchers* and the discourse that has grown around it, which in turn enables him to shoplift one of the greatest, most enduring themes of the American experience – sexual repression and its relation to the creation of minatory doppelgängers, dark doubles of the forest and the city, to be confronted and exorcised through regenerating violence. Schrader's penchant for allusionist annotations of his texts is notorious. In *Taxi Driver,* which Schrader scripted, Travis Bickel's deep alienation is signaled by running *Diary of a Country Priest* ('50) up the flagpole, while the *redemption* of the protagonist (through his being able, finally, to receive love) in *American Gigolo* ('79) is italicized by a reprise of the ending of *Pickpocket* ('59).[11]

If Schrader seems a particularly extreme case of one whose "serious" ambition and big themes drive him to heavy allegory and pedantry, it is important to remember that his delight in allusion is not different from that of the more commercial, lowbrow whiz kids. In *Assault on Precinct 13* ('76), a film that owes a lot to *Rio Bravo* ('59), Carpenter has the embattled black policeman heave a shotgun to a dangerous prisoner in imitation of a famous moment in *Red River* ('48) when Walter Brennan comes to John Wayne's aid. For the viewer not aware of the reference, the scene is a rather typical one in which the cop, in a tight predicament, has no alternative but to trust the outlaw. For those in the know, however, the gesture also has the aura of the sort of mystic male bonding that cements the Hawksian brotherhood; we know that a special understanding – of the type, you know, only men can have – now exists between the lawman and the thug.[12] Steven Spielberg, no one's idea of an artist possessed, also enjoys allusions, especially to cartoons. His flying saucers zip along the highway like Road Runner, a reference that he is careful to parade; while the endings of both *Close Encounters* and *Raiders* feed off the "Night on Bald Mountain" sequence of *Fantasia* ('40) in order to swathe their supernaturals in Disneyesque wonderment.[13]

Though it is harder to put one's finger on, it seems to be the case that recent filmmakers depend not only on references to explicit genres, films, scenes, and so forth, but also on references to themes that have dominated film discourse and which have been enshrined therein – for example, Hawksian professionalism. Walter Hill's alterations of *Alien* ('79), culled in large part from *The Thing* ('51), unambiguously show his indebtedness to Hawks. And some of his own films, like *The Driver* ('78), appear to make sense only in the light of the Hawksian cult of the professional. As one might argue of *The Warriors* ('79), the title of *The Driver* is the name of the profession or skill of the central character. The film is a compendium of elegant car stunts, outpacing *Bullitt* ('68) and *The French Connection* ('71), and opening the eyes of even the most jaded veteran of the last decade's infatuation with the guns-and-gas subgenre. The protagonist has no psychological motivation other than the need to prove that he is the best at what he does; his room and his personal interactions are as empty and uneventful as his inner life. He has nothing to say and he doesn't, and he has nothing to do but drive. The hiatuses between action scenes are as willfully flat as the escape episodes are hair-raising. The obsession with the driver's skill, his profession, is monomaniacal. To an outside observer, the film might appear to be naught but mindless action. But to an insider, the action itself is an icon of an existential commitment; through years of discussions of Hawks's professionalism, we know to take the action of *The Driver* as Hill's philosophical position – the ultimate personal reality is skill; meaning in life comes through excellence. Hill's professionalism is different from Hawks's. Hill lacks the master's humor and sense of camaraderie. And yet without the critical hypostasization of Hawksian professionalism, Hill's professionalism would not be particularly comprehensible. The exact increments of Hill's allusion to Hawks are more difficult to pin-point than are allusions made to a scene or a camera movement or even to a story; there is no structural element, no object or image that we can hone in on that is being imitated. So without a handle on the global reference to the professional-cult theme, the spectator is likely to find *The Driver* unintelligible. If, however, we keep Hawks in mind, we can at least begin to answer the question, "Why does the driver do what he does?" by saying with the accumulated profundity of feeling allowed us by Hawks's criticism, "Because it's his *job.*"

Langian paranoia also has become an important referent of films of the seventies and eighties. This level of allusion is even more slippery to deal with than Hill's dependence on Hawksian professionalism. The notion of Langian paranoia, as galvanized by recent film discourse, has a certain specificity. It does not apply to just any thriller/crime film with a conspiracy in it, but only to conspiracies that are virtually all-encompassing while also appearing innocent and ordinary. The Langian myth, as conceived in film discourse, is that of a vast, almost undetectable evil scheme disguised by an illusory patina of things-as-usual. The hero is alone in seeing through the veil of everydayness and is pitted against something or someone of the demonic proportions of a Mabuse. The seventies saw the development of the paranoia subgenre – for example, *Parallax View* ('74), *Three Days of the Condor* ('75), *Capricorn One* ('78), *Hangar 18* ('81) – which often had as its presiding point, "In government, we distrust." These films do not look like Lang's. And yet their provenance is in themes that were refined, discussed, and interrelated in reference to Lang's work. The Lang of criticism, a far more rarified and coherent being than the Lang of celluloid, has provided the undermeaning and standards for the subgenre. The films need not directly allude to Lang, and yet to be appreciated they must be weighed on a paranoid fantasy scale whose interrelated criteria were originally tagged and popularized in terms of Lang. That is, we decide whether such films are good examples of the Langian-paranoic kind by asking how claustrophobic, how all-enveloping, how omnipotent, omniscient, and all-malevolent is the conspiracy in the film while everything on the surface appears to be normal.

Styles as well as historic themes are often alluded to in a way that gives them a special expressive, iconic function. Style in the generative (explanatory) sense as opposed to style in the classificatory (descriptive) sense, of course, is intrinsically connected to expression – we isolate stylistic units in terms of looking for the formal variations that give rise to the expressive and discursive effect we already intuit. But, in the recent films I have in mind, the style, because it is mediated through allusion, works by iconic reference rather than by expressive implication. That is, the historical reference of the lighting in a specific scene or its color may allow it to be taken as the use of style-as-symbol. For example, in the early seventies, the discussion of one historical style, *film noir*, reached the proportions of a popular sport. As a result, what the composition of *film noir* was said to express can now be appropriated simply by dimming your lights and tightening your framing. In Schrader's *Blue Collar* ('78), the images grow ominously dark while the story still seems comic and high-spirited. *Blue Collar* starts to look like a *film noir*, or at least to satisfy enough of the criteria to be said to look like a *film noir* – a style, by the way, which Schrader as a critic wrote about in a major article – before the tension in the plot begins to build. But you feel the allusion strongly, and, sure enough, as time goes on, the stylistic reference turns out to have been a premonition of things to come. The number of recent films in the style-as-symbol category that revive *film noir* as a means of commenting on their dramatic material is legion: *Night Moves* ('75), *Elephant Man* ('80), *All the President's Men* ('76), *Taxi Driver*, *Hardcore*, and *Body Heat*. Nor is *film noir* the only archaic style available for quotation. Scorsese opens *Alice doesn't Live Here Anymore* ('74) with a precise *homage* to the Hollywood musical, explicitly recalling *Hello, Frisco, Hello* ('43) and *The Wizard of Oz* ('39). The glorious studio-framed set contrasts strongly with the open style of the rest of the film. Scorsese uses this overdetermined allusion to characterize Alice's ambitions as full-color, Hollywood fantasies on the boundary of childlikeness and childishness. Scorsese is an addicted allusionist, as his asides through clips of *The Searchers* and *The Big Heat* ('53) in *Mean Streets* attest. *New York, New York* is probably the wildest experiment in style-as-symbol of the new Hollywood, combining compositions from period dramatic films, plot lines from musical biographies, and dashes of Visconti a whirligig of allusions that requires a viewer with the knowledge of a film historian like William K. Everson or Miles Kruger.[14]

American filmmakers are not alone in their taste for allusion. It is also a popular practice in the new German cinema. Fassbinder's periodic exhumation of Douglas Sirk is the most publicized example. Wenders is also a crafty allusionist; his *American Friend* ('77) is the most sophisticated use of *film noir*-as-symbol that we have so far. Even Herzog dabbles in historiography; his *Nosferatu* ('79) is more about Murnau's film and its symbolic implications than it is a vampire movie. Nor is the shared allusionism of the new Hollywood and the new German cinema a mere caprice of the zeitgeist wending its mysterious ways. The correlations can be explained genetically; the two movements have a common ancestry, the French New Wave. In the sixties, aspiring American and German filmmakers looked to Paris for role models, as did aspiring film connoisseurs and buffs. The filmmakers learned, or though they learned, what is meant to be serious and ambitious about film from the French. They also got tips about how to behave which included not only pointers on editing, composition, and improvisation, but also the idea of allusion. I am not trying to equate the New Wave, New German cinema, and the new Hollywood. Each differs considerably from the others. Where there are tangencies, however, such as allusionism, that is a function, for good or ill, of the influence of the New Wave. The Americans were very selective in what they took from the French, and they left a great many fecund ideas to wither on the vine. As well, they transplanted their graftings to a very unique climate, Hollywood, where strange mutations occurred. The Germans, on the other hand, took on the spirit as well as the techniques of the New Wave, and seem consequently to have evolved in a more satisfying aesthetic direction than the Americans.

Much of the American film craze of the sixties and early seventies was underwritten by the French; many a film buff recited a litany of film directors garnered from French auteurism; and, of course, the preoccupation with the Director was itself originally French. In many cases, perhaps the majority, American auteurists did not know their progenitors from the original sources, but secondhand from synthesizers, summarizers, and imitators. A great deal of information circulated by word of mouth; if French auteurism was not widely read in this country, it nevertheless supplied an increasingly suffusive coloration to the American film-consciousness movement. New Wave films were initially seen to go hand in hand with auteurism, of either the French or the American variants. A number of the American auteurs of the new Hollywood were early admirers of Godard. Some features of Godard that caught their eye included his loose form, mood shifting, improvisation, jump-cutting; his attempt at combining formalism and realism, documentary techniques, and Eisensteinian montage; and, of course, his use of allusion to film history and pop culture (as opposed to his allusions to the rest of culture). But the Americans never bought into the whole of Godard's program, not even to all of its implications in terms of the use of allusion to film history. Specifically, they were not interested in what has been called Godard's critique of illusionism. They did not seek to drive the kind of wedge between their fictions and the process of filmmaking that was at the heart of Godard's enterprise. The Americans were never taken by the notion of Brechtian distance as Godard interpreted (or, to be more truthful, misinterpreted) it. The Americans did not mind distance but they preferred the smart-alecky, wise-guy distance of a precocious film buff to the cerebral intensity of Godard's progressively more modernist phases. Godard's allusions to film history, either when they functioned to communicate the show-off exuberance of every young cinéaste's self-discovery of film, or when they functioned as comments on the fictional world of a film, were fine. But allusionism as a means of interrogating the nature of cinema was foreign to Godard's American acolytes.

The New Wave practice of reworking genres – for example, *Shoot the Piano Player* ('60), *The Bride Wore Black* ('67), *Fahrenheit 451* ('66), *Mississippi Mermaid* ('69), *Alphaville* ('65), *Made in U.S.A.* ('66) – offered the Americans a fertile concept not only because it accorded with their own rediscovery of film history and because it gave them a well-charted, easily manipulated expressive vocabulary, but because it provided a road to their dreams, working in Hollywood *and* still being artistically and intellectually respectable. But as a consequence of the American lack of any full-blooded commitment to modernism, their work evolved less in the direction of Godard's and more in the direction of the later Truffaut's and that of Chabrol, of whom it can be said "the genre is the man."[15]

The rise and fall of allusionism, the distance between great expectations and Alexandrianism, can be profitably reviewed in the career of Brian DePalma. He became interested in film through his work in theater in the sixties. He absorbed the rich Manhattan film culture, participated in varied art-world activities, and wanted to become the American Godard. His early works have strong affinities with other avant-garde work of the period. *Wotan's Wake* ('62) is an absurdist self-parody of male fantasies of sexual repression in which Wotan, a satirically grotesque, horny rag of an underground man, pursues comely coeds in the style of silent comedy chases – imagine Mack Sennett's adaptation of the Return of the Repressed. *Wotan's Wake* culminates in what in 1962 was a hilariously awkward and intentionally tacky allusion to the last scene in *King Kong* ('33), transforming into bathos the male self-pity inherent in the original. *Dionysus in '69* ('70) covered some of the same territory as *The Brig* ('64) while, like *Hallelujah the Hills* ('63), *The Wedding Party* ('64) tried to join European experimentalism – jump-cuts, episodic transitions, and improvisation – with American humor. Allusionism is the fundamental strategy in *Murder à la Mode* ('68), an exercise in style in which each part of the film is done in a distinctive pop idiom that metaphorically comments on its content (for example, soap opera style equals soap opera people). In the young DePalma, one sees the best of the cinéphile turned filmmaker. He is irreverent, topical, satirical, experimental, and stylistically icono-clastic while assuredly in command of his forms in a way that seethes with brashness, confidence, and talent.

Uudeniably, many of these qualities continue to be visible in DePalma's later work, especially *Phantom of the Paradise* ('74). His flair for experimentation is still evident in his always creative fascination with the split screen. And he is an awesomely formidable formalist; in *Carrie* ('76) he takes little more than a handful of scenes and through camera movement and editing erects a full-length feature film on a plot more meager in complications than many TV dramas. It is a tour de force of what was once called the cinematic. But with each new film, DePalma's ambition seems to recede a little further. He clamors for the mantle of Hitchcock and spins variations on *Vertigo* and *Psycho*. He wants Hitchcock's themes, like voyeurism; but by working through allu-sion, does he ever inherit them except in name only?

I have already introduced *Blow-Out*. The reference there to Antonioni enables us to see that the film is *about* more than the action without the reference would suggest. It is about art and representation, and about what is given (directly in Antonioni; derivatively in DePalma) as the enigmatic inadequacy of the attempt of art to do something like "capture" (represent) life/reality. DePalma's artist figure is "deeper into" technique than Antonioni's and DePalma himself seems far more inter-ested in showing the audience exactly how his recording toys work than Antonioni was. And DePalma's artist-cypher is finally more disgruntled than the hippyesque affirmation of Antonioni's disappearing stand-in. But without *Blow-Up* as a hermeneutic key, *Blow-Out* has very little to say about the purported problem of the relation of representation and reality. Most of its energy is invested in the convolutions of its thriller plot and its everyday-exotic realism – that is, the detailed discovery of folkways and places never before seen in film – for example, what goes on in Philadelphia phone booths. Of course, the problem is not just that DePalma has nothing theoretically staggering to offer; the problem is that whatever he does feel about the issue is so elliptically signaled and so tangential to the pulse of the action that it lacks any urgency. Yes,

DePalma has made a big statement about a matter of putatively great importance to him. But it is so deferred that no one, including DePalma, could say that reflexivity was the central or even *a* central preoccupation for anyone watching the film. There is nothing wrong with allusions per se, but *Blow-Out* indicates the greatest risk involved in allusionism as it is currently practiced in the new Hollywood – self-deception. Filmmakers and audiences are both deceiving themselves if they think that by merely "mentioning" great themes about which great artists have expended great energies, a two-tiered, allusionistic genre film will be saying anything substantive of its own.

*

The industrial conditions that led to the rise of the new Hollywood and its allusionist auteurs are complex, overlapping, and causally interconnected. In rough sequential order they include: the steady decline of the movie audience since 1946, the industry's final divestiture of its theater holdings, its overinvestment in production in the mid-sixties, the disappearance of the studio system's experienced leaders (the quondam moguls), and the takeover of the industry by huge corporate conglomerates. These interrelated factors conspired in multiple ways to make the late sixties and early seventies a time of ferment, uncertainty, and experimentation – a period in which no one was sure which way to turn. As a result chances were taken in every direction. The failure of high-budget, general entertainments like *Star!* ('68) terrified Hollywoood in the late sixties.

Around the same time, however, the condign success of low-budget "youth" films, notably *Easy Rider* ('69), suggested a possible avenue of retrenchment. Hollywood focused its energy on special-interest audiences, especially youth. Remember *Getting Straight* ('70), *RPM* ('70), *Vanishing Point* ('71), *Alice's Restaurant* ('69), *Dealing* ('72), *Drive, He Said* ('70), *The Last Movie* ('71), *Electra Glide in Blue* ('73), *Scarecrow,* ('73), *Move* ('70), *Zabriskie Point* ('70), *The Strawberry Statement* ('70), *The Revolutionary* ('70), *Brewster McCloud, Jesus Christ Superstar* ('73), *Two-Lane Blacktop* ('71), *Out of It* ('69), *Little Fauss and Big Halsey* ('70), *Five Easy Pieces* ('70), *The Landlord* ('70), *Steelyard Blues* ('72), *Panic in Needle Park* ('71), *The Christian Licorice Store* ('70). The idea of special-interest films not only made revisionist westerns popular, but also made hyper-morbid comedies like *Where's Poppa?* ('70) and *Harold and Maude* ('71) possible (even if the industry was not always enthralled with the results), as well as "personal" films like *King of Marvin Gardens* ('72). Though at the time the cascade of different kinds of films seemed ructious and confusing, in retrospect it was a rich period. Hollywood's insecurity made it open to new ideas and new blood. This provided an entry into the industry for many of the sixties cinéphiles who are today's major directors. Once inside the industry proper, the young auteurs had a distinct advantage over the corporate managers who bankrolled Hollywood – they knew about movies. They consolidated their power by helping fellow cinéphiles begin their careers, and gradually the aesthetic predispositions of American auteurism became a significant force in Hollywood. The settling down of the industry in the mid-seventies through the increasing reliance on genres strengthened rather than weakened the position of the cinéphiles, who adjusted via the two-tiered system of allusion. But the question remains whether the DePalmas, Schraders, Carpenters, and Spielbergs are putting the old genres through their paces or vice versa.

Just outside the gates of the old Hollywood in the sixties were a number of those who would become lords and ladies of the new Hollywood. They were encamped and waiting at a small studio called American International Pictures. Among those who passed through AIP were Bogdanovich, Coppola, Scorsese, Milius, Hellman, Hopper, Jonathan Demme, Robert Towne, Jack Nicholson, Robert DeNiro, Bruce Dern, John Alonzo, Laszlo Kovacs, and Verna Fields. For financial reasons, AIP gave many young cinéphiles an opportunity to work – they were dirt cheap and they labored unstintingly for love of cinema. When the industry proper became interested in special-audience and youth films it was natural that AIP would be a source of talent, since for years it had, almost alone, farmed the fields of special-interest genres (such as motorcycle movies) and youth (and even younger) films. But AIP was important for the creation of the new Hollywood not only because it was a stepping-stone for future luminaries but because it provided an atmosphere which was not just congenial but also conducive to the aesthetic proclivities of the cinéphile.

The major artistic force at AIP was Roger Corman, a figure of great symbolic and inspirational, as well as instrumental, value for cinéphiles of the sixties. His was a life of film, the closest approximation around to the life of the American studio contract directors the American auteurists idolized. The very existence of Corman answered the cinéphiles' wish to believe that it was still possible to live and work like a Ford or a Walsh. Corman plied the *old genres,* moving from one to another, doing his job at a constant rate of productivity. Corman's individual films were less important than the fact that he was always immersed in the process of *film*. Corman appeared to be able to toss off films as quickly and as confidently as Mozart could symphonies. The number of camera setups Corman could run through from dawn to dusk was legendary; he could churn out a feature in three days, though he usually gave himself two to three weeks for a project. He worked quickly, improvising with surety, evoking the same kind of admiration for craftsmanship that Balanchine and Cunningham do in outsiders witnessing them in the thick of choreographing. Corman's creative speed and enormous output made him seem like a visitor from a bygone era.

His working procedures also recalled the hurly-burly days of early films – jumping into a car to drive over to a friend's house for some location shooting or cooking up a second film on the days remaining on the contract for the first. The working schedule was grueling, but it seemed tinged with adventuresomeness, freedom, and the fun of filmmaking. Corman's low budgets were often the mother of formal inventiveness; in the middle of an unadorned, almost TV-documentary-looking run of shots, his film might burst into an assertively edited sequence, a strikingly self-demonstrative camera movement, or a cheap, glaringly garish special effect that felt bold and experimental in contrast to the staid prevailing dicta of sixties Hollywood realism. Though overstated, his Poe films were refreshingly stylized in their use of color in a period of gray flannel films. Corman's indulgence in layers of albeit often strained religious and ritual allegory and literary conceits, as well as his willingness to shift from flat, homely, mundane images to self-declaiming stylization, gave his work a personal signature, a sense of irony; Corman was a literate director who stood apart, somewhat amused but also genuinely involved and entertained by his generally silly but at the same time oddly compelling little films. The films looked thrown together, a bit amateurish; they were often wooden, but would suddenly evince a feat of cinema that would appear to hail from nowhere. They could leap from cheap economical realism to montage to broad shtick. This gave his work a quality of freedom or free play that could be mistaken for Godard's, especially as the latter was misperceived in America.

Corman made parodies like *Bucket of Blood* ('59), *Little Shop of Horrors* ('60), *Creature from the Haunted Sea* ('61), and the funny, belligerently avant-garde *Gas,* ('70) that were directed at a special hip audience that accepted the *Mad Magazine, Comix* premise that being sophomoric can be sophisticated – an article of faith not unrelated to the mind set required to become a committed film fiend. In works like *St. Valentine's Day Massacre* ('67) Corman includes self-conscious bows to the historical gangster film, while in *Bloody Mama* ('70) he madly careens from dramatic to comic tones, from brutal to lyrical ones, while also taking potshots at media-made America. Increasingly Corman's cinema came to be built with the notion of two audiences in mind – special grace notes for insiders, appoggiatura for the cognoscenti, and a soaring, action-charged melody for the rest. In this, he pioneered the two-tiered system.

It was the not-so-secret daydream of many a cinéphile to run away from school and join Corman – to make the old genres dance to new themes, topical and metaphysical, and to lard them with personal touches like the ones people were always finding in Ford, Hawks, Lang, and company. Everyone wanted to make a film rather than to write the Great American Novel; those with auteurist leanings wanted to be directors, directors of American genre films, ones with highly personal preoccupations showing. Some actually carried through on their dream. And Corman was demanding, hard-driving, yet permissive taskmaster. The cinéphiles could have all the personal touches and artistic flourishes they wanted so long as they stayed on schedule, stayed within their budgets, and kept the sex and violence moving along briskly enough so that the drive-in audiences didn't start honking their horns. Corman asked no more of his epigones than he asked of himself.

The result was films like *Boxcar Bertha* ('72), in which one is suddenly jolted by the imitation of an editing pattern from *Shoot the Piano Player,* Scorsese thereby striking a blow for cinema literacy on the drive-in circuit. Of course, the seminal film of this two-tiered variety was Bogdanovich's *Targets*('68), the most enterprising early exercise in allusionism. In *Targets,* Bogdanovich, as a character, explicitly tutors the audience in the creed of American-style auteurism. He also uses film history – in the person of Boris Karloff – to defend film violence from its puritanical detractors; the melodramatic and stylized horrors of cinema, according to *Targets,* are piddling compared to the banality of evil spawned by American life. I do not wish to defame *Targets*; it was an artistic success, partly because its allusionism was woven into its overall expressive point and partly because the mad sniper was, for a number of reasons, including the war, a timely, chilling image. The issue is not whether *Targets* is a good film but whether it and Bogdanovich's other ventures in allusionist film provide a satisfactory prototype for film now.

*

The rise of allusionism is part a of more general recent tendency toward strident stylization that began in the mid-sixties. If the late fifties and early sixties settled into a comfortable, non-self-demonstrative black-and-white form of realism à la Stanley Kramer, Sidney Lumet, John Huston, William Wyler, and others, then the later sixties, through the zoom lens, rapid montage, slow motion, freeze frame, emphatic use of angulation and close-ups, of lenses of varying focal lengths, of narrative ellipses, and so on, explored the expressive potentials of shamelessly aggressive and conspicuous displays of technique. The shift away from an understated, "classical" realist style toward expressive stylization is uneven and sporadic, popping up here and there – for example, Lester's Beatles films, Frankenheimer's *Seconds* ('66), Penn's *Mickey One* ('65), all of which painlessly integrated, while muting, European innovations into the popular cinema. There are, of course, numerous other forerunners of this tendency, but it can be said that by the time we reach *Bonnie and Clyde* and *The Graduate* ('67), the idea that style is something that an audience should see and consciously unpack as part of the overt meaning of the film had become the wave of the future.

In *The Graduate* not only is the editing studdded with fancy match and shock cuts, but almost every setup reeks with symbolism which the audience is nudged to interpret. For example, toward the end we see the protagonist divided from his true love by a pane of glass, which we refer back to some strong arm shots of a toy diver in an aquarium (through which we see the "alienated" protagonist disconsolate in the background), which we refer back even further to an earlier shot of the hero at the bottom of a swimming pool "drowning (well, submerged) in materialism." Though dated now, *The Graduate* seemed daring when it was realeased; every shot looked like it was planned according to the rules of a textbook such as *Film as Art*. But the student-exercise quality was less immediately apparent than the possibilities heralded by *The Graduate:* that popular film could be self-consciously, "cinematically" intelligent, and that assertive stylization was authorized so that the audience could be expected to perceive and decipher stylistic choices.

These are unquestioned operating presuppositions for making and seeing film in the seventies (and beyond), that is, for those who regard themselves as serious filmmakers and film goers. As presuppositions, these are salutary, even if the results are often mixed, and they produce extremely agreeable working conditions for film-school directors. Allusionism is part and parcel of this tendency toward demonstrative expressiveness through markedly deliberate style. Indeed, allusionism probably follows from the larger tendency through a natural series of events: a concern with style leads to the study of examples and thereby opens the possibility of both learning from the examples and quoting them outright. There is no reason in principle to scorn either the increasingly presupposed sensitivity to style or the use of allusion. Allusionism as it is currently being employed, however, is problematic.

The generation that came to film consciousness in the sixties was embarked on a very special project – the attempt to create a common cultural heritage, a repertoire of shared references to be used the way the bible or Aristotle or Shakespeare had been used in the past. The film craze had the dimensions of a crusade; the film fanatic felt moral indignation over the denial or belittling of film, especially American film. It was our popular art, our great art – how could anyone fail to see its splendor? Hollywood was touted as a twentieth-century creative counterpart to the golden ages of the past. Allusionism, at least initially, was an expression of this utopian urgency, this desire on the part of many members of the generation that grew up in the fifties to establish a new community, with film history supplying its legends, myths, and vocabulary.

It is important to remember that the generation which rediscovered film also rediscovered radical politics. Many cinéphiles participated in the political upheavals of the mid-sixties, becoming politically conscious at the same time that they came to film consciousness. This fact is still evident indirectly in the thriving leftist tenor of a significant portion of our contemporary film journals, many of whose editors and contributors became involved with film during the Vietnam War, when they also were active politically. For many, film and politics seemed to blend into each other easily – perhaps all to easily – in the sixties and early seventies. It seems plausible, then, to speculate that the politics and the film craze of the sixties may have had the same or very similar causes – the identity crisis (or identity construction, if you prefer) of the generation that grew up in the fifties. The film boom was a call for the democratization of art – for the admission of the lowly genre film into the canon of aesthetic and academic worthiness. The film generation chose movies as an emblem of self – movies, something deeply part of their youthful experience, but something whose existence was ignored, disparaged, and sometimes even "forbidden" by the established "adult" culture. What better sounding board for selfhood? The battle against the injustices of art history toward film was energized by the same self-righteous rebelliousness that activated the social movements of the sixties. The completion of their task by the visionary company of cinéphiles was to have supplied and codified the sacred texts of this most promising new generation's new community. American auteurism is best understood as

part of a quest for identity through the construction of a new and, needless to say, improved culture, one to be implemented by political and
alternative life-style activism, one whose common vocabulary would be
found at the movies. The early inclusion of film-conscious allusions in
genre films and their recognition by stalwart cinéphiles was symbolic
interaction of great emotional resonance in the sixties and early seventies, when the rediscovery of film was bound up with both a general
utopian project, the creation of a brand-new common culture, and a
concurrent process of self-definition and discovery, the adoption of a
new sensibilty, one customized to order for the postwar generation. But
with the foreclosure of the prospects for utopia allusionism loses much
of its glitter. It can deteriorate into mere affectation, nostalgia, and, at
worst, self-deception when filmmakers[16] or now middle-aged viewers
think that in and of itself allusion to film history is still charged with
the psychocultural importance it had when the sixties turned into the
seventies.

There is an arresting analogy to be drawn between the film-school
allusionism of the new Hollywood and certain tendencies of recent
avant-garde film, viz., the Althusserian – Lacanian "New Talkie." Both
are examples of film styles that testify to the victory of certain critical-
theoretical positions – American auteurism, on the one hand, and
Anglo-French psychoanalytic semiotics on the other. Both artistic practices try to incorporate the prejudices of their critical lights in their
works and deeds. In the new Hollywood, the filmmakers model themselves on the great-director notion of American auteurism, as well as
making allusions to film history that require knowledge, on the part of
audiences, of the commonplaces and criticism of American auteurism in
order to make sense. Likewise, the New Talkie often takes its guidelines
(for example, don't make eyeline matches, don't connect, don't suture)
from the writings of reigning semiological tastemakers, while the works
themselves, such as *Dora* ('80), are illustrations of ideas, controversies,
and arguments that preexist the films in the world of academic film writing, and they presuppose spectators familiar with that literature in order
to be understood. In many instances, artists of the new Hollywood and
the New-Talkie wing of the avant-garde appear to be taking their march-
ing orders from established criticism. This, at the very least, is a reversal
of the conventional order of things in which the artist is envisioned as
creating works that impel the critics and theoreticians to alter their conceptual frameworks. Now we have works designed for a particular kind
of criticism. Perhaps this reversal is what accounts for the feeling that

much of the production of the new Hollywood and the semiological wing of the avant-garde is dull, predictable, and authority-bound. It is as if the unprecedented, extended process of film education that many contemporary filmmakers have undergone has resulted in an unexpected catastrophe – through overexposure to the medium, the cinéaste has succumbed to the essentially authoritarian features of the film-viewing situation. Or perhaps it was the authoritarianism of the medium that attracted these particular cinéastes to film in the first place.

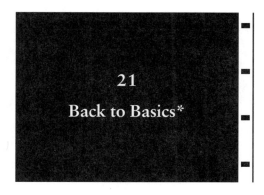

21

Back to Basics*

Vampires from outer space, pirate treasure, time machines, cowboys defending homesteaders, dinosaurs, a half-naked warrior vanquishing hordes of enemies, a house that turns into the biggest popcorn machine in history.

These are the images you would have seen in some of Hollywood's major productions of the past year – in *Lifeforce*, *The Goonies*, *Back to the Future*, *Silverado*, *My Science Project*, *Rambo: First Blood Part II*, and *Real Genius*.

This list may remind some older Americans of the kinds of movie choices they faced when they were children during the 1930s '40s, or '50s. Those films could be neatly defined – as science fiction, horror, Westerns, war pictures, and slapstick comedies. For critics and movie-makers, these labels, along with others, such as musicals, mysteries, and thrillers, sort out the major film "genres."

A decade and a half ago, the genre film seemed close to becoming an endangered species. Hollywood had largely turned away from the old standbys, seemingly forever (although it still produced a fair number of them), in favor of more experimental films in the vein of *Steelyard Blues* and *Five Easy Pieces*. "What these films – and others – had in common," writes Arthur Knight, a film historian, "was their articulation of contemporary attitudes and emotions, in a language that had its own modern rhythms and nuances."

But Hollywood attentively follows ticket sales at the box office, and by the mid-1970s, the movie-going public was telling studio executives that it wanted old-fashioned genre films again. This time, instead of churning out simple copies of past hits, Hollywood produced fairly sophisticated confections, larded with in-jokes and arcane allusions to motion picture history. Few in the audience understood those references,

* "Back to Basics," *Wilson Quarterly*, Vol. X, no. 3, (Sammer '86), pp. 58–69.

but crowds flocked to the new movies – science fictions, Westerns, and other variations on old recipes.

Genres, of course, have shaped film production almost since the beginnings of cinema.[1] The Frenchman George Méliès enthralled turn-of-the-century audiences with "trick" films that exploited special effects in frame after frame of miraculous disappearances, apparitions, and transformations. Later, chase, escape, and rescue films, perfected during the 1910s by D. W. Griffith and others, introduced suspense as a staple ingredient of the cinema. The 1920s call to mind the great slapstick comedies of the Keystone Kops and Charlie Chaplin; the years of the Great Depression seem inextricably bound up with escapist musicals, swashbucklers, gangster films, and horror shows; the late 1940s recall the *film noir*; the 1950s, Westerns, science fiction, and thrillers.

During Hollywood's Golden Era, the general notion of genres provided filmmakers with ready-made formulas for large numbers of films. A genre label, the studios discovered, helped a film find an audience. Musical fans could be counted on to turn out for the latest Busby Berkeley creation; werewolf lovers would pay to see many of the movies of that genre. Moreover, the reliance on genre production supplied a sort of common language for the filmmaker and the audience. Knowing that the audience was aware of the assumptions and conventions of the form – that, for example, in horror films vampires abhor daylight – directors could spare lengthy exposition in favor of continuous action.

In the hands of an especially talented director, the shared genre "vocabulary" was not just a short cut but a means of creative expression. When Orson Welles opened *Citizen Kane* (1941) with a shot of an old, dark house on a hill, for example, he artfully used the imagery of the horror movie to convey the sense that his film (a thinly veiled portrait of ambitious newspaper magnate William Randolph Hearst) would deal with the hidden and unholy. And Alfred Hitchcock often invoked the conventions of the thriller in order to make jokes. In *Strangers on a Train* (1951), the murderer and the hero's wife take a ride in an amusement park's Tunnel of Love. A shadow appears; there is a shriek. But when the pair reappears, the audience discovers that they have simply been flirting.

From the studios' perspective, genres were useful in plotting production strategy. Genre films come in cycles: On the principle that nothing succeeds like success, Hollywood would follow one box-office genre hit with many clones. Each would be refined in its own way. "It is as if with each commercial effort, the studios suggested another variation on cinematic conventions," writes Thomas Schatz, a University of Texas film scholar, "and the audience indicated whether the inventive variations would . . . be conventionalized through their repeated usage." As the audience for one genre was exhausted, the studios could then revive and promote another genre that had lain dormant for several years.

During the late 1930s and early '40s, for example, Hollywood tried, without much success, to repeat the popular horror cycle of the early Great Depression years. Make-up men busied themselves with *Son*, *Ghost*, and *House of Frankenstein*, as well as *Son* and *House of Dracula*. During the same era, comedians Abbott and Costello met monsters W, X, Y, and Z.

More than one film critic has seen the constant repetition and recycling in the history of popular movies as a sign that celluloid is a significant repository of contemporary myth. "When a film achieves a certain success," the French director François Truffaut observed in 1972, "it becomes a sociological event, and the question of its quality becomes secondary." Laconic cowpokes, bug-eyed monsters, singing sailors, and sinister, domineering gangsters rehearse on the screen the audience's hopes and fears, its notions of loyalty and authority, of masculinity and femininity.

The chief preoccupations of each genre tend to change very little over time, but the inflections shift from one cycle to the next. Take the horror film. Its essential ingredient is *Otherness*, epitomized by a monster. Frankenstein, Dracula, and the Mummy made their screen debuts during the early 1930s, when distraction from the day-to-day difficulties of the Depression was good box office. Often, the movie monsters of the 1930s were themselves creatures of some pathos: Not a few tears were shed in movie houses over the demise of King Kong. But when Hollywood recycled the horror genre during the 1950s, the early Cold War years, things had changed. There was nothing sympathetic about the giant insects and repulsive aliens who ravaged the cinematic Earth during those years. In *The Invasion of the Body Snatchers* (1956), for example, aliens from outer space slowly infiltrate a California town, taking over the bodies of its human inhabitants. Only one telltale sign gives the aliens away: They lack emotion. The Other had become a completely repulsive force bent on dehumanizing us, a stand-in for the Soviet menace.

By the late 1960s, however, it appeared that the curtain was coming down on genre movies. Amid growing domestic disarray over the war in South Vietnam and black riots in the nation's big cities, none of the old formulas seemed to work, on the silver screen or in real life. Most clearly, there was bad news at the box office.

In their perpetual quest to offer something TV could not, the studios had hit on two new high-budget genres during the early 1960s. Epic spectacles such as *Ben Hur*, *Lawrence of Arabia*, and *Spartacus* often seemed to use Pax Romana and Pax Britannica as metaphors for Pax Americana to illustrate the trials and tribulations of imperium. (Other epics, such as *The Longest Day* and *Fifty-five Days at Peking*, meditated more directly on American military history.) The runaway success of *The Sound of Music*, starring Julie Andrews, in 1965 marked the apogee of a series of lavish musicals celebrating the bright optimism of the times with uplift and gaiety: *Music Man*, *Mary Poppins*, and *Hello Dolly*.

When the big-budget genre balloon finally burst, notably with the flop of 20th Century-Fox's $15 million *Star!* in 1968, it blew up with a bang. In 1969, five of the Big Eight studios were deeply in the red, and Wall Street was bearish on their future.

In that same year, the year of Richard Nixon's inauguration, Hollywood witnessed the monumental success of *Easy Rider*, a low-budget motorcycle tour of America's emerging counterculture starring Peter Fonda and the then-unknown Jack Nicholson. The studios were quick to climb aboard the new bandwagon, ushering in a period of cinematic experimentation unprecedented in a half century of American filmmaking.

Traditional genre films were thrust into the background by a slew of original offerings that included: *Alice's Restaurant*; *Zabriskie Point*; *Drive, He Said*; *Brewster McCloud*; *Harold and Maude*; *Mean Streets*; *Five Easy Pieces*; *M*A*S*H*; and *Carnal Knowledge*.

These films reflected the nation's (or at least Hollywood's) Vietnam-afflicted, antitraditional mood. *Carnal Knowledge* was sexually explicit; *M*A*S*H*, a black satire on war; *Harold and Maude* recounted the love affair of a teen-age boy and an 80-year-old woman. The films were experimental in form and composition as well as content. The plots were loosely constructed and the editing disjunctive, reflecting the influence of Jean-Luc Godard and other directors of the French New Wave.

The most remarkable genre pictures of this period – such as *Bonnie and Clyde*, *McCabe and Mrs. Miller*, *The Long Goodbye* – were not straightforward genre exercises, but self-conscious and reflexive. Their directors were well aware of the old formulas and turned them upside-down in order to thumb their noses at the established order. In *McCabe and Mrs. Miller* (1971), for example, Robert Altman set up McCabe as a typical Western hero, a rugged individualist and founding father of a pioneer town, then exposed him as a weakling and a loser. The unrelenting hail of bullets in many of these movies echoed the domestic and international strife of the day, so the critics said, while the astounding stupidity and seediness of the new "anti-heroes" made it hard to tell who wore the white hats and who wore the black ones.

This is not to say that "experimental" and revisionist genre features monopolized the nation's movie screens. Hollywood still churned out standardized Westerns (*The Stalking Moon*) and cops-and-robbers pictures (notably, *Bullitt* and *The French Connection*). These films, too, indirectly reflected popular anxieties about the war against evil, foreign and domestic. In Clint Eastwood's *Dirty Harry*, a San Francisco cop deals with a psychotic terrorist named Scorpio the old-fashioned way: He kills him. And a spate of disaster films – *The Poseidon Adventure*, *Airport*, *Skyjacked*, *Earthquake*, *The Towering Inferno* – exploited the theme of entrapment, whose political and social correlates were easy to identify.

But these efforts were the exception. For a time, experimentation thrived, commanding much greater critical and public attention than the more pedestrian genre offerings.

It was an unexpected string of blockbuster hits – William Friedkin's *The Exorcist* in 1973, Steven Spielberg's *Jaws* in 1975, and then George Lucas's *Star Wars* two years later – that sent Hollywood producers rushing back to genre films. Or, as one film title later put it, back to the future.

One by one, the blockbusters slowly rose to high rank on *Variety's* list of all-time hits. Indeed, today all of *Variety's* top 10 are movies made since 1975.[2]

The success of these genre features underscored the fact that movie audiences had changed. No longer was Hollywood mainly in the business of offering entertainment for all ages: More than half of the people lining up at the theaters were under 25, many of them teen-agers. The older folks were staying home with TV. "If Hollywood keeps gearing movie after movie to teen-agers," quipped comedian-director Mel Brooks, "next year's Oscar will develop acne."

Youth was also making its mark in Hollywood. Spielberg (who was 24 when he agreed to make *Jaws*) and Lucas were among the first "movie brats," a new cadre of young filmmakers who were beginning to make their way up the Hollywood ladder when *Jaws* swam onto the scene.[3] Raised in the age of television, the newcomers had watched endless late-night reruns of Hollywood's trash and treasures. Many were also trained in university film schools when the reigning form of criticism, *auteurism*, accorded special emphasis to such Hollywood classics as Hitchcock's *Psycho* and John Ford's *The Searchers*. In the view of the auteur critics, Hollywood's previously unrecognized contract directors were maestros of film who made sharp personal statements in their works. The new directors were more than ready to follow in their footsteps.

Whatever else might be said of these filmmakers – that, as some critics contend, their works are clever but often empty – they know their craft. Spielberg, Lucas, and company can put the old genres through their paces with awesome precision, invent new plot twists, graft old tricks onto contemporary subject matter, and combine genres into new alloys.

But that is not all that they do. Often, the works of these new directors contain sly and not-so-sly allusions to film history – a camera movement here, the re-creation of a famous scene there. *Time* said of *Star Wars* that it was "a subliminal history of the movies, wrapped in a riveting tale of suspense and adventure." The new genre films often appear to have been designed with two audiences in mind: the connoisseurs on the lookout for "scholarly" references, and a mass of younger viewers in search of thrills.

One of the first genres to reappear was horror. Revived by the success of *The Exorcist*, which generated a half-dozen spinoffs, the trend did not appear long for this world. However, *Jaws* and *The Omen*, with its Grand Guignol stagings of stylized murders, gave the cycle a second push. Every kind of monster that audiences had ever seen rose up from its Hollywood grave: werewolves (*The Howling, American Werewolf in London*), vampires (*Dracula, Lifeforce, The Hunger, Fright Night*), psychics (*Firestarter*), zombies (*Dawn of the Dead, The Fog*). With *The Car* and *Christine*, the studios added a new family of monsters to the Hollywood immortals: old cars.

Many of these movies share the same basic plot structure. First the monster appears, committing ghastly atrocities (the shark's mauling of a young girl in *Jaws*). Next, someone (the boy next door in *Fright Night*) discovers the agent of death (a vampire, in this case). Then, he must convince unbelievers that there really are vampires, big sharks, or whatever. And together the good guys go off to confront the monster in a final showdown.

This kind of plot seems to appeal to young audiences because it is a kind of parable about growing up. It highlights the discovery of hidden knowledge, while also dramatizing a moment when adults are finally forced to listen seriously to the young. And many horror films stress biological deformity and Otherness, thus broaching adolescent anxieties about the body.

Sometimes just the act of viewing a film can be a kind of rite of passage for teen-age boys: Are you man enough to sit through a gruesome "slasher"[4] film (e.g., *Halloween, Friday the 13th* and its sequels, *Prom Night*), or an even gorier "splatter" film like *Scanners* or *The Evil Dead?*

A sizable share of the current menu of science fiction offerings – such as *Alien, The Thing, The Dark* – are really horror films, films about monsters. They are classified as sci-fi only because their monsters hail from outer space. A new twist in this old genre is the beatific, in contrast to horrific, sci-fi movie: *Close Encounters of the Third Kind, E. T., Cocoon.* These films, with their friendly extraterrestrials, confirm the adolescent wish for a universe filled with warm and compassionate beings.

Even more appealing to teen-age audiences is that these pictures involve quests or rites of passage. *The Last Starfighter,* for example, not only enacts the notion of a trial in cosmic proportions but exploits the desire of every girl and boy to escape the humdrum world of school and family. Because of his prowess in video games, Alex, otherwise an ordinary earthling boy next door, is drafted by the Star League of Planets to defeat the forces of the traitorous Xur.

The projection of adolescent fantasies onto big screens does not happen by accident. When Lucas was working on the script of *Star Wars,* he recalls, "I researched kids' movies and how they work and how myths work." "Do not call this film 'science fiction,'" he told the marketing men at 20th Century-Fox. "It's a space fantasy."

The commercial success of the space operas spawned several variants built around the quest and rite-of-passage themes. In the sword-and-sorcery genre – *Excalibur,* the *Conan* series, and, in 20th century garb, *Time Bandits* and *Raiders of the Lost Ark* – swords and whips replace ray guns, and magic, science. The *Mad Max* series depicts a post-apocalyptic world cloaked in imagery of the Dark Ages. Castles and chargers are made out of old cars, the barbarians are at the gates, and the spark of civilized life hinges on the outcome of stock car races between knights in punk regalia.

Today's comedies are not much closer to reality. With the exception of such sex farces as *10* and *Unfaithfully Yours,* both starring Dudley Moore, most of them are keyed to younger sensibilities. This is apparent in the flurry of films about high school romance, often in a light comic mood (*Sixteen Candles, Risky Business*). It is even more obvious in the aggressive irreverence of the gross-out/fraternity house humor of *Animal House* (and its numerous progeny) and the Burt Reynolds redneck car films. When they decide to sabotage their college homecoming parade with "a really futile, stupid gesture," Bluto and his *Animal House* brothers sum up the new comedy's attitude toward adult values.

Physical humor – slapstick, sight gags, and comic chases – has also gained a new lease on life. But the same sense of unreality prevails. Slapstick shares several traits with science fiction and supernatural films. All three genres demand the suspension of the laws of physical probability: The world becomes a kind of playground. In Woody Allen's *Zelig*, for example, a man metamorphoses into whomever he is with; in *The Purple Rose of Cairo*, a character steps off a movie screen that the characters are watching. This assault on the reality principle is so extreme that it verges on vulgar surrealism in films such as *The Blues Brothers*, the *Cheech and Chong* series, and *Pee Wee's Big Adventure*.

Fantasy prevails even when the settings seem real. In 1976, Sylvester Stallone restored the power of positive thinking to the screen with *Rocky*, a story about a "ham 'n egg" prize fighter who nearly wins the heavyweight boxing crown from the glamorous Apollo Creed. *Rocky* paved the way for a slew of uplifting sports films, of which Britain's *Chariots of Fire* is aesthetically the most noteworthy, as well as success stories about all sorts of down-and-outers, such as *The Verdict*.

There have been three *Rocky* sequels so far, all of them exercises in improbability. In *Rocky IV*, a boxing match becomes the solution to East–West tensions. Some of the most effective wish-fulfillment films, such as *Breaking Away* and *The Karate Kid*, have adolescents in the leading role. And, of course, the resurgence of the teen musical, spearheaded by *Saturday Night Fever, Fame*, and *Flashdance*, owes much to the success story motif.

The darker side of adolescent fantasy is evident in Stallone's two *Rambo* pictures. The Rambo movies have several ingredients that make them especially compelling to young audiences: the figure of the misunderstood loner, and the themes of betrayal and revenge. In *Rambo: First Blood Part II*, the Pentagon dispatches Rambo back to Vietnam to rescue American soldiers who have been declared "missing in action" (MIA). But then officialdom deserts him claiming that there are no MIAs. So he uses his perfect, high school weightlifter's body to execute unstoppable rampages, leading his MIAs back to the United States over the dead bodies of scores of his foes. On the screen, Rambo transforms teen-agers' feelings of alienation and frustration into cinematic delusions of grandeur.

Of course, Hollywood has always emphasized escapism. Yet, it is astounding what a high percentage of its products today are literally fantasy films – horror, sci-fi, and absurdist comedies – or, in the case of *Rocky* and its kin, psychological fantasies. Even during the Great Depression, the heyday of Hollywood escapism, the studios released a fair number of gritty "realistic" pictures. But *The Grapes of Wrath* has no real counterpart today. *The Color Purple*, Steven Spielberg's effort to explore the unhappy history of the black family in America, was filmed like a fairy tale. *Country* and *The River*, two recent films that dramatized the plight of the nation's farmers, were thoroughly drenched in sentimentality. And there were many empty seats in the theaters where they were shown.

Lucas and the other new university-trained directors, with only a few notable exceptions, are no more interested in the "real world" than are their audiences. During the 1970s, they set out to rescue their heroes – not only Alfred Hitchcock and Howard Hawks, but Superman and Flash Gordon – from critical contempt and oblivion. In their eyes, the Hollywood genre movie was one of America's great art forms: How could so many people fail to see that?

In a sense, the movie brats have accomplished their revivalist mission in grand style. Indeed, they have managed to achieve a level of financial success and celebrity beyond the imaginings of their predecessors. But now they have nothing left to do. Movies have become the subject of movies, as though the most vital elements in our contemporary environment are representations and images rather than the "real world."

If today's directors are paid handsomely to indulge themselves, it is because their audiences make it profitable for the studios to sign the checks. And the youthful ticket-buying public seems to find more comfort and authenticity in honey-spun fantasy films than in those that confront political and social themes or simply dramatize the often painful realities of everyday life. Until the nation's movie audiences change their minds, Hollywood is sure to travel ever deeper into its past in search of its future.

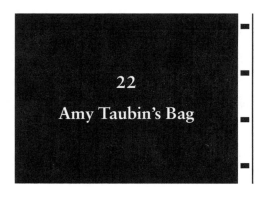

22

Amy Taubin's Bag

In the Bag (1981) is the first completed film of Amy Taubin, noted avant-garde critic, actress and performance artist. Roughly twenty minutes long, the film records a search through a tattered, patchwork-quilt shoulder bag for something – we know not what. Like *Wavelength*, a film many misremember as a single tracking shot, *In the Bag* is also easily misremembered and wrongly described as a stationary long take à la Warhol which relentlessly records Taubin's relentless rummaging. However, in fact, the film is intensively edited – full of what we come to understand as flash forwards, and cross-cuts between the primary search, set on a brown table, and an almost identical search, set on and amid the blue sheets of a bed. Taubin – her "cold/preoccupied" shoulder to the camera, her face generally occluded from us by her long brown hair – is the only person in the film; her manner is concentrated, suggesting a total obliviousness to onlookers. This plus her silence and the methodical character of her search gives *In the Bag* a meditative air which, in turn, places the film on a continuum with Taubin's solitary performance pieces – all solo meditations on the nature of the self.

Taubin began making theater pieces in 1978.[1] These include *Pimping for Herself* (1975), *Double Occupancy* (1976), and *Performance Which Began with a Train Ride on Which the Rider Realized but Not Until the Last Moment That She Had Been Seated Backward, Or Half of an Unbalanced Situation* (1978). Like *In the Bag*, each of these pieces is short, each is structured in a way that is transparently manifest to the audience – indeed, one takes it that grasping the structure of each work is something the audience is expected to achieve – and each features Taubin as a soloist. In the last two performances especially, acting is de-emphasized in favor of reading, and the text rather than the performer/performance is foregrounded. This has the effect of locating the

"Amy Taubin's Bag," *Millennium Film Journal*, no. 12 (Fall/Winter 1982–83), pp. 68–77.

energy of the pieces in ideas rather than spectacle, which, in the context of these works, stands for a concern with mind rather than body. The solo format refines this reference further, suggesting itself, via soliloquy, as an illustration of or symbol for ego.

Moreover, Taubin's theatrical emblems of ego are embarked on a very particular task: the attempt of the self to clarify its nature to itself. The first piece, *Pimping for Herself*, is an exercise in applied Sartrean psychology in which Taubin subjects each member of the audience to the existentialist's Look of the Other.[2] This results in palpitations of self-consciousness and intersubjectivity among spectators while also, reflexively, erecting the performer-as-symbol into a privileged instance of self-awareness. *Double Occupancy* explores the homology that mind is to body as male is to female in an effort by Taubin to examine her identity as a woman, while *Performance Which Began* ... literalizes the French Structuralist metaphor of identity – in this case, the female identity – as a *position*. Though *In the Bag* lacks the monologues of the theater pieces, its imagery – significantly dominated by Taubin's head in a backward close-shot, and complete with that avant-garde icon of the self, the mirror – signals Taubin's continued commitment to artworks conceived of as meditations, meditations concerned with identity. Specifically, *In the Bag*, it seems to me, expresses the idea that an identity is not a matter of discovery – of finding something that already exists – but rather a matter of decision.

In the Bag introduces its central topic obliquely in its first and only title card; screen right, there is a torn reproduction of Vermeer's *The Lace Maker*.[3] Retrospectively, one might take this item as another of the many casualties of Taubin's merciless search. But a better interpretation might be to regard it as an allusion to the idea of the fragmented ego. The grounds for this attribution rest on contextual factors. In the avant-garde filmworld, of which Taubin is an avid participant, it is commonplace to hold that the self is a representation. Consequently, it makes perfect aesthetic sense to portray the ego as fragmented – another prevailing idea of the avant-garde filmworld and one quite relevant to the rest of *In the Bag* – by tearing up a *representation*, notably a portrait.

While reading the credits, we hear airport-terminal sounds, and the advertising phrase, "... twenty-two minutes and we'll give you the world." The slogan is repeated and followed by laughter as we see the first image – a scarlet shoulder bag, with blue patches, lying on a brown, walnut-colored table. Barely visible in the background, we see slivers of the surfaces of three stand-up mirrors. Throughout the film, the playing space never seems to exceed nine square feet in area. The bag dominates many shots and it is rifled again and again.

The opening audio-visual imagery sets up a strong contrast. Formally, the sound presents us with the world and travel in opposition to the claustrophobic playing space. This juxtaposition can also be glossed in terms of a public place versus a private one, an open space versus a closed one, a random zone versus a controlled one, and outside versus inside. Perhaps, these all can be subsumed under the broader dichotomy of world versus self. Furthermore, the dominance of the visual track fixes Taubin's subject as the "inner" world. Thematically, the sound-track evokes the idea of a journey while the visual imagery is of a search. Both metaphors are conventionally combinable as figures describing an investigation of self. The commentary promises that in twenty-two min-utes – a prediction of the length of the film – we will be given the world. But it is an inner world rather than the outer world of the advertisement that *In the Bag* delivers.

The image of the bag on the table gives way to some brief shots of torn papers. Later we recognize these as residues of newspapers, letters and notebooks that Taubin shreds to bits – as if to find what she is look-ing for hidden, literally occulted, *inside* the pages of her various reading materials, along their frayed edges. These flash inserts have a visually explosive, disruptive appearance, intimating the violent urgency that underwrites Taubin's otherwise measured search.[4]

Next, we see the bag – with a copy of the *New York Times* underneath – on the blue bedspread, before returning to the search on the brown table. There, large items are first disgorged from the bag: pink panties, various purses, pouches, notebooks and so on. The bag is turned inside out. Its contents are piled onto the table and then cleared off to prepare for a systematic investigation. Various receptacles inside the bag undergo the same fate as their container; pouches inside pouches are emptied and turned inside out – glasses are dumped from their case, and scissors, lipstick and other beauty aids are removed from a make-up kit and lined up for inspection. Similar activities transpire on the bed-spread. As things are emptied, piled, sifted, turned over and cleared away, we begin to notice and to discriminate certain objects: an airmail overseas letter, a checkbook, a copy of H. D.'s *Tribute to Freud*, a pass-port, a red pouch, a diary-type notebook, a brown pouch embossed with golden leaves, a drugstore photo-machine strip of four pictures of Taubin, etc. Though the bag seems to be excavated in one continuous process, it is, in reality, emptied more than once. All of the objects that pour out of it convey a strong sense of the personal – some because they stand in an intimate metonymical relation to their owner; others because they are symbols of identity, e.g., photos, identification papers, make-up, the diary and even the checkbook as a sort of capitalist day book.

The search escalates in desperation. Taubin begins tearing apart, cutting and breaking up various articles in her bag. The blue overseas letter is scrutinized intently and then – like the brown pouch and the bag itself earlier – the envelope is turned inside out. Next the envelope is ripped and Taubin runs her hand along the edge as if to discover a message in Lilliputian braille. A flashforward shows us the letter torn to smithereens; the sudden mismatch rocks the visual field, suggesting that some magical combustion has blown the letter into a million, neatly squared, scraps. The remnants of the dissected letter are spread out on the bed where they, tellingly, blend into the bedclothes.

Other objects are dismembered: a red pouch, a diaphragm, the diary-notebook. The word "cut" appears on the soundtrack in a way that ambiguously alludes to what is going on in the frame, to splicing and to castration.[5] A hand-mirror is broken, as is a pair of sunglasses; a string is unraveled. A fist of tin-foil, balled as if containing marijuana, is undone. These images, especially those of cutting, seem to be figures for the process of analysis. At the same time, they imply either that whatever Taubin is searching for is so small that it is virtually invisible (one view of the self), or that the existence of what Taubin is searching for is somehow dubious – the word "imaginary" springs to mind in the context of Taubin's "Lacanian" mirrors.

Throughout *In the Bag*, there are repeated cuts to slow motion images of Taubin's rustling through the bag with her arms extended fully into it. These shots differ from the standard speed shots in terms of orientation, i.e., Taubin tilts screen left to right in the normal speed shots but faces screen right to left in the slow motion images. The repetition of these shots, as well as the ritual quality imbued by the slow motion, abet one of the most striking features of *In the Bag*: obsessiveness. Even the orientation shifts come into play here; they remind one of the permutating camera angles that in Structural Film stand for thoroughness and systematicity. Yet, at the same time, the shifting camera positions recall the right/left befuddlement of *Performance Which Began . . .* , and they promote the feeling that the image is being rotated, in vain, to catch a glimpse of something that is missing.

An atmosphere of obsessiveness pervades *In the Bag*. Specific actions are repeated: cutting, tearing, dismantling, turning things over and inside out. Objects are constantly piled for re-examination, and then cleared away, with anal finickiness, to begin again. Moreover, this is all extremely methodical. For example, various papers are decomposed into the most precise little squares, and ruled, rectangular strips. Also, Taubin's hand repeatedly touches every article on the table in a manner that conveys the feeling of an anxious inventory. At points, Taubin seems engaged in what could be called a preoccupation with composition. She reaches into the pile and extracts some objects – e.g., a yellow-capped pen, broken sunglasses and a flashlight – and she tries to array them in a satisfactory still-life. But she rejects their arrangement, brushing them away in a swipe of obsessive fussiness; they do not correspond to some unnamed idée fixe.

One could describe the basic procedure of *In the Bag* as a parade of objects before the camera. These objects are often framed alone in the visual field as Taubin examines them, thereby affording us a virtual string of close-shots. Given our lack of knowledge about what Taubin is looking for, our interest in the basic narrative function of these items quickly evaporates, leading us to peruse the objects for their metaphoric and symbolic values.[6] The bag itself, especially in the slow motion shots, becomes a body of sorts, an enormous after birth that Taubin searches for a sign. The bag, at the very least, is a yonic image, an interpretation enhanced by the fact that Taubin removes a diaphragm from it. Pens, glasses, a flashlight shaped like a movie camera, notebooks, all seem to herald Taubin's identity as a writer, artist, filmmaker while the inclusion of *Tribute to Freud* acts as an emblem of the interphase of art and psychoanalysis. Taubin's gestures also seem full of symbolic portent. For instance, as Taubin rips apart the red pouch – in slow motion, from reverse angles – the image suggests the skinning of a small, helpless animal. The air of violence seething beneath the surface is also apparent in the shot in which Taubin snips her diaphragm apart. Though this act is performed in a matter-of-fact manner, it is one that many spectators read as full of anger and renunciation.

In the Bag rushes into a kind of finale as Taubin conjoins a flurry of brief shots of her hand passing through mounds of square, small scraps of paper in two locales: on the brown table and on the blue sheets. In each set-up, Taubin faces myriad pieces of paper, scattered like parts of a giant jigsaw puzzle, with rather the same connotations as the puzzle/identity correlation in *Citizen Kane*. As the editing weds disjunct spaces, Taubin's hand movements seem continuous from shot to shot as a result of what I have elsewhere called weak ampliation.[7] But both the background colors (brown and blue), and the contours of the piles of paper in the alternating shots clash, yielding a pulsating flicker which is disruptive and violent. Thus, though Taubin's hand movements are even, steady and deliberate from shot to shot, the speed of the editing and the phenomenal explosions of the flicker effect suggest a ferocity and a consternation underlying and shielded by the obsessive rituals practiced throughout the film. Finally, Taubin clears the bed and the table. Her hand runs over the wooden grain in a last effort to find something lodged in the cracks between the boards. There is nothing to discover. Taubin's hand returns and places two pens and the camera shaped flashlight on the table. She has not found her identity in one piece, so to speak. Rather she has asserted it. From the contents of her handbag, she has chosen the tools of a writer and a filmmaker – ink and light.

At first glance, *In the Bag* is deceptive: it initially looks like a film of a minimalist or a structural persuasion. The obsessive clearing-off of the table, for example, recalls Richard Serra's *Hand Scraping*; indeed, the very idea of creating a film around the execution of a single concrete action suggests an allegiance to the minimal-art-inspired genre of the task-dance and the task-performance.[8] The impression that the camera set-up at the table – the core of the film – is a single long take from a fixed position evokes memories of Warhol, *Wavelength*, *Soft Rain* and *Still*. As in these earlier films, Taubin's camera adopts an intent, obsessive stare, and, given the relatively banal, minimal interest of the imagery, we have a distinct feeling that duration – one of the prized qualities of phenomenological filmmaking – is an issue for *In the Bag*. Taubin's cutting between images that closely resemble each other, the concomitant animation and flicker effects and the creation of an object that is at once placid and full of commotion remind one of *Serene Velocity*. Yet, for all the analogies and lines of influence that might be traced between *In the Bag* and various of its minimal-art-inspired forebears, Taubin's film is not in that camp. It aims at expressive effects rather than formal, phenomenological or reflexive ones; it has a humanistic theme and it uses objects symbolically. It is not about seeing, seeing afresh, or about baring its devices. Rather, it uses its devices to articulate a theme of some apparent urgency to its central character; it is somewhat like a lyric poem, but on film.

Taubin's performance pieces have the same ambiguous status. Their austere scenography; rigorous, dramaturgic symmetries; and their obvious subdivision into discrete but systematically related components invite one to identify them as examples of Structuralist Theater.[9]

However, in fact, her scenography is better understood as a metaphoric field and her texts are indubitably allegorical. Taubin could be called an expressionist who uses a minimalist's vocabulary. Several things need to be said about this.

First: what Taubin derives by striking a minimalist pose are certain expressive qualities that constitute the dominant tone of *In the Bag*: precision; an aura of hard, clean, clear thinking in contrast to ecstatic, romantic rambling; an atmosphere of intellectual intensity – obsessiveness and thoroughness – a dogged, penetrating, ever-observant and inexhaustible attentiveness, the minimalist's capacity to continue to see subtleties where others see nothing to see. These qualities characterize the tenor of Taubin's meditation. It is an anti-sentimental, hard-minded, no-nonsense, just-the-facts interrogation with a realist, anti-utopian bias. Taubin acquires these qualities by splitting minimalist stylization from minimalist concerns (such as the examination of the conditions of perception), and by then imitating only the mannerisms of minimalism.[10]

One might argue that the apparent minimalism of *In the Bag* can be accounted for biographically. Minimalism was the dominant prejudice in various art forms as they were practiced in New York during the term of Taubin's artistic apprenticeship. Thus, she automatically turns to minimalism in creating her first film. Undoubtedly this has some truth in it. Yet, it is also important to remember that the aesthetic of the sixties and seventies was equally dominated by the ideas of "moves" and "countermoves"; art was conceived of as a Duchampian chess game. In this light, *In the Bag* represents a sneak attack on minimalism. It has the look of a minimalist film but uses the données of minimalism to make direct, albeit metaphoric, statements. An analogous kind of contrariness is in evidence in the way that *In the Bag* tempts the viewer into categorizing it as an exercise in real-time realism despite the appearance of taunting flourishes of editing. In both cases, Taubin makes the issue of categorizing the film – as minimalist or expressionist, and as realist or montagist – a nagging tension one feels while viewing the work. Our inclination is to take the most complacent line or interpretation – e.g., call it a minimalist film and then tag it with the by-now formulaic, modernist rhetoric which is usually applied to Structural Films. But while strongly tempting us with this easy out – there are so many minimalist cues – *In the Bag* resists this interpretation. Too much of it would have to be ignored to carry off this hermeneutic ploy. We might call the exploitation of this sort of tension, in Taubin's film, categorical contrariness. Moreover, the employment of categorical contrariness as an emphatically stressed structural dimension in a film about identity has an obvious aesthetic aptness. For not only does the topic of stylistic identification seem an analogue to identity, but the film's resistance to complacent cataloguing can be seen as a parallel to the resistance to roles and labels that could motivate a quest for identity.

The primary symbolic structure that Taubin employs in her subversion of minimalism is the verbal image, i.e., the production of visual metaphors through literalization.[11] In charade-like fashion, Taubin presents the audience with a series of metaphors – such as "the search for self" – by composing the film from concrete actions – in this case, lookings-for – that are literally describable as "searches"; once the audience has the word "searches" in its possession, it can go on to mobilize the figurative, non-literal role the word plays in entrenched metaphors, such as "the search for self" or "searching for oneself." The reference of the film to the self as its subject is established by several factors: the bag itself – one remembers the Humean metaphors of the self as a bundle or a collection;[12] the mirrors – a popular avant-garde as well as a fashionable psychoanalytic symbol for the self; contextual factors – identity is one of the dominant themes in avant-garde film (and consequently, elliptical references to said theme should always be given special weight if there is no countervailing interpretation); Taubin's previous work. Thus, once the subject of the film is fixed as the self, the audience can use the invocation of the word "search" in its literal sense to infer the metaphor "search for self."[13] Furthermore, a similar process operates in regard to the other metaphors the film evolves for thinking about the self – turning over, turning inside out, breaking up, dissection, decomposition into parts, puzzling out, the journey, the inventory, clearing away, etc.

That *In the Bag* contains verbal images is not the source of its aesthetic merit. Verbal images are common cinematic devices, and, as such, they can appear in good films and in bad ones. What is artistically significant about *In the Bag* is not the fact that it contains verbal images but the way it organizes the verbal images it does contain. In the first place, Taubin taps into families of *related metaphors* with her verbal images, and she develops them in a way that is analogous to the method of literary conceits. For example, she starts with the general metaphor of the search as her trope for meditating about the self, and then she develops (or extends) her imagery in terms of related, "investigatory" sub-metaphors such as "turning things over" and "turning things inside out." The effect of this is to give the film a sense of coherence over time, a feeling of the appropriateness and the exfoliating thematic unity of the character's various gambits. That is, we do not have the reaction that *In the Bag* is monotonously repeating the search metaphor, but that it is, from gesture to gesture, expanding it coherently.

Secondly, Taubin also taps into related families of *distinct metaphors* – e.g., the search, the journey, the puzzle – and she combines them sequentially in a way that characterizes the notion of meditating in a variety of its aspects as we commonly conceive them. A more technical way of putting this point is to say that Taubin's verbal images explore the overlapping metaphorical systems that serve the complex cultural purpose of encapsulating our concept of a meditation.[14] One might analogize this to the trajectory of certain sonnets which develop, *ad seriatim*, separate literary conceits in successive stanzas.[15] Yet, these fit together coherently because, when read in context, the various mixings of metaphor have overlapping implications when referred to the subject at hand. *In the Bag* has a similar sort of aesthetic unity. The different families of metaphors that its verbal images evoke hang together as the film pursues its linear pathway because Taubin has drawn her images with an eye to remaining within the bounds of the intersection of the metaphorical systems we typically rely on to characterize the act of meditation. This enables Taubin to proffer a progression of images which, from the point of view of narrative motivation, would appear diverse and obscure, but which, because the system of verbal images reflects pre-existing, metaphorical systems, appears integrated, cognitively satisfying and emotionally right.

I have expounded the idea that *In the Bag* is a subversion of minimalism. Historically this places the film as part of a larger trend that has been gathering momentum since the mid-seventies: the revolt against Structural Film, especially in virtue of the reintroduction of content, and experimentation in the direction of narrative and metaphoric discourse. At the same time, *In the Bag* evinces strong personal, biographical traces. The various artworld minimalisms of the sixties and seventies provided Taubin with her artistic training ground and, therefore, with the source of her anxiety of influence. Consequently, it is hard not to interpret her subversion of minimalism as a revolt against her masters. In this respect, her film is autobiographical. It not only concerns the affirmation of her decision to become a filmmaker but it defines her relation to her predecessors as one of studied antithesis. Of course, by describing *In the Bag* as autobiographical, I am aligning it with yet another major framework of avant-garde American filmmaking.

Needless to say, I do not think that the fact that *In the Bag* elicits references to so many preoccupations of the avant-garde filmworld is accidental. Rather I think it is part and parcel of its aesthetic achievement; it is a hallmark of the elegance of its conception that *In the Bag* is able to segue comments on, contributions to, and acknowledgments of so many filmworld concerns – such as the Structural Film debate, minimalism, identity, the realist/montage debate, autobiographical film-making, and the theme of anxiety of influence – within its brief compass. That its modest design incorporates such complicated and multi-faceted resonances is a testament to Taubin's ingenuity.

One filmworld context that I have not mentioned in relation to *In the Bag* is feminism. Yet, this is perhaps the most important context for the film, as one might expect, since for many years Taubin has been one of New York's most outspoken feminist film critics. From this perspective, to call *In the Bag* only a revolt against minimalism is to tell merely half the story. For, insofar as *In the Bag* repudiates minimalism by reinstating content, that content – the concern with discovering one's identity as a woman filmmaker – is feminist content as conceived within the dialectics of the filmworld (where the topic of the female subject is the crux of extensive discussion). Moreover, as a symbolic gesture, the assertion of Taubin's artistic identity against her male, minimalist mentors makes *In the Bag* one woman's declaration of independence.

In the Bag is not a didactic feminist film in the tradition of *Amy!* or *Dora*. It does not elaborate an approach to the issue of woman's identity, but it is informed by current ciné-feminist theorizing, and it takes a stand – it regards the futility of finding an identity among the fragments of the ego as an occasion for decision. However, instead of didacticism, *In the Bag* symbolically portrays the experience of a woman becoming a filmmaker through expressive and metaphoric imagery that is essentially poetic. In this respect, *In the Bag* is an example of a growing tendency in feminist filmmaking – that includes works such as Su Frederich's *Cool Hands, Warm Heart*, and Leslie Thornton's *Jennifer, Where Are You?* and *Adynata*. These films all adopt the resources of metaphor, and what might be thought of as the imagery of psycho-drama and psycho-narra-tive to convey the experience of women in a society still, in the main, ruled by men.

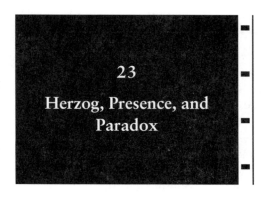

Herzog is a filmmaker of whom it is often said that he is difficult to categorize. For example, it is common to announce that he is unique among
New German Filmmakers. And, of course, the notion that Herzog is
unclassifiable contributes to the myth that he has created for himself of
the director identified with abnormal, extreme characters, who are at
times possessed, but are generally extraordinary social misfits, or better,
"nonfits." Herzog is the visionary Fitzcarraldo, for instance, doubling
his character's obsession, as the promotional material surrounding that
film made abundantly clear. If the characters that Herzog creates defy
classification, is it at all surprising that the director who claims he is his
films should equally desire to appear resistant to cataloguing?

And yet, Herzog is not alone when seen in the context of international cinema. He falls into a group of filmmakers devoted to what might be
called the primacy of experience. Stan Brakhage and Terrence Malick
would also be notable representatives here. These are filmmakers concerned to acknowledge or to disclose the often ignored richness that is
nevertheless believed to be always available to experience. These filmmakers share an advocacy of the immediacy of experience, that is, an
avowal of the possibility of experience – or, at least, of dimensions of
experience – independent from routine, social modes of schematization.
Indeed, all three regard normal practices of perceiving and of otherwise
organizing the world – such as, most dramatically, language – as filters
that exclude whole, existing dimensions of qualities and feelings from
our ken. Nor is this exclusion taken to be benign. Rather, all three hold
that these feeling-tones and qualities are irreducible parts of reality to be
recovered and celebrated in their work.

Herzog, Brakhage, and Malick espouse that there are qualities and perhaps even forces in the world and in us that are available for experience

"Herzog, Presence, and Paradox," *Persistence of Vision*, no. 2 (1985), pp. 30–40.

and that cannot be reduced to the categories of language or science or of psychology or bureaucracy. Their animus, of course, is directed at what might be called eliminative reductionism – that is, the kind of reductionism that denies the existence of whatever escapes its conceptual scheme or fails to be translatable into the basic terms of its framework. Herzog, Brakhage, and Malick are, in this sense, anti-eliminativists, which, in turn, commits them to foregrounding various nonreligious "ineffables," though of course, the ineffable in question differs from filmmaker to filmmaker. In short, for these filmmakers there are more things – experientially available things – than are represented by our languages, sciences, and bureaucracies, and no account of what is can be descriptively adequate unless it acknowledges this. Indeed, given the partisan stripe of their advocacy, their position often seems stronger than this, viz., that the properties, qualities, feeling-tones, and powers ignored and effectively repressed by routine schematization may have some claim to priority.

Whereas the philosophical commitments of these filmmakers can be captured by the title experiential anti-eliminativism, their aesthetic programs and affinities might be approximated by the use of the word "presence." In their films, sights and events are portrayed as "too much there," resistant to satisfying description or explanation in terms of narration, psychology, and sometimes even physics. "Presence," in this context, denotes a quality of an experience wherein the percipient encounters a phenomenon that – because it is not readily assimilable via language or the routines of instrumental reason – evokes a feeling of strangeness or alien-ness such that, rather than prompting the percipient to discount the phenomenon as an hallucination, instills a sense of the utter and inexplicable thereness of the object of attention. The object or event at issue looms before us with an irresistible and undeniable force – as, to take a famous example from Heidegger, a tool appears when it breaks down.

When I apply this notion of presence to film, I do not mean to say that the percipient believes the referent of the screen image is in the screening room. The viewer recognizes an image marked by presence to be a film image like any other. But as a film image, the represented object has an aura of inexplicability, i.e., it is hard to articulate the purposes, especially the narrative purposes, for which we are seeing the image at the particular given moment in the particular way and with the particular intensity with which it is being shown.

Two conditions, then, of this experience of presence are the sense of inexplicability and, secondly, that of immediacy – since the object is not referable to ingrained habits of seeing. Phenomenologically the phenomenon seems to "hop out of time," or, to adopt another metaphor, to subsist in an elongated present, disjunct from a continuous sense of its relation to the past or the future. The phenomenon may suggest, as well, an uncanny impression of uniqueness or singularity, which, of course, is bound up with its appearance of immediacy. Herzog, Brakhage, and Malick each consistently contrive, through different strategies, to produce imagery that provokes the feeling of presence as part of the rhetoric of anti-eliminativism, supplying, thereby, cinematic correlates for the putatively always available and honorifically mysterious riches of experience. Perhaps Brakhage's films most pervasively embrace this aesthetic of presence, while Malick's and Herzog's invoke it more intermittently. Yet presence as an emblem of the potential of experience in general – as opposed to a quality of only art or film – is a distinguishing trait of all three.

Undoubtedly, it may seem bizarre to group these three filmmakers together. Their films look so different and belong to such different cinematic traditions – the avant-garde film, the European Art Film, and the Hollywood Action Film. However, at the level of film viewing rather than of film analysis, all share one thing in common that I hope will convince you to suspend whatever skepticism you may have about my amalgamation of these three filmmakers into a single tendency. That common feature is their approach to landscape. Each of these filmmakers obsessively returns to arresting, even ravishing, awe-inspiring images of enormous natural vistas. In *Days of Heaven* (1978) and *Aguirre, der Zorn gottes/Aguirre, the Wrath of God* (1972), these dwarf the human action with their implacable, inert, "silent" presence. Or, in Brakhage's *Western History* (1971), an endless expanse of clouds stands monumentally stolid as the camera records the passenger plane barely inching across the sky. These landscapes are the sort that Kantians are wont to call sublime. They are associated with a sense of infinity. They may suggest either infinite expanse or eternity. They are often literally breathtaking. We are tempted to declare the effect of such landscapes or vistas to be inexpressible or indescribable. And it is for this very reason, I submit, that these three filmmakers revert to such images so often.

Admittedly, the idea of experience used above is a bit slippery. It cannot refer to experience *tout court* for that would encompass all those aspects of experience that are assimilable to schematization, especially by language. Rather, the relevant variety of experience – the "real," "really real," or genuine experience – for Brakhage, Malick, and Herzog is identified by its purported inaccessibility to language. Somewhat extravagantly and tendentiously, these filmmakers regard experience as the logical contrary of language. Authentic experience is that which is left over undescribed or unexplained after language has done its work. In Malick, the opposition between language and experience is worked out in the counterpoint between the voice-over narration and the action. The commentator's limited understanding, often highlighted through catastrophic understatement, is repeatedly emphasized. Perhaps Malick got the idea of the disjunction of the "facts" from the commentary on the justly famous juxtaposition of the psychiatrist and Norman Bates at the end of *Psycho* (1960). Malick has turned that originally sequentially ordered device into a trope of simultaneous juxtaposition which repeatedly underscores the theme that language, as represented by the voice-over commentary, is inadequate to the task of explaining or of even portraying the events and passions presented in *Badlands* (1973) and *Days of Heaven.*

Of course, it is not just language, literally construed, that these filmmakers distrust, but everything that language – conceived of as a socially inculcated filter of experience – can, in a rather broad sense, be made to stand for. And that can be quite a lot. Here is how Brakhage opens his *Metaphors on Vision.*

Imagine an eye unruled by man-made laws of perspective, an eye unprejudiced by compositional logic, an eye which does not respond to the name of everything but which must know each object encountered in life through an adventure in perception. How many colors are there in a field of grass to the crawling baby unaware of "Green"? How many rainbows can light create for the untutored eye? How aware of variations in heat waves can that eye be? . . . Imagine a world before the "beginning of the word."[1]

For Brakhage, in a paroxysm of the Whorf hypothesis, language determines what we routinely see. Perspective and education come to be linked under the rubric of language. Language is made to stand as the negative, repressive side of acculturation. Brakhage's mission then becomes the invention of a vocabulary or iconography of forms – ranging from painting on, scratching, and punching the film stock to the use of multiple layers of superimposition, and out of focus shots – to approximate and, thereby, to recover aspects of visual experience putatively repressed by culture, such as myopia, hypnogogic vision, and the phosphenes of closed-eye vision. We are supposed to grasp these figures in a gasp of prelinguistic recognition, portending presence. In addition, Brakhage's films, in general, are not sequentially structured in a way that affords anticipation. This too is meant to result in an experience of presence – the films suggesting some sort of immediate access to the continuum that supposedly evades the vectorial category of time.

In Herzog as well, the enemy comprises the various forces of culture that can be seen as functioning to suppress authentic experience. These include, first and foremost, language, which, in turn, is associated with practical and instrumental reason, with science and bureaucracy, with religion and civil society. In what follows I will attempt to sketch some of what I believe are Herzog's major strategies in light of his commitments to the acknowledgment of authentic experience and presence. I will conclude then with some comments on what I take to be a paradox in his program which has led to certain problems in his recent work.

The easiest place to begin is to outline Herzog's attitude toward language. Though he clearly disdains the practical use of language, especially insofar as it facilitates regimes of instrumental reason, there is nevertheless a use of language that intrigues him. He has referred to this by speaking of word combinations that are wrong but which convey a very definite feeling, indeed a particularly arresting feeling. For example, at the conclusion of *Of Walking in Ice* – a title which itself suggests both a semantic short-circuit and a physical impossibility – Herzog addresses Lotte Eisner by saying "Together... we shall boil fire and stop fish."[2] Herzog cherishes the phrase because in its semantic oddity it discloses or conveys the intuition of an otherwise inexpressible, i.e., unnameable, quality. Herzog reveals his affection for visionary word salads, as well, in his discussions of the hypnotic experiments that occasioned the making of *Herz aus Glas/Heart of Glass* (1976). He told his hypnotized actors that they were about to see a poem inscribed in an emerald by a great writer. Each actor was made to believe that he or she was the first person to lay eyes on this inscription. Each trance-subject was instructed to read the nonexistent poem when Herzog touched his shoulder. Of one experiment, Herzog remarks:

And so I put my hand on the shoulder of a man who was at least fifty-five years and who was working in a horse-stable – a stable cleaner without any formal education – and this man started to "read" a poem that was really very beautiful. With a very strange voice, he started to recite, and here is what he said: "Why can't we drink the moon? Why is there no vessel to hold it?" and it went on and on like this, and it was very, very beautiful.[3]

In short, the semantical mistake here results in the disclosure of a feeling that is unnameable or unparaphrasable in other terms. That Herzog is fascinated by the effects achieved in what might be thought of as the abuse of ordinary language – i.e., language employed in accordance with standard communicative norms – is evident in his *How Much Wood Would a Woodchuck Chuck* (1976). The auctioneers in that film employ a language that is virtually indecipherable to the uninitiated. Their performance is something that Herzog views as a kind of chant, expressively revelatory of the spirit of capitalism. Even though this language is ostensibly functional, it is extreme in a way that foregrounds or depicts a spirit or feeling. It is not the overt message of this discourse that interests Herzog but its tone which manifests an otherwise unnoticeable quality.

Of course, *Jeder für sich und Gott gegen alle/The Mystery of Kaspar Hauser* or *Every Man for Himself and God Against All* (1974) is the Herzog film that most deeply explores the oppositions between language and experience, between the communicative and the expressive uses and misuses of language and the relations of these oppositions to social power and freedom. The theme of the film is unmistakable – language is death; the man who gives Kaspar Hauser language finally takes his life. Kaspar's inculcation in language and his concomitant integration into society correlates with his progressive immiseration. His acquisition of language is described as a fall. Like Handke in *Kaspar* and in stark contrast to the Taviani brothers in *Padre Padrone* (1977), Herzog, in *Kaspar Hauser*, regards language learning as regimentation rather than humanization.

Throughout the film, we are clearly urged to regard Kaspar's resistance to language as heroic. His semantic dislocations and his refusal or inability to grasp fundamental categorical oppositions – such as animate versus inanimate – are framed as victories of the human spirit. This is perhaps most vividly evinced in the scenes concerning Lord Stanhope, Kaspar's prospective patron. Stanhope uses language to assert his power; his conversation is slightly veiled, artificial speechifying. When Stanhope presumes to explain Kaspar elegantly, however, Kaspar blurts out "Your Honor, there is nothing more that lives in me but my life." The idea that a life lives inside one – rather than that one simply lives – sounds like a linguistic confusion and a metaphysical howler. However, it expressively conveys the tenacity and intensity of Kaspar's subjectivity – the strength of what we might call his "inner life," in triumphant contradistinction to the facade Stanhope creates by his purportedly exquisite manipulation of language.

Kaspar's apparent refusals to grasp some of the deep categorical distinctions that subtend language-use not only provide moments of hilarity but are endorsed as wisdom by the film through the reliance on the traditional theme of the naif dumbfounding the doctors by his unprejudiced clarity. Kaspar doesn't abandon the idea that apples are sentient agents when his teachers' crucial experiment goes awry. Similarly, Kaspar rejects the logic of inside and outside in the discussion of the relation of his prison cell to the tower, and he never seems fully convinced of the distinction between reality and dreams. For example, he says that he did not dream during his captivity, but this strongly suggests, to me at least, not an earlier lack of dreaming but a failure to demarcate dreams and reality in the stream of experience. Kaspar's confrontations with clergymen and the logician are cast in terms of power relations, and Kaspar's obdurate rejections of the niceties of their technical jargons register as resistance to domination. Throughout Herzog's work, figures of public authority are portrayed as agents of specialized languages – languages often of instrumental knowledge and, therefore, languages connected with the exercise of power. Moreover, Herzog takes special pleasure in depicting these jargons and their attendant modes of reasoning as absurd. The doctor in *Woyzeck* (1978) with his utterly fantastical murmurings on scientific method is a prime example of this, as is the figure of Van Helsing in *Nosferatu* (1978), who, in advance of logical positivism, argues vociferously that vampires are just unscientific.

The inability of representatives of specialized knowledge to transcend their conceptual framework is a recurrent cause for black comedy in Herzog. In *Aguirre*, the priest Carvajal shows an Amazonian Indian a Bible, explaining that the word of God is within. Perplexed, the Indian puts the mysterious object to his ear and hearing no words throws the book to the deck in a mixture of disgust and terror. Carvajal regards this understandable confusion as blasphemy and dispatches the Indian straightaway, apparently himself confusing murder with conversion. Similarly, an alderman at the end of *Nosferatu* impotently calls for Van Helsing's arrest even though all the judges, lawyers, policemen, and gaolers are dead. Herzog's view of organized society is that it is a form of self-perpetuating madness – a vision signaled by his recurrent image of the circle as a symbol for society, e.g., the trucks in *Auch Zwerge haben klein angefangen / Even Dwarfs Started Small* (1970) and *Stroszek* (1977), and the final circular helicopter shot around Aguirre's "empire." This negative view of society is constantly reaffirmed in Herzog's films by proposing dramatic situations in which the application of specialized language and associated modes of instrumental thinking completely miss the mark – such as Emperor Fernando de Guzman's ridiculously formalistic and legal, yet absolutely idle, expropriations of the "real estate" of his kingdom as the raft drifts down the river in *Aguirre*.

Land des Schweigens und der Dunkelheit / Land of Silence and Darkness (1971) is a film in which the relation between language and experience is not primarily situated in the arena of social criticism – unless the peripheral question of society's insensitivity to the handicapped is taken to be the resounding social point of the film. Yet, *Land of Silence and Darkness* is the Herzog film that most compellingly raises the issue of language and experience. It is a documentary about people who are both deaf and blind. The principal character is Fini Staubinger, a woman who is deaf and blind and who works toward forging a community between herself and others like her.

Language and the acquisition of language are the major elements in the creation of this community. Herzog pays close attention to the intricacies and enormous patience required to teach language to the deaf-blind as well as for the deaf-blind to learn language. One cannot leave the film without an overwhelming sense of admiration for the ingenuity, effort, and will power expended by and for the deaf-blind in their acquisition of language. Nor would one dare to disparage facilely the use of language as a central cohesive force in the community of the deaf-blind. And yet one who is sighted and can hear also feels an irrepressible sense of alienation from the language of the deaf-blind. For though we share what is a common language with the deaf-blind – one that runs relatively smoothly in terms of our mutual reference and ordinary practical concerns – we cannot but ask ourselves about the radically different associations the deaf-blind must correlate to the words we share with them. Indeed, the fact that we share a common language – one produced in a culture whose reliance on seeing and hearing is far more intensive than its reliance on other sense modalities – brings to the fore a recognition of the necessary disparity and otherness that must be phenomenologically the experience of the deaf-blind. Nor can we capture that experience by closing our eyes and stopping our ears, for we then would only be sighted and hearing people momentarily without sights and sounds.

Throughout *Land of Silence and Darkness*, Herzog chooses compositions that make the disparity of point-of-view (!) between the audience and the deaf-blind characters a disparity that is tangibly felt. For example, he frames an image of the bedroom of the insane asylum in such a way that while Fini and Else Fehrer sit in the foreground, a depressive sits on the cot behind them, obsessively touching herself and changing her pose for the camera. We realize that the two deaf-blind women will never be aware of this micro-drama, while also the full force of what it is to pose for a camera is outside their experience. When we watch Vladimir Kokel, a sort of forerunner of Herzog's Kaspar Hauser, play with his ball, it is hard not to ask what in the world he can possibly think is going on when it bounces back and beans him on the head. Similarly, when we watch the deaf-blind introduced to new sensations during the visits to the botanical gardens, to the zoo, and the plane flight, we can only wonder what thoughts and feelings these outings can kindle in them. When the film ends and the deaf-blind man hugs the tree trunk – for what seems several minutes – we sighted viewers have the sense that we could never recognize the subjective significance that that gesture holds for that man. For that is, one surmises, literally inexpressible.

Land of Silence and Darkness repeatedly invites us to contemplate the indescribability and inexpressibility of the experience of the deaf-blind. For though language functions well enough – both referentially and socially – throughout the film, the alien context in which it is used makes us strongly aware of the presence of a realm of experience effectively beyond the reach of language. That is, language remains serviceable between us and the deaf-blind, but when it comes to the thoughts and feelings, or better, the associations attending such discourse, we sense a radical problem of translation.

In several ways, *Land of Silence and Darkness* is the emblematic Herzog film. For in underscoring the inaccessibility of the feelings and experiences of the deaf-blind, the film presents these figures as paradigmatic Herzog heroes. Whether Woyzeck or Stroszek, Aguirre, Fitzcarraldo, Nosferatu, or Kaspar Hauser, these characters are moved by inner forces that for Herzog remain inexplicable, unnameable, and indescribable. The inscrutability of the springs that move them erects a certain affective distance – a kind of obdurate clarity – between us and them. Such figures are virtually canonized by Herzog for the uniqueness and the inaccessibility of their passions and their inner life. At the same time, *Land of Silence and Darkness* counterposes a feeling of the tenuousness of language when weighted against the awesome, inarticulate experience of the deaf-blind.

Filmmakers committed to the celebration of the primacy of experience suspect language insofar as it is identified as an unacknowledged filter of experience. In this, language is simply one – though certainly the most prominent – form of schematization. There are others, such as the relation of cause and effect, which, of course, has obvious importance for instrumental reason. In a number of his most striking images, Herzog seems preoccupied with challenging the pride of place accorded to causal relations in our experience of the world. In this he does not strive to deny causality, but rather to displace it from the center of our way of seeing the events in his films. That is, without questioning the existence of causality, Herzog attempts to make us see events in such a way that our causal conception of them recedes. We see instead from a noncausally directed point-of-view, which, in turn, raises a strong feeling of presence in us.

In general, Herzog achieves this by presenting us with events which are causally comprehensible within the narrative but which at the same time so incongruously combine elements that we view the events as images – luminously strange images – rather than as effects. In *Dwarfs* pots burn while the truck circles and the dwarfs throw dishes and type-writers at it. The narrative explains how each of these elements has come into play, but the image is more than the sum of the causal effects and actions that gave rise to it. The image is also more than a microcosmic vision of the frenzy and destructiveness of the human condition. It is unflinchingly strange, surreal, and abnormal. So, also, is a similar scene at the end of *Stroszek*.

Throughout *Aguirre* the power of the oxymoronic is unavoidable. We are constantly brought up short by the incongruity of Renaissance culture transplanted to the Amazon. Cannons, armor, and courtly gowns never seem to fit in the environment. And though the narrative fully explains the juxtaposition, one's thoughts often shift away from the place of a given image in the narrative to remark upon and savor how insanely strange these images are. It is not that we question Herzog's historical accuracy. But instead we are dumbfounded rather than skeptical that all these ill-matched elements could go together. I remember especially the image of the virtually medieval European warhorse, thrown from the raft, standing knee deep on the bank of the rainforest. Or the sedan chairs being hoisted through the bush. The monkeys scrambling over the cannon, of course, is a famous example of this, one repeated with mice in *Nosferatu*. And the ship in the tree is also relevant here since, though the dialogue suggests that it may be a hallucination, we see it in a shot from behind Aguirre, from no one's point-of-view, in a way that invites us to regard it, imponderably enough, as a European ship unaccountably aloft in a jungle tree.

Images like this, whose full account in terms of our experience appear to exceed a causal account – that tempt us to speak of *mere* causal accounts – are frequent in Herzog: the attire and defense system of the blind twins in *Dwarfs*, for example, and the images from *Nosferatu* of scores of identically dressed pallbearers carrying identically designed coffins. Or, there is the scene of Fini at the swimming lesson in *Land of Silence and Darkness*. On the one hand, it recalls an ordinary enough, mundane event: an elder – a mother, a grandmother, or an aunt – watching a child being taught to swim. But when we realize that neither the child nor Fini can see or hear each other, this folksy tableau becomes unalterably strange and disconcerting. For sighted and hearing people, the whole purpose for going to a child's swimming lesson has fallen away because, as far as we know, neither Fini nor the child can be directly aware of each other's presence in any way we are familiar with. The event, though narratively motivated, drops out of the web of sense for us, i.e., out of the realm of our habitual expectations concerning action, motive, and purpose. The image, thereby, arrests us through its incongruity.

One of the most striking examples of the kind of image that I have in mind occurs in *Fitzcarraldo* – viz., the scene where the boat is pulled over the mountain. There is no question of denying the existence of causality here, but nevertheless, attention to the mechanics of the scene at a certain point gives way to the appreciation of the scene's incongruity. The central camera position is a long shot taken in a way that the boat, obliquely angled, gives the impression, impossibly, of powering itself up the mountain side as it would through a body of water. A ridge blocks our view of the bottom of the boat, enabling us to see the boat as if it were chugging up the side of the hill. Then Fitzcarraldo stops the proceedings in order to play a record. The boat no longer seems merely steaming up the mountain, but it appears to be propelled by Caruso's voice. We know about the way that this feat has been causally executed but this is less important than looking at the image from a perspective outside normal causal thinking. It strikes one as delirious but not as hallucinatory. It invites us to appreciate the strangeness of human enterprises, if we open ourselves experientially to seeing that strangeness through suspending our routine modes of practical cognition. Such images throughout Herzog's work engender a sense of presence for the concomitant purpose of encouraging us to experience the world and especially human affairs afresh and as estranged, perhaps with the eyes of an anthropologist from another galaxy. One continually has the feeling that Herzog believes human life is inherently bizarre, though with what such bizarreness is meant to contrast remains unstated.

If Herzog offsets our habitual routines of causal apprehension by means of the compellingly incongruous image, he also has various strategies for displacing our standard relation to space in film. This displacement, as well, promotes a sense of presence. That is, Herzog often mobilizes certain compositional strategies that reaffirm his preoccupation with presence and experience. The images produced via these strategies are intermittent – not every shot in every film is an example of the strategies in question. Rather, the images I have in mind appear at certain moments, and once they have had their effect, Herzog returns to a more customary mode of composition. Landscapes and cityscapes are often the subjects of these images.

One compositional technique Herzog uses to evoke presence is to hold a long shot of a landscape or a cityscape for a duration that is greater than that required to recognize what the image represents. Here I have in mind shots such as that of the townscape in *Woyzeck*. The composition has no center of interest, so our eye begins to roam around inside the image. We quickly grasp the narrative significance of the shot, so all that is left for us to do is to look in a digenically disinterested way that compels us to greet that which is represented as a visual fact apart from the horizon of narrative meaning. Our conscious experience of looking becomes more intense than it is in most narrative films. Such images appear throughout Herzog's work and also in Malick's *Days of Heaven*.

I have already mentioned Herzog's penchant for shots describable in terms of the sublime. In this regard not only does he present vistas that suggest infinite expanse, eternity, and the giganticism of nature – e.g., the low horizon line of the vistas on the river in *Aguirre* – but he also returns again and again to icons of the sublime such as mists and clouds. One thinks of the clouds and cascades of the Borgo Pass scene in Nosferatu or the blue-tinted dream of the mountain in *Kaspar Hauser*. Material objects seem to blend into the atmosphere. Herzog uses the rhetoric – clouds and mists – of a religious view of nature not to render the landscape spiritual but to promote a related oceanic but secular feeling. That is, by emphasizing clouds and mists he foregrounds the lighting and opticality of scenes rather than their object-properties. The secondary qualities of scenes, rather than their primary qualities, are stressed, underscoring a "subjective" dimension rather than the "objective" dimension of the image. Whereas this kind of imagery in the work of

Caspar David Friedrich implies that the vista is spiritually charged, in Herzog's hands this symbolism suggests that the image is subjectively charged, thereby proposing a correlative to the prized experiential fusion of subject and object.

Though the preceding interpretation originated with a discussion of the effect of Herzog's affection for clouds and mists, its conclusions bear on much of Herzog's treatment of landscape. Through the use of the decentered image, through the use of clouds and ghostly colors, the optical qualities rather than tactile qualities of the image shine forth and objects as such – objects as material, individuated things – are demoted in terms of their relative importance. Landscapes and cityscapes lose some of their substantiality, appearing dreamlike, ethereal, and somewhat immaterial. A good example here can be found in the opening shots of Aguirre where the mist, the softly plummeting camera, the choir-like soundtrack, the initial lack of scale-correlatives, and the absence of natural noise render the massive mountain almost weightless, giving us a feeling that the mountain is nearly floating. One has the conscious feeling of being presented with something almost purely visual, which in our culture has the association of being subjective.

This emphasis on the optical is also apparent in Herzog's use of color. Color, of course, is not only something associated with subjective secondary qualities but is also a favored and frequent example of phenomena richer than language can accommodate. Color often serves as Herzog's emblem of the world swathed in mysteries available only to intense subjectivities. Herzog makes his attitude toward light and color explicit in *Heart of Glass*, where the plot hinges on the futile efforts to reproduce a certain shade of red crystal. Herzog makes light and color symbolize the immaterial and the experiential, the inexpressible and the unnameable as well as making color project his sense of wonderment. Moreover, the audience can at times be drawn into a corresponding sense of rapture over the mystifying effects of color as when in *Nosferatu* reds are gradually introduced into the image as the film nears the domain of the Count. We experience a dramatic and palpable change in the image as it gains redness, but we are initially unable to identify this as the cause of our feelings. Instead, the image exercises a sensuous power over our experience which, because we cannot pinpoint its source, imbues the imagery with a commanding, unstatable insistence.

In the main, Herzog's manipulation of the temporal dimension of his narratives is not as distinctive as several of his visual strategies. The theme of experience, that is, is not as evident in his temporal organization. It is true that the temporal links between his scenes are often loose; one could not construct a very precise chronology between many of the events in his films. Often, as in *Kaspar Hauser*, events seem to be included as repeated illustrations of the basic ideas behind the film, so many variations on a theme that could have been ordered differently. Perhaps this looseness is meant to suggest some slackening of temporal schematization, but most often the effect is faint since we do tend to presume that the stories are vaguely chronological. However, a striking exception here is Herzog's book, *Of Walking in Ice*, a memoir of his pilgrimage from Munich to Paris. Though the walk was undertaken to save a languishing Lotte Eisner, the diary rarely adverts to getting closer to the goal of the trip. As a result, all sense of anticipation and suspense is oddly absent. The primary temporal connective in the book is "and then." Furthermore, Herzog mixes straightforward descriptions with unmarked memories, dreams, plans, and incidental surrealist reports – e.g., brief mention is made of a public official beheaded in a helicopter accident in the middle of an account of a restaurant. Reverie and matter-of-fact description are indiscriminately run together at a steady temporal pulse. Images pass by without comment, yielding a strong sense of a stream of undifferentiated consciousness. Things seem to float in and out of experience.

The Herzog film, it seems to me, that most closely approximates this effect is *Aguirre*, in which sights, fantastical and oneiric, appear to drift past the raft as the raft drifts past the shore. The world appears to be flowing past the raft even though in fact it is the raft that is floating. In this sense, the point-of-view from the raft serves as a metaphor for consciousness, as sights and visions pass "through" or by it. The river comes to symbolize the "streaming quality" of experience which addresses the audience in terms of a temporal sense of drifting, freed from purpose and expectation. In this way, Herzog seems to attempt to dramatize the conditions of an "ungrasping" state of consciousness, ironically enough, in the context of a story about a rapacious, all-too-grasping conquistador.

Earlier I said there is a paradox in Herzog's program. It is this. On the one hand, Herzog, and other celebrants of experience, seek to acknowledge the unexpressed or ineffable aspects of experience that have been filtered out and suppressed by routine forms of schematization, such as language. For them, there are more things in heaven and earth than are canvassed by our dictionaries. Most of us, I think, would assent to this. However, what the celebrants overlook is that by pointing to unacknowledged properties and feelings, they not only make them salient for others to experience, but they also make them available to language. Indeed, these filmmakers may bequeath their own names to the very qualities they disclose.

That is, part of the cognitive function of art is undoubtedly to make us aware of features of the world and of experience. Often artists discover properties or qualities or feelings that were previously ignored. But when they do this, their artworks come to function as the symbol of these newly recognized qualities, and often the artist's own name is used to label the phenomenon, e.g., Turner light, Rembrandt light, Rubensesque flesh, Langian paranoia, Hawksian professionalism. Thus, in successfully depicting a quality of either experience or the world, the artist provides us with a new symbol that refers to the property, and, sometimes, the artist's own name becomes part of the name of the property. So when I walk down Spring Street in New York's Soho district and I see a seedy man behind the wheel of a Rolls Royce, dressed and bearded like a buccaneer, listening to Bach while reading Stephen King's *Christine* and munching on a quiche, I can say to my companion "how like a Herzog film" or, better yet, "how Herzogesque." In short, paradoxically, the more successful in clarifying unexpressed and unacknowledged aspects of experience an artist like Herzog is, the more likely that his prized ineffables are to become part of a cultural schematization. The filmmakers' artworks become manipulable symbols, names, and labels, within a culture's language game, broadly construed. A cognitive function of art is to provide symbols and expressions for what was hitherto unknown and unexpressed. Thus, in vouching for something ineffable – in pointing it out and symbolizing it distinctly – Herzog makes those dimensions and properties of experience that he champions more and more effable.

In practice, this is perhaps not a very vexing paradox. It may be easy to live with as long as the symbols that refer to these once ineffable properties and feelings do not lose their aura of originality, like so many dead metaphors. If properties cannot remain ineffable once they are symbolized, the symbols can at least preserve some of the original sense of the discovery of the property by remaining fresh themselves. But here is where the paradox becomes a real problem. In recent works like *Fitzcarraldo*, Herzog's approach is becoming predictable, a repetition of mannerisms from earlier films – e.g., South American exoticism, an impossible vision, the worship of the ineffable power of music, a physically dangerous feat, Kinski, etc. The extraordinary is reduced to the formulaic; the mysterious becomes routinized; the ineffable hackneyed. I feel a similar plight overtook Brakhage's representations of forgotten aspects of perception. Through repetition, these initially unsettling symbols become code-like. Undoubtedly, any artist runs the risk of repeating him or herself. But for celebrants of the ineffable, the stakes are higher. For when their practice becomes predictable, the unfamiliar becomes all too familiar and their project self-defeating.[4]

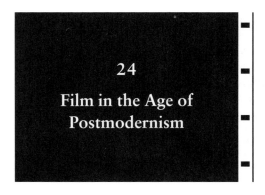

24

Film in the Age of
Postmodernism

The recent history of the avant-garde film in America mirrors the general pattern of cultural experience over the last two decades. The sense of a unified oppositional movement concerned with the war in Vietnam, student protest, and opposition to racial and sexual domination gives way to a sense of the collapse of that unified energy into a range of heterogeneous projects. If in 1971, one could feel part of the cutting edge of history, that feeling is no longer available. Where in the early seventies the future seemed promising, few today have much confidence about where we are headed.

Avant-garde film of the early seventies appeared to propose, at least to many of its most vocal adherents, a privileged relation to history. It witnessed the ascendency of structural film, which asserted a decisive break not only with commercial entertainment film, but also with the previously dominant tradition of the avant-garde, which was highly expressionist in its practices and theory. At the same time structural film proposed a revolutionary break with several cinematic pasts, it also seemed to afford filmmakers with something like a paradigm for working out a project that could be expatiated endlessly into the future. In the early seventies, there was momentary euphoric agreement about the task of film and about the shape that the future of film should take. A language of criticism, quasi-theory, and appreciation took hold that invited everyone to board the train of film history and to ride into a bountiful future.

Uudoubtedly the sense that structural film provided a unified project was illusory – both historically and theoretically. However, and more importantly, even the illusion of unity was short-lived. By the middle and late seventies, numerous reactions arose against the structural ethos. These took the form of the reintroduction of various of the concerns

"Film," in *The Postmodern Moment*, ed. S. Trachtenberg (Westport, CT : Greenwood Press, 1985), pp. 100–133.

missing from the formalistically austere structural film – narrative, personal obsession, expression, reference, politics – in short, what we might loosely call "content." Yet the forms of reaction to the structural film were multiple and various. Structural film was not superseded by a single movement – that is, a program like surrealism – but by a set of alternative movements, genres, and sensibilities, including the deconstructionist film, the New Talkie, punk film, psychodramas, and, lastly, a return to imagery that is expressive, aesthetic, elusive, and enigmatic, a kind of "new symbolism." These reactions to structural film are often quite different from each other. Nevertheless, they each bear testimony to the extreme hold that structural film exerted upon the imagination of the early seventies, insofar as each gains much of its energy from the repudiation of the structural film mystique. At the same time, these alternate movements form a rough grouping inasmuch as they are all vexed by the ostensible (rather than actual) repression of content, broadly construed, in structural film. Needless to say, each of these movements differs in the content that it wishes to restore to film. However, they do represent a loose family of movements, sensibilities, and genres that we may think of as antistructural or as poststructural.

There are several reasons I have written "poststructural" rather than "postmodern." The term "postmodern" is unsettling. It can apply to Nietzsche if we are speaking of philosophy, Venturi if the subject is architecture, Creeley if our focus is poetry, Longo and Goldstein in painting, Rainer and Paxton in dance. But what has Rainer to do with Nietzsche, or Venturi to do with Creeley? And if this could be answered by a single formula, how would that formula work for the variety of avant-garde films of the late seventies and eighties?

These rhetorical questions should signal hesitation about belief in some broad movement called "postmodernism" that manifests itself uniformly in philosophy and various artistic practices in different centuries and countries (Nietzsche and Venturi), and in different generations (Creeley and Longo). On the positive side, however, the label "postmodern" should not be ignored as a means of marking a stylistic or theoretical break within a specific ongoing discourse or art form. There is something that the term "postmodern architecture" refers to that is rather specific, just as there is something "postmodern dance" refers to. Indeed, these labels were used within certain communities of artistic practice – by actual practitioners (working artists, critics, programmers, curators, patrons, etc.) – to denominate specific historical changes of emphasis and program. "Postmodern architecture" names a style opposed to the ideal of the modern found in someone like Le Corbusier, while "postmodern dance" was antimodern dance as the latter was exemplified in the projects of Graham, Humphrey, and Limón, among others. When the scope of postmodern is appropriately limited to a particular arena of practice and to a particular time frame, and where the term is used by practitioners to highlight their differences and conflicts with their predecessors, the term "postmodern" can be found to have concrete reference and can be given a perfectly operational meaning.

However, the above considerations are exactly what gives rise to a second reservation about applying the term "postmodern" to film or, even more specifically, to avant-garde film.[1] Namely, the term "postmodern" is not indigenous to film practice. The middle seventies did not witness the emergence of self-proclaimed postmodernist filmmakers nor was that label often applied by film critics. Instead, movements like punk film arose. Consequently, insofar as we speak of postmodern film, we will only, in general, be talking about film activity that is somehow analogous to activity in other arts which, in that other-art context, is already called postmodern.

In light of the preceding, antistructural film is our likeliest nominee for the title postmodern film. For the past two decades – because of the nature of the venues for avant-garde film (often museums) and because of the tendency for avant-garde filmmakers to be trained in art schools (as well as to teach in such schools) – film and fine art have been a major locus of interaction. Now, in fine art, we have witnessed the transition from modernist essentialism, whose apotheosis was minimalism, to a reaction formation called postmodernism, which reintroduced cultural content. The result was a form of politicized pop art. Similarly, in avant-garde film, the structural moment can be regarded as the celluloid correlate to painterly and sculptural minimalism. This, in turn, implies a certain loose appropriateness to employing the term "postmodernism" to the various antistructural efforts – that is, if we wish to apply it to anything at all.[2]

I prefer to speak of antistructural rather than postmodern film. For though postmodern film makes some sense homologously, it is not even as precise as the admittedly imprecise notion of antistructural film. Thus, a compromise is to write of avant-garde film in the age of postmodernism, that is, the seventies and eighties, when, in a quest for the identity of our epoch, we have become obsessed with the idea of the postmodern.

I will begin by proposing a characterization of the structural film and then proceed to chart and to describe, in some detail, major reactions to structural film, notably: deconstructionism, the New Talkie, punk film, the new psychodrama, and the new symbolism.[3] These tendencies are not mutually exclusive, nor do they provide a systematic set of categories, and, lastly, they neither comprehend nor exhaust the full range of contemporary avant-garde film activity.[4] After all, we are not dealing with a closed canon, like ancient Greek tragedies, and these shortcomings must be accepted by anyone who pretends to offer a historical framework for understanding the present. Also, some of these categories may at times appear overly stretched by the amount of material packed into them. Nevertheless, at present these categories provide an initially useful, albeit primitive, survey of avant-garde film.

One final caveat: By describing the field in terms of movements and genres, there is the danger of obscuring what is perhaps the most significant feature of avant-garde film in the late seventies and the eighties, namely, that the most vital and productive source of contemporary avant-garde film derives from feminism. This phenomenon transcends genre and movement classification. In each of the genres and movements discussed, women filmmakers – most often self-professed feminists – are among the leading figures. So the careful reader should take special note of the incidence of feminist activity in each of the categories. And in several categories, such as the New Talkie and the psychodrama, feminism is the dominant force. Feminism cuts across the categories of contemporary film in a way that demands special attention. Moreover, there are many seminal women filmmakers whose pioneering work does not fit neatly into the fledging taxonomy presented here.[5]

Structural Film

In 1969, P. Adams Sitney, the foremost chronicler of the American avant-garde (until the mid-seventies), declared, "suddenly a cinema of structure has emerged."[6] By this dramatic pronouncement, Sitney meant to call attention to a major shift with the development of the American Avant-garde. From the birth of this enterprise, in the forties, through the accomplishments of Maya Deren, to the middle sixties with the work of Gregory Markopoulos, James Broughton, Harry Smith, Kenneth Anger, Sidney Peterson, and Stan Brakhage, the American avant-garde was highly expressionist, concerned with myth, dream, trance, heightened states of consciousness, and the mysteries of personality, sexuality, and metaphysics. Sitney himself referred to this dimension of the American avant-garde as "mythopoetic."[7] However, in the late sixties and early

seventies a new group of filmmakers appeared, including, according to
Sitney, Michael Snow, George Landow (aka Owen Land), Hollis
Frampton, Paul Sharits, Tony Conrad, and Ernie Gehr. These filmmakers shared many affinities with the minimalism then emerging in fine art.
And, like the minimalists in their reaction to the psychodramatic and
mythic pretensions of abstract expressionism, these new filmmakers
adopted strategies to depersonalize, distance, and "cool-out" their
medium. Thus they came to adopt generative strategies that removed a
great deal of moment-to-moment decision making, and, therefore,
expressivity from their work.

These strategies came to be lumped under the label "structural." In
general, two major structuring approaches were most popular. The
first was to give the work a discernible, geometric shape in time. For
example, Anthony McCall's *Line Describing a Cone* (1973) begins as a
laserlike beam of light and, over thirty minutes, widens into a cone
whose apex is at the projector lens. Similarly, Michael Snow's ↔ (1969)
involves repetitive lateral and then vertical camera movements. The
shapes inscribed by this plan, rather than the imagery of the locale photographed, is the locus of attention. The emphasis upon highly legible,
geometrical shape in these films recalls the hard-edge, linear iconography of painters like Frank Stella, though, of course, with this difference:
the filmmaker's shapes evolved over time.

The second major family of strategies adopted by structural filmmakers might be called the systemic approach. Like Noland's paintings and
LeWitt's sculptures, films were built on generative plans, upon repetition, repetition and variation, and quasi-recursive procedures. A major
part of the point of such films was that the audience was supposed to
grasp the underlying system that generated the imagery and, more
importantly, its order. Undoubtedly artists of this period were deeply
impressed by the general cultural interests in such things as generative
and transformational grammar, the rise of the computer, and the pervasive talk of systems analysis. And they certainly found an iconography
with which to project these preoccupations.

A strong example of the systemic approach to structural film is Hollis
Frampton's *nostalgia* (1971). The film involves a parade of individual
photographs, each set on a slow burning hot plate. Each shot lasts until
each respective photograph turns to ash. On the sound track we hear a
description of the photo we are about to see in the next shot while we
watch the photo we previously heard described incinerate. The effect of
this sequence of description and image is to call our attention to the

difference between verbal language and pictures. None of the descriptions ever fully prepares us for the picture we later see. In this contrast, we encounter a major concern of structural filmmaking: reflexivity. Like gallery formalists, the structural filmmaker embraces the task of revealing the nature of his medium through the use of the medium itself. *Nostalgia* shows us the appropriately ineffable distinction between word and image – that is, the photographic image – as two contrasting forms of representation. At the same time, the topic of reflexivity is not restricted by the structuralist filmmaker to reflection on the medium but is also concerned to reveal the nature of our cognitive and perceptual responses to the medium. In *nostalgia*, we remark upon the way in which language primes us to look at the photos, as well as the way in which it sets up false expectations. Our visual versus our verbal capacities are set out for examination as we struggle to correlate the photo we presently view with the description we just heard. Such structural films often took on the aura of amateur, self-administered, psychological tests, providing the spectator with the opportunity to reflect apperceptively on his or her own cognitive style as well as on the forms of cognition and on memory, imagination, and expectation-formation. Of course, it is the austere restriction of interest to simple, repetitive structures that impels the spectator to such an apperceptive stance, for there is little to attend to save the process of attending.[8] Furthermore, in its concern with cognition and perception, the structural film reflects the obsession of the sixties with perception, an interest evinced as well by the drug culture and the popularization of anthropology, phenomenology, and cognitive psychology.[9]

The accomplishment of structural film is suggested in three of the masterpieces of this movement: Snow's *Wavelength* (1966), Frampton's *Zorn's Lemma* (1970), and Ernie Gehr's *Serene Velocity* (1970). Snow's film is the paradigm of the shape approach to structural film; Frampton's is the seminal systemic film; and Gehr ingeniously combines both approaches in the process of creating what looks like an animated minimalist painting.

Wavelength is a generally continuous zoom shot of a loft that takes forty-five minutes to move from a broad shot, encompassing the whole space, to a tight close-up of a photograph of waves. Though human events, such as a death, occur in the course of the film, one's attention is dominated by the forward propulsion of the camera. The film has a characterizable shape as it slowly closes on the apex of a cone, and, then, ironically, opens out again, like an hourglass, as the frame enters the perimeter of the diminutive photograph of the seascape. For once inside the seascape, the tiny photo effectively assumes the proportions of a long shot. This gesture makes two reflexive points about what Snow takes to be the nature of cinema. First, that cinematic space is ambiguously flat and deep – a point underscored by the photo, which is at first classified by us as a flat surface in the room but which becomes a virtual deep space when the camera "enters" it. And second, that designations such as long shot or close-up are relative insofar as, in certain senses, the shot of the photo is both.

At the same time, *Wavelength* has important implications for the notion of apperceptive reflexivity. That is, it is said to make the viewer aware of certain generic features of film perception, if not of all perception. This interpretation is set forth magisterially by Annette Michelson in her famous article "Toward Snow." Michelson notes the way in which the film captures the viewer in its trajectory and engenders a sense of anticipation about where it will stop. Will it light on the image of the seascape, or on an adjacent image of a walking woman, or will it pass through the window and out onto the street? Tension builds, revealing, Michelson believes, a basic condition of the experience of temporality, namely, narrative. She writes

And as the camera continues to move steadily forward, building a tension that grows in direct ratio to the reduction of the field, we recognize, with some surprise, those horizons as defining the contours of narrative, of that narrative form animated by distended temporality, turning upon cognition towards revelation. Waiting for an issue, we are "suspended" towards resolution. And it is as if by emptying the space of his film... Snow has redefined filmic space as that of action. The eye investigates the length of the loft, moves towards that conclusion which is a fixed point; in its movement toward that point, alternate conclusions and false "clues" have been eliminated, as street signs and movement and certain objects pass from view. That object is indeed another surface, a photograph of the sea. The view is held, as the sound mounts . . . [and] the photograph is re-projected in superimposition upon itself. The eye is projected through a photograph out beyond the wall and screen into a limitless space. The film is a projection of a grand reduction; its "plot" is the tracing of spatio-temporal données, its "action" the movement of the camera as the movement of consciousness.[10]

Frampton's *Zorn's Lemma* is the archetypal systemic film. It is divided into three sharply contrasting parts. The first introduces the theme of the alphabet as a structural device. The screen is black, but we hear a voice recite a grammar school text called *The Bay State Reader*. For each letter of the alphabet, a theologically didactic sentence is intoned whose key word corresponds to the appropriate letter of the alphabet (e.g., for "A" we hear of Adam's Fall).

The next section, lasting approximately forty minutes, is silent. It begins as block-letter images of the alphabet flash by, in their proper order, at the rate of one letter per second. These letters then give way, in a successive run, to scenes that are projected at the same, one-second-per-image pulse. Like the sentences of the first section, each of these scenes has embedded somewhere in it (e.g., in a piece of graffiti or in a sign) a word whose first letter corresponds to the letter of the alphabet whose place in the order of the shot chain the scene has taken over. We learn to assimilate the successive images as rows of alphabetic exemplification. Then the lettered scenes are gradually replaced by ones without letters. An image of a fire substitutes for the letter "X." Over time, all the alphabetic images are replaced by unlettered scenes, by images with no writing in them.

The last section of the film is an artificially contrived long take in which we watch a man, woman, and a dog cross a snow-covered field while six women read Grossetestes' "On Light, or the Ingression of Forms," a metaphysical generative system that proposes an account of creation not unlike the generation of words through the combinatory resources of the alphabet.

When structural film is mentioned, the first thing that comes to many people's mind is the central section of *Zorn's Lemma*. Its very title, derived from set theory, is a playful tribute to systematicity. The alphabetic structure of the image rows is immediately grasped by the spectator, who then occupies himself in a game resembling the old TV show *Concentration*. Using the alphabet as a mnemonic device, we attempt to memorize the unlettered shot chain while also anticipating the replacement of lettered scenes by unlettered ones which, in turn, leads us to anticipate the completion of the second section of the film (which we infer will come when all the alphabetic substitutions transpire). In terms of the way in which *Zorn's Lemma* engages the spectator, the second section is a field day for apperceptive reflexivity. Our responses are strongly restricted to acts of memory and anticipation, and we begin to observe apperceptively some of the ways in which these mechanisms operate.

At the same time, the film invites us to regard it as an encyclopedia of cinematic forms and as a reflection upon the nature of cinema. The second section, for example, might be interpreted as an inventory of cinematic devices. The unlettered replacement images display a differentiated battery of cinematic techniques, a kind of "vocabulary" of film, including fast motion, slow motion, superimposition, split frames, long shots, close shots, moving camera shots, and so forth. Indeed, the whole section seems to exemplify the notion of parallel editing as the alphabetic replacement series "races" to completion. Thus, the second section could be construed as a primer in cinematic technique.

The reflexive dimension of *Zorn's Lemma* not only is articulated in the inventory of devices developed in the second section, but also is worked out in the various interrelations between the film's three parts. This relies upon a dialectic of spiraling contrasts. The first section has spoken words but no images; the second part is essentially a silent film – images and written words, but no sounds – the third part has both sound and image. Moreover, the second part of the film is notably an edited film, a montage film, while the third part of *Zorn's Lemma* is a piece of long-take realism, the often privileged form of sound filmmaking, just as montage was the often privileged form of silent filmmaking. Thus, the structure of *Zorn's Lemma* alludes to a series of debates and distinctions concerning the nature of film.

The opposition of the first part to the second part, like the relation between speech and image in *nostalgia,* reminds the viewer of the difference between these forms of representation, while the stylistic opposition between the second part and the last exemplifies the alternate conceptions of film sponsored by the Soviet-surrealist tradition, on the one hand, and the Bazinian-neorealist tradition on the other. The third part might read in contrast to both of the earlier sections. If part one stands for language, and part two for film-as-language, then part three opposes both of them with what, in the context of film history, could be viewed as an aesthetic of reality. Significantly, the film ends as the snow falling on the field becomes indistinguishable from the grain of the film. Hence another vision of the nature of film is broached, the modernist idea that a film is really flat, an object in the world, like the photos that burnt up on the hot plate in *nostalgia.* That is, if the third section begins as a cinematic celebration of realism, then it ends its reductive dialectic with an affirmation of the art of the real.[11]

In many ways, Gehr's *Serene Velocity* represents the most elegant triumph of structural film. It has both a legible shape and a legible system. Like *Wavelength*, it is based upon a zoom shot. The camera moves down a greenish, institutional hallway whose spare but regular features, when flattened by the action of the zoom lens, recall the plainness and symmetricality of a minimalist painting. At the same time, the film ultimately pretends to the shape of a line as the camera pushes down the passageway to a door at the rear. But experientially this is a broken or stuttered line. This is where the element of systematicity plays its role. Sitney describes the system and its phenomenological effects thusly:

The filmmaker positioned his tripod within the corridor and then proceeded to alter his zoom lens every four frames. At first the shifts are not dramatic. He alternates four frames at 50mm with four frames at 55mm. After a considerable period the differential increases: 45mm to 60mm. Thus, the film proceeds with ever increasing optical shocks. In this system, the zoom never "moves." The illusion of movement comes about from the adjustment of the eye from one sixth of a second of a distant image to one sixth of a second of a nearer one. Although the absolute rhythm never changes, the film reaches a crescendo because of the extreme illusions of distance by the end. Furthermore, Gehr cyclically shifts the degree of exposure every frame in the phrases of four. In its overall shape *Serene Velocity* moves from a vibrating pulse within an optical depth to an accordion-like slamming and stretching of the visual field.[12]

Generated by a simple decision procedure, *Serene Velocity* evokes a series of effects that can, within the context of structural film and minimal art, be interpreted as dialectically reflexive comments on the nature of film. The hallway is initially experienced as a deep space. But at times, the juxtaposition of the four frame segments are such that they appear compressed in a single, flat frame. At one point, the image appears to constitute a large, black X, squashing the corridor in what Sitney characterizes as a slamming, accordion effect. Given the polemics of minimalism, this operation might be glossed by saying that though the film image appears deep, it is revealed to be actually flat.

Another important effect of the juxtapositions is that at times the eminently still images become alive with movement. This is an optical effect that involves our mind's imputation of movement to sequentially displayed visual arrays that are closely but not exactly aligned in regard to their figural outlines. This, of course, is the principle that makes animation possible, but also that makes all film possible. For all film movement is based upon the optical illusion of motion that results when two similar still photos are juxtaposed to each other. What Gehr has done in *Serene Velocity* is to set up a cinematic context in which the film viewer can observe for himself the origin of cinematic movement. We see the images are still: we see that certain juxtapositions result in the impression of tumultuous movement. By attending to our own perceptual response to the image, we recognize the secret of cinema. It is, in a manner of speaking, a "serene velocity" – "serene" because it begins in *stillness*; "velocity" because from stillness comes quickening *movement*. Like most structural film, *Serene Velocity* addresses its audience didactically, striving to reveal the nature of cinema and the dynamics of film through elusive and elliptical "experiments."[13] The triumph of *Serene Velocity* is that it is able to allude to so many theoretical themes and to project such stark beauty by means of such a simple, that is to say minimal, initial decisional procedure.

The intense didacticism of structural film is also especially apparent in the British version of the movement, which is generally referred to as structural/materialist film, whose major practitioners and proponents are Malcolm LeGrice and Peter Gidal. As the title of this movement suggests, its aim was to educate the spectator in the true, *material* nature of the medium. These filmmakers regarded representational film as illusionistic, and they sought to free the spectator from this supposed deception by adopting structures that would lead us to appreciate the real nature of the medium as a material object. Thus in LeGrice's *Dejeuner Sur L'Herbe, After Manet, Giorgione, etc.* (1974), a picnic scene is represented by four separate cameras. In terms of shape, the structure is a matter of one large square divided into four quadrants, each composed of projections resulting from one of the initial cameras. In terms of systematicity, the structure is one of disparity, since the projectors run in and out of synchronization and since four different film stocks are employed (color, color negative, black and white, and black and white negative). The effect of these disparities, is to frustrate the enjoyment of the depiction at an anecdotal level, and is said to call our attention to the materiality of photographic representation.[14]

Initially structural/materialist film appeared to be a local variation of structural film. However, it quickly differentiated itself by contending that its commitment to revealing the ultimate materiality of film evinced a commitment to materialism in the political sense, that is, a commitment to Marxist materialism.[15] Simultaneously, proponents of structural/materialist film denounced the attempts of exegetes of structural film to claim an emancipatory role for the reflexive didacticism of the American output. Whether either or neither structural film nor structural/materialist film is actually politically emancipatory or even politically significant is less important than the fact that in the shouting matches between these two competitors, the charge that American structural film was essentially formalist stuck. And this, added to other dissatisfactions with what was becoming a genre, would result in the decline of structural film in the late seventies.

Another key factor in the demise of structural film was that its early success led predictably to wide-scale imitation. This was especially the case in the area of optical printing where, through processing, images within images could be constructed in Chinese boxes of delicate games of theme and variation. In Ken Kobland's *Frame* (1976), for example, the ground of an image is a set of row houses, while the figure is an inset of the same row of houses compositionally reversed.[16] But as each new reworking of the premises of structural film appeared, audiences and commentators became increasingly disenchanted.

Since the style to a large extent relied upon seizing a simple structuring principle, it was easily imitated. And this, plus the immense volume of imitations, led to charges that the structural film was unimaginative, too facile, unchallenging, rote, and possibly trivial.[17]

In the hands of what seemed to be a horde of second-generation structural filmmakers, including Tom DeBiaso, Dana Gordon, Vincent Grenier, Peter Rose, James Benning, Joanna Kiernan, and others, the enterprise seemed to be hardening into a genre and a highly academic one at that. Strategies such as partitioned images recurred with frequency. These films were very respectable efforts and showed thorough knowledge of the tradition of avant-garde film and the other arts. But they were hardly innovative, nor did they expand greatly on the breakthroughs of first-generation structural filmmakers. The apperceptive themes of structural film – the play of memory and attention – were repeated again and again as were the reflexive, anti-illusionist comments on the nature of film.[18] These notions came to appear standardized rather than a matter of new insights. The idea that film is material became shrill with repetition, while the generic apperceptive discoveries about the operation of memory and attention were numbingly familiar even if each new film brought them to the spectator's awareness in a different way. Indeed, a constant diet of structural film, doting on the processes of one's own memory and attention, could result in a disquieting and uncomfortable sense of solipsistic monotony. This is not to deny the original accomplishment of the first structural films, nor to reject the possibility that exciting structural films can still be made – for example, Peter Greenaway's brilliant *The Falls*. However, the flood of respectable, careful but nonground breaking structural films left the impression that the genre was threadbare if not finally empty. And this, combined with the charges of rank formalism, routinization, and lack of imagination, led to a consensus from all sides that structural film was a dead end. Moreover, if the problem with this genre was one of barrenness, this seemed to suggest content as a line or at least a slogan of reclamation.[19]

Deconstruction

Whereas structural film can be characterized as a genre, deconstruction is more of the nature of an aim or goal that can be pursued in many ways, by many means, and across many different genres. Thus, structural/materialist films can be championed in the name of deconstruction as can found footage films, optically printed films, New Talkies, and so on. Deconstruction, in short, is a catchphrase that marks the predominant sensibility of the seventies and eighties in film of the avant-garde variety, and it supplies a major source of energy for such film making into the present.

Many readers are familiar with the term "deconstruction" from the influential writings of Jacques Derrida. There the concept, roughly speaking, denotes the isolation and explication of what are supposedly the *inevitable* contradictions of a text – that is, the collapse of any attempt to sustain the logical contrareity of such concepts as nature/culture, original/copy, speech/writing, and so on. This is *not* the way in which filmmakers and film critics use the term. Rather, for them to deconstruct is to take apart, to dismantle, or, more fashionably, to subvert the dominant conventions of filmmaking: that is, this dismantling usually has a destructive connotation to it.

One deconstructs the conventions of Hollywood editing by mismatching the eyelines in a conversation scene, by failing to show the source of a striking off-screen sound, or by breaking the 180° rule in shooting an action scene. By disregarding these conventions one purportedly subverts the audience's expectations and thereby calls their attention to the putatively conventional and artificial nature of the dominant forms of filmmaking. Like the structural film, deconstruction is underwritten by a zeal for didacticism or at least a presiding metaphor of a learning situation. Furthermore, educating audiences in this way about the contrivances of dominant cinema is thought to be political because it reveals the mechanism by which ideology is disseminated in the dominant cinema. Deconstructionism answers the call for content, supposedly, by dismantling dominant cinema through supplying spectators with the knowledge necessary to see through its artifice.[20]

Obviously the idea of deconstruction is not completely alien to the project of structural film. Artists in that vein did subvert the approach of dominant cinema in order to reveal to spectators what they thought to be the real nature of film and of the perception of film. But structural filmmakers and their proponents often spoke as if they believed that they were disclosing the *essence* of film and the *nature* of perception. It is this combination of essentialism and naturalism in the structural filmmakers' conception of reflexivity that puts them at odds with the main line of deconstruction in the late seventies and eighties. For most deconstructionists do not believe that film has an essence or that our practices of perception are natural. All is cultural and conventional.[21] Thus, structural film itself has to be deconstructed, for essentialism is politically suspect, a means of mystifying a set of conventions.

Of course, the deconstructionist' emphasis on conventions and codes marks the immense influences of semiology and poststructuralism on the imagination of the seventies and the eighties, whereas phenomenology, cognitive psychology, math, and natural science provided the preferred rhetoric of much structural film. And yet, despite these theoretical (or polemical) differences, the techniques of deconstructionists often grow out of and resemble those of structural filmmaking, though of course the deconstructionist will argue that his political perspective enables his work to avoid charges of formalism and to claim redeeming social content.

One area where deconstructionism and structural film appear close is, as might be expected, in the practice of structural/materialist film. But structural/materialist film did succeed in appropriating the vocabulary of politicized deconstruction, whereas this option was denied to structural film. The simple reason for this is probably that structural/ materialists took on this rhetoric first and then refused to be convinced by proponents of structural film who attempted to do likewise.

In any case, the deconstructionist aspect of recent structural/materialist film is in place. In his *Emily – Third Party Speculation* (1979), LeGrice records adjacent off-screen sounds without cutting immediately to their source, for example, to a record player.[22] He claims that this subverts the Hollywood convention of field-reverse-field editing, thereby deconstructing and unmasking Hollywood artifice for the spectator. Whether it is true that Hollywood films always immediately cut to the source of off-screen sounds (horror films? mystery films?) and whether or not viewers of *Emily* experience the critical awakenings LeGrice claims for them is less important than the fact that the rhetoric he uses to justify his artistic choices is politicized deconstruction. For in that he exemplifies the dominant trope of contemporary avant-gardists.

To deconstruct in film is always of necessity to deconstruct something, that is, something else, something other than the deconstruction itself. That object is usually of the nature of a familiar cultural artifact – a preexisting film, genre, TV program, ad, a traditional compositional schema, traditional iconography, or even the conventions of narration. Since deconstruction always requires an object, one of the most literal-minded avenues along which to pursue the deconstructive goal is the found footage film.

A found footage film is one that is composed of old films, photographs, TV programs, or fragments thereof which are rearranged through reediting or rephotography in a way that suggests to many commentators an analogy with collage. Once images are taken out of their original context, dislodged, and placed in a new and generally disjunctive setting, the image can be made to appear strange, and initially unnoticed features of it may be said to be unmasked. Imagine taking a close-up of Fay Wray screaming out of *King Kong* and juxtaposing it to an image of a Coke bottle. Displaced to this new context, we will look at this screaming in a fresh light. It will appear bizarre and its contrivance will be manifest. We may wonder how we were ever able to overlook its strangenesss.

This is the method of the found footage film. Its potential usefulness for deconstructionism should be apparent; it is a ready means for reassessing and unmasking the significance of familiar iconography and narrative form.

The found footage film predates deconstructionism. It was employed in the thirties in such films as *Rose Hobart* by the surrealist Joseph Cornell, who reedited a Hollywood pot-boiler called *East of Borneo* in such a way that the narrative dissolves and his obsessive infatuation with actress Rose Hobart and her special qualities becomes central. In 1958 Bruce Conner made *A Movie,* a disjunctive compilation of movie fragments that projected a pop art vision of the madness of contemporary civilization rushing toward apocalypse. Conner has continued to work in the found footage style and has proven that the form is the avant-garde approach with the most popular appeal, undoubtedly because even audiences untutored in avant-grade aesthetics can recognize the images in such films and follow the filmmakers' subversions, parodies, and effacements of them. Found footage films can also be found in the structural film tradition in the work of Ken Jacobs, whose classic *Tom, Tom the Piper's Son* (1969) involves the analytic rephotographing of a Biograph film made in 1905. *Tom, Tom...* and subsequent films by Jacobs, such as *The Doctor's Dream*, provide influential models for contemporary deconstructionists.[23]

Perhaps the influence of Jacobs on deconstructionists is most apparent in the work of J. Hoberman. Hoberman is not only a filmmaker but the most widely published and most influential journalistic critic of avant-garde film today. Working as a resident reviewer of the *Village Voice* in New York City, Hoberman employs the notion of deconstruction overtly in his criticism, praising those films, such as the works of Jacobs' beloved Oscar Micheaux, which appear to Hoberman to transgress the politically repressive conventions of the dominant cinema. Hoberman also brings his war with Hollywood to the editing bench. In *Broken Honeymoon #3*, he reedited an episode of *Bewitched*, a TV sitcom from the sixties. He chopped the shots of the episode into one second lengths and reordered them while taking whatever remained of the shots that were under one second and stringing them in reverse chronological sequence at the end of the film. Commenting on *Broken Honeymoon #3*, a sympathetic critic, Jonathan Buchsbaum, writes

The episode [of *Bewitched*] concerns a visit by one of the in-laws to Dick York's family, but its appeal for Hoberman lay in the sequence when Dick York attempts to show some home movies, but has difficulty with the sound synchronization. He must start the projector several times before he gets synchronization. Clearly, recutting the sitcom, with an optical track, automatically wreaks havoc on the synchronization because of the 26 frame sound advance. Since television and film build their "illusion of reality" on the base of synchronization, Hoberman has "broken" the "honeymoon" usually enjoyed by the audience of such constructions, for the audience must work at reconstituting the union of sound and image.[24]

The importance of the found footage film for aspiring deconstructionists extends beyond the fact that the genre supplies a ready modus operandi for designating the target of one's deconstruction and (literal) intertextual play. The found footage film is economical; it can be built from outtakes and discarded films. This is especially important at a time when rising film costs threaten the extinction of avant-garde film. Also, found footage films have a degree of accessibility that other avant-garde approaches may lack. Among the charges leveled at structural film was the notion that it was elitist as well as too hermetic to sustain general audience interest in avant-garde experimentation. The accessibility of the imagery of the found footage film along with its audience-pleasing parodic potentials make it immediately attractive to the avant-garde polemicist seeking to reach wider audiences. Nor has this aspect of the use of recycled imagery been lost on avant-garde video makers, such as Bruce Tovsky, whose *Invaders* (1983) deconstructs a fifties sci-fi film recorded off his TV set.

The deconstructionist who employs found footage finds his material ready-made, so to speak. But one may also remount the type of narrative or genre one wishes to subvert, and in the course of that remounting, through strategies such as exaggeration, repetition, disjunction, oxymoron, and condensation, one can deconstruct as one goes along. An example of this is Manuel DeLanda's *Raw Nerves: A Lacanian Thriller* (1980), which, among other things, deconstructs the *film noir* by foregrounding the paranoid fear of women found in the genre. Jonathan Rosenbaum writes:

The ensuing paranoid plot owes a lot both to *Kiss Me Deadly* and the Mickey Spillane novel it's based on (which furnishes part of the dialogue – although the script is credited to Joan Braderman, Paul Arthur and DeLanda, among others), with iconographic (and graphic) lifts from forties and fifties *noir* as well: shadowy grill patterns on walls, colors like the inside of a fruity Fifties jukebox. In a surprise ending, the off-screen narrating voice of the hero proves to belong to a woman, who declares "Never trust a first person pronoun" before shooting him dead.[25]

Of course, the targets of the deconstructionist need not be the artifacts of popular culture but those of high culture as well. In *Misconception* (1977), Marjorie Keller offers a subversion of the childbirth film, a subgenre of the personal, avant-garde cinema made famous by Stan Brakhage. In what Keller calls "a loving critique of [Brakhage's] *Window Water Baby Moving*," she injects far more ominousness than the celebratory Brakhage in her vision of the "blessed event" via foreboding images of the demolition of a house.[26] Perhaps these anxious premonitions should be explicated as proto-feminist reservations about the male outlook that dominates the most well-known examples of the childbirth genre.

One strategy of deconstruction might be thought of as the autodestruction of the film itself through the staged collision of the elements within it. Michelle Citron's *Daughter Rite* (1978), for example, mixes documentary and fictional modes in a way that is said to call both forms of representation into question E. A. Kaplan writes:

The use of home movies and old photographs is crucial as a device that establishes continuity through time and that reflects the fiction-making urge that, as Metz and Heath have shown, pervades even the documentary. Used as unproblematic representations, the past images function to seal individual change instead of providing evidence of the way women and their bodies are constructed by the signifying practices of both the social and the psychological institutions in which they are embedded. Interestingly enough, this construction makes a main theme in Michelle Citron's *Daughter Rite* (1978) where the slowing down of home movies enables us to see that the representations are far from an "innocent recording," that the process of making the movies itself functions to construct the place for the female child.[27]

Whether the theoretical premises that Kaplan mobilizes above are correct, of course, is not of particular significance historically, for Kaplan has accurately captured Citron's deconstructionist intentions. Those intentions, indeed, are even more explicit in the next group of avant-gardists to be reviewed – the practitioners of the New Talkie.

The New Talkies

As the title of this genre implies, the New Talkies are dominated by language. Indeed, as a first approximation, one might say that an identifying feature of the New Talkie is that in this genre language is ultimately more important than image. Language has often been a matter of central concern to structural filmmakers – for example, Frampton's *nostalgia* and his *Poetic Justice* (1971), and Snow's *Rameau's Nephew* (1974) and his *So Is This* (1982). However, structural filmmakers appear primarily concerned with the limitations and possibilities of language (e.g., the polysemy of words and their materiality) as a form of representation as such. Practitioners of New Talkie, on the other hand, are preoccupied not only with these issues but also with using language to say something, something of political-theoretical-cultural significance. That is, key examples of the New Talkie – such as Peter Wollen's and Laura Mulvey's *Riddles of the Sphinx* (1977); Anthony McCall's and Andrew Tyndall's *Argument* (1978); and McCall's, Tyndall's Claire Pajaczkowska's, and Jane Weinstock's *Sigmund Freud's Dora*, (1980) – tend to espouse politicized versions of semiology and poststructuralism, which are believed thereby to become didactically available to audiences through film viewing. The goal of the majority of new talkies is to educate spectators in the role of "signifying practices" in the maintenance of political domination that is not only economic but sexual. This is what the New Talkies have to tell us. Thus, unlike the structural film, the new talkie utilizes discourse – while also interrogating it – to tell us, putatively, about the content of our lives.

Another significant difference between the New Talkie and the structural film regards narrative. In the main, the structural film was antinarrative or oblivious to it. Structural film was far more concerned with the visual and cinematic elements of films. However, in the New Talkie, narrative is again center stage. This phenomenon is yet again another example of the revolt against structural film in the name of content. That is not to say that the new talkies are predominantly engaged in telling stories (though some of them do tell stories). Rather, in the New Talkie narration itself as a form of representation with purported social significance is a fundamentally recurring topic. Stories are presented to be deconstructed as in the feminist film *Sigmud Freud's Dora*, which rereads Freud's case study of the same name in order to plumb the lacunae of the original. In this respect, the new talkie strives to be essayistic, though the topic of the essay is often narrative. Specimen-stories are deconstructively subverted to unmask their structural, political, and psychosexual presuppositions.

An important influence on the New Talkie is the work of Jean Luc Godard. In Godard proponents of the New Talkie found a model for a cinema that is at once intellectual, discursive, oppositional, and political. In Godard's work, such as *Le Gai Savoir* (1968), the possibilities and vagaries of language and discourse are interrogated and challenged, as they are in structural film; however, the relations of language and signs to social reality are also subject to scrutiny and criticism. Thus, in the jargon preferred by practitioners of New Talkies, the signifier (e.g., the word, image, and so on) is investigated by Godard, at the same time that the signified (here best thought of first as what the signifier refers to and then metaphorically expanded to comprehend reality, or socially constructed reality) is not forgotten and, thereby, is available for political analysis.[28]

The new talkie also derives stylistic strategies from Godard. Just as Godard mixes documentary with fictions and facts with fancies in *Two Or Three Things I Know About Her* (1966) and studio shooting with cinema verité style in *Passion,* so the new talkie favors pastiche. The parents of the new talkie, Peter Wollen and Laura Mulvey, in many of their works – including *Penthesilea* (1974), *Riddles of the Sphinx* (1977), and *Amy!* (1982) – divide the film into segments marked by different styles and often by different media (film, video, painting, photography, theater, and so on). The effect of this pastiche is supposed to be the dawning awareness that the audience is confronting representations whose structure is contingent rather than necessary. At the same time, these segments – stories, lectures, documentation – do not segue into a unified discursive flow; they are juxtapositional in a way that suggests that they are mutually inflective or commentative. Yet, the substance of those comments must be deciphered by an actively participating spectator. In other words this disjunctive style, like Godard's, functions to raise questions that the audience must wrestle with. Moreover, this maieutic effect is, of course, what many thought to be Godard's most salutary accomplishment.[29]

The films of Jean-Marie Straub and Daniele Huillet also provide a touchstone for the New Talkie. In films like *Moses and Aaron*(1975), an adaptation from Schoenberg, and *Class Relations*(1983), a screen version of Kafka's *Amerika,* Straub/Huillet evince an interest in radically remounting and, thereby, radically reinterpreting known cultural artifacts in a way that brings the very question of interpretation to the fore insofar as Straub/Huillet's austere versions of these works subvert the expectations of viewers familiar with the earlier works. That is, radical reinterpretation is supposed to reveal the fact that received ideas about such works are also interpretations. Similarly, New Talkies often play off known originals – *Penthesilea* enacts Kleist's play as a mime; *Sigmund Freud's Dora* subversively retells Freud's account with a feminist's eye for incongruities, interspersing the narrative with telling sexist TV ads and porno films and flanking the whole proceedings with feminist meditations.[30] In each case the act of radical reinterpretation is predicated on the desire to disrupt complacency toward accepted interpretations and, thereby, to reveal the interests believed to be behind those interpretations.[31]

Sally Potter's *Thriller* is arguably the most successful of the New Talkies. It retells *La Bohème* as a detective story, but as the film proceeds the question of "Why did Mimi die?" demands an answer greater in scope than the identification, in the style of a "whodunit," of a single culprit. Rather, we are to understand the meaning of that death in terms of what it epitomizes about the operation of a capitalistic and sexist, psycho-sexual system. While simultaneously deconstructing the detective genre and the operatic melodrama, *Thriller* offers forays into Lacanian psychoanalysis, the privileged metaphysic of the New Talkie, in order to discover a feminist explanation for Mimi's death that accounts for both its narrative necessity in the opera and for the social significance of that very plot structure. Mimi

...finally understands why she had to die. Had she lived, she and Rodolfo would have borne children and she would have had to work even harder to feed them. Seen in this light motherhood is not romantic, and again, it makes the woman a subject; children activate *her* desire, and she is not able simply to be the object of male passion. She had to die because "an old seamstress would not be considered the proper subject of a love story."[32]

At present, the future of the New Talkie is uncertain. Part of the reason for this may be that the New Talkie did not succeeed on its own terms. Politically activist proponents of the New Talkie sought to reach wider audiences than the limited number of cognoscenti informed enough and willing enough to follow the refined dialectics of the gallery aesthetics of structural film. But simply trading art theory for political (content-oriented) theory – the amalgam of Lacan, Althusser, and feminism – did not make the New Talkie either more accessible or more attractive to nonspecialized audiences. After all, one has to be extremely well versed in Marxist psychoanalytic theories of representation to follow these films, especially since the tenets of this philosophy were, in typical avant-garde style, only elliptically alluded to rather than coherently spelled out, with appropriate background information, in the films in question. This, of course, raises the issue of how didactically successful such films can be. But perhaps even more pressing is the possibility that didacticism, the major mode of avant-gardism since the sixties, is itself a problem for filmmakers seeking wider audiences. With this in mind, it seems that some proponents of the New Talkie are headed in the direction of straight narrative feature production. Wollen and Mulvey have made *The Bad Sister* for British TV, while Bette Gordon, creator of the New Talkie *Empty Suitcase*, has directed *Variety*. From dominating the avant-garde at the turn of the decade, the New Talkie presently appears in danger of extinction.

A Digression: Yvonne Rainer

In the discussion of the New Talkie, mention of one figure whom many may feel is the exemplar of the genre, namely, Yvonne Rainer, has been omitted. However, though Rainer's work bears affinities to the New Talkie and though it was influential for and respected by practitioners of the New Talkie, it is distinct. For in Rainer's work neither didacticism nor affirmation of the tenets of politicized poststructuralist theory is central. Instead, her program to date appears, broadly speaking, novelistic.

Of avant-garde filmmakers who emerged in the seventies, Rainer is the major filmmaker at work today. She came to film from a career as a choreographer, in which, during the sixties, she gained a reputation as the leading figure of the postmodern dance movement.[33] That movement, eschewing the preoccupation with the emotions found in the choreography of artists like Graham and Humphrey, was rigorously minimalist. Rainer turned from dance to film, in part, in order to find a medium that she thought would be better attuned to the exploration of the emotional life than was dance.

From an art world and a dance world background of minimalism, Rainer entered an avant-garde American film scene dominated by structural film. Yet her own films – such as *Lives of Performers* (1972), *Film About a Woman Who...* (1974), and *Kristina Talking Pictures* (1976)– pushed against the prevailing tide, offering narratives, albeit modernist, distanced, and disjunctive ones, of the lives of characters. Her films are narratives profuse with inner dialogue, comment, and memories, layered with quotations, observations, and contesting voices. During the seventies, Rainer was the single major American avant-garde filmmaker concerned with narrative and with the extensive use of language (spoken, written, and generally elliptical) to broach substantial issues about such things as the battle of the sexes. Rainer's allegiance to narrative and to the substantive use of language, along with the implicit feminism of her concerns with sexual power relations, inclined proponents of the New Talkie to regard her as both a forerunner and a fellow traveler.

The influence of Godard also supplies a point of convergence between Rainer and the New Talkie. For example, she remains particularly impressed by his Brechtian refusal to permit audiences to identify empathetically with characters. Thus, in certain of her films she will have the same character played by different performers in order to block empathy while also using printed statements or deadpan voice-over expressions of inner feelings to cool our engagement with the characters. For though Rainer wishes us to explore with her the contours of contemporary life and feeling, she wants that exploration to be detached, sober, and tough-minded, aware of complexity, conflict, and contradiction and not homogenized by strong reactive emotions.

Despite the points of tangency between Rainer and proponents of the New Talkies, her work differs from theirs in its refusal to embrace and to promote a unified theory as the perspective from which to answer all the pressing moral, political, and sexual problems of contemporary life. This is apparent in her recent film *Journeys from Berlin / 1971* (1980). The film can be viewed as a choir of disparate, but associatively related conversations, secondarily supported by visuals that illustrate, baldly represent, or are associated with material in the discourse of the text. The voices of the conversation include an exposition of the history of the Baader-Meinhof terrorists (mostly in printed titles); selections from a morally concerned, teenage woman's diary; a stylized enactment of a psychiatric session; an offscreen discussion between a couple about revenge and terrorism; memoirs of Russian anarchists; an interview with Rainer's nephew; a videotaped "letter" from Rainer to a fictive mother. Out of this welter of material certain themes emerge about the incommensurability of private experience versus public life, about the psychiatric examination of motives and its relation to the evaluation of political action, about the fractured nature of the self and the moral significance of this. These issues are attacked from a number of perspectives – through reminiscences, dramatic enactments, lectures, and examples – in a way that suggests a protracted dialogue. The film does not resolve these problems by means of an implied theory, in the fashion of the New Talkie, but rather presents an affecting tapestry of personal, moral, and political quandaries, sensitively reflective of the paralyzing knots and contradictions confronting someone who realistically yet ethically seeks to assess the significance of contemporary political life. [34]

Punk Film

As must already be evident, the development of avant-garde film over the past two decades is marked by a high seriousness, intellectualism, and a penchant for debate that frequently reaches academic proportions. The emergence of punk film in the late seventies is an explicit rejection of this. Many of the works of this genre are modeled on low-budget Hollywood films, signaling an interest in action rather than thought and abandoning the burdens of reflexivity in the name of entertainment.

Growing out of new wave music, punk filmmaking projected a similar view of the world, one that was sensationalist but that lacked affect or moral sensibility. The punk world combines qualities of violence and detachment. It is populated by egotistical characters, grasping, unashamed of their wants, undisturbed by the reactions their   often crude frankness might elicit. They are cold and morally unresponsive. Their urban environment, often the Lower East Side of Manhattan, is pictured in a way that makes it appear like a bombed-out no-man's land sometime in the future. The punk film portrays a kind of postapocalyptic state of nature where life is nasty, brutish, but immediate, and where the punk hero survives through the sort of dumb sang-froid found in a Mike Hammer. Punk heroines are often pure machismo. Other denizens of this world are hysterics wallowing in alienated, incoherent, and paralytic remorse, somnabulists, and representatives of the bourgeoisie, rendered in vicious caricature.

In 1978, the New Cinema was opened in the East Village in New York by Eric Mitchell, Becky Johnstone, and James Nares. Here films were showcased via video projection. Films were also shown in bars, clubs, and cabarets in lower Manhattan. The punk filmmakers wanted popular venues outside what they believed was the staid avant-garde circuit.

A surprising number of long films were produced very quickly, most often in the inexpensive format of super-8. Mitchell made *Kidnapped* and *Red Italy* in 1978; the married team of Beth B. and Scott B. made *G-Man* and *Black Box* in 1979 and *The Trap Door* in 1980; Becky Johnstone made *Sleepless Nights* in 1980; while Vivian Dick made *Guerillere Talks* and *She Had Her Gun Already* in 1978.

In *Black Box*, a twentyish young man, fresh from his girlfriend's arms, is kidnapped in front of an apartment building somewhere in the East Village. He is brought to a torture chamber where the minions of a secret religious organization plan to purify him using knouts, cudgels, chains and electric shocks. The film is an homage both to sleaze and to adolescent images of evil. The villains, with thick New York accents, recall hectoring parental nagging more than the stage diction of the evil-doers of traditional B-films. Mixed with the broad shtick are sadomasochistic interludes in which the boy is beaten by his maniacal captors. The torture appears to be meant to titillate but at the same time it is comic, until finally the naked, bound, and bleeding captive is thrust into a black box, and he and the audience are assaulted at length with abrasive electric sound waves that provide an effective, horrific symbol of totalitarian repression.

The levels of irony in the film are complicated. Banality in both film and life is alternately embraced, celebrated, and satirized while the sadomasochism signals an unresolved fascination with sexual repression at the same time that such repression is derided. The sophomoric irony appears to be a disguise for a great deal of pain, which is both denied and expressed through the enactments of comic/horrific victimization.

The punk film movement was involved in a war on two fronts, rejecting mainstream Hollywood professionalism, on the one hand, and the still influential structural avant-garde, on the other. Films were originally made in the super-8 format not simply because it was inexpensive but because the primitive, amateurish look was a flag of identity belligerently flown in the face of Hollywood polish. Pariah genres, like low-budget crime films and shoe-string sci-fi, were cannibalized, their bad taste, outrageous logic, and crudity further exaggerated in such a way that the cheapness and mindlessness of these wretcheds of the film industry were intensified to the point where they could function as symbols of the punk self. At a stylistic level, the exaggerated adaptations of pulp genres stated themes of transgression of norms, of outsideness, of the valorization of the authentic, even romantically heroic, significance of bad taste. The punk filmmakers exploited the brazenly antireflective address of the genres while also expropriating the raw if rather crude energy available in their structure. At the same time the violence endemic to the Hollywood genres could be rechanneled in stories that plotted revolutionary acts against the bourgeois culture.

Like the new German cinema, punk film has an ambivalent relation to Hollywood, whose imagery it refashions into emblems of the self, projecting the signs of identity for a new generation. Often, this refashioning takes the form of parody and allusion. Like postmodernist art in other media, the punk filmmaker often gives the impression of cobbling his or her intentionally amateurish and rough-hewn films out of fragments of a defunct culture – art as the practice of referring to shards and pieces of a once-vibrant civilization; art in the ruins. Into the tempos of action genres, punk filmmakers imploded long stretches of dead, hanging-around time in order to canonize the cadences of life lived outside the margins of the workaday bourgeois world.

The parodic dimension of punk recyclings of genres both resembles deconstructionism and does not. On the one hand, it is transgressive and subversive. However, this seems less a matter of teaching the audience to be aware of Hollywood conventions – though that may happen–than a means of expressing a disdain and a superiority for an established culture. The choice of action genres, as well, relates to another key punk theme: the anesthetization of feeling. Punk films seem dominated by characters who refuse to be touched emotionally or moved. By taking

Hollywood genres notable for their emotionally affecting potential and their immediacy and by distancing them through low-key irony, punk filmmakers raise the theme of anesthetization to the level of style.

In opposition to the structural film, punk film aligned itself with narrative content even though the Hollywood prototypes it commandeered were subversively remodeled if not deconstructed. Moreover, the address of the punk film was expressive rather than reflexive, its point directed at finding objective correlatives for the textures and feelings of a certain way of being-in-the-world, the alienated ethos of the urban punk.

One of the most successful punk films is Slava Tsukerman's *Liquid Sky*, which was theatrically released in 1983. An independent film made by Soviet emigrés, J. Hoberman describes it as the

... not unfamiliar witch's brew of decadent fashion, smacked-out club life and political terrorism. The latter, appropriately, is extraterrestrial: attracted by the presence of heroin, an alien spacecraft hovers over a Lower East Side tenement, apparently drawing energy from human sexual secretions and, in any case, killing at climax the hapless lovers of the rangy, petulant model (Anne Carlisle) who lives inside.[35]

The self-consciously outlandish science fiction conceit, the apocalyptic ending, the alternately amateurish, stilted, and affectless acting and the juxtaposition of glitter and squalor mark *Liquid Sky* as pure punk as does the humor of the dialogue, which is based on a mix of parody, naiveté, and ruthlessness. Most horrifying in this allegory of alienated sexuality is that survival and power are based in the "ability" not to be excited sexually, but to be anesthetized. For to have an orgasm leads to death by an intergalactic ray. Sexual lethargy, the faculty to be unmoved and untouched, to be in an emotional deep-freeze, is the closest approximation of freedom – which is equated with survival – in *Liquid Sky*. The film is composed of brutal sexual victimizers – sex as rape – on the one hand, and the victimized, emotionally anesthetized Carlisle on the other. Urban romance has rarely been envisioned as so completely and unredemptively savage.

The punk film flourished during a period in which the rediscovery of the sleazy, the grubby, and the debris of modern life was also being celebrated in the broader culture, for example, in the weekly TV program *Saturday Night Live* and in its offshoots like *The Blues Brothers*. Thus it is no surprise that, at present, the aesthetic proclivities of the punk film are, in modified form, finding their way into the broader distribution networks of commercial film. The current high visibility of *Repo Man* (1984), for example, suggests that the punk sensibility is on its way to finding mainstream expression.

The Psychodrama

The American avant-garde film was inaugurated in the forties by films that, under the probable influence of Jean Cocteau's *Blood of a Poet*, presented themselves as dream states or as the fantasies of the protagonists. Maya Deren's *Meshes of the Afternoon* (1943) is the reverie of a young wife who envisions the death of her virgin self at the hands of her emerging sexual self, while Kenneth Anger's *Fireworks* (1947) is an imaginary testament to a homosexual's coming of age. In the psychodrama, the filmmaker creates a cinematic dreamwork in which, through fragmented narrative and charged imagery, anxieties and wishes are portrayed symbolically. The rise of structural film momentarily eclipsed the acceptability of psychodrama. But the yearning for a return to content, in reaction to the structural film, has predictably led young filmmakers to reassess the potentials of the psychodrama.

The mode of address of the structural film, as that of much deconstructionism and of many new talkies, is didactic. The psychodrama, on the other hand, reverts to a much more familiar mode of address, that of expression. The psychodrama presents a situation in which feeling tones, indicative of emotions, anxieties, wishes, and moods are emphasized. The audience responds by recognizing the particular emotional colorations by which the filmmaker characterizes the situation portrayed. At the very least the spectator's interest in the film is in how a certain life or a certain situation feels. Some might even claim that the spectator is moved to share whatever mood or emotion the film projects or even to be infected by it. But in the psychodrama the currency of the discourse is primarily feeling rather than theory.

In James Nares' *Waiting for the Wind* (1979) a solitary sleeper lies fitfully on a mattress on the floor of a tenement apartment. Suddenly furniture – hurled at the walls with tremendous force – flies about the room, propelled by some invisible force. It is a telekinetic spectacle of the sort one sees in films of demonic possession. But there is no Satan here to be exorcised. One interprets the violence as a dream, fantasy, or hallucinogenic state of the protagonist. The rage inscribed in the whirling furniture incongruously contrasts to the vulnerability we attribute, at first, to the sleeper. This juxtaposition projects a strong sense of the magical thinking involved in the belief in the omnipotence of the will, here appropriately situated in a context suggestive of urban loneliness, alienation, and helplessness.

The area in which psychodrama has especially come to the fore is that of feminist filmmaking. Feminists have found in the psychodrama a means of communicating the particular anxieties they suffer under patriarchal society. At the same time the genre can be used to symbolize their wishes and desires, as well as their accusations. Through the psychodrama, the feminist filmmaker can address emotional questions in their own terms rather than in the didactic, theoretical voice of the New Talkie.

Discussing Su Friedrich's dream like journey, *Cool Hands, Warm Heart* (1979), Lindly Hanlon says that it

... is a defiantly feminist film, chronicling in rite after ritual the deep violence which women have accepted as part of their daily attempts to refashion their nature into a cleaned-up, pared-down image of glossy magazine mannequins. In stark, contrasty, grainy, black-and-white silent images, we watch a woman travel through a series of encounters with other women who perform daily female rituals on a raised, public platform where passers-by observe them awkwardly and curiously. In these street-performer, side-show acts a woman juggles a weapon (razor, knife or scissors) against her body or other natural entity, a piece of fruit. Out in the open, out of the bathroom closet, so to speak, for all to see, shaving legs and underarms, paring an apple, and cutting off a braid of hair look like bizarre, sado-mascochistic acts that one would have to be perverse and deranged to perform.[36]

If *Cool Hands, Warm Heart* expressively reveals the latent violence and cruelty in ordinary womanly practices in patriachy, then Leslie Thornton's *Jennifer, Where Are You?* (1981) explores the ambivalences of growing up female. The central image is of a close-up of a very young girl playing with lipstick, presumably her mother's. The film begins as a nostalgic, humorous memory. Perhaps the girl is hiding in the attic as she plays, smudging lipstick all over her face, playing at being Mommy. Offscreen, we hear a voice (her father's) calling her. As the voice repeats, it seems to become angrier and angrier. What started as a pleasant memory begins to fill with anxiety. We begin to realize that the girl's play is really preparation for the role and costuming she will have to master to succeed on male terms in modern society. The play takes on burdensome connotations. As the girl's features grow consternated, she unknowingly signals to us the ambiguity of her "harmless" play acting.

The psychodrama is a serviceable form for feminists because it can express pain and anxiety while at the same time it can allegorically accuse the social formations that give rise to that pain and anxiety. Writing of *Marasmus* (1982), by Laura Ewig and Betzy Bromberg, Paul Arthur notes

The central figure of *Marasmus* moves through a series of brightly hallucinatory spaces, alternating roughly between the insular offices of a sterile skyscraper, bleak industrial sites, and even bleaker canyon terrain. There are multiple references to and metaphors for birth, death and abortion. The protagonist's body lies near an oil pipeline covered by a clear plastic shroud, the stillborn of this blight or its murdered victim. The relation between industry, female reproduction, and disease is signalled by the film's title, a children's ailment found in urban slums and rural poverty areas – almost entirely in the Third World – and caused by gross malnutrition; a disease where infants acquire the blank inanition, pained movement, and wrinkled skin of the aged, with bloated bellies that grotesquely recall pregnancy. The plastic shroud, a dry bush held in front of the woman's face, and skin shown through water, all suggest an attempt to empathize with this condition of starvation.[37]

The New Symbolism

The options explored in the reemerging psychodrama are an element in a larger phenomenon, the revival of interest in imagery not in terms of its deconstructive significance but because of an interest in its expressive and/or aesthetic qualities. The psychodrama pursues a concern with expressive qualities, employing quasi-narrative and dreamlike structures. However, the current interest in imagery need not occur in narrative contexts, nor need the image play be notable solely in terms of the projection of expressive qualities, that is qualities associated with human feelings, such as anger, anxiety, fearfulness, and so on. In Pat O'Neill's work, as Paul Arthur points out, there is a recurring imagistic theme in which the natural and the mechanical are conflated.[38] Through optical processing, in an O'Neill film like *Saugus Series* (1976), "natural elements such as clouds move with the speed or rhythm of mechanical objects; water is granted the colors of an industrial paint job; a potted cactus soars like an airplane."[39] Thus in O'Neill's work the viewer attends to a flow of images, remarking upon the arresting and unexpected way in which O'Neill qualitatively characterizes the objects he depicts. Water may suddenly appear metallic or a piece of paper organic.

Noting these aesthetic appearances becomes, in short, the focus of the spectator's preoccupation.

This concern with image play and with the projection of expressive and aesthetic properties is a major motive for Stuart Sherman, whose twenty or so short films represent one of the most original developing bodies of filmmaking today. Sherman is a performance artist. He specializes in a form of solo that he calls "spectacles." Most often he stands behind a folding table, like a magician. On the table, he arrays small objects – toys, paper clips, pieces of paper, glasses, cards, pocket-sized souvenirs – which he manipulates, for example, grouping all the similar objects together, touching every object with every other object, or proposing visual puns. The spectator follows these spectacles by catching onto the patterns of association that underlie Sherman's manipulations of objects, his image play. At times these associations are metaphorical but they are often simply systematic, the following through of a formal plan such as changing the position of every object on the table until they are all spatially reversed.

Turning from performance art to film, Sherman continues to be concerned with image play. *Flying* (1979), a film that is only a minute long, is a strong example of his procedure. The second shot is of a metal railing – an airport bannister – that runs horizontally across the screen; on the left, a hand mysteriously holds a suitcase handle, without a suitcase. The camera moves rapidly along the railing from left to right. Then there is a cut to a shot of the plane taking off in the same direction. This shot is executed from the perspective of a passenger inside the plane. As the camera rises at a gradually expanding acute angle, the hand is superimposed on the image, the handle still without a bag. This is an elegantly elliptical symbol for travel, charged expressively by the haunting partial absence of the traveler and his belongings. The image deftly and economically makes the point that they are now elsewhere.

Sherman's films are sometimes like short poems and sometimes like riddles that call attention to the expressive qualities of objects or that urge us to encounter familiar objects in a new light – comparing ice-skating rinks with diminutive ice-cubes, for example, in *Skating* (1978). By calling attention to the qualitative dimension of the world, Sherman reacts against the structural filmmaker's preoccupation with the qualities of film (or of filmic perception). In this way, Sherman's work is concerned with the return to content, though in this context "content" does not have the political connotations found in many contemporary filmmakers. Moreover, Sherman's reliance upon the associative play of images enables him to avoid the problems of didactic address that tends not only to take an academic approach to much academic film but to alienate it from wider audiences. Sherman's films are imaginative games or puzzles, in which any sensitive viewer can take part; they afford a forum for aesthetic and interpretive play on the part of spectators. Sally Banes notes that in *Roller Coaster/Reading* (1979).

Sherman proposes, through editing and parallel camera movement, that the act of reading is exhilarating, like riding a roller coaster. The conjuction of the two actions is established in the first shot, in which Sherman gets into the car of the roller coaster without looking up from the book he is engrossed in reading. In a series of symmetrical camera movements and compositions, a bookcase and the white wooden structure of a roller coaster are scanned and compared, with the camera moving upward or to the right (as if reading), or zooming in and out. The final pair of shots shows Sherman still reading, walking into the enormous roller coaster structure (whose double doorway resembles an open book) as the bookcase recedes.[40]

The theme of play pervades the films of Ericka Beckman, a leading figure in the return to expressive or qualitative imagery. In *We Imitate; We Break Up* (1978), a super-8 color, sound film, Beckman allegorically portrays the tensions she sees in male/female relationship through juxtaposed imagery. The film begins by cutting between the imaginary male protagonist – a pair of puppet legs manipulated by a rope and called Mario – and a young woman, played by Beckman, dressed as a schoolgirl. At first the girl imitates all of the puppet's movements, as if she too were on a string. The schoolgirl outfit and the imitation motif are symbols of being dominated. The man and woman play kickball, first cooperatively, then vengefully. In the middle of this symbolic quarrel, the girl takes the ball and comically runs away while the legs, now gigantic and threatening, pursue her interminably. A male figure bowls the kickball into animated household furniture that jumps aside into piles, literalizing the idea that the relationship has broken up. The songs that accompany the images are repetitive, like childish chants, while the images themselves are quite simple and easily understood in terms of their symbolic import. Shots, for example, of the girl "running away," are repeated endlessly so that they will be comprehended as metaphors. But also, their obsessive recurrence expressively indicates fixations that Beckman strives to ironize and distance through comedy and repetition. Yet the childhood references and the clarity of exposition give the piece an overall feeling of lightness rather than of brooding.[41]

Of course, in speaking of the return of the expressive or otherwise qualitative use of imagery, a single genre is not being discussed, but a refocusing of interest that can cut across genres. For example, one might make a found footage film, in the tradition of Cornell's *Rose Hobart*, whose purpose was not deconstructive but expressive. Conner's recent *Valse Triste* is a good example of this. Yet even though it is not isolatable to a genre, the discussion of a renewal of interest in expressive or qualitative imagery is not totally amorphous. For this renewal of interest takes place against a backdrop of both structural film and cinematic deconstructionism, which were concerned with images primarily in terms of their functioning as signs. Images were presented and were to be viewed at an analytic remove, like specimens under a microscope. This stance toward imagery is part and parcel of the tendency toward didacticism that has dominated the avant-garde imagination for two decades. The reinstatement of the image as a locus of expressive and aesthetic properties and as a symbol to be engaged in terms of interpretive play may supply a way out of the didactic impasse.

Diagnostically, it is helpful to note that the didacticism of structural film and later of cinematic deconstruction corresponds to the rise of the academic approach to film after the boom in movie connoisseurship in the sixties. Supporters of structural film and then deconstructionism were often academics involved themselves in trying to discover the nature of the medium or the symbol system about which they sought to erect a discipline. It should come as no surprise, then, that they had a special interest in films that were concerned with an enterprise similar to their own (and also, for that reason, eminently teachable). Moreover, it is easy to understand how, in this context, didactic rhetoric would be positively reinforced. Thus, even when deconstructionists claimed a political content for their work, in opposition to the supposedly contentless structural film, the preoccupation with the model of film as a lesson in the operation of symbol systems continued. Reflexive didacticism remained the presiding metaphor of avant-garde filmmaking.

But it is now quite some time since the movie boom led to the intensive study of film. We have examined the processes of filmmaking in academic writing and reflexive filmmaking for nearly twenty years. In regard to avant-garde filmmaking, it may be the case that the time for reflecting on the processes of filmmaking – even where that reflection is political – is past. The time has come again to use those processes to make images that are expressive and aesthetic, to make narratives and psychodramas, political and personal, that reflect first and foremost on life and the world rather than primarily on the medium and the sign. At present, the avant-garde film is in a state of crisis. The dominant movements of the last two decades appear to have either exhausted themselves or ground to a halt. There is no telling what will happen.

Notes

Introduction

1 For a definition of "moving images," see Noël Carroll, *Theorizing the Moving Image* (New York: Cambridge University Press, 1996).

2 For arguments against the film/language correlation, see Carroll, "Film, Attention and Communication," *The Great Ideas Today: 1996* (Chicago: Encyclopaedia Britannica Inc., 1996), pp. 2–49.

3 In America, auteurist criticism was best represented by the pioneering work of Andrew Sarris.

4 An example of descriptive criticism is Lois Mendelson and Bill Simon, "*Tom, Tom, the Piper's Son,*" *Artforum*, vol. 10, no. 1 (September 1971). Though descriptive criticism was encouraged by Annette Michelson – as both a professor at NYU and an editor at *Artforum* – I think that it is accurate to say both that she herself was not a descriptive critic, and that she did not take herself to be one.

5 See, for example, Susan Sontag, "Against Interpretation," *Against Interpretation* (New York: Dell, 1996), pp. 13–33.

6 I do not mean to suggest that these were the only available options at the time. Rather, they were the ones that addressed me where I lived. Perhaps some readers are struck by my failure to mention semiotics and Lacanian psychoanalysis here. Those approaches arrived on my horizon only after my commitment to close analysis was already fixed. When they arrived on the scene in New York, I did my best to resist them, often at tedious length. For some of my arguments against these approaches, see Carroll, *Mystifying Movies* (New York: Columbia University Press, 1988).

7 Here I take myself to be agreeing with David Bordwell's point that film interpretation may concern the meaning, the effects, *or* the functions of a feature of a film or an ensemble of film features. See David Bordwell, *Making Meaning: Inference and Rhetoric in the Interpretation of Cinema* (Cambridge: Harvard University Press, 1989), p. 262. See my "Interpreting *Citizen Kane*" (this volume) for an example of an interpretation that is not simply a matter of what might be called semantic meaning.

8 Bordwell, *Making Meaning*, p. 42.

9 I should also note that Bordwell and I probably disagree about the importance and usefulness of the notion of semantic fields and possibly over the question of whether meanings are projected rather than detected.

10 Here I should stress that I take appreciation to be an activity, one that when successfully engaged yields satisfaction (some might say pleasure) when it accords with the criteria of achievement internal to the activity. A key element of appreciative activity is sizing up or understanding (some might say contemplating) how a film works. In this sense, interpretation is a medium of appreciation and can be construed as an opportunity to derive satisfaction autotelically and, therefore, as a source of value. Here, of course, my emphasis is on the process of interpretation, rather than merely its propositional output. For further remarks on interpretation and value, see Carroll, "Art and Interaction," *Journal of Aesthetics and Art Criticism*, vol. 45, no. 1 (Fall 1986), pp. 57–68.

11 For an account of why I am not an autonomist, see Carroll, "Moderate Moralism," *British Journal of Aesthetics*, vol. 36, no. 3 (July 1996), pp. 233–238.

12 Janet Staiger, *Interpreting Films: Studies in the Historical Reception of American Cinema* (Princeton, NJ: Princeton University Press, 1992), pp. 97–131.

13 For some sense of what I mean by objectively plausible attributions, see Carroll, "Art, Intention and Conversation," in *Intention and Interpretation*, ed. Gary Iseminger (Philadelphia: Temple University Press, 1992), pp. 97–131.

14 Bordwell, *Making Meaning*, chap. 4.

15 Claude Levi-Strauss, "The Structural Study of Myth," *Structural Anthropology*, ed. Claude Levi-Strauss (Garden City, NY: Anchor Books, 1967), pp. 202–228.

16 Pierre Macheray, *A Theory of Literary Production* (London: Routledge and Kegan Paul, 1978).

17 Louis Althusser, "A Letter on Art in Reply to Andre Daspre (April 1966)" and "Cremonini Painter of the Abstract (August 1966)," in *Lenin and Philosophy*, ed. Louis Althusser (New York: Monthly Review Press, 1971), pp. 221–249.

18 Editors of *Cahiers du Cinema*, "John Ford's *Young Mr. Lincoln*," in *Narrative, Apparatus, Ideology: A Film Theory Reader*, ed. Philip Rosen (New York: Columbia University Press, 1986), pp. 444–482.

19 H. G. Gadamer, *Truth and Method* (London: Crossroad, 1986).

20 George Wilson, *Narration in Light: Studies in Cinematic Point of View* (Baltimore: Johns Hopkins University Press, 1986), p. 203.

21 Both essays are in Carroll, *Theorizing the Moving Image*.

22 The course was George Amberg's Introduction to Film Theory.

1. The Cabinet of Dr. Kracauer

1 For example, Erwin Panofsky, "Style and Medium in the Motion Pictures," in *Film Theory and Criticism*, ed. G. Mast and M. Cohen (New York: Oxford University Press, 1974), p. 169.

2 Siegfried Kracauer, *From Caligari to Hitler* (New York: Noonday Press, 1959), pp. 61–76.

3 For example, David Robinson, *The History of World Cinema* (New York: Stein and Day, 1974), p. 91.
4 Kracauer, 66–67.
5 Morton Schatzman, "Paranoia or Persecution: The Case of Schreber," *History of Childhood Quarterly: The Journal of Psychohistory*, vol. 1, no. 1, (Summer 1973), p. 81. For a more detailed account also see Schatzman's *Soul Murder: Persecution in the Family* (New York: Signet, 1973).
6 Walter Sokel, *An Anthology of German Expressionist Drama* (Garden City, NY: Doubleday, 1963), p. xvii.

3. The Gold Rush

1 Rudolf Arnheim, *Film as Art* (Berkeley: University of California Press, 1957), p. 107.
2 Northrop Frye, *Anatomy of Criticism* (Princeton: Princeton University Press, 1957), p. 39.
3 Ibid., pp. 43–44.
4 Roman Jakobson, *Studies on Child Language and Aphasia* (The Hague: Mouton, 1971), p. 70.
5 André Bazin, *What Is Cinema?* trans. by Hugh Gray (Berkeley: University of California Press, 1967), vol. 1, pp. 145–146.

4. Keaton: Film Acting as Action

1 For sustained analyses of the doubling structure throughout Keaton's narratives, see Daniel Moews, *Keaton: The Silent Features Close-up* (Berkeley: University of California Press, 1977).
2 For analyses of these gags from *The General*, as well as others not discussed in this paper, see Noël Carroll, *An In-depth Analysis of Buster Keaton's The General* (Ph.D. dissertation, New York University, 1976). The director of that thesis was Annette Michelson, whose influence on my approach to Keaton and to film in general has been profound.
3 The gags that I describe in terms of a duality of viewpoint can also be seen as a subset of what Bergson calls the reciprocal interference of (event) series: see Henri Bergson, *Laughter in Comedy*, ed: Wylie Sypher (Garden City: Doubleday Anchor Books, 1956), p. 123.
4 Bergson, p. 67.
5 Norman Maier, "A Gestalt Theory of Humor," *The British Journal of Psychology*, vol. XXIII, part I (July 1932), pp. 69–70.
6 David Robinson, *Buster Keaton* (Bloomington: University of Indiana Press, 1969), p. 79.

5. Buster Keaton, *The General*, and Visible Intelligibility

1 Penelope Houston, "The Great Blank Page." *Sight and Sound*, vol. 37 (April 1968), p. 65.

6. For God and Country

1 Sergei Eisenstein, *Film Form*, ed. and trans. Jay Leyda (New York: Harcourt, Brace and World, 1949), p. 63.
2 Ibid., pp. 62–63.
3 Eisenstein, *Film Sense*, (New York: Harcourt, Brace and World, 1942), p. 33.
4 Eisenstein, *Film Form*, p. 63.
5 Ibid., p. 82.
6 Quoted by Eisenstein, *Film Sense*, p. 32.
7 Ibid., p. 32.

8. Notes on Dreyer's *Vampyr*

1 See Mark Nash. "*Vampyr* and the Fantastic," *Screen*, vol. 3 (Autumn 1976): 29–67; Mark Nash, *Dreyer* (London: British Film Institute, 1977), pp. 56–57; David Bordwell, *The Films of Carl-Theodor Dreyer* (Berkeley: University of California Press, 1981), pp. 93–116.
2 Bordwell, *The Films of...*, p. 217.
3 Tzvetan Todorov, *The Fantastic* (Ithaca: Cornell University Press, 1975).
4 See Noël Carroll, *The Philosophy of Horror, or Paradoxes of the Heart* (New York: Routledge, 1990).
5 Carroll, *Philosophy of Horror*, chap. 3.
6 Ibid.
7 It should be stressed that the connection between Dreyer's film and LeFanu's novella is extremely tenuous. At most, it seems to me, both include suggestions of lesbianism and perhaps both converge somewhat, though in different ways, on the legend of Elizabeth Bathory.

   Another story by LeFanu from which Dreyer probably derived some inspiration is the non-horror mystery story "The Room in the Dragon Volant." In Chapter 26 of that story, the narrator Richard Beckett is drugged in such a way as to appear dead, although he is conscious and aware that he is about to be buried alive. This recalls the dream/funeral sequence in *Vampyr* in certain respects: most notably, Beckett hears the working of a turnscrew on the coffin while Gray sees it. This story is anthologized in Sheridan LeFanu's *Ghost Stories and Mysteries*, selected and edited by E. F. Bleiler (New York: Dover, 1975).

9. *King Kong*: Ape and Essence

1 Specifically, *Journey to the Center of the Earth* is a fictional tour through Lyell's *Principles of Geology* with a touch of John Cleves Symmon's hollow-earth thesis, Charles-Claire Deville's theories of volcanoes, and a strong dose of Cuvier.
2 In the mid-seventies AIP released two passable adaptations of Burroughs' prehistoric world tales under the titles of *The Land That Time Forgot* (1974) and *At the Earth's Core* (1976) .

3 The centrality of the abduction of women is also manifest in Burroughs' Pellucidar series, a total of seven novels, beginning with *At the Earth's Core* (1914), which are also in the prehistoric vein. The fauna of the underground world of Pellucidar has many similarities with Caspak's. Besides various pre-historic species, there are Sagoths (ape-men), humans, and Mahars. The Mahars are super-intelligent, winged reptiles who dominate Pellucidar and who kidnap humans to serve as slaves and for vile rituals as well. The Mahars are as nasty as the Weiroos and perform a similar narrative func-tion. Whereas the Weiroo are all male, the Mahars are all female. As a result of their science, they have learned to reproduce without males by using a secret formula. When a surface-side human hero, a savior-from-above fig-ure, steals that formula, the Mahars literally become endangered species.

The Mahars are virtually emotionless, cruel, highly intellectual, and hypnotic, like many fifties' sci-fi aliens who, in turn, bear strong resem-blances to certain earlier comic book, pulp fiction, and movie portraits of Nazis (and then Communists). The Mahars are also political tyrants, a proto-master race, who view humans suspiciously as potential threats. In *At the Earth's Core* and *Pellucidar* (1915), the surface-side human heroes (using their superior knowledge and technology) mount what we would call a war of national liberation which, given the prehistoric setting, is portrayed as a matter of species liberation in which the Mahars face extinction if the humans are the fittest. There is a long tradition of political allegory in lost world and Atlantean tales, both in the earlier satiric tradition and in the later adventure/melodrama strain. In the prehistoric tale à la Burroughs, the saga of a purportedly innate Anglo-Saxon loathing of tyranny is reinforced by biological metaphors which themselves reflect the Social Darwinist idiom that was used at the turn-of-the-century to talk "scientifically" about politics.

4 *Tarzan of the Apes* (1914) shares certain structures with the prehistoric novels, employing abductions/rescues and repetitive confrontation compli-cations, but it is also a more intricately designed and more interesting book than anything in the Caspak or Pellucidar series. This is not the place to explain why this is. However, *Tarzan* does seem worth considering vis-à-vis *King Kong* since Kong is somewhat of a fusion of two characters in *Tarzan*. Kong is, at first, Terkoz the ape, the abductor of Jane, but gradually he comes to resemble Tarzan, not only because he is a forest god who torments the natives and because he is ostensibly some kind of jungle orphan, but because he defends Ann Darrow in the wilderness as Tarzan defends Jane; though, of course, Kong is not as "civilized" (he can't read) as Tarzan.

5 One index of the popularity of Social Darwinism in the U.S. was the Spencer fad: from the 1860s to 1903, 368,755 copies of Spencer's works were sold in America, quite a heady turnover for sociological tomes in the nineteenth century. Social Darwinism was enough a part of the American vernacular for discussing politics that Burroughs' virtual allegorization of it was accommo-dated unflinchingly.

6 For some examples consider James J. Hill, ". . . the fortunes of the railroad companies are determined by the law of the survival of the fittest"; John D.

Rockefeller, "The growth of large business is merely the survival of the fittest . . ."; Andrew Carnegie, ". . . while the law may sometimes be hard for the individual, it is best for the race because it assures the survival of the fittest in every department." For these speakers, as for many Social Darwinists, evolutionary metaphors were a means to justify the status quo.

7 Perhaps this is why Harryhausen has felt the need to invent a new fantastic species – the mythological robot of which Minoton in *Sinbad and the Eye of the Tiger* (1977) is a prime example.

8 American prints of *Kong* were darker than British prints in order to avoid the censor's disapproval of streams of visible blood that oozed down the gorilla' s chest.

10. Becky Sharp Takes Over

1 Tom Milne, *Mamoulian* (Bloomington: Indiana University Press, 1969), p. 91.

2 Mitchell's play is available in *Monte Cristo and Other Plays*, ed. J. B. Rusak (Princeton, NJ: Princeton University Press, 1941).

3 For information on Jones see *The Theater of Robert Edmond Jones*, ed. Ralph Pendleton (Middletown, CT: Wesleyan University Press, 1958). Interestingly, Jones designed the sets for a production of Mitchell's *Vanity Fair* during the 1928–29 theater season.

4 In both the novel and the film, there are suggestions that Becky is to be understood as somewhat "Napoleonic."

11. Interpreting *Citizen Kane*

1 Ian Jarvie, *Philosophy of the Film: Epistemology, Ontology, Aesthetics* (London: Routledge and Kegan Paul, 1987), pp. 268–69.

2 Ibid., p. 271.

3 Ibid., p. 269.

4 Jorge Luis Borges, "*Citizen Kane*," in Focus on *Citizen Kane*, ed. Ronald Gottesman (Englewood Cliffs, NJ: Prentice-Hall, 1971), p. 127.

5 James Naremore, *The Magic World of Orson Welles* (New York: Oxford University Press, 1978), pp. 92–93.

6 Jarvie, *Philosophy of the Film*, p. 272.

7 It should be added that if the charge of "*ad hocery*" here can be made to stick, it will be especially problematic for Jarvie. For as a Popperian, he, himself, is especially critical of attempts to render hypotheses unfalsifiable by the addition of *ad hoc* explanations.

8 André Bazin, *Orson Welles* (New York: Harper and Row, 1978), p. 66.

9 Parker Tyler, *The Hollywood Hallucination* (New York: Simon and Schuster, 1970), pp. 199–207.

10 Naremore, *The Magic World* . . . , p. 93. Similarly, David Bordwell, who wants us to take Rosebud seriously, identifies the sled as an image of the absence of love and establishes the intellectual respectability of the device by arguing that "like Elizabethan tragedy, the film proposes that action

becomes an egotistical drive for power when not informed by love." See Bordwell's "The Dual Cinematic Tradition in *Citizen Kane*," in *The Classic Cinema*, ed. Stanley Solomon (New York: Harcourt Brace Jovanovich, 1973), p. 186. I should also note that I think that Bordwell's way of putting it is closer to the way the film characterizes Kane than is Naremore's.

11 Perhaps the emphasis Welles puts on changing Kane's makeup is also connected to the sense the audience has of Kane as a collection of selves.

12 The visual theme of the multiplicity of Kane is also in evidence in the enormous billboard that bestrode the marquee at the opening of the film in New York. For a photograph of this billboard, see Robert Carringer, *The Making of Citizen Kane* (Berkeley: University of California Press, 1985), p. 116.

13 Throughout his *The Making of Citizen Kane*, Robert Carringer is quite adept at tracing the collision of artistic styles in the decor of the film. See, for example, p. 54.

14 In the confrontation between Kane and Leland after the election failure, Kane offers a "Toast, Jedediah, to love on my terms. Those are the only ones anybody ever knows. His own."

15 Leland says that Kane has problems with the people because he (mistakenly) thinks he owns them; this problem disappears with his statues, since he does own them.

16 For most viewers, I suspect, the connection between Leland's mockery and the opening shots can be made only in retrospect and after re-viewing the film. But one thing that is notable about *Citizen Kane* is that it is designed for re-viewing. It rewards repeated viewings because of its camera style, as Bazin noted, but also because of the cross-correlational style of its interview structure: objects and events are constantly reframed from different perspectives. Amplifying Bazin, one might say, metaphorically, that to a certain extent the film has an "open temporal field" as well as an "open" spatial field. Thus, we notice the trophy the staff of the *Inquirer* earlier gave Kane in the warehouse scene at the end of the film; or we notice the glassy snowscape of the opening of the film amidst the clutter on Susan's vanity table in the scene where Kane first meets her. Tracing these cross-correlations affords a great deal of aesthetic pleasure in successive re-viewings of the film. Later, I shall argue that the kind of intellective play that encourages the re-viewing of the film is also encouraged by the narrative structure of the film in terms of what can be called its dialogical aspect. As well, the potential for re-viewing by participant audiences is part of what marks *Citizen Kane* as a work of *art* in one traditional, honorific sense of that notion; and this is relevant to the issue of mass art versus kitsch, with which this article will conclude.

17 Indeed, the sled literally figures as an important implement in the struggle (tussle) to separate young Charles from his family.

18 This recurring snowscape, of course, also refers back to Kane's separation from his family, which separation occurs during an idyllic winter's scene. The shots of the sled – being covered with snow – at the end of that scene would appear to associate visually the themes of that scene with Susan's glass bauble.

19 Again the statue imagery seems relevant, for statues are "people" Kane can own. Also, Susan Alexander dragoons the statues in her argument against Kane; he merely buys her things rather than giving her something of himself – and buying a bracelet is said to be emotionally equivalent to giving someone money for a statue that remains uncrated.

20 David Bordwell, "The Dual Cinematic Tradition in *Citizen Kane.*"

21 Indeed, the word "rosebud" may provide a psychological clue worth speculating about in this context. The second supplemented edition of the *Dictionary of American Slang* identifies "rosebud" as a slang expression, of homosexual origin, for the anus. In this respect, "Rosebud" may signal the anal character of Kane's obsession in a way that corresponds to the obvious anal-retentive play for control evinced in Kane's collecting. See Harold Wentworth and Stuart Berg Flexner (compilers), "Supplement," in *Dictionary of American Slang* (New York: Thomas Crowell Publishers, 1975), p. 737. Moreover, this connotation of the word "rosebud" might be used to reinforce Naremore's interpretation, which was cited earlier in this article.

22 That is to say that the strategy being discussed is not simply of formal significance but provides a way to draw viewers into a more general reflection upon the structure of human life and their culture's conception of it.

23 In their article, "Propositions," Noël Burch and Jorge Dana dismiss *Citizen Kane* for what they believe to be its conformism. This conformism amounts to the film's deployment of commonplace conceptions of human life. By denigrating the putative conformism of the film, Burch and Dana are ostensibly speaking politically. But I am not persuaded by their diatribe. In order to engage a general audience in reflection on the culture's views of human life, it seems appropriate to address them in terms of perspectives and problems which they are likely to find accessible and recognizable. To disallow this – in the name of some theoretically sophisticated view – seems to me, at the very least, utopian. It would suggest that no interchange with a general audience can ever be practicable. And the political efficacy of such a stance is surely dubious. See Noël Burch and Jorge Dana, "Propositions," *Afterimage*, vol. 5 (Spring 1974), pp. 40–65.

24 As I indicated earlier, I see the philosophical dialogue as a model for *Citizen Kane*, and it is in that sense that I attribute a "dialogical" structure to the film. I realize that the term "dialogical" is also presently employed by followers of Bakhtin. Since their use of the term would appear to require a much more radical play of meaning than I argue is relevant to *Citizen Kane*, my usage should not be confused with theirs.

25 See, for example, André Bazin, "Theater and Cinema – Part One," in *What Is Cinema?* Vol. I, ed. and trans. Hugh Gray (Berkeley: University of California Press, 1967), p. 92.

26 See, for example, André Bazin, *The Cinema of Cruelty* (New York: Seaver Books, 1982), pp. 7–8.

27 It has been remarked, by commentators like Brian Henderson (in "Two Types of Film Theory," in his *A Critique of Film Theory* [New York: Dutton, 1980]), that Bazin's approach to film lacks an appreciation of narrative. This is not completely true, as the preceding footnote indicates. Bazin does con-

ceive the importance of his favored cinematic style in terms of an overall narrative ensemble of effects. That is, he sees the significance of spatial realism in the context of an animating narrative project. Spatial realism, for Bazin, is consistent with a certain narrative effect. What *is* true is that this is not sufficiently or explicitly emphasized in his most famous essays on filmic style. However, I believe that an implicit commitment to the sort of narrative that prompts audience participation is in evidence in most of Bazin's writings.

At the same time, recalling that Bazin does conceive of the importance of spatial realism in concert with a concern with a certain form of narrative may help resolve one of the apparent puzzles people have concerning Bazin's approach. For though Bazin talks endlessly about spatial realism, it is often noted that full-blooded examples of shots of this sort are statistically rare even in some of the masterpiecs of the style Bazin defends. So the question becomes: Why did Bazin declare spatial realism to be so pervasive? One answer, which is part of the truth, is that those occasions when the camera style of spatial realism is mobilized are of particular significance. But another answer may be that, in Bazin's thinking, spatial realism is so enmeshed with an overall narrative approach that those famous deep-focus shots stand as an emblem for the narrating style that dominates whole films. Though statistically these shots are, at best, only intermittent, they galvanize the overall perspective of films like *Citizen Kane*. Thus, Bazin is correct in emphasizing them, insofar as they "summarize" an entire attitude toward narration.

Moreover, if the preceding analysis is correct and Bazin is really interested in spatial realism only in the context of an overall narrative ensemble, then it is clear why he pays scant attention to the presence of depth-of-field photography in much of what is called primitive cinema for though depth-of-field photography may be evident there, it is not integrated into an overall narrative style of the sort that Bazin favors.

28 Clement Greenberg, "Avant-Garde and Kitsch," in *Art and Culture* (Boston: Beacon Press, 1961). The political and cultural significance of this article is analyzed in: Serge Guilbaut, *How New York Stole the Idea of Modern Art* (Chicago: University of Chicago Press, 1983); and Victor Burgin, *The End of Art Theory* (Atlantic Highlands, NJ: Humanities Press International, 1986).

29 See Michael Denning, "Towards a People's Theater: The Cultural Politics of the Mercury Theater," *Persistance of Vision*, 7, 1989.

30 Douglas Gomery and Paul Arthur were somewhat puzzled by the concluding sections of this paper and demanded to know explicitly what its connection was to the earlier discussion of the enigma and Rosebud interpretations of the film. As I see it, if *either* the Rosebud or enigma interpretation of the film is correct, then the film would turn out to be kitsch according to Greenberg's conception of it. If, however, the film is dialogical, then it promotes the kind of participatory spectatorship that Greenberg regards to be the hallmark of genuine art. Thus, if the film is structured in the way that is advanced in the earlier parts of this paper, it is an example of mass art that is a candidate for consideration as genuine art, at least by Greenberg's lights.

This, of course, entails that movies can be authentic art, again under Greenberg's conception, and that the attempt to stimulate mass audiences by means of a mass medium is not automatically kitsch. And, this, in turn, suggests a way in which the elitism and/or hermeticism of Greenberg and subsequent avant-gardists is not inevitable, even on their own terms. One can, that is, make mass popular films, for example in the manner of *Citizen Kane*, for general audiences in, so to say, good aesthetic conscience. The significance of this for cultural politics should be obvious: there is no deep conceptual pressure, of the sort Greenberg suggests, for art to sever its relations with the general audience. Avant-garde isolationism is not the only alternative, even within the somewhat special, traditionally derived, theoretical framework that Greenberg invokes. That is, happily, a good aesthetic conscience *can be* compatible with a good political one.

13 Mind, Medium and Metaphor in Harry Smith's *Heaven and Earth Magic*

1 P. Adams Sitney. "Harry Smith Interview," *Film Culture,* no. 37 (Summer 1965), p. 10. Readers interested in descriptions of Smith's other films should consult the *Film-Makers Co-operative Catalogue,* Vol. 3 (1965), pp. 57–58.
2 Sitney, *Visionary Film* (New York: Oxford, 1974), p. 291.
3 Ibid.
4 Errol Harris, *Fundamentals of Philosophy* (New York: Holt Rinehart and Winston, 1969), p. 233.
5 John Locke, *Essay Concerning Human Understanding*, 11, 11, 17.
6 see Coleridge's *Biographia LITTERIA*.
7 Aron Gurwitsch, "On the Intentionality of Consciousness," II, *Philosophical Essays in Honor of Edward Husserl,* ed. by Marvin Farber (Cambridge, Mass.: Harvard, 1940), p. 125.
8 David Hume, *Treatise on Human Nature*, 1, 4, 2.
9 Hume. 1.4.6.
10 For example, Locke. 1, 2, 4.
11 Hume, 1, 4 6.
12 Hume, 1, 1, 3.
13 Sitney, "Interview," 10.
14 Sigmund Freud, *The Interpretation of Dreams* (New York: Avon, 1965), pp. 327–330.
15 Freud, *On Dreams* (New York: Norton, 1952), p. 50.
16 Eisenstein footnotes Freud in "Word and Image." *Film Sense* (New York: Harcourt, Brace, and World, 1942), p. 7.
17 Sitney, "Interview," p. 11.
18 Freud, *Interpretation of Dreams,* p. 328.
19 This type of association is specifically discussed by Freud.
20 Sitney, *Visionary Film,* p. 292.
21 Freud, "Psychoanalytic Notes on an Autobiographical Account of a Case of

Paranoia." *Standard Edition. The Complete Works of Sigmund Freud.* Vol. 12 (London: Hogarth Press, 1958).

14. Welles and Kafka

1 Erich Auerbach, *Mimesis* (Garden City, NY: Doubleday, 1957), chap. 1.
2 Georg Lukacs, *Realism in Our Time* (New York: Harper, 1971), pp. 47–92.
3 Franz Kafka, *The Trial* (New York: Modern Library, 1956), p. 123.
4 Theodor Adorno, *Prisms* (London: Neville Spearman, 1967), p. 255.
5 Kafka, *The Trial,* p. 135.
6 Boris Eikhenbaum, "Problems of Film Stylistics," *Screen* (Autumn 1974), p. 30.
7 Thomas Kavanagh, "*The Trial* as Semiology," *Novel* (Spring 1972), pp. 242–253.

16. Identity and Differences: From Ritual Symbolism to Condensation in Anger's *Inauguration of the Pleasure Dome*

1 The historical information concerning Inauguration throughout this article is based on P. Adams Sitney, *Visionary Film* (New York: Oxford, 1974), pp. 104–115. I have benefited not only from Sitney's impressive research but from his careful interpretation of the film. I think the present interpretation is compatible with most of Sitney's account. I also hope that it adds something new to our understanding of *Inauguration* by analyzing the overall structure of the film in terms of more reductive categories than Sitney's mythopoetic vocabulary. By this, I do not mean to criticize Sitney but to explain why I am bothering to write in an area where such authoritative criticism already exists.
2 Norman O. Brown, *Love's Body* (New York: Vintage, 1966), p. 161.
3 Some readers may wonder why I talk about ritual symbolism at such length, arguing that I could analyze the entire film by means of dream symbolism. Such readers might hold that since ritual symbolism has its psychic provenance in the structures of the primary process, the emphasis on a contrast between the tropes of ritual and dream is really a distinction without a difference. My justification for the ritual/dream cleavage is twofold. First: whether or not ritual symbolism can be explicated by the operation of oneiric processes, the imagery in *Inauguration* is experienced as more stable, public, and historical in its meanings than the imagery of dream. Thus, in explaining how these images function communicatively, it seems appropriate to situate them in the public setting which gives them meaning, viz., ritual. Second: the hieratic gestures, the clothing, the pacing, and events resemble those of ritual. It seems *prima facie* correct to examine the film as it is presented, i.e., to unravel its meanings in a ritual context.
  As a side note, it should be added that the type of magico-metaphysical ceremony found in *Inauguration* has precedents in theatrical pieces done by

both MacGregor Mathers and Aleister Crowley. These mages, like Anger, artistically projected oceanic, symbolist cosmologies, reconciling fundamental opposites through strategies of synethesia. For information see J. F. Brown, "Aleister Crowley's *Rites of Eleusia*," *The Drama Review*, vol. 22, no. 2 (T78, June 1978), pp. 3–27.

4 Sitney is also pushed to narration as the natural means of explicating *Inauguration*.

5 Most often I think we can discuss avant-garde films quite adequately by suggesting the types of effects the film is designed to engender and then supplying some concrete examples of how those effects are achieved. For an example, see the section on flicker films in my "Toward a Theory of Film Editing," in *Millennium Film Journal*, no. 3.

6 Arnold Van Gennep, *The Rites of Passage* (Chicago: University of Chicago Press, 1960), p. 113.

7 I interpret the introduction of the Scarlet Woman this way because the tilt up the body reminds me of the way one examines one's attire in a looking-glass.

8 Van Gennep, p. 54.

9 Van Gennep, pp. 20–21.

10 For an account of decomposition see Robert Rogers, *The Double in Literature* (Detroit: Wayne State University Press, 1970). In discussing the mirror imagery I have not made reference to the Lacanian notion of the mirror-stage because I believe Anger is deliberately employing the motif of the mirror/*doppelgänger*. I do not believe that it is historically plausible to postulate that Anger's mirrors allude to Lacan (whereas, of course, I emphatically agree that LeGrice's and Wollen's and Mulvey's reflectors are beamed directly at Paris). My primary concern is with what the mirrors signify in *Inauguration*. To dissenters who would argue that the mirror/*doppelgänger* association can ultimately be explained in terms of Lacan's analysis of the mirror stage, I must reply that I think that that is an interesting debate for meta-psychologists, but not for film critics. And it is as a film critic that I assert that the mirror/*doppelgänger* association is the most appropriate exegesis of the mirror as it functions symbolically in *Inauguration*.

11 Victor Turner, *The Ritual Process* (Chicago: Aldine 1969), pp. 131–165.

12 Robert Rogers, *Metaphor, A Psychoanalytic View* (Berkeley: University of California Press, 1978), pp. 25–26.

13 Van Gennep, p. 29.

14 Sitney, p. 113.

15 I suspect Sitney's rejoinder would be that the beating is a displacement for the sacrifice. And this could be the case. Yet, I think the data is woefully indeterminate on this issue. That is, the beating might be a displacement for a whole range of ceremonies. It might be a purification. My point is simply that we are not compelled to interpret it as *sparagmos*.

16 This particular connotation of fire is exploited by Sylvia Plath in "Lady Lazarus."

17 Sigmund Freud, *The Interpretation of Dreams* (New York: Avon Books, 1965), p. 172.

18 Ibid., p. 328.

20. The Future of Allusion : Hollywood in the Seventies (and Beyond)

1 If Kasdan's work on *Continental Divide* ('81) seems less derivative than the films named here, one must still remember the degree to which it is simply an updating of the classic Hollywood battle-of-the-sexes motif.

2 By this I mean that in interpreting recent films, the appearance of a correspondence between a new film and an old film is used as a criterion or ground for asserting that the new film is making a comment of some sort. That is, it asks us to apply what we know of the old film to the new film's point of view on its materials. To see how this operates, consider a literary, noncinematic allusion from *Ragtime*, one that the film repeats from Doctorow's novel. The Coalhouse Walker episode bears several similarities, including the onomastic resemblance, to Kleist's *Michael Kohlhaas,* the story of a man who leads a peasant revolt because his horses are destroyed at an aristocrat's illegal tollgate. In recognizing the allusion to Kleist's novella, we feel the reinforcement of the theme of the rage of justice as well as its universalization across time and culture. In *Reds* ('81), some viewers have taken the dog as a reference to Asta, which, in turn, is taken to cast the Reed/Bryant relationship under the metaphor of the relationship of Nick and Nora Charles. The tenuousness of this fit suggests that something has to be added to similarity or that the relevant modes of similarity have to be refined in order for a given similarity to amount to an allusion. My claim is that, with contemporary film viewing, similarity can generally be used as a starting point for isolating an allusion even if it is not a sufficient condition for allusion. The Steady-cam point-of-view shots of the creature in *Halloween II* ('81), for example, are not allusions to *Halloween* ('79) but are rather a continuation of a stylistic donnée of the original. On the other hand, the clips from Romero's *Night of the Living Dead* ('67) in *Halloween II* are allusions to Romero's film because of their obvious aptness as an annotation of what is happening in the new film. This suggests that aptness needs to be joined to similarity in order to constitute an allusion.

The preceding paragraph jumps easily from the discussion of high art to low art. This may surprise readers who are more accustomed to essays in art and literary criticism than film criticism. Those older disciplines focus attention on a limited range of works of roughly the same degree of (high) ambition. Such works belong to a commonly agreed upon canon. Film criticism, though often in search of a canon, has no agreements about how to close off entry to its proposed canons in such a way that lowly genre films like *Night of the Living Dead* can be differentiated a priori from the lofty ambitions of films like *Reds*. Anything can be taken seriously in film criticism; this is the price auteurism paid in its effort to redeem American film from the denigration it suffered at the hands of the high-art, especially the literary, establishment. This entire essay reflects the film-world tendency to take any kind of film as potentially serious, that is, as aspiring to seriousness. I do not do this because I am attempting to construct my own canon, but because one cannot understand the current practices of the film world unless one takes an insider's viewpoint. One tenet of that viewpoint – shared by certain filmmakers, critics, and viewers – is that any kind of film, from a chintzy horror film to a multimillion-dollar "personal" film, can be a candidate for consideration as a major work.

3 Paul Mazursky might also seem to be a nominee for this company, but his fetishism of Fellini is too pronounced.

4 Though this essay for the most part emphasizes recent dramatic film, it should be clear that mainstream film comedy in the seventies also evinced an obsession with film history and allusion – were not Woody Allen and Mel Brooks the regnat comic directors of the period? Even Richard Lester's stunning swashbucklers – *The Three Musketeers* ('74), *The Four Musketeers* ('75), and *Robin and Marion* ('76 – depend on some awareness of film history, since their humor is often the product of the subversion of the bodily gracefulness associated with the classical costumer. Their expressive qualities – their roughness and joie de vivre—rely on the interruption of the flawless acrobatics, boundless energy, and good manners of a well-entrenched Hollywood form.

5 The idea that the modern filmmaker *should* be a director with personal touches, concerns, themes, etc., is also a consequence of American auteurism, which has served to define the proper expectations that contemporary auteurs should set for themselves. Furthermore, the idea of the Director, initially inspired by auteurism, has within the last decade come to be increasingly reinforced by film criticism, which, also influenced by auteurism, uses the category of the Director as central for cataloging films and plot developments (i.e., changes in so-and so's style, etc.). As a category, the Director is a convenient means for keeping track of the mass of information a reviewer must process as well as a rhetorical device through which a critic claims authority.

Throughtout this essay I continually advert to the relation between serious film viewing and serious filmmaking. Obviously within the class of serious film viewers there is a very special group, the ever-expanding numbers of historically savvy film critics. Often they act rather like conductors in the game of allusion. That is, by constantly noting allusions in their writings, they implicitly tell the audience that this is how to watch a film while simultaneously rewarding filmmakers for their allusions in a way that invites more of the same. Needless to say, allusionism is also valuable to the critic because it affords the opportunity to adopt the role of guardian of specialized knowledge.

As the foregoing suggests, the kinds of influences and, to a certain extent, the role of the critic have been changing during the seventies. The relation of Hollywood to the critics has altered as Hollywood's symbol systems altered. And these, of course, are terms connected within a complex network of causal interaction.

6 Along with genres, remakes of classic films have been embraced by Hollywood as a hedge against an insecure future. The logic behind both moves is related: if something worked once it will work again. Also, remakes, like genres, can provide ready-made pretexts for studied rework-

ings. Witness *Invasion of the Body Snatchers* ('78), *The Postman Always Rings Twice* ('81), and even *The Incredible Shrinking Woman* ('81).

7   Though this section deals with genres, it is important to note that Altman's relation to historical film styles is also complex. Altman's debts to the Renoiresque tradition of realism are many, including the openness of his frame, his blocking, the busyness of his soundtracks, his direction of actors, and his commitment to accommodating the conflicting viewpoints of different characters in his "grand scheme of things." Concerning this, I am at least tempted to say that Altman is not just someone who was influenced by the Renoir tradition but someone who essentially imitates it and rather expands it. If this is true, then it would seem that much of Altman's meanings are primarily a function of allusions to a style that already has strongly associated values, such as freedom, spontaneity, vitality, and so forth. To clarify this point, contrast Altman to Kubrick. Kubrick works in the tradition of Welles (rather than that of Renoir); Kubrick emphasizes monumental compositions of great solidity, and he is also a montagist. But Kubrick is not parasitic on Welles for his expressive qualities. Though formal properties are shared, Kubrick uses them to create a greater distance, sense of circumspection, and feeling of implacability than does Welles. Whereas Altman often depends on his tradition to fix the meaning of his formal choices, Kubrick, while belonging to a tradition, uses it to generate his own original cluster of expressive qualities.

Throughout the seventies, perhaps as a result of *Battle of Algiers* ('65), directors self-consciously adopted styles with established connotations as a means of making comments about the fictional worlds of their films. For example, Scorsese tells us as clearly as he can that the culture of Little Italy is "raw," "authentic," and "real" in *Mean Streets* ('73) by using a cinema-verité style – that is , a style linked to these very adjectives. I suspect that Altman is involved in the same type of allusionism.

Like *Battle of Algiers*, *Psycho* ('60) is an influential forerunner in this particular use of allusion, which we might call style-as-symbol. In *Psycho* Hitchcock stresses the banality of his fictional world by intentionally adopting, after the florid stylization of *Vertigo* ('58), the modest look and style of a TV program. The use of this style is not mysterious or obscure; think of vulgar examples like *What a Way to Go* ('64).

8   Other revisionist westerns are *The Culpepper Cattle Company* ('72), *Dirty Little Billy* ('72), *Little Big Man* ('70), (probably) *Bad Company* ('72), *Pat Garrett and Billy the Kid* ('73), *The Great Northfield Minnesota Raid* ('72) in terms of the portrayal of Jesse James especially, *The Ballad of Cable Hogue* ('70), and *Missouri Breaks* ('76) as a late entry. During the height of the genre's popularity in the late sixties and early seventies, many cowboy-films, such as *War Wagon,* were anything but reworkings, and there were genre reworkings made that were not revisionist, such as *The Shootist* ('76). By the mid-seventies, the western had spent itself, its residual energies absorbed by cop films.

Attempts to revive the genre, mostly through reworking, have appeared in the last few year. *Comes a Horseman* ('78) and *The Long Riders* ('79) have attempted to do this by elongating the pace of the past, giganticizing the everyday. *Days of Heaven* ('78) also adopts a drawn-out cadence to rework the genre, as well as a battery of other defamiliarizing techniques that makes the old West seem like Mars. The disaster of *Heaven's Gate* ('80), however, should put a damper on any wholehearted attempt to reinstate the genre in the near future.

9 Clark's *Murder by Decree* ('79) is also an interesting example of expression by genre variation. It works through combining two subgenres – the classical detective and hard-boiled modes – in order to underscore the enormity of its outrage over governmental conspiracy; it does this by having Sherlock Holmes behave like a private eye, showing feelings and dealing in fisticuffs. The genre transgression is meant to mirror the seriousness of the crime. Clark is an old hand at using genres as a tool of political statement. His *The Night Walk* ('72)exploits the vampire film to comment on the Vietnam War in relation to the social values that produced it.

The British have also been very active in detective reworkings throughout the seventies. Hodge's *Get Carter* ('71) and Frear's *Gumshoe* ('72) are examples of allusionist English films that take the historical mystery film as a starting point. Though many would disagree, I would argue that Winner's *The Big Sleep* ('78), an Anglo-American coproduction, is also a respectable mystery reworking.

Throughout this essay the majority of examples are in the nature of allusions to the narrative, dramatic, and thematic content of earlier films rather than to their cinematic style. This, I think, reflects the direction of allusionism as it is currently practiced. One reason for this might be that auteurist criticism, despite its proclaimed antiliterary bent, tended primarily toward narrative/dramatic/thematic analysis rather than to the discrimination of visual, audio, and cinematic modes of stylization. Thus, contemporary allusionists, depending on the codified commonplaces of received criticism, recapitulate the tendencies of American auteurism. Of course, there are many exceptions to this observation; perhaps Martin Scorsese is the most notable.

10 On the other hand, Romero's *Dawn of the Dead* ('79) was quite a financially successful reworking and one far more loaded with inside allusions (for example, to motorcycle films) than Kubrick's *The Shining*. The moral seems to be that you can have hermeticism as long as the action keeps moving fast enough that the general audience isn't annoyed.

For the past several years the horror film has been a major vehicle for reworking. One looming tendency in this field is the use of the horror format to illustrate metaphors of pop psychology, for example, all of Cronenberg's films and *The Howling* ('81). It is interesting to note that the current horror-film cycle correlates with several other social preoccupations that, in turn, are related to the latent content of horror-film imagery. What I have in mind are the seventies' obsessions with sexual experimentation, ecology (especially pollution), and the resurgence of religion – cults, established and otherwise, are flourishing a decade after the death of God.That horror is the major genre of the seventies may be explained by the fact that no other genre combines sex, themes of pollution, and religion so well.

The horror genre is also allusionistically invoked in nonhorror films such as *Apocalypse Now* ('79), the last section of which effectively becomes a monster film through its use of lighting, scale, and mystifying spatiality. This, of course, is meant as a visualization of the theme of "the horror" that issues in the dialogue. (Perhaps Coppola got the idea of an allusion to the horror-film genre from *Citizen Kane*, a film whose opening uses thirties-Gothic stylizations as a means to metaphorically introduce the monster in the mansion and the "ghost" in Kane).

11 In *Taxi Driver* Schrader joined a director who more than matched his own passion for cross-reference. For instance, towards the end of the film, Scorsese footnotes his violence as Fulleresque by copying a widely admired camera movement from *Park Row* ('52).

12 In *Escape from New York* ('81),Carpenter has the hero, Snake, speak in that choked whisper Clint Eastwood perfected as the man-with-no-name in the Leone series and *Hang 'em High* ('68); thus we know how really mean this guy is.

13 Spielberg also used the Road Runner allusion in *Sugarland Express* ('74), where it worked quite effectively, first as a comparison and then ultimately as an ironic contrast to the pursuit in the film. While not alluding to specific cartoons, Russ Meyer relies on references to Hollywood, especially Warner Brothers, cartoons to evoke his particular comic-plastic view of the body. What is important in this context is that both Spielberg and Meyer differ from someone like Tashlin. Tashlin treated live-action film as if it were capable of cartoon physics. Meyer alludes to cartoons to suggest that the pornographic urge is antirealistic, essentially a form of caricature based on deformation through exaggeration. The content of Spielberg's references is even more specific, grounded in the use of very definite sources which make exact comments about given scenes and stories.

14 Midnight cult films such as *The Rocky Horror Picture Show* ('75) and *The Love Thing* ('80) also rely on allusion; however, they are not constructed on the two-tiered model of communication. Their meaning remains hermetic, hidden in the system of allusion. Undoubtedly this is one reason they succeed as cult films – one must have knowledge of the allusions as well as grasp their sub rosa connotation; to do this is to be of the select. Such Morrisey/Warhol collaborations as *Heat* ('72) are relevant forerunners of this type of allusion.

Douglas Crimp pointed out to me that the extreme emphasis on historical references and historical pastiches involved in the Hollywood practice of allusionism raises questions about its relation to the phenomenon of post-modernism in the other arts. Though social factors – such as the rise of the arts-education system – may be common causes of Hollywood allusionism and the various postmodernisms, Hollywood allusion as currently practiced diverges from, for example, postmodernist activity in the visual arts as represented by such artists as Laurie Anderson, Robert Longo, Sherrie Levine,

Cindy Sherman, Richard Prince, Jack Goldstein, and Troy Brauntuch. Two immediate distinctions to be drawn between Hollywood allusion and these postmodernists are: first, Hollywood allusionism involves a two-tiered system of communication whereas these postmodernists operate on a one-tiered system of recondite meanings (even though they justly point out that they are more accessible than the minimalists); and second, Hollywood allusionism is undertaken for expressive purposes whereas postmodernism, like modernism, refers to artifacts of cultural history for reflexive purposes, urging us to view the products of media as media. Undoubtedly some of these postmodernists were influenced by the auteurist project; their knowledge of the history of film is often evident. But their use of that knowledge subserves their deeper commitment to the esoteric dialectics and unflinching reflexivity of modernism. Perhaps Hollywood allusionism is more akin to postmodernist architecture, for example, a work such as Charles Moore's Piazza d'Italia in New Orleans. Postmodern architecture is a two-tiered system; while building structures for public use, it packs its edifices with esoteric quotations. At the same time, however, Hollywood allusionists are essentially respectful of their forebears whereas postmodernist architects are repudiating their predecessors.

15 I do not mean to suggest that the Americans should have slavishly imitated Godard in every respect. The last thing cinema needs is still more earnest, gaseous, self-proclaiming philosopher-manqués drifting on the ether of undigested ideas. Nevertheless, some sustained American commitment to modernism might have been beneficial. Perhaps Brecht himself could have served as a model for a cinema that would have been both reflexive and popular.

16 Some people, hearing my argument, have asked why I believe allusionistic filmmakers are deceiving themselves. These critics seem to think that filmmakers like DePalma put allusions in their work but don't think that the allusions come to much or are very important. The filmmakers are just goofing around. I find this psychological explanation hard to swallow. Why waste your time on these allusions? Why array them so carefully (and coherently) unless you really want them to mean something special? Admittedly this is not an absolutely conclusive rejoinder to my critics – people, yes, even filmmakers, have been known to act in peculiar ways. But I think that on any model of artistic psychology and artistic communication that presupposes purposiveness on the part of contemporary filmmakers, we must assume that they have a reason for what they are doing and that that reason is probably connected with the obvious communication they are achieving. This is another way of saying that they must be serious. But if they think that the way they are attempting to be serious in unproblematic, then they are self-deceived.

    In conversation David Bordwell has noted that one reason that the allusion/pastiche style is attractive to filmmakers is that it provides a perfect forum in which a director can display consummate virtuosity – mastery of all and every style. Though Bordwell has not yet developed this idea, we can conjecture that allusionism in this light might be seen as a celebration of skill and professionalism for their own sake. This is certainly a preoccupation of this decade. Allusionism becomes the means of presenting the artist in terms of ultra-competence rather than genius, as technically brilliant rather than profound, as a manipulator rather than an innovator.

This clearly sounds like the profile of ambition for many walks of life since the mid-seventies. A defense mechanism is obviously at work when one's social world is defined by cynicism, disillusionment, and a sense of impossibility. If you can only survive as a movie apparatchik, then you might as well at least let everyone know that you are as skilled as any apparatchik can be, or was in the past.

21. Back to Basics

1 The word *genre* comes from the Latin *genus*, a kind or a sort, a category based on regularly recurring patterns. Westerns, for example, repeat certain settings (the American West in the 19th century), actions (gunfights), and certain hero-villain plot structures. But there is no one set of criteria for identifying genres. A Western must be set in the West, but a musical can be set in any time or place, as long as there is singing and dancing. A *film noir*, on the other hand, has more specific demands: a downbeat mood, signaled by dark lighting and rain-slick streets, a contemporary setting, and a pessimistic plot line. Horror films, to cite a final example, are named after the emotion they provoke.

2 At the top of *Variety*'s list, with $228 million in U.S. and Canadian film rentals collected by its distributor, Universal, is *E.T: The Extra-Terrestrial*. It is followed by *Star Wars, Return of the Jedi, The Empire Srikes Back, Jaws, Ghostbusters, Raiders of the Lost Ark, Indiana Jones and the Temple of Doom, Beverly Hills Cop*, and *Grease*.

3 The newcomers and their credits include: Joe Dante (*Gremlins*), Brian DePalma (*Body Double*), Tobe Hooper (*Poltergeist, Lifeforce*), Lawrence Kasdan (*Body Heat, Silverado*); John Landis (*National Lampoon's Animal House, The Blues Brothers*); Nicholas Meyer (*Star Trek II: The Wrath of Khan*); Ivan Reitman (*Ghostbusters*); and Robert Zemeckis (*Romancing the Stone, Back to the Future*).

4 "Slasher" films, in the tradition of *Psycho*, are those in which victims are done in by knives and axes. "Splatter" movies take advantage of sophisticated new special effects: Victims either explode on-screen or deteriorate in gruesome ways.

22. Amy Taubin's Bag

1 For a fuller description of Taubin's work in theater, see Carroll, "Amy Taubin: The Solo Self," *The Drama Review*, vol. 23, no. 1 (T81, March 1979).

2 Jean-Paul Sartre, *Being and Nothingness*, trans. Hazel Barnes (New York: Philosophical Library, 1956), especially part III, chap. 1, sec. IV.

3 The *Lacemaker* is a painting with intertextual significance for avant-garde filmmakers. It appears as early as *Un Chien Andalou* where Bunuel and Dali, like Taubin, abuse it. In that film, it is parodied by being juxtaposed to a transvestite bicyclist who wears a collar mockingly similar to that of the woman in the portrait. A more recent historical reference which Taubin might have in mind could be Michael Snow, who has claimed Vermeer as a source of inspiration for *Wavelength* and ↔ ("Letter," *Film Culture*, vol. 46, no. 5). Insofar as *In the Bag* is a repudiation of minimalism, the destruction of *The Lacemaker* might be read as part of a larger campaign of aggression.

The picture also bears a series of overdetermined relations to *In the Bag*. The woman in the painting is hunched over, riveted to her work with a quality of undivided attentiveness which one finds in other Vermeer paintings such as *The Geographer, The Astronomer, The Milkmaid, Lady Reading a Letter by the Window*, etc. That quality of preoccupation is, of course, echoed by Taubin in the film. Also, the lacemaker is sewing a tapestry of that sort that figures as a detail in many Vermeer paintings, e.g. *Girl Drinking with Gentlemen*, and that tapestry has a great deal of blue in it. Taubin's bag is also a sewn thing made of pieces of Middle Eastern fabric, a quilt with many blue patches. At the same time, Taubin defines herself against the lacemaker, that woman is making a work of art by putting together tiny little things whereas Taubin makes her work by tearing small things apart.

4 The color throughout the film – soft blues and browns and deep reds – is very soothing in a way that imparts an added quality of "quietness" to the imagery. However, in this section of flash inserts, and the one at the end, the colors no longer softly blend but clash harshly. The color timing seems to have been altered to make the colors harder and colder, thus increasing the sense of turmoil.

5 What is susurrated on the soundtrack is a cluster of idioms about "cutting" – "cut down to size," "cut ups," "cut off," etc. These apply not only to the action in the film but to the concurrent, assertive, rapid editing. It is also interesting to note that this favoring of clusters of idioms corresponds to Taubin's use of verbal images which I discuss later in the essay by means of the idea of literary conceits.

The other burst of language in the film centers around idioms of "losing" – "lose ground," "lose face," "lose sight of" and so on. The original title of the film was to have been *Cutting Her Losses*.

6 With a Structural Film, it would be customary to say that once the narrative interest is denied, we would be forced to become attentive to the objects *qua* objects. However, once the overarching search metaphor is in place in *In the Bag*, we look for further metaphors.

7 See Carroll "Causation, the Ampliation of Movement and Avant-Garde Film," *Millennium Film Journal*, nos. 10/11.

8 For information on task-dances and task-performances see Sally Banes, *Terpsichore in Sneakers: Post-Modern Dance* (Boston: Houghton Mifflin Co., 1980). For some discussion of the theoretical significance of the task-genre see Noël Carroll and Sally Banes, "Working and Dancing," *Dance Research Journal*, vol. 15, no. 1 Fall/Winter 1982–1983.

9 For discussions of Structuralist Theater see the issue of *The Drama Review* devoted to that subject – T83.

10 This section of the essay may seem obscure to some readers because it is often claimed that minimalist works do not have expressive qualities. I, on the other hand, believe that they necessarily have certain types of expressive qualities. My argument is stated in "Post-Modern Dance and Expression," *Philosophical Essays on Dance*, ed. Gordon Fancher and Gerald Myers (Brooklyn: Dance Horizons, 1981).

11 For an account of the verbal image, see my "Language and Cinema: Preliminary Notes for a Theory of Verbal Images," *Millennium Film Journal*, nos. 7/8/9.

12 David Hume, *A Treatise of Human Nature* (Oxford: Oxford University Press, 1978), p. 252.

13 Obviously the fact that we can consistently derive the idea of "the search for self" from the film also lends further confidence to the imputation that the film is about the self. In the preceding paragraph I have supplied reasons independent of the explanatory coherence imparted by the "search for self" metaphor for claiming that *In the Bag* is about the self. However, this should not be taken as a denial that explanatory coherence is relevant to the plausibility of my interpretation.

14 For a detailed explication of the concept of overlapping metaphorical systems see George Lakoff and Mark Johnson, *Metaphors We Live By* (Chicago: University of Chicago Press, 1980), especially chap. 17. As the paragraph above suggests I, at least, think that the idea of overlapping metaphorical systems might be adapted fruitfully to study the structure of certain forms of poetry.

It should be noted that like Lakoff and Johnson, I regard the existence of commonplace metaphors as salutary. There is an opposing position that regards them as ideologically pernicious, and which might scorn artworks based on them. For an ideological attack on commonplace idioms see Anton C. Zijderveld, *On Clichés: The Supersedure of Meaning by Function in Modernity* (London: Routledge and Kegan Paul, 1979). Personally, I find this an example of Critical-Theory-type sociology at its worst, most specious, speculative extreme.

15 Another loose correspondence between *In the Bag* and certain sonnet forms is that the film concludes with a dramatic reversal.

Though I have analyzed *In the Bag* using the concept of the literary conceit, it may be possible to derive a similar explication employing Michael Riffaterre's notion of a *hypogram*. See his *Semiotics of Poetry* (Bloomington: Indiana University Press, 1978).

23. Herzog, Presence, and Paradox

1 Stan Brakhage, *Metaphors on Vision*, ed. with an introduction by P. Adams Sitney, a special issue of *Film Culture* 30 (Fall 1963), unpaginated.

2 Werner Herzog, *Of Walking in Ice*, translated by Matje Herzog and Alan Greenberg (New York: Tanam Press, 1980), 90.

3   "Images at the Horizon," a workshop with Werner Herzog, conducted by
    Roger Ebert at the Facets Multimedia Center, Chicago, Illinois, April 17,
    1979. Translated, annotated, and edited by Gene Walsh, p. 20.

4   The research for this paper was conducted in late 1982 and early 1983 in
    preparation for its delivery at the conference on New German Cinema held
    in 1983. It is for this reason that no Herzog film released after *Fitzcarraldo* is
    included in the discussion. I owe special thanks to New Yorker Films for
    allowing me to review a number of Herzog films and to Joyce Rheuban,
    Stuart Liebman, Tony Pipolo, and John Locke for their comments and
    encouragements.

24. Film in the Age of Postmodernism

1   Throughout I am making the assumption that to the extent that one would
    want to speak of postmodern film, one would want to restrict one's compass
    to avant-garde film. For an argument denying the label "postmodern" to
    commercial film, see Carroll, "The Future of Allusion: Hollywood in the
    Seventies (And Beyond)," *October*, vol. 20 (Spring 1982). That essay is also
    contained in this volume.

2   From the above, the reason should be clear as to why I want to restrict the
    application of "postmodernist" to films of the late seventies and eighties.
    For immediately prior to that period, the avant-garde film entertained a
    modernist aesthetic via the structural film. Obviously, the postmodernist
    moment could emerge only *after* the modernist interlude.

3   The reader should not assume that these labels are standard throughout the
    film word; they are partly borrowed and partly of my own invention.

4   For example, it does not include the efforts of autobiographical filmmakers
    such as Jonas Mekas or Howard Guttenplan. These have not been consid-
    ered in my review primarily because their work, which is often quite
    striking, appears to me to be concerned with issues that predate the rise of
    structural film and is, therefore, not part of the dialectical narrative of anti-
    structural film. Similarly, Brakhage, who in one sense is very antistructural
    and who continues to make exciting films in the wake of that movement, is
    not part of the story I have to tell.

5   For example, M. Duras, C. Ackerman, and C. Schneemann, among others.

6   P. Adams Sitney, "Structural Film," anthologized in *Film Culture Reader*,
    ed. Sitney (New York: Praeger, 1970), p.326.

7   This is major category in P. Adams Sitney's *Visionary Film* (New York:
    Oxford University Press, 1974 and 1979).

8   A third kind of approach that is often called "structural" but which empha-
    sizes neither shape nor system involves showing long, uninterrupted takes of
    locales bereft of narrative or dramatic interest, for example, Andy Warhol's
    Empire (1964). I suspect that the reasons for calling such films structural are
    twofold. First, the decision that generates the film can certainly be called
    minimal while also denying the moment-to-moment expressivity of the film-
    maker. And, second, the choice of such a strategy throws the spectator into

an apperceptive stance, reflecting upon the way his attention is drawn when it is not guided by the interests of narrative, drama, or allegory. Thus, if such films are to be called structural, it is because they promote a kind of apperceptive reflexivity in the spectator.

Needless to say, though I have spoken of the shape, system, and single image approaches as distinct, they are not mutually exclusive, and they can all appear in a single film, for example, Ernie Gehr's *Serene Velocity* (1970).

9 In terms of psychology, I have in mind the popularity of books such as R. L. Gregory's *Eye and Brain* and *The Intelligent Eye*. One difference between the sixties and the seventies, it may be noted, is a shift from the preeminent concern with perception to a concern with language, a shift, moreover, that is reflected in the respective fortunes, with the intelligentsia, of phenomenology followed by semiotics.

10 Annette Michelson, "Toward Snow," *The Avant-Garde Film*, ed. P. Adams Sitney (New York: New York University Press, 1978), p. 175.

11 Throughout the sixties and the seventies, a film like *Zorn's Lemma* would have been described as theoretical, suggesting that such a film actually proposes a theoretical argument. This notion that avant-garde films literally make theories continues into the present. I do not believe that this rhetoric, often employed by critics in the process of explicating a film, is accurate; I prefer to say that the relation of such films to theory is better characterized by saying that generally such films allude or otherwise refer to theories. My case for this approach is stated in Carroll, "Avant-garde Film and Film Theory," *Millennium Film Journal*, nos. 4/5 (Summer/Fall 1979), pp. 135–145. This essay is also contained in my *Theorizing the Moving Image* (N.Y.: Cambridge UP, 1996).

In this essay I am writing as a historian and a critic, not as a theoretician. If I present the theoretical presuppositions of film movements uncritically, it is not because I believe them but because my task here is to help the reader understand these movements in terms of what the filmmakers believed they were doing. As a theoretician I have grave reservations about all the various theories that filmmakers presupposed in the period under consideration.

12 Sitney, *Visionary Film*, p. 438.

13 Of course, it remains an open question as to how didactivally viable such films really are. For it would seem that only viewers steeped in avant-garde polemics could recognize and decipher the allusions to film theory made by such films and, thereby, "learn" what the film wants to tell them. But it is not obvious that such a process is really a matter of learning insofar as the spectator must already know what he or she is supposed to be taught.

14 See Joanna Kiernan, "To Films by Malcolm LeGrice," *Millennium Film Journal*, no. 3 (Winter/Spring 1979); pp. 56–71.

15 See Peter Gidal, "Theory and Definition of Structural/Materialist Film," in *Structural Film Anthology*, ed. Gidal (London:British Film Institute,1976).

16 See Lindley Hanlon, "Collision Course: Ken Kobland's Optical Prints," *Millennium Film Journal*, nos. 7/8/9 (Fall/Winter 1980–81), pp. 253–259.

17 The most acerbic of these criticisms can be found in Gary Doberman's "New York Cut the Crap," *CinemaNews* (Spring 1980).

18 Perhaps the reason for this was because in this genre the mode of articulation more closely resembles a rebus than an essay. This may place limitations on how specific a point it is possible to make about the nature of memory or attention. That is, general themes rather than refinements of themes may be all that can be expected in this sort of avant-garde symbol system. Refinement may require the kind of logical connectives, contrast, process of conjecture, experiment (or report of experiments), and refutation that is unsuitable to an avant-garde genre committed to an elliptical, allusive intentionally disorienting, and initially obscure mode of presentation.

19 It is also true that the structural film was based upon certain expectations whose failure to be realized may have influenced the decline of the movement. The structural film emerged from the gallery scene connected with minimalism. Undoubtedly it was hoped that structural film would become as financially viable as minimalist painting and sculpture. However, the galleries were either unwilling or unable to turn structural film into a collectible on a par with paintings and sculpture. The reproducibility of film along with the questions of how a collector would appropriately display such an "object" were obvious problems. The growing awareness of the limitations of the economic prospects of structural film correlates with the dissipation of the energy behind the movement. Moreover, filmmakers had to turn to the academy rather than to the art world for support. And this, of course, has led some to propose economic reasons for the academic approach to structural film.

20 The most popular source for the gross misinterpretation and misunderstanding of the philosophical concept of "deconstruction" is, without a doubt, "Propositions" by Noël Burch and Jorge Dana, published in *Afterimage*, vol. 5 (Spring 1974).

21 Throughout, I refer to the theoretical prejudices of film movements in order to illuminate their practices and history. At no point should the theoretical (as opposed to critical) biases be mistaken for my own. For a statement of my own opposition to the essentialism of structural film, see my "Medium Specificity Arguments and the Self-Consciously Invented Arts: Film, Video and Photography," *Millennium Film Journal*, nos. 14/15 (Fall/Winter 1984–85), pp. 127–154. This essay is also contained in my *Theorizing the Moving Image* (N.Y.: Cambridge UP, 1996).

22 For a description of this film, see my review of LeGrice in the *Soho Weekly News*, April 12–18, 1979. It should be said that in answer to my point about affinities to structural film, LeGrice would probably retort that he is deconstructing narrative, something he conceives of as cultural and conventional, whereas the structural filmmakers attempt to disclose essential features of film as such.

23 For an account of *Tom, Tom the Piper's Son*, see Lois Mendelson's and Bill Simon's article of the same name in *Artforum*, 1971. For information concerning *The Doctor's Dream*, see Tom Gunning's "Doctor Jacobs' Dream Work," *Millennium Film Journal*, nos. 10/11 (Fall/Winter 1981–82), 210–218. Also of interest is Lindley Hanlon's interview, *Ken Jacobs* (Minneapolis: Filmmakers Filming Monographs, 1979).

24 Jonathan Buchsbaum, "Independent Film and Popular Culture: The Films of J. Hoberman," *Millennium Film Journal,* vol. 6 (Spring 1980), pp. 111–112.

25 Jonathan Rosenbaum, *Film: The Front Line, 1983* (Denver: Arden Press, 1983), p. 76.

26 "Discussion Between Marjorie Keller and Amy Taubin," in *Idiolects*, vol. 6, parenthetical information added.

27 E. A. Kaplan, "Theories and Strategies of Feminist Documentary," *Millennium Film Journal* 12 (Fall/Winter 1982–83): 53, parentheses removed. It is also important to state that *independent* filmmakers in the seventies and eighties, in their search for a means to express content, often turned to documentary filmmaking. This is especially true of feminist filmmakers. I have not included a chronicle of this important development here because my focus is avant-garde film, not all independent film. The Kaplan article just cited is one place for the interested reader to obtain information about the state of independently produced, feminist documentaries.

28 Undoubtedly the preference for at least "equal time" devoted to the interrogation of the signifier *and* to the ramifications of its operation in the construction of (a presumably repressive) social reality is what accounts for the lack of interest of politicized post-structuralists in the works of George Landow (aka Owen Land). In films such as *Remedial Reading Comprehension* (1971) and *On the Marriage Broker Joke* (1980), Landow has deconstructively subverted popular discourse – for example, ads, the jargon of institutional testing, and so forth – in order to raise questions about audience reception and interpretation. Because of its humor, his work is often accessible to wide audiences. Yet, in spite of his affinities to many of the aims and concerns of the new talkie, he does not appear to be of major interest to proponents of that genre because he does not address what for them are broader issues of reception, namely its place within a social reality that is politically, sexually, and economically oppressive.

29 The preferred format many of new talkies involves the filmmakers appearing after the film in order to answer questions and to discuss and debate issues with the audience. As with Godard's work, the New Talkie is thought of as a way of initially engaging issues. It is incomplete if it does not lead to further discussion. This underscores the genre's commitment to political work and is also related to a desire for greater accessibility by these avant-gardists. It might be further connected to a more general stance by these filmmakers against the kind of "repugnant" closure found in commercial films and "aesthetic" art.

30 For an analysis of this film, see E. A. Kaplan, "Feminist Approaches to History, Psychoanalysis and Cinema in *Sigmund Freud's Dora*," *Millennium Film Journal*, nos. 7/8/9 (Fall/Winter 1980–81).

31 The intertextual preoccupations of these New Talkies, rooted in a theoretical commitment to semiology and post structuralism, corresponds to the Barthesian tendencies of postmodernists in the fine arts such as Cindy Sherman. She too presents us with representations of recognizable cultural representations for the purpose of pithing their semiotic operation. The

similarity between practitioners of art world postmodernism and proponents of the new talkies may suggest to some a reason to designate *the* latter as *the* cinematic postmodernists.

32 E.A. Kaplan, "Night at the Opera: Investigating the Heroine in Sally Potter's *Thriller,*" *Millennium Film Journal*, nos. 10/11 (Fall/Winter 1981–82), pp. 115–122.

33 See Sally Banes' chapter on Rainer in her *Terpsichore in Sneakers* (Boston: Houghton Mifflin Co., 1980).

34 For more information on Journeys..., see my "Interview with a Woman Who..." in *Millennium Film Journal* nos. 7/8/9 (Fall/Winter 1980–81), pp. 31–68. For general information about Rainer see: Annette Michelson, "Yvonne Rainer, Part One: The Dancer and the Dance," *Artforum* (January 1974), pp. 1157–1163; Michelson, "Yvonne Rainer, Part Two: Lives of Performers," *Artforum* (February 1974), pp. 30–35, and B. Ruby Rich, *Yvonne Rainer* (St. Paul, MN: Filmmakers Filming Monograph, 1981).

35 J. Hoberman, "The Divine Connection," *Village Voice*, July 26, 1983.

36 Lindley Hanlon, "Female Rage: The Films of Su Friedrich," *Millennium Film Journal*, nos. 12 (Fall/Winter 1982–83), pp. 79–86.

37 Paul Arthur, "The Western Edge: Oil of L. A. and the Machined Image," *Millennium Film Journal*, no. 12 (Fall/Winter 1982–83), pp. 17–18.

38 Ibid. pp. 22–25.

39 Ibid.

40 Sally Banes, "Theatre of Operations: Stuart Sherman's Fifteen Films," *Millennium Film Journal*, nos. 10/11 (Fall/Winter 1981–82), pp. 87–102.

41 For an account of Beckman's career, see Sally Banes, "Imagination and Play: The Films of Erica Beckman," *Millennium Film Journal*, no. 13 (Fall/Winter 1983–84), pp. 98–112.

Index